Photoshop
Elements 4
one-on-one™

Advance Praise for *Photoshop Elements 4 One-on-One*

Also from Deke Press

Photoshop Elements 4
one-on-one™

DEKE McCLELLAND

WITH GALEN FOTT

deke™
PRESS
O'REILLY®

BEIJING • CAMBRIDGE • FARNHAM • KÖLN • PARIS • SEBASTOPOL • TAIPEI • TOKYO

Photoshop Elements 4 One-on-One

by Deke McClelland with Galen Fott

This title is published by Deke Press in association with O'Reilly Media, Inc., 1005 Gravenstein Highway North, Sebastopol, CA 95472.

O'Reilly Media books may be purchased for educational, business, or sales promotional use. Online editions are also available for most titles (*safari.oreilly.com*). For more information, contact O'Reilly's corporate/institutional sales department: 800-998-9938 or *corporate@oreilly.com*.

Managing Editor:	Carol Person	**Interior Designer:**	David Futato
Associate Editor:	Susan Pink, Techright	**Production Designer:**	Karen Montgomery
Indexer:	Julie Hawks	**Video Directors:**	Denise Maffitt, Barbara Stillwell
Technical Editor (& Dearly Departed):	Jason S. Woliner	**Video Editors:**	Jennifer Erickson, Andrew Jasper, Eric Vitner
Production Manager:	Claire Cloutier	**Queen of Motion:**	Barbara Ross
Manufacturing Manager:	Sue Willing	**DVD Graphic Designer:**	Barbara Driscoll
Marketing Manager:	Betsy Waliszewski	**Video Compression:**	Carey Matthew Brady
Publicist:	Theresa Pulido	**Interface Programmers:**	Melissa Symolon, Marc Johnson
Galactus Editoriali:	Steve Weiss, Colleen Wheeler	**DVD Quality Assurance:**	Anthony Packes, Andrew Coughlan
Cover Designer:	Emma Colby		

Print History:

November 2005: First edition.

Special thanks to John Bell, Brian Maffitt, David Murcott, Jerry Yen, Connie Quach, Steve Johnson, Richard Lainhart, James Thomas, J. Scott Klossner, Mikkel Aaland, Fifi Shenay, David Rogelberg, Sherry Rogelberg, Stacey Barone, Katrina Bevan, Renee Midrack, Laurie Petrycki, Mark Brokering, and Tim O'Reilly, as well as Patrick Lor, Val Gelineau, and the gangs at iStockphoto, PhotoSpin, NAPP, Peachpit Press, and Adobe Systems. Extra special thanks to Amy Thomas Buscaglia and our relentlessly supportive families, without whom this series and this book would not be possible.

This book was typeset using Adobe InDesign CS and the Linotype Birka, Adobe Rotis, and Adobe Futura typefaces.

0-596-10098-1
[C]

RepKover™ This book uses RepKover,™ a durable and flexible lay-flat binding.

So brave, so strong,
so tough, so young:
Sam and Max.

CONTENTS

PREFACE

HOW ONE-ON-ONE WORKS

Welcome to *Photoshop Elements 4 One-on-One*, the latest in a series of (what I hope I conservatively term) lavishly visual, full-color titles that combine step-by-step lessons with two hours of video instruction. As the name *One-on-One* implies, I walk you through Photoshop Elements 4 just as if I were teaching you in a classroom environment. Except that instead of getting lost in a crowd of students, you receive my individualized attention. It's just you and me.

I created *One-on-One* with three audiences in mind. If you're a digital photographer or graphic artist—professional or amateur—you'll appreciate the hands-on approach and the ability to set your own pace. If you're a student working in a classroom or vocational setting, you'll enjoy the personalized attention, structured exercises, and end-of-lesson quizzes. If you're an instructor in a college or vocational setting, you'll find the topic-driven lessons helpful in building curricula and creating homework assignments. *Photoshop Elements 4 One-on-One* is designed to suit the needs of beginners and intermediate users. But I've seen to it that each lesson contains a few techniques that even experienced users don't know.

Read, Watch, Do

Photoshop Elements 4 One-on-One is your chance to learn and have fun with Photoshop Elements under the direction of a professional trainer with 20 years of computer design and imaging experience. Read the book, watch the videos, do the exercises. Proceed at your own pace and experiment as you see fit. It's the best way to learn.

Figure 1.

Photoshop Elements 4 One-on-One contains twelve lessons, each made up of three to seven step-by-step exercises. Every book-based lesson includes a corresponding video lesson (see Figure 1), in which I introduce the key concepts you'll need to know to complete the exercises. Best of all, every exercise is project-based, culminating in an actual finished document worthy of your labors (see Figure 2). The exercises include insights and context throughout, so you'll know not only what to do but, just as important, why you're doing it. My sincere hope is that you'll find the experience entertaining, informative, and empowering.

All the sample files required to perform the exercises are included on the DVD-ROM at the back of this book. The DVD also contains the video lessons. (This is a data DVD, not a video DVD. It won't work in a set-top device; it works only with a computer.) Don't lose or destroy this DVD. It is as integral a part of your learning experience as the pages in this book. Together, the book, sample files, and videos form a single comprehensive training experience.

Start with a file...

follow the steps...

and end with an effect you're proud of.

Figure 2.

One-on-One Requirements

The main prerequisite to using *Photoshop Elements 4 One-on-One* is having Photoshop Elements 4 installed on your Microsoft Windows-based PC. You may have purchased Photoshop Elements as a stand-alone package (see Figure 3) or as part of a bundle that includes Photoshop Premiere Elements. Photoshop Elements 4 also ships for free with some brands of scanners and digital cameras.

At the time of this writing, Elements 4 is not available for Apple's line of Macintosh computers. (If you are a Macintosh user and you have Photoshop Elements 3, check out my six-hour video series, "Total Training Presents: Adobe Photoshop Elements 3 Unleashed," from *www.totaltraining.com*.) I look forward to the day when Elements is once again a truly cross-platform product. But in the meantime, it's available exclusively for the PC.

Any computer that meets the minimum requirements for Photoshop Elements 4 also meets the requirements for using *Photoshop Elements 4 One-on-One*. Assuming you own a PC, you'll need an Intel Pentium III, 4, or Centrino processor, 800MHz or faster, running Windows XP with Service Pack 2 or better.

As if that's not enough, your computer must also meet the following minimum requirements:

Figure 3.

- 256MB of RAM (512MB recommended)

- 1.1GB of free hard disk space (900MB for Elements and 200MB for the *One-on-One* project and video application files)

- Color monitor with 16-bit color video card

- 1024-by-768-pixel monitor resolution

- Microsoft DirectX 9-compatible display driver

- DVD-ROM drive

To play the videos, you will need Apple's QuickTime Player software version 5.0.2 or later. (QuickTime offers superior playback functions, which is why I choose it over the Windows Media Player.) Many computers come equipped with QuickTime; if yours does not, you will need to install the free QuickTime Player using the link provided on the DVD included with this book.

Finally, you'll need to install the *One-on-One* project files and video software from the DVD that accompanies this book, as explained in the next section.

One-on-One Installation and Setup

Photoshop Elements 4 One-on-One is designed to function as an integrated training environment. Therefore, before embarking on the lessons and exercises, you must first install a handful of files onto your computer's hard drive. These are:

- QuickTime Player software (if it is not already installed)
- All sample files used in the exercises (130MB in all)
- Total Training video training software
- Nearly 100 custom layer styles, which you'll be using throughout the exercises in this book

All these files are provided on the DVD that accompanies this book. To install the files, follow these steps:

1. *Quit the Organizer and Editor workspaces.* If Photoshop Elements is running on your computer, you must exit the program before you install the *One-on-One* files. Choose the **Exit** command from the **File** menu or press Ctrl+Q or Alt+F4.

2. *Insert the One-on-One DVD.* Remove the DVD-ROM from the back of the book and place it in your computer's DVD-ROM or DVD+RW drive.

3. *Open the Photoshop Elements 4 One-on-One Launchpad.* With any luck, the Launchpad window (see Figure 4) opens automatically. If it doesn't, choose **My Computer** from the **Start** menu. In the ensuing window, double-click the *DKPSE4* DVD icon.

Figure 4.

The Launchpad includes all you need to install the files and play the videos. Just click the blue buttons under the red *one-on-one training* text.

---

4. *If necessary, get QuickTime.* Click the **Install** button to copy to your hard drive all the files required to complete the exercises in this book. The installer software starts by performing a compatibility test to see if QuickTime is available. If you see some clouds float by and hear some watery music, click the **Continue** button, as in Figure 5 on the facing page. If not, click **Get QuickTime** and follow the on-screen instructions. After you finish installing QuickTime, proceed to the next step.

5. *Install all support and training files.* After you accept the terms of the licensing agreement, the installer software displays a plain gray but highly informative **Installation** screen, which tells you that you can skip a step in the installation process (see Figure 6). Don't believe it; I want you to perform *all* the steps. Here's a quick tour:

Figure 5.

- Click the **Continue** button. Most likely, you'll see another screen asking to determine the files that need to be installed. Click **Proceed** to move on.

- A moment later, up comes the **1 Install Lesson Files** screen. By default, the installer wants to create a folder called *Lesson Files-PE4 1on1* on your computer's desktop. You'll need this folder to complete the exercises in this book. The desktop is the most convenient location for the lesson files, but if you'd like to put them elsewhere, click the **Browse** button and specify a location.

- Click the **Install** button. A progress bar tells you that the installer is writing a total of 115 files. A few moments later, a message tells you that the lesson files have been successfully copied, as in Figure 7. Click the **OK** button.

- At the **2 Install Deke's Presets** screen, click the **Install** button again. The installer copies the custom layer styles to Photoshop Elements 4's Presets folder. Click **OK** when this brief process completes. The styles will load the next time you start Elements' Editor workspace.

Figure 6.

- At the **3 Install Training Application** screen, click the **Install** button one last time. This installs the software required to run the video training. After a few seconds of progress bar, another message tells you about another successful installation. Click **OK**.

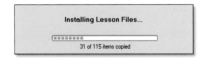

- At the final screen, click the **Finish** button to return to the Launchpad.

You should see a new folder called *Lesson Files-PE4 1on1* on your computer's desktop. You'll be referencing this folder a lot over the course of the lessons in this book.

Figure 7.

6. *Close the Launchpad (or don't).* We're finished with the Launchpad for the moment. If you like to keep your on-screen world tidy, close the Launchpad by clicking the **Exit** button in the top-right corner. But bear in mind, the Launchpad is your gateway to the videos. If you plan on watching them in the near future (as explained in the upcoming "Playing the Videos" section on page xvii), leave the Launchpad open.

7. *Check your screen resolution.* To use Elements effectively, your monitor should be set to display 1024 by 768 or more pixels. If it isn't, or you aren't quite sure, right-click an empty portion of your on-screen desktop. Then choose **Properties** from the shortcut menu. Click the **Settings** tab in the top-right corner of the **Display Properties** dialog box. Then increase the **Screen Resolution** setting to at least **1024 by 768 pixels** or as high as you can take it and still comfortably read type on-screen. Click the **OK** button. Your screen may flicker on and off. That's perfectly normal. Follow the instructions you see on screen and you should be fine.

Figure 8.

8. *Start Photoshop Elements.* Double-click the **Adobe Photoshop Elements 4.0** program icon on your desktop or, if there isn't an icon, click the **Start** button and choose **Adobe Photoshop Elements 4.0**. (If you don't see the program listed on the left-hand side of the Start menu, you'll have to dig for it. It may be located in the **Programs** or **All Programs** submenu, possibly inside an **Adobe** submenu.)

9. *Launch the Organizer.* Unless you've specifically asked it to do otherwise, Elements starts you off on the Welcome screen. Click the **View and Organize Photos** button, which I've circled in Figure 8. This launches the Organizer workspace, which lets you organize images.

10. *Turn on color management.* Photoshop Elements ships with a killer color management engine that helps ensure that your colors remain consistent from one computer to another, as well as from your monitor to your printer. But it needs a bit of tweaking. Choose **Edit→Color Settings**. Inside the **Color Settings** dialog box, select the **Allow Me to**

Choose option, as in Figure 9. This lets you adjust the color management settings for a single image at a time, as we will in Lesson 2 (see Step 3, page 55). To accept your changes, click the **OK** button. Now the colors of your images will match (or at least more closely match) those shown in the pages of this book.

11. *Maximize the Organizer workspace.* Does the Organizer workspace take up your entire screen? If so, skip to the next step. If not, maximize the interface by clicking the ☐ icon in the upper-right corner of the window.

12. *Quit the Organizer.* You've come full circle. Choose **File→Exit** or press Ctrl+Q. Quitting the Organizer not only closes the program but also saves the changes you made to the color settings and window size.

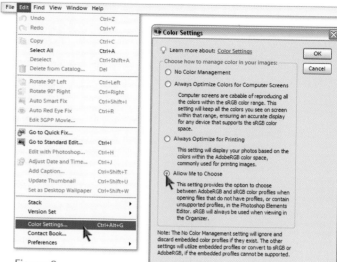

Figure 9.

Congratulations, you and I are now in sync, and you're ready to begin following along with the exercises in this book.

Playing the Videos

At the outset of each book-based lesson, I ask you to play the companion video lesson from the DVD-ROM. Ranging from 9 to nearly 19 minutes apiece, these video lessons introduce key concepts that make more sense when first seen in action.

Produced in concert with the computer training pioneers at Total Training, the video lessons are not traditional DVD movies. They're much better. A standard NTSC movie on DVD is limited to 720-by-480 non-square pixels, of which only 720-by-240 update at a time (an antiquated and generally unfortunate phenomenon known as *interlacing*). We have no such restrictions. Our movies play at resolutions as high as 960-by-540 pixels (see Figure 10 on the next page), and every pixel updates 30 times a second, with no interlacing. The result is a picture that approaches the quality of HDTV. (If the video looks smaller than you might expect on your screen, bear in mind that a computer monitor packs in far more pixels than a standard TV.) Total Training employs state-of-the-art capture technology and gold-standard Sorenson compression to pack these vivid, legible videos into a trim file that plays smoothly, even on older-model computers. This is video training at its finest.

Figure 10.

To watch a video, do the following:

1. *Insert the One-on-One DVD.* You must have the DVD in your computer's DVD drive to watch a video.

2. *Open the Photoshop Elements 4 One-on-One Launchpad.* Again, the Launchpad window should open automatically on your PC. But if it doesn't, choose **My Computer** from the **Start** menu, and then double-click the *DKPSE4* DVD icon.

Figure 11.

3. *Click the Start button.* Click the button in the middle of the Launchpad, which is circled in Figure 11. Assuming that you installed the Total Training video training software as directed in Step 5 on page xv, you'll be treated to the animated Total Training splash screen followed by a welcoming message from your genial host, me.

4. *Switch to the video lesson that you want to watch.* The twelve videos are divided into four sets of three lessons each. To get around, first choose a set of lessons from the top-left pop-up menu, then choose the desired lesson from the pop-up menu immediately to the right. (I've labeled the two

pop-up menus in Figure 12.) Set 1 contains Lessons 1 through 3, Set 2 contains Lessons 4 through 6, and so on. Each set also contains a personal introduction by me. You can watch any video lesson in any order you like. However, each video lesson makes the most sense and provides the most benefit when watched, in order, at the outset of the corresponding book-based lesson.

Set pop-up menu   Lesson pop-up menu

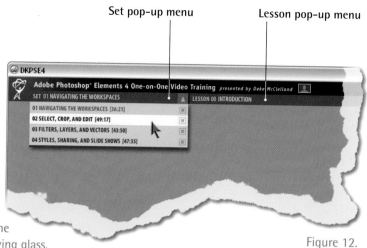

Figure 12.

The video is surrounded by a matrix of navigation buttons and play controls. To hide these controls and view only the video, move your cursor inside the video image. When the cursor changes to a magnifying glass, click. If you prefer to magnify the video so it fills your entire screen, press the Alt key and click. To restore the video to its normal size and state, with all controls and other interface elements, click anywhere inside the video.

Use the play controls in the lower-left corner of the screen (see Figure 13) to play, pause, and fast-forward the video. You can also take advantage of the following keyboard shortcuts:

Figure 13.

- To pause the video, press the spacebar. Press the spacebar again to resume playing.

- To skip to the next lesson, press the ⇢ key. This is also a great way to play the next lesson after the current one ends. For example, after viewing my initial and enthusiastic personal introduction, press the ⇢ key to play Video Lesson 1, "Welcome to the Organizer."

- To return to the preceding lesson, press ⇠. For example, you might revisit one of my personal introductions after watching a lesson.

- Adjust the volume by pressing the ⊡ and ⊟ (plus and minus) keys.

Finally, for help on any element of the interface, click the **?Help** button in the lower-right portion of the screen.

Take note that the video lessons do not include follow-along project files. It works like this: You work along with me inside the book; you sit back and relax during the videos.

Structure and Organization

Each of the dozen lessons conforms to a consistent structure designed to impart skills and understanding through a regimen of practice and dialog. As you build your projects, I explain why you're performing the steps and why Photoshop Elements works the way it does.

Each lesson begins with a broad topic overview. Turn the first page of each lesson, and you'll find a section called "About This Lesson," which lists the skills you'll learn and directs you to the video-based introduction.

Next come the step-by-step exercises, in which I walk you through some of Elements' most powerful and essential image editing features. A DVD icon, like the one on the right, appears whenever I ask you to open a file from the *Lesson Files-PE4 1on1* folder that you installed on your computer's hard drive. To make my directions crystal clear, command and option names appear in bold type (as in, "choose the **Open** command"). Figure references appear in colored type. More than 600 full-color, generously sized images diagram key steps in your journey so you're never left scratching your head, puzzling over what to do next. And when I refer you to another step or section, I tell you the exact page number to go to. (Shouldn't every book?)

PEARL OF WISDOM

Along the way, you'll encounter the occasional "Pearl of Wisdom," which provides insights into how Photoshop Elements and the larger world of digital imaging work. Although this information is not essential to performing a given step or completing an exercise, it may help you understand how a function works or provide you with valuable context.

More detailed background discussions appear in independent sidebars. These sidebars shed light on the inner workings of the Quick Fix mode's Auto buttons, the mysteries of the visible-color spectrum, the mechanics of print resolution, and other high-level topics that are key to understanding Photoshop Elements.

A colored paragraph of text with a rule above and below it calls attention to a special tip or technique that will help you make Photoshop Elements work faster and more smoothly.

Occasionally, a project is a bit ambitious. My enthusiasm for a topic may even take us beyond the stated goal. In such cases, I cordon off the final portion of the exercise and label it "Extra Credit." If you're feeling oversaturated with information, go ahead and skip to the next exercise. If you're just warming up, by all means carry on; you will be rewarded with a completed project and a wealth of additional tips and insights.

Each lesson ends with a "What Did You Learn?" section, which features a multiple-choice quiz. Your job is to choose the best description for each of 12 key concepts outlined in the lesson. Answers are printed upside-down at the bottom of the page.

The Scope of This Book

No one book can teach you everything there is to know about Photoshop Elements, and this one is no exception. If you're looking for information on a specific aspect of Elements, here's a quick list of the topics and features discussed in this book:

- Lesson 1: An overview of the Organizer workspace, including getting photos into a catalog, zooming and rotating images, creating and applying tags, finding photos by date, and comparing similar photos

- Lesson 2: The Quick Fix mode, including automatic color corrections and lighting and focus adjustments, as well as ways to save your edited images as independent files or in sets

- Lesson 3: Color and brightness adjustments, including the Remove Color Cast, Adjust Color for Skin Tone, and Color Variations commands; Hue/Saturation and Levels; the Shadows/Highlights command; and the Camera Raw dialog box

- Lesson 4: Selection tools, including the lasso, magic wand, and marquee tools, as well as the selection brush, magic selection functions, and the commands in the Select menu

- Lesson 5: Ways to crop and transform an image, including the crop and straighten tools; as well as the Divide Scanned Photos, Image Size, and Canvas Size commands

- Lesson 6: Painting and retouching, including the paintbrush, dodge, burn, and red-eye removal tools, as well as the healing brushes and the various brush settings in the options bar

- Lesson 7: The Editor's extensive collection of filters, including the Unsharp Mask, High Pass, the many effects in the Filter Gallery, and the powerful Liquify function

- Lesson 8: Layer functions, including the Layers palette, stacking order, blend modes, transformations, and the eraser tools

- Lesson 9: Text and shape layers, including the type and shape tools, formatting attributes, scalable vector objects, and the Warp Text dialog box

- Lesson 10: Layer styles and adjustment layers, including the Styles and Effects palette, the Style Settings dialog box, the Gradient Map command, and layer masks

- Lesson 11: Ways to share your digital images, including printing single images and multiple photos, as well as emailing image files and posting them online

- Lesson 12: The wide world of multimedia Creations, including photo albums, greeting cards, wall calendars, Web galleries, and panoramas that comprise several photos stitched together

To find out where I discuss a specific feature, please consult the Index, which begins on page 397.

While I touch on almost every aspect of Photoshop Elements in some degree of detail, a few specialized topics fall outside the scope of this book. In the Organizer, I don't cover how to use File→Backup to make duplicates of your photos for safekeeping, nor do I explain how to use File→Burn to copy images to a CD or DVD. And although I provide a general and, I think, very educational lesson on filters (Lesson 7, "Filters and Distortions"), I don't cover all of the Editor's filter commands. It's a pretty small list of missing functions, but I want you to know up front.

I now invite you to turn your attention to Lesson 1, "Getting and Organizing Photos." I hope you'll agree with me that *Photoshop Elements 4 One-on-One*'s combination of step-by-step lessons and video introductions provides the best learning experience of any Photoshop Elements training resource on the market.

LESSON

1

PHOTOSHOP ELEMENTS 4 may be the most phenomenal bargain in the history of digital imaging. Modeled after the professional-grade, industry-standard Adobe Photoshop CS2, Photoshop Elements delivers far and away more capabilities than any other image-editing program in its price range.

From the tadpole that was Photoshop LE (short for Light Edition)—a freebie version of Photoshop in which many of the program's most powerful functions were merely turned off—Photoshop Elements 4 has matured into a unique piece of software that incorporates many of Photoshop's best features and tosses in a few dozen tricks of its own. It's an easy matter to chart the top capabilities of the two Photoshops and make Elements come out the winner. Admittedly, such a table is unfair, which is why it appears barely rescued from the dustheap in Figure 1-1. Elements provides only rudimentary support for some features, and most of Photoshop CS2's strengths are so rich and deep that they put the program in a class by itself. Still, the table makes a point. For a fraction of the price of the full-blown Photoshop CS2, Elements provides more features than most digital photographers will ever use. Photoshop Elements is a consumer-level program for folks with professional-quality aspirations.

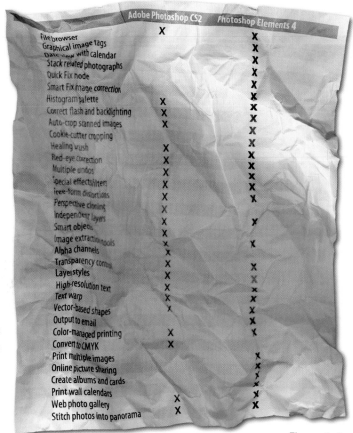

Figure 1-1.

What Is Photoshop Elements?

Photoshop Elements 4 is really a combination of three programs running in tandem. Adobe calls these programs *workspaces*. The first is the Welcome screen, which invites you to the software and

ABOUT THIS LESSON

Project Files

Before beginning the exercises, make sure you've installed the lesson files from the DVD, as explained in Step 5 on page xv of the Preface. This should result in a folder of images called *Lesson Files-PE4 1on1* on your desktop. We'll be working with the files inside the *Lesson 01* subfolder.

Before you can set about correcting and modifying your digital photographs, you must know how to import and organize image files. In the following exercises, you'll learn how to:

Video Lesson 1: Welcome to the Organizer

When you first run Elements 4, the program greets you with an interactive Welcome screen, which walks you through the various operations you can perform. Click the ⊞ icon (labeled View and Organize Photos) to launch the Organizer, which lets you create catalogs of images and view the images as thumbnails.

The Organizer is so useful that I've made it the subject of the first video lesson on the DVD. To view this video, insert the DVD, click the **Start** button, and choose **Lesson 1, Welcome to the Organizer** from the second pop-up menu at the top of the screen. The movie lasts 12 minutes and 19 seconds, during which time you'll learn about the keyboard equivalents and shortcuts listed below:

Operation	Keyboard equivalent or shortcut
Create a new catalog	Ctrl+Shift+C, Enter
Get images from a digital camera or card reader	Ctrl+G (or insert memory card into reader)
Zoom in or out of thumbnails	⊡ (plus) or ⊡ (minus)
Rotate an image clockwise or counterclockwise	Ctrl+→ or Ctrl+←
Hide or show details below thumbnails	Ctrl+D

explains some of the tasks you can accomplish. The second workspace, the Organizer, is a *file browser*. It lets you import images from a digital camera or scanner, preview many images at a glance, name and otherwise label those images, and decide which (if any) you want to edit and print. The final workspace, the Editor, is an *image editor*. It lets you open a photograph and change it. You can adjust the brightness and contrast, alter the colors, move things around, sharpen the focus, retouch a few details, and even combine two photographs. When you're finished, you can save your changes, print the result, attach it to an email, or post it online.

But it doesn't end there. You can also use Photoshop Elements to enhance artwork that you've scanned from a hand drawing or created with another graphics program. If you're artistically inclined, you can start with a blank document and create a piece of artwork from scratch. If that's not enough, Elements offers a wide variety of illustration tools, special effects, and text-formatting options.

In this lesson, you'll take your first look at the Organizer. Specifically, you'll look at how you acquire images, collect them into libraries, review and evaluate them, keep them organized so you can quickly find an image in the future, and compare one photo to another.

Getting Photos into Elements

After you've successfully opened the Organizer workspace (as explained in Video Lesson 1, "Welcome to the Organizer"), the next step is to tell the Organizer where your photos are. Happily, the Organizer gives you a number of easy ways to do this. You can direct the program to scour your hard drive for any image files it can find. From that point on, you can rely on Elements to transfer new photos from your camera to your hard drive automatically. Just insert your camera's memory card into a card reader or connect the camera directly to your computer via a USB or FireWire connection, and Elements automatically sets about importing the photos.

Elements keeps track of imported images in a *catalog*, which remembers the links to the images on your hard drive and stores any information that you might want to associate with the images. By default, Elements creates a catalog for you, giving it the apt but generic name *My Catalog*. A single catalog can manage hundreds or even thousands of photos, even if the images are scattered in multiple folders on different hard drives or even on backup CDs.

To see the Organizer import images from a digital camera media card, watch Video Lesson 1, "Welcome to the Organizer," included on the DVD (see page 4). In this exercise, however, you won't be working with your photos. Instead, I want you to import a select group of images that I've provided. This will ensure that what happens on your screen exactly matches the steps and figures shown in this book. It's sort of a control group, as the scientists say. If you've been experimenting on your own and have already imported some photos into Elements, don't worry. We'll begin this exercise by creating a fresh new catalog file just for this lesson. If you've worked in the program before, the *My Catalog* file that you've been using will be saved exactly as you left it. And I'll tell you how to open it again at the end of the exercise, so that you can regain access to your personal photos.

Figure 1-2.

1. *Launch Elements.* You'll start this exercise in the Organizer workspace. Start up Photoshop Elements 4. In the Welcome screen, click the **View and Organize Photos** button. If this is the first time you've launched the Organizer, it'll ask you whether you want to import photos into your default *My Catalog* file. For now, click **No**. (You can always import photos later by choosing File→Get Photos→By Searching. Then click the Search button and away you go.)

2. *Create a new catalog.* Choose the **Catalog** command from the **File** menu or press Ctrl+Shift+C. As pictured in Figure 1-2, the resulting **Catalog** dialog box provides a few helpful instructions on the left and a column of buttons on the right. The buttons work as follows:

   • Click the New button or press the Enter key to make a new catalog file, which will initially appear empty.

   • Click Open to open a catalog you created in the past.

   • Use Save As to change the name of your catalog file.

   • If your catalog becomes damaged by a power failure or a computer glitch, try clicking the Recover button to relocate the original images and rebuild the catalog file.

   Leave the check box at the bottom of the dialog box turned on to import Elements' free music files into your catalog, which you can use to accompany slide shows and the like. Next click the **New** button to display the **New Catalog** dialog box.

3. *Name the new catalog and confirm a few settings.* Enter "PE4 1on1" in the **File name** field. Leave all other options unchanged and then click the **Save** button. The Organizer workspace should appear as pictured in Figure 1-3. Note that the Organizer window is empty and the title bar at the top of the window sports the new catalog name, *PE4 1on1.psa*.

Figure 1-3.

Just to make sure that you and I are in perfect agreement—and thus avoid the possibility of confusion later—check the settings of the following options (all circled in Figure 1-3):

- Select **Photo Browser** in the shortcuts bar in the top-right portion of the workspace. This tells Elements to display multiple thumbnails at a time. Or you can press Ctrl+Alt+O.

- Set the pop-up menu in the lower-left corner of the screen to **Date (Newest First)**.

- Make sure the next-door **Details** check box is turned on.

- Do you see a couple of palettes along the right side of the window? If so, good. If not, click the ◀ **Organize Bin** text in the lower-right corner of the workspace.

- If you see big blue icons for the 13 music files (most likely you won't, but just in case), choose **View→Media Types**, turn off the **Audio** check box, and click **OK**. (Leave the **Photos**, **Video**, **Creations**, and **PDF** check boxes on.)

4. *Add photos to the catalog.* Click the camera button in the shortcuts bar in the top-left corner of the Organizer. Choose **From Files and Folders** from the pop-up menu to display the **Get Photos from Files and Folders** dialog box, as in Figure 1-4. (For the record, you can also choose File→Get Photos→From Files and Folders or press Ctrl+Shift+G.)

Figure 1-4.

5. *Navigate to the Lesson 01 folder.* Click the **Desktop** button on the left side of the dialog box to navigate to your computer's desktop. Locate and double-click the *Lesson Files-PE4 1on1* folder that you installed as directed in the Preface (see Step 5, page xv) to open this folder. Inside you will see folders for each of the 12 lessons in this book. Click the *Lesson 01* folder to select it. (Do not enter the folder; just select it.)

6. *Turn on the check boxes.* Turn on both the **Get Photos from Subfolders** and the **Automatically Fix Red Eyes** check boxes. The first option tells Elements to import all photos inside any and all folders that may reside in the *Lesson 01* folder. The

second option enables a new feature in Elements 4, one that promises to eliminate the dreaded flash-induced red eye before you ever get a chance to see it. In a moment, we'll see how well Elements performs this task.

7. *Get the photos.* Click the **Get Photos** button. Elements displays a fleeting window titled **Getting Photos** as it imports each of the 30 photographs contained inside the *Lesson 01* folder (see Figure 1-5). The browser window then fills with image thumbnails. A moment later, a progress bar appears as the program examines images that might contain red eye (see Figure 1-6). In all, about 60 percent of the photos are under suspicion. Just sit back and let the program do its thing.

Figure 1-5.

8. *Dismiss the messages.* After it checks for red eye, the Organizer presents you with the message in Figure 1-7. In the end, Elements decides that just two of the images contain subjects with red pupils. The message explains that both the corrected and original versions of each of these two photos have been preserved in special groups called version sets, about which we'll learn more later. Good to know, but not the sort of news you need to read every time you import images. So click the **Don't Show Again** check box and then click **OK**.

Figure 1-6.

Figure 1-7..

Next you must contend with the message pictured in Figure 1-8. Turns out, this one is irrelevant. Here's the gist: The program wants you to know that if your new catalog already contained some photos, the older images will now be hidden. But the catalog was empty, so no worries. Again, turn on the **Don't Show Again** check box and then click **OK**.

9. *Click the Back to All Photos button.* Or press the Backspace key. The newly imported photos are the only images in the catalog, so clicking **Back to All Photos** doesn't really change things. But you might as well get in the habit for when it does, right?

Figure 1-8.

10. *Make the thumbnails their absolute smallest.* Click the little ▦ button (the one that appears circled in red in Figure 1-9) to shrink the thumbnails to their smallest possible size. You should now be able to take in all 30 thumbnails at once—even though, it must be said, the thumbnails are very tiny. Incidentally, you might be tempted to play with the slider to the right of this icon. But I'd be much obliged if you would save at least some playing for the next exercise, during which I'll introduce you to the wonders of this seemingly innocuous slider.

Figure 1-9.

PEARL OF ⬤ WISDOM

If at any point you'd prefer to work with your own photos, choose File→ Catalog, click the Open button, select *My Catalog.psa*, and click yet another Open button. Your catalog is reinstated just as you left it. Use this same technique to switch back to the *PE4 1on1.psa* catalog when you're ready to move on to the next exercise.

Organizing Your Photos

The Organizer is obviously great at showing you a "big picture" overview of the photos in your catalog. But when you want to examine one of those photos in closer detail, the Organizer can also show you—quite literally—the *big picture*. This flexibility makes the workspace ideal for sorting through a large catalog that contains a few thousand images. You can zoom in to inspect the most minute details of a particular photo and then zoom back out to view the thumbnail in the context of its mates.

However, the Organizer is much more than a means to view your photos. It also lets you make important changes to images, including correcting rotation problems and changing filenames, precisely what we'll be doing in this exercise. But first we'll learn how to use the Organizer's flexible controls to examine image thumbnails—which is, after all, one of the workspace's most fun functions.

1. *Open the catalog.* If the *PE4 1on1* catalog remains open from the preceding exercise, skip to Step 2. Otherwise, choose **File→Catalog** or press Ctrl+Shift+C. Then click the **Open** button and double-click the *PE4 1on1.psa* file to open it. The contents of the catalog appear inside the Organizer.

   If necessary, click the ▦ icon to zoom all the way out, as you did at the end of the preceding exercise (see Figure 1-9 on the facing page). Notice that the month and year in which an image was taken appears below its thumbnail. If this information does not appear on your screen, turn on the Details check box at the bottom of the Organizer workspace.

2. *Enlarge the photos.* Slowly slide the thumbnail scale slider in the lower-right corner of the photo browser all the way to the right. Don't release the mouse button until you've reached the end of the slider. If you've a keen eye, you'll notice several things as you move the slider:

   - The thumbnails grow bigger, and therefore you see fewer of them on screen at a time.

   - At a certain point, Elements adds the date to the details displayed below each thumbnail. Then it adds the time of day when each photo was taken.

   - After you've moved the slider as far as it will go to the right (see Figure 1-10), you've entered what the Organizer calls the *single-photo view.* Elements also displays any caption information that you may have entered for the image. In our case, the Olympus-brand camera used to take these photos has automatically captioned each image *Olympus Digital Camera.* This information doesn't exactly help differentiate one photo from the next, but you can always click the caption below the large thumbnail, press Ctrl+A to select it, and enter a new caption.

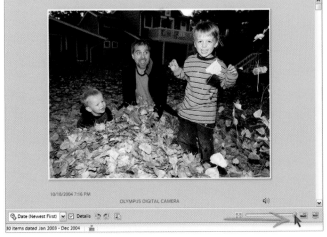

Figure 1-10.

The Organizer Interface

Your journey with Photoshop Elements 4 begins with the Organizer, which is where you acquire and manage your digital photographs. To make sure that you and I are speaking the same language as we venture through the exercises in this lesson, I'd like to take a moment to introduce you to this essential workspace. Labeled in the figure below, the key elements of the Organizer interface are as follows, in alphabetical order. (Red labels indicate terms that are discussed in the context of other interface elements.)

- **Catalog title:** The Organizer uses catalogs to keep track of the images on your hard drive, CDs, and other media. You can create a catalog using File→Catalog, or just accept the one the Organizer creates for you by default.

- **Cursor:** The cursor (sometimes called the *pointer*) is your mouse's on screen representative, moving to keep pace with your mouse. Use the cursor to select items, choose commands, and adjust settings.

- **Details:** In the photo browser mode, the Organizer lists information about a photograph below its thumbnail. You should at least see the date when the image was captured. To see the filename as well, press Ctrl+K and turn on Show File Names in Details.

To show or hide details, turn on or off the Details check box at the bottom of the workspace or press Ctrl+D.

- **Image thumbnail:** In the digital realm, the word *image* is a general term for any photograph or piece of scanned artwork. The Organizer previews images by displaying them as reduced *thumbnails*, varying in size from postage-stamp tiny to dollar-bill big. Clicking a thumbnail selects it and gives it a heavy blue outline. Press Shift while clicking to select a range of thumbnails; press Ctrl and click to select multiple nonadjacent thumbnails.

- **Menu bar:** Click a name in the menu bar to display a list of commands. Choose a command by clicking it. A command followed by three dots (such as Catalog...) displays a window of options called a *dialog box*. Otherwise, the command works right away.

- **Organize Bin:** Aligned to the right edge of the workspace, the Organize Bin contains the Tags, Collections, Order Prints, and Properties *palettes*, which are windows of options that can remain visible on the screen even when you are performing other tasks. Many palettes contain multiple panels. Move a palette by dragging the title bar at the top of the palette. Display a palette by choosing it from the Window menu or by clicking the tab that contains the palette's name.

Of the four palettes, I judge Properties to be the most critical for day-to-day work. The Properties palette lets you change filenames, add captions, and examine the EXIF metadata captured by a digital camera. To hide or show the Properties palette, press Alt+Enter. To free the Properties palette from the Organize Bin so it appears *free floating*, choose the command Window→Dock Properties in Organize Bin to turn it off.

- **Organizer views:** Click one of the two buttons in the top-right corner of the workspace to switch between the photo browser and date view modes. The *photo browser* shows a collection of thumbnails in the order defined by the sort order pop-up menu in the bottom-left corner of the workspace. Not shown in the figure, the *date view* organizes thumbnails into calendars, either by year, month, or day.

- **Shortcuts bar:** Located below the menu bar, the *shortcuts bar* offers quick access to some of the Organizer's most common functions. Icons with tiny down-point-ing triangles next to them (as in ▼) display menus of commands. Others produce immediate effects.

- **Shortcut menu:** Click the right mouse button (*right-click*) to display a shortcut menu related to the item you clicked. The Organizer provides shortcut menus in the photo browser and the date view, as well as inside some portions of the Tags, Collections, Order Prints, and Properties palettes.

- **Timeline:** Perched atop the photo browser window, the *timeline* charts the number of images that you captured on a month-by-month basis in the form of a standard-issue column graph. Each vertical bar is a month; a taller bar means more photos were shot in that month. Drag the blue month marker or click in the timeline to view a different month of thumbnails in the photo browser.

- **Window controls:** The top-right corner of the Organizer window sports three controls that let you hide, resize, and close the workspace, respectively. Except when the Organizer is maximized (as when you click the ☐ icon), you can drag the size handle in the bottom-right corner of the workspace to make the window bigger or smaller.

- **Zoom slider:** Click or drag along the slider bar in the lower-right corner of the workspace to change the size of the scalable, always-smooth thumbnails. Or press the ⊡ or ⊟ key to zoom incrementally. To zoom all the way in or out, click one of the icons on either side of the slider. You can also zoom all the way in—so that you see just one big thumbnail at a time—by pressing the Enter key. The icon on the far right of the slider launches the *full-screen view,* a built-in slide show for viewing images free from the distractions of the Organizer interface.

3. *Display filenames.* Turns out, I've already given these files something every bit as good as captions—distinctive filenames. So let's show the names. Choose **Edit→Preferences→General** or press Ctrl+K to open the **Preferences** dialog box. Then turn on the **Show File Names in Details** check box and click **OK**. (Depending on your default email client, Elements might request that you take a moment to fill out the Your Name and E-mail Address options. You can either do so or just set the E-mail Client option to something other than Adobe E-mail Service.) With any luck, the Organizer will display the filename *Leaves Max & Sam-1.jpg* beneath the date and time.

4. *Return to the small thumbnail size.* Previous to this, you've clicked the ▦ icon to switch to the small thumbnail view. This time, I want you to try something different: Click the green **Back** arrow (◉) in the upper-left corner of the Organizer workspace or press the Backspace key (or Alt+←). This option works like the Back button in a Web browser, taking you back to the most recent view.

5. *Switch to the largest thumbnail size.* Take your pick and do any one of the following:

   • Click the right-pointing arrow icon (the one that looks like ◉).

   • Press the equivalent keyboard shortcut, Alt+→.

   • Click the little picture frame icon (▣) to the immediate right of the thumbnail-size slider bar.

   Whichever method you choose, you will once again maximize the *Leaves Max & Sam-1.jpg* image in the photo browser. And in case you're wondering why we're going back and forth between views, I'm just trying to give you a sense for the many ways you can scale thumbnails in the Organizer.

Here's another: You can also make the thumbnail size shrink and grow by pressing the ⊟ and ⊞ keys, respectively. (That's the minus and plus keys, in case you can't quite identify them without reading glasses. And I say that as one who quite unfortunately identifies with your lack of identification.)

6. *View the first several photos.* To cycle through the images in single-photo view, press the ⇢ and ⇠ keys. Press ⇢ to advance through the photos of me and my boys playing in the leaves. (I'm the big kid with the facial hair.) Three presses of ⇢ takes you to the image named *Leaves Max & Sam-6_edited-1.jpg*, which you might notice has a small version set icon (⬛) in its upper-right corner.

PEARL OF ⬤ WISDOM

This is one of the two photos that Elements chose as having a red-eye problem. But as you can see, Elements was wrong. In fact, all eyes are closed. The high contrast between the pink areas of flesh and the dark, shadowed background fooled the software. We'll examine the program's success rate in the red-eye department more closely in the next lesson.

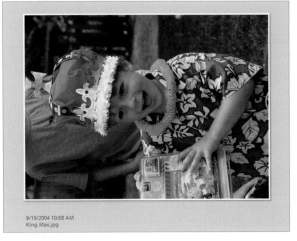

9/19/2004 10:58 AM
King Max.jpg

Figure 1-11.

Stop pressing ⇢ when you get to the *King Max.jpg* photo shown in Figure 1-11. As you can see, this photo is in need of some rotation.

7. *Rotate the photo.* You can use the icons at the bottom of the screen to rotate images 90 degrees counterclockwise or clockwise. Max needs a clockwise rotation, so click the ⬚ icon (circled in red in Figure 1-12) or press Ctrl+⇢. Figure 1-12 shows the result.

8. *Shrink the thumbnail view size.* Several other images need rotation, so we might as well correct them all at once. Drag the thumbnail slider triangle to the left or press the ⊟ key until you can see all 30 thumbnails clearly.

9. *Select the other thumbnails that need rotating.* Select the thumbnail for the next photo that needs rotating (dated 9/14/2004). Then press the Ctrl key and click the other photos that appear on their sides. You should end up with 14 selected thumbnails, as in Figure 1-13 on the next page.

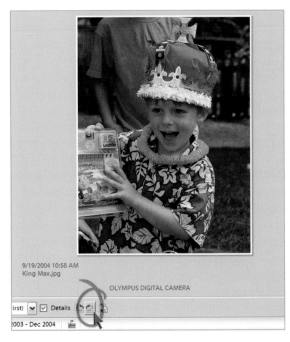

9/19/2004 10:58 AM
King Max.jpg

OLYMPUS DIGITAL CAMERA

irst) ☑ Details

2003 - Dec 2004

Figure 1-12.

10. *Rotate the selected thumbnails.* All the photos rest on their left sides. (Most built-in flashes perform best when the camera is tilted clockwise.) Press Ctrl+··→ or click the ⬆ icon. A moment later, the Organizer rotates the selected thumbnails upright.

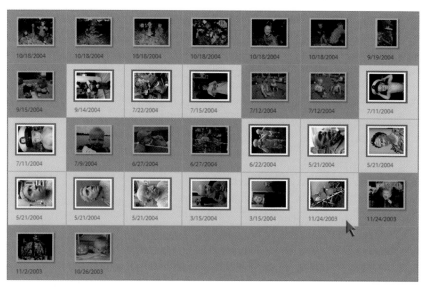

Figure 1-13.

11. *View the last photo in single-photo view.* Just one more problem to correct: All the images in the photo browser except the last one have descriptive filenames. So let's give it one. Double-click the last thumbnail. The selected image fills the photo browser window, as shown in Figure 1-14. I used a slow sync flash—that is, a flash that fired after a long exposure—to create the ghostly visage of my younger son. Chills the bone, doesn't it? As witnessed below the thumbnail, the photo still subscribes to the nondescript name assigned by the digital camera, *P7230025.jpg.* Chills the marrow.

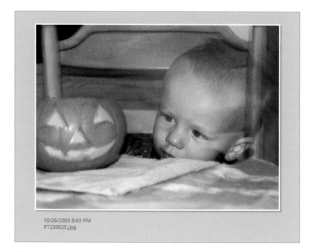

Figure 1-14.

12. *View the Properties palette.* Click the ▤ button to the right of the rotation icons at the bottom of the workspace, or press the keyboard shortcut Alt+Enter to display the **Properties** palette. If the Properties palette even slightly blocks your view of Sammy, choose **Window→Dock Properties in Organize Bin**. This takes what is otherwise a *free-floating palette* and anchors it to the Organize Bin. The Properties palette displays an abundance of information about the selected image. You can even use the palette to edit the image information.

13. ***Rename the selected photo.*** Let's change both the caption and the filename assigned to this photo:

- Click the **General** icon in the top-left corner of the Properties palette. This displays the Caption and Name fields.

- Click the **Caption** field. Press Ctrl+A to select the existing Olympus advertisement and replace it with "Sammy examines a Jack-O'-Lantern," or words to that effect.

- Press the Tab key to advance to the **Name** option and replace it with "Sam & pumpkin.jpg." Then press the Enter key to accept the change.

Figure 1-15 shows the new caption and filename as they appear both in the Properties palette and under the magnified image preview.

Figure 1-15.

Creating and Using Tags

Computers and digital cameras have transformed the way we capture photographs. But although the trappings are different, the methods are often familiar. Consider storage and organization, for example. Where once we had shoeboxes, now we have hard drives. More often than not, our pictures reside in those digital shoeboxes just as pell-mell as in their physical counterparts. But what the traditional shoebox doesn't have is the Organizer. Assuming that you're willing to invest the time—a big *if*, to be sure—you

Figure 1-16.

can document photos in minute detail, which permits you to later search through them in a matter of seconds. This feature is so fantastic that many Photoshop users also own Elements simply to use the Organizer's unique image management capabilities.

Photoshop Elements lets you assign labels to images using tags. Strictly speaking, a *tag* is a descriptive keyword that you can associate with a photo. The tag also includes a tiny graphic, giving it some visual presence and making it easier to identify. You can apply a tag to many photos at once, and a single photo may have multiple tags attached. For instance, if you and your brother take a vacation to Guatemala, you might create a Guatemala tag and apply it to all those vacation photos. You might also want to create a tag for your brother, which you would naturally apply to all the photos you shot of him, including those taken in Guatemala (as symbolically illustrated in Figure 1-16). You can create tags for virtually anything—people, pets, places, events, you name it—and share them between images as much as you like.

All this tagging pays off when you're searching through thousands of digital photos for a specific shot. Double-click the Guatemala tag, for example, and the Organizer displays only the photos with that tag attached. Add the tag for your brother to the mix, and the Organizer displays only those photos that show your brother in Guatemala. Or, you could *exclude* your brother's tag from the Guatemala shots, displaying only brotherless vacation photos. The virtual nature of tags makes it possible to group, sort, and arrange photos in multiple ways. If you've ever been frustrated trying to organize a large number of physical objects—should your *Tommy* CD be filed under Opera or The Who?—you'll love the infinite flexibility of tags.

In this exercise, we're going to create and apply tags to some of the 30 imported photos in the *PE4 1on1* catalog. Because tags are so flat-out amazing, this exercise is a little longer than some. But trust me, your time will be well spent. Just imagine the payoff when you apply tags to not just 30 photos but also your own vast and ever-growing library of photographs.

You create and manage tags in the Tags palette. (If you don't see the Tags palette at the top of the Organize Bin, click the Tags tab to bring it forward.) Every catalog starts out with a few starter tags as well as some categories and subcategories to keep the tags organized. (Turns out, you can also assign categories directly to thumbnails, too.) As you tag your own images, you'll likely want to create a hierarchical system of tag categories and subcategories. Just remember that the tags you create are saved in a particular catalog file, not with the associated images. If you start a fresh catalog, the Organizer makes only its default tags available to you.

1. *Open the lesson catalog.* This exercise starts exactly where the last one left off. Open the *PE4 1on1* catalog, if it's not already open, by using the **File→Catalog** command. Then scroll to the last thumbnail, *Sam & pumpkin.jpg*, and double-click it so that you see it in the single-photo view.

2. *Close the Order Prints palette.* We're not going to be ordering prints anytime soon, so click the ✕ in the upper-right corner of the **Order Prints** palette. Then drag the horizontal line between the Tags and Properties palettes so the two palettes are about equal in size. Now we have room to work.

If you ever want the Order Prints palette to return, just choose it from the Window menu. If the Properties palette is not available, choose Window→Properties or press Alt+Enter.

---

3. *Create a new tag.* Choose **New Tag** from the **New** pop-up menu or press Ctrl+N to display the **Create Tag** dialog box. Enter the information shown in Figure 1-17, like so:

   • This tag will be applied to pictures of my pumpkin-curious son Sammy, so type "Sam" in the **Name** field.

   • As is often the case, our new tag fits handily in an existing category. Go to the **Category** pop-up menu and select **Family**, which is a subcategory of People.

   • Click the **OK** button to create the new tag. The ▼'s next to the People and Family categories automatically twirl open to reveal the Sam tag.

You can choose View→Collapse All Tags or press Ctrl+Alt+T to twirl closed all the categories in the Tags palette. Choose View→Expand All Tags or press Ctrl+Alt+X to twirl them all open.

Figure 1-17.

Graphical creatures that they are, tags display little thumbnails to tie a visual reference to the tag. The Sam tag sports a question mark because we haven't yet applied it to an image. We'll remedy that in the next step.

Incidentally, don't double-click the tag. I mention this because it's such a natural operation—seemed logical to me, anyway—but it runs a search, one that comes up empty. If I didn't catch you in time and you have accidentally double-clicked, just click the 🏛 icon in front of the Sam tag to turn off the search results. Then press the End key to advance to the final image in the catalog, the one of Sam.

4. *Apply the Sam tag.* Instead of double-clicking, drag and drop the Sam tag onto the picture of Sam and the pumpkin. You'll notice that several things happen:

   - The tag appears momentarily in the lower-left corner of the thumbnail, and then disappears.

   - The details area below the thumbnail shows the Sam tag and the People category icon, circled in Figure 1-18.

   - Also circled in the figure, Elements replaces the question mark on the tag with an itty-bitty Sammy.

Figure 1-18.

As it so happens, this particular photo of Sam doesn't make a good tag graphic because we can't see all of his face and he's lost in the tiny 22-by-22-pixel icon. We'll correct that in Step 12 (see page 24). In the meantime, let's add an event tag that tells us that this is a Halloween photo.

5. *Create a Holidays tag category.* We could place the Halloween tag in the predefined Events category, but I reckon holidays are sufficiently special to deserve their own category. That's the great thing about tags; you can organize them any way you like. Here's how (as documented in Figure 1-19):

- Click the **New** button at the top of the **Tags** palette and choose **New Category** from the resulting pop-up menu to display the **Create Category** dialog box.

- Click the **Choose Color** button to select a color to represent this category. This color will be used to color the tops and edges of all subcategories and tags, just as the current Family and Friends subcategories and the Sam tag use the orange color of the People category. Turquoise is the default color; click **OK** to accept it.

- Type "Holidays" in the **Category Name** field.

- Select a representative category icon. My suggestion: click the third option, the desk calendar. Click **OK** and the Holidays category appears at the bottom of the Tags palette.

Figure 1-19.

PEARL OF WISDOM

By default, you can move categories up or down in the Tags palette in any order you want, but tags are alphabetized within their categories. If you don't like this behavior, choose Edit→Preferences→Tags and Collections. Then click the options to switch categories, subcategories, and tags between Manual and Alphabetical modes.

---

6. *Create a Halloween tag.* Instead of going back to the New button at the top of the Tags palette, just right-click the **Holidays** category and choose **Create new tag in Holidays category**. The Holidays category is already selected in the **Create Tag** dialog box. Simply type "Halloween" in the **Name** field and click **OK**. The new tag sports a question mark and the Holidays category's turquoise color.

7. *Apply the Halloween tag.* This time, drag and drop the image of Sammy and his orange friend onto the **Halloween** tag in the **Tags** palette. As you can see, tagging images works both ways. The Holidays icon and Halloween tag appear alongside the People icon and Sam tag below the image preview.

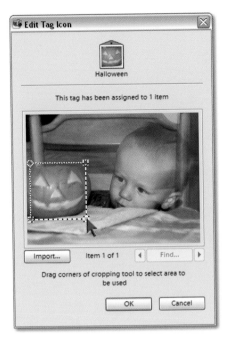

Figure 1-20.

8. *Edit the Halloween tag icon.* If you ask me, the jack-o'-lantern makes a good icon for the Halloween tag, but we need to edit the icon to make it more legible. With the Halloween tag still selected, do the following:

- Click the pencil icon (✐) at the top of the Tags palette to display the **Edit Tag** dialog box.

- Click the **Edit Icon** button to display the **Edit Tag Icon** dialog box. The animated square marquee on the big image thumbnail shows the cropping area for the tag icon.

- Resize and reposition the marquee so that it frames the pumpkin's face, as in Figure 1-20. Drag a square corner handle of the marquee to shrink it; drag inside the marquee to move it. Notice that the preview at the top of the dialog box updates to show you what the tag icon will look like. When you're happy with the preview, click **OK**.

- Click **OK** again in the Edit Tag Icon dialog box to change the Halloween tag in the Tags palette.

9. *Apply the Halloween tag.* One more image needs the Halloween tag. To locate it, press the ⊟ key until you can see all 30 thumbnails. Most likely, the tag details will disappear from below the final thumbnail, replaced by a blue tag icon, which tells you that at least one tag is applied. Then locate the photo of Max in a Batman costume. It's the ninth image in the list, dated 9/14/2004. (Max was trying on his costume a bit early.) Then do like so:

- Double-click the thumbnail to zoom in on it.

- In the spirit of discovering yet another way to apply tags, right-click the *Maxman.jpg* image preview. Then choose **Attach Tag→Holidays→Halloween**. Sort of cumbersome, but it's a technique. The Halloween icon appears momentarily, shortly replaced by the Holiday icon and Halloween tag below and to the right of the preview.

Whether your images appear large or small, you can still inspect the tags applied to a thumbnail. Just select the thumbnail in the Organizer and click the Tags icon at the top of the Properties palette.

---

10. *Search for faces in the photos.* To help us finish applying the Sam tag to the appropriate photos, we'll use a hot new feature in Photoshop Elements 4 that automatically searches a collection of photographs for faces.

Here's how it works:

- First, zoom out from the thumbnails by pressing the ⊡ key a couple of times.

- Then press Ctrl+Shift+A to deselect all the thumbnails so you can search the entire catalog at once.

- Now choose **Find→Find Faces for Tagging**. Or click the little face icon (🔍) at the top of the Tags palette.

Elements asks if you're sure you want to analyze every single image in the photo browser (see Figure 1-21). This is a small catalog, so it won't take much time. Click the **OK** button to display the **Face Tagging** window. Elements searches through the 30 images in the catalog and creates thumbnails for more than 20 faces, as in Figure 1-22. (Note: your faces may vary.)

Figure 1-21.

PEARL OF ⚪ WISDOM

All 30 photos in the catalog contain at least one face. (Including the statues, I count 43 human faces in all, plus a sheep and a pumpkin.) But while the program can find multiple faces in a single image, it can't see faces in profiles, nor can it identify the backs of people's heads. On the bright side, virtually everything tagged as a face actually *is* a face. (One tag features hands.) One of the ancient statues was apparently realistic enough to rate identification. My jack-o'-lantern carving skills, on the other hand, have a long way to go.

---

11. *Apply the Sam tag to other photos.* The fact that the Tags palette is built right into the Face Tagging window means we can apply the Sam tag to the found faces.

- In the Face Tagging window, click the first image of Sammy's face, which (if you're having trouble telling my kids apart) is the fourth thumbnail.

- Ctrl-click on each of the other thumbnails to select the other pictures of Sammy, which appear circled in Figure 1-22. (Your thumbnails may appear in different locations.) You should end up with a total of nine faces selected.

- Go to the **Tags** palette and twirl open the **People** category and the **Family** subcategory. Then drag the **Sam** tag onto any one of the selected thumbnails.

Figure 1-22.

This tags all the selected thumbnails, making it the fastest way to tag a group of images in one fell swoop.

Rather abruptly, the tagged images disappear from the main window. To redisplay the Sammy faces, turn on the Show Already Tagged Faces check box at the top of the Face Tagging window.

---

12. *Modify the Sam tag icon.* Still inside the Face Tagging window, create a more legible icon for Sam's tag as follows:

   - With the **Sam** tag selected, click the ✐ icon at the top of the Tags palette to display the **Edit Tag** dialog box, which says you've assigned the tag to 10 images.

   - Click the **Edit Icon** button to open the **Edit Tag Icon** dialog box. There you'll see Sam and his pumpkin.

   - Notice that the Find button is flanked by two arrowheads, ◄ and ►, which allow you to scroll through the tagged images. That's great, but it's even easier to click the **Find** button, which displays a scrolling list of all the tagged images.

   - See that photo of Sammy with the silver juice packet (selected in Figure 1-23)? It's a good full-on face shot, even if Sammy has a bit of a trail running out of his nose. (If you're grossed out by baby goop, do yourself a favor and don't inspect the picture too closely.) Select the image and click **OK**.

   - Back in the Edit Tag Icon dialog box, adjust the marquee until it focuses on Sam's face, as in Figure 1-24. Then click the **OK** button.

   - Click **OK** once more to escape the maze of dialog boxes and update the Sam tag. (If you still see the old icon in the bottom-right corner of the window, don't worry. The tag really has been updated.)

Figure 1-23.

13. *Create a tag for Max.* In the **Face Tagging** window, right-click the **Family** subcategory in the **Tags** palette and choose **Create new tag in Family sub-category**. Enter "Max" in the **Name** field. Even though you haven't applied this tag to a thumbnail—heck, you haven't even finished creating the darn thing yet—you can click the Edit Icon button and hunt for a picture of Max on your hard drive. But it's much easier to choose a tag icon after the tag has been applied to an image or two. So click **OK** to add the Max tag (with question mark) to the Family subcategory.

14. *Select the faces of Max.* All but three of the remaining faces belong to Max, so the easiest thing to do is press Ctrl+A to select all the face images, and then Ctrl-click the three that aren't Max. (I trust you can tell which ones those are.) Figure 1-25 below shows the selected faces. If you don't see the exact Max images shown in the figure, no biggie; select the ones you can see.

15. *Apply the Max tag to the selected photos.* Drag the Max tag onto the *Captain Max.jpg* thumbnail that I circled in orange in Figure 1-25. Not only does Elements apply the Max tag to all the selected thumbnails, it assigns the *Captain Max.jpg* image as the tag's icon. If you drag a question mark tag onto a selected thumbnail, that thumbnail becomes the tag icon. The icon could probably use a little cropping, so feel free to click the ✏ icon and adjust the marquee at your discretion.

16. *Create a subcategory.* If you have a large family, you might want a category for each branch of the family tree. Luckily, the Organizer lets you create an unlimited number of categories. Right-click the **Family** item to display a shortcut menu and choose **Create new sub-category in Family sub-category**. Then type "Kids" in the **Sub-Category Name** option and click **OK**.

17. *Place the tags inside the subcategory.* Drag and drop the **Sam** and **Max** tags onto the **Kids** icon to place them inside the new subcategory.

18. *Close the Face Tagging window.* Leaving the headshots of me and the statue (I believe that's Nero) untagged, click the **Done** button to close the Face Tagging window and return to the Organizer.

19. *Do some clean-up tagging.* The Face Tagging command isn't quite perceptive enough to identify all the faces. So you'll need to do a little manual clean-up tagging to make sure Sam and Max are properly identified in all the photos. The catalog includes 6 photos of Sam by himself and 8 of Max (see Figure 1-26 on the next page). Another 11 photos, including all the leaf pictures, feature both boys. Again, if you miss a couple of images, no big deal. I won't be grading you on how well you identify my family. The purpose of this exercise is to provide a complete picture of how tagging works so you can better identify family.

Figure 1-24..

Figure 1-25..

Figure 1-26.

By now, you've done a lot of work. You've created tags and categories, you've assigned the tags to images, and you've edited tag icons. Plus, you've spent a fair amount of time meticulously selecting thumbnails, which is great practice for working in the Organizer. But truth be told, applying tags is only half the battle. The big payoff comes when you want to find pictures fast. If you want to take a break, now's a good time. Otherwise, stick with me as we exploit the true power of tags: searching.

20. *Search for thumbnails with the Sam tag.* In the Tags palette, notice the empty square to the left of each tag and category name. Click inside the square to the left of the **Sam** tag (circled in Figure 1-27 on the facing page) to display a 🔍 icon and view only those thumbnails that are associated with the tag. The tag that governs (or *filters*) the search appears in the top-left corner of the Organizer window. The Matching information on the right shows that the 17 images that include Sammy best fit the search while the 13 that don't include him do not fit the search at all. (This assumes that you took care to tag *all* the Sammy images in Step 19 on the preceding page.)

21. *Add the Halloween tag to the search filter.* Scroll down the **Tags** list and click in the square to the left of the **Halloween** tag. This displays another 🔍 icon and refines the search to only those images that contain both the Sam and Halloween tags (not one or the other, as you might expect). Thus, only one image appears in the Organizer, the one of Sam and his pumpkin.

You can also search by dragging tags from the Tags palette directly into the Find area above the thumbnails.

22. *View the closely matching search results.* Notice that the check box labeled 1 Best is selected above the thumbnails, which indicates that the one thumbnail that best matches the search is being displayed. Turn on the **17 Close** check box and deselect the **1 Best** check box. As Figure 1-28 shows, the Organizer now reveals the images that fit the search filter closely, but not the one that matches exactly. In other words, the

Visible thumbnails
match this tag

17 images match the
Sam tag, 13 do not

Figure 1-27.

2 tags filter thumbnails

1 image includes
both tags, 17 include
one or the other, and
12 include neither

Figure 1-28.

17 images visible in the photo browser include either the Sam tag or the Halloween tag, but not both. If you were to turn on the 12 Not check box, the Organizer would show you the dozen images that have neither tag.

23. *View all the images.* Click the **Back to All Photos** button above the photo browser window. The Organizer cancels the search filter—both 🔍 icons disappear from the Tags palette—and the photo browser once again displays all 30 thumbnails.

24. *Search for all images having the Max tag.* To search for images linked to a single tag, you can double-click the appropriate tag. For example, double-click the **Max** tag in the **Tags** palette and the Organizer displays the 19 images with the Max tag.

25. *Filter out the Sam tag images.* Right-click the **Sam** tag in the Tags palette and choose **Exclude photos with Sam tag from search results**. A red ⊘ icon appears next to the Sam tag, showing that any image featuring Sammy is excluded from the search (poor guy). In other words, the Organizer shows the 8 images that feature Max but not Sam, as pictured in Figure 1-29.

Figure 1-29.

Incidentally, just in case you're wondering whether you can search for thumbnails that have *no* tags, the answer is, oh gosh yes. Just choose Find→Untagged Items or press Ctrl+Shift+Q.

Now that you know how to create tags—and just how powerful they can be—a few quick words about getting rid of them: To remove a tag from a thumbnail, right-click the thumbnail and choose Remove Tag. Then select the tag that you want to remove from the ensuing submenu. If you want to delete a tag from the Tags palette, either select the tag and click the trash can icon at the top of the palette or right-click the tag and choose the Delete command. You can delete any of the Organizer's default tags except the Favorites and Hidden tags (the latter of which lets you hide thumbnails without removing them from a catalog). Deleting a tag removes it from any photos to which it has been applied; the photos themselves stay put.

Making Collections

If tags are virtual Post-it notes that you affix to your images, then *collections* are virtual paper trays that permit you to sort your photos. Simply put, they let you assemble minicatalogs of images, related by whatever topics you might dream up. Elements implements collections very much like it implements tags. You create and modify collections in a palette, and then drag and drop them from the Collections palette onto thumbnails in the photo browser window.

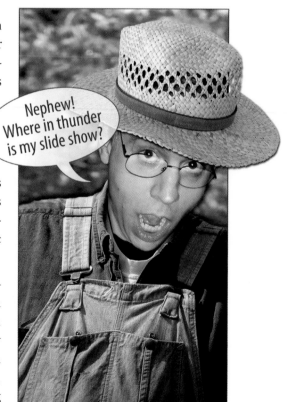

Figure 1-30.

The one big advantage collections have over the search results produced by tags is that you can change the order of your photos in the browser window and save that sort order with the collection. So if you need to arrange a sequence of images in a specific order inside a group, collections are the way to go.

You might also think of tags and collections this way: Generally speaking, tags are designed to organize images that share a common subject; collections are for images that share a common destination. And in Photoshop Elements 4, you can now instantly share a collection through an online photo service. (You'll learn how to share photos online in Lesson 11.) In this brief exercise, we'll create a collection of images with the intent of turning them into a slide show to send to my Uncle Zeke. (The fact that I don't really have such an uncle, and if I did, he might or might not look like the guy in Figure 1-30, is of no consequence.) We'll add a few photos to the collection and then arrange them in a specific order. Having just completed the preceding exercise on tags, a lot of this exercise will seem familiar, but never fear; I'll point out many subtle but important distinctions as we go along.

1. *Open the Organizer.* If you have the Organizer open from the last exercise, skip to Step 2. If not, choose **File→Catalog**, click the **Open** button, and open the *PE4 1on1.psa* file. I'm assuming that you've completed the three previous exercises. If you haven't, you'll have the most luck if you perform them in order first.

2. *Display the Collections palette.* Click the **Back to All Photos** button at the top of the photo browser to see all 30 thumbnails. Then click the **Collections** tab to the right of Tags.

3. *Create a new collection.* Click the **New** button at the top of the Collections palette to bring up a pop-up menu that lets you create a new collection or a new collection group. Like tag categories, *collection groups* let you organize collections into, well, groups. If you're feeling fussy, you can even create (or *nest*) one collection group inside another. But unlike tags, collections do not have to be organized. Whereas a tag must belong to a category, a collection can roam free. So there's no need to create a collection group unless you really want to.

That said, here's what I want you to do:

- Choose **New Collection** to display the **Create Collection** dialog box.

- Select the desired group from the **Group** pop-up menu. If you already created one or more collection groups, they would appear in the Group pop-up menu. As it is, your only choice is **None (Top Level)**.

- Type "Slide show for Uncle Zeke" in the **Name** option, as in Figure 1-31. (If you can't bring yourself to enter that, name the collection whatever you want.)

- Click **OK** to add the new collection to the Collections palette, complete with a question mark to show that it's empty.

4. *Select a few photos.* Now to add some photos to the collection. Scroll to the bottom of the photo browser. Select the five sculpted busts by clicking the first one and then Shift-clicking the last. Shot in the Victoria and Albert Museum in London, these heads hail from the famous Fakes and Forgeries gallery. Being an art forger by trade, Uncle Zeke should be interested.

Figure 1-31.

But since he's also a family guy, we need to add a picture of my kids and me. So press Ctrl+Home to move to the top of the catalog without deselecting the statues. Then Ctrl-click the first thumbnail—the one of my boys and me in the leaves—to add it to the selection.

5. *Add the images to the collection.* As with tags, you can right-click one of the selected thumbnails and choose the Add Selected Items to Collection command from the shortcut menu. But better to drag the question mark icon from the **Collections** palette onto the first sculpture thumbnail. This way, the bearded fellow becomes the icon for the collection, as illustrated in Figure 1-32. If you don't like the way the icon is cropped or centered, click the ✏ icon at the top of the Collections palette and then click the Edit Icon button, as directed in the preceding exercise (see Step 12, page 24). Personally, I think that dignified old phoney looks pretty swell as he is.

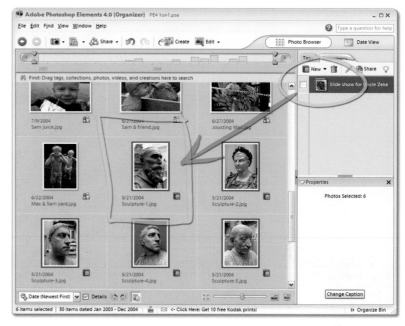

Figure 1-32.

Depending on your zoom level, you may notice that the sculpture thumbnails sport blue tags; they have in essence been "tagged" with a collection. (As I implied earlier, the distinction between tags and collections can be a little cloudy.) Larger thumbnails sport little book icons when they're part of a collection.

6. *View the photos in the collection.* Click the box to the left of the **Slide Show for Uncle Zeke** collection in the Collections palette to display the 🔖 icon. As in Figure 1-33 on the next page, the photo browser displays the 6 images in your collection. Although this might seem identical to filtering images with tags, there is a difference: You can't combine multiple collections to filter thumbnails as we did with the Sam and Halloween tags in the preceding exercise. One collection search cancels the other.

Notice that each thumbnail presents a number in its upper-left corner. Because you added the thumbnails at the same time, they remain in date order, as in the Organizer. If you had added thumbnails to a collection one at a time, they would appear in the order in which they were added. But regardless of their initial order, you can re-sort the thumbnails any way you like.

7. *Reorder the images.* Let's save the image of me and the lads for the end of the slide show. Drag the first thumbnail to the end of the collection. As you drag, notice that a vertical yellow line shows you where the photo will land. When the yellow line appears after the sixth thumbnail, release your mouse button.

Because I'm particularly fond of the expression that adorns the last of the sculpted busts—he has a sort of "What, me awake?" thing going on—drag it to the front of the collection. Make sure your thumbnails are arranged as they appear in Figure 1-34.

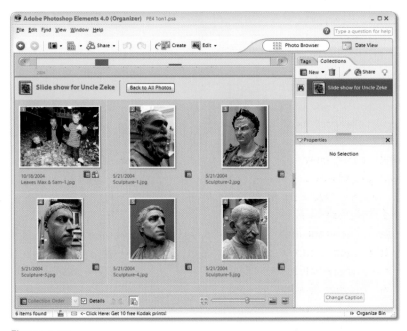

Figure 1-33.

Much to my delight, the images now appear in the order that I want to show them to my dear Uncle Zeke. To preview this collection of images as a slide show, choose View→View Photos in Full Screen or press the F11 key. For this collection, I recommend that you turn off the Include Captions check box and set the Background Music option to None. Then click the OK button to enter the full-screen photo review mode. Click the play button (◉) in the top-left corner of the screen to set the slide show playing. When you've had enough, click the stop button (⊗) or press the Esc key. For complete information on this photo-reviewing mode, read the last exercise in this lesson, "Comparing Similar Photos," which begins on page 41.

Finding Photos by Date

Often, a photo's most distinguishing feature isn't the who, the what, or the where—it's the *when*. And if you need to search for photos by when they were taken, the Organizer gives you the *how*. I'm speaking of the *date view*, which fills your screen with a calendar and shows thumbnails of your images in the date cells. It's a great way to view your photos in the context of time, giving you an illustrated calendar of your very own special events.

The Organizer draws a photo's date from its *EXIF metadata*. Although this sounds technical, EXIF (pronounced *eks-if*) is actually a common standard that imparts such basic information as the time the photo was taken, the make and model of camera, the aperture setting, the focal length, and whether the flash fired. Most digital cameras save EXIF metadata when the shot is taken. If no EXIF info exists, as in the case of a scanned image, the Organizer uses the date the image was last modified.

Figure 1-34.

This system works extremely well—except when the Organizer assigns a date that's just plain wrong. And it's pretty easy for that to happen. For example, if you don't set your camera's clock, the EXIF metadata will be inaccurate. And if you scan in an ancient photo, you'll probably want the Organizer to manage the image according to when the photo was originally taken, not when you last edited the scan. Luckily, the Organizer gives you the power to override the recorded info and assign new dates and times.

In this exercise, we'll do just that, adjusting the time for a few photographs to account for shifting time zones. Then we'll move on to explore the timeline and see how it lets you limit searches to a specific period of time. Finally, we'll take a look at the date view's various calendar settings and see how to change the display of thumbnails and important events.

1. *View all imported thumbnails.* As in previous exercises, take a moment to make sure the *PE4 1on1* catalog is open inside the Organizer. Also, if necessary, click

the **Back to All Photos** button at the top of the workspace to make sure all 30 images are available in the photo browser.

2. *Examine the recorded date and time for the first piece of sculpture.* Check that the **Properties** palette is open. (If it isn't, press Alt+Enter to bring it up.) Then double-click the thumbnail for the *Sculpture-1.jpg* photo—the one of the fellow with the great beard—to magnify the image so it fills the screen. Now view the **General** settings in the Properties palette. As

shown in Figure 1-35, Elements seems to be under the impression that I shot the photo on May 21, 2004 at 7:27 A.M. Strange, that, because I distinctly remember still being in bed at that time, dreaming about things that thankfully had nothing to do with Photoshop Elements or digital photography. Meanwhile, the V&A museum doesn't even open until 10 A.M.

I shot these photos in London. But my camera, an Olympus C-5060, was still on Colorado time, seven hours earlier. And so the camera—being unable to gauge my position on the planet's surface or the sun's altitude in the sky—embedded Colorado's time of day into the metadata of all the London photos.

Figure 1-35.

3. *Adjust the time of day for the V&A pics.* Zoom out and select all five sculpture photos by clicking the first one and Shift-clicking the last. Then choose **Edit→Adjust Date and Time of Selected Items** or press Ctrl+J to display the winsome dialog box shown in Figure 1-36. This dialog box presents you with four options:

   • The first allows you to set all selected photos to a single date and time, according to your specifications.

   • The second option tells the Organizer to ignore the EXIF metadata and instead sets the date and time of each file to the last time it was modified.

   • The third option allows you to enter a new date and time for the earliest of the selected photos and then shifts the others relative to the first. If your camera's clock was set incorrectly, the relative increments from one wrong time to the next are accurate. In other words, correct the earliest photo in the sequence and the others will be updated in kind.

- The fourth option lets you adjust the time of each photo by a set number of hours, just what we need to correct the time zone problem.

Users of Elements 3 may remember being able to simply click the date under the image to bring up the dialog box in Figure 1-36, but that no longer works automatically. To reactivate this handy feature, press Ctrl+K to go to the General panel of Preferences and turn on the final check box, Adjust Date and Time by clicking on Thumbnail Dates.

Figure 1-36.

Select the final option, **Shift by set number of hours (time zone adjust)**, and then click **OK**. Elements displays another dialog box (also shown in Figure 1-36) that lets you move the time forward or backward a prescribed number of hours. Select the **Ahead** option and set **Hours** to 7. Then click the **OK** button. Once again, click the first thumbnail bust and note the new time: 3:27 P.M. The Organizer now records the time just as if I had advanced my camera's clock when I was in London.

PEARL OF ● WISDOM

It's worth noting that the new times are recorded within the context of the catalog file only. Photoshop Elements scrupulously avoids changing the EXIF metadata embedded in the files because Adobe's lawyers regard EXIF as legal data, potentially admissible in a court of law. Although I personally consider this notion ridiculous—it's an easy matter to fake EXIF information with no one the wiser—the cogs of the great legislative wheel turn slowly. For now, EXIF is (supposedly) off-limits.

4. *Take a look at the timeline.* That long strip between the shortcuts bar and the photo browser is the Organizer's *timeline*. Pictured in Figure 1-37, the timeline contains a series of pale blue bars. As in a standard bar graph, each bar represents a month in which the photos in the catalog were originally captured by a digital camera. The taller the blue bar, the more photos there are for that month. Click a blue bar to display the dark blue marker (the one with the green bar inside it). You can drag this marker along the timeline to focus on a particular month, or just click a different bar to reposition the marker.

Figure 1-37.

5. *Change the thumbnail size and view.* To appreciate how helpful the timeline can be, we need to adjust our view of the photo browser a bit. First, click the **I▶ Organize Bin** item in the bottom-right corner of the workspace to hide the palettes along the right side of the screen. Then drag the thumbnail-size slider to the right or press the ⊡ key until three or four thumbnails fit on the screen horizontally. Finally, press Ctrl+End so you're viewing the final images in the catalog. As you may recall, these are the earliest images in the catalog, with the last photo captured October 2003.

6. *Focus on the tallest bar.* To switch to a different point in time, click the third bar from the right in the timeline, which represents the seven photos from July 2004. As Figure 1-38 shows, the photo browser jumps to display the first thumbnail for that month, which shows Max on a four-wheeler. Just to make sure you don't miss the thumbnail, Elements temporarily outlines it in green and flashes the time marker. No need to wonder what photos you shot in a specific month; Elements couldn't make it any clearer.

Figure 1-38.

7. *Narrow the timeline's date range to 2003.* In addition to the vertical bars, the timeline features *range markers*—the blue down-and-up pointers on either side of the timeline—that you can use to narrow a specific period of time. Drag the right range

marker to **2004** under the timeline. As witnessed in Figure 1-39, this limits the photo browser photos so we are seeing photos shot only after 2003.

Dragging the range markers lets you limit the time range in one-month increments. If you need to set specific start and end dates for your range, choose Find→Set Date Range or press Ctrl+Alt+F, and then specify the start and end dates for your search. To clear a date range, choose Find→ Clear Date Range or press Ctrl+Shift+F.

---

8. *View images that have the Max tag.* The timeline interacts with tag filters to help you find exactly the photos you're looking for. Bring back the Organize Bin and display the **Tags** palette. Then double-click the **Max** tag. Despite the fact that the catalog includes 19 images tagged to Max, only the 2 from 2003 appear on the screen. If you look closely, you may also notice that the timeline changes to reflect the influence of the tag. Of the 3 images for November 2003, 2 feature Max, so the bar for that month is two-thirds blue and one-third empty. The preceding month, October 2003, includes a single photo and Max isn't in it; therefore, that bar is empty.

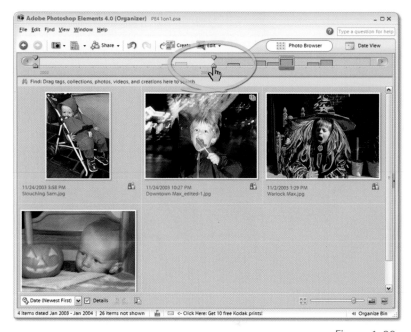

Figure 1-39.

9. *Switch to the date view.* Now let's check out the date view. Click the large **Date View** button in the upper-right corner of the workspace. You should now see a month calendar; if not, click the **Month** button at the bottom of the screen.

Click the ◐ and ◑ buttons on either side of the month name at the top of the calendar to switch from one month to another. Or you can press the bracket keys, ⬚ and ⬚.

---

10. *Navigate back to October 2004.* Whether by button or by bracket key, make your way backwards in time to October 2004. As pictured in Figure 1-40 on the next page, the calendar displays the holidays of Thanksgiving (Canada) and Halloween in lavender. Even more significantly, an image thumbnail appears in the cell for October 18, which happens to be the very

day that my wife shot the photos of the boys and me playing in the leaves. That's the beauty of the month view—the photos you take on a given day are automatically assigned to the corresponding cell in the calendar.

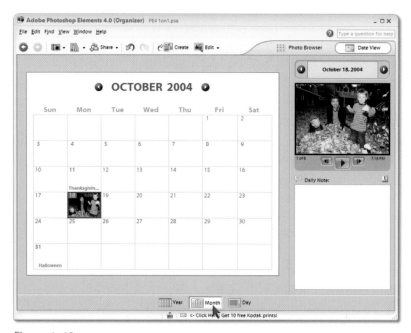

Figure 1-40.

The right side of the workspace lets you view photos and modify information associated with the selected day, October 18:

- Click the big blue ▶ button to the right of the calendar to play an instant (albeit tiny) slide show of all the images for the selected day. Click the blue ◀ or ▶ button to move through the images one at a time.

- The tiny desk calendar icon (🗐) below the right side of the inset slide show window lets you add special events to the calendar. You'll learn more about this shortly.

- Directly below the slide show is the Daily Note area, where you can click to enter any information that occurs to you about the selected day. I very much recommend it. Just a few notes can spark a lot of memories later.

Because the timeline, tags, and collections aren't features of the date view, the various limits and filters of the photo browser have no effect here. All photos for a specific month are available from the date cells and inset slide show window.

11. *Navigate to May 2004.* This time, click the word **October** at the top of the calendar to display a pop-up menu that lists the other months of the year. A photo icon indicates that a month includes pictures. Choose **May** from the menu.

May has four holidays, and I'd like to add a special event, Uncle Zeke's birthday. I could accomplish this by clicking the cell for his birthday, May 23, and then clicking the desk calendar icon on the far right side of the workspace. But for holidays and events, I prefer to go to command central: the Calendar preferences.

12. *Customize the Calendar preferences.* Choose **Edit→Preferences→Calendar** to display the dialog box shown in Figure 1-41. The first category of calendar preferences is Options, of which there is only one: Whether to use Monday as the first day of the week or keep it as Sunday. Leave this check box turned off.

Take a scroll through the Holidays list, and you'll see that the folks at Adobe have perversely decided to deactivate just one holiday from their long list: April Fools' Day. Someone at Adobe probably figures it inspires too much inner-office ruckus. But heck, it's such fun ruckus. So turn on the **April Fools' Day** check box. If you want to eliminate the bad ruckus, I say turn off **Valentine's Day**. (Gents, back me up here.)

Finally, here's the category of options we're looking for: Events. Figure 1-42 on the next page shows what I want you to do. This list tells you to:

- Click the **New** button to display the **Create New Event** dialog box.

- Enter "Uncle Zeke's Birthday" in the **Event Name** field.

- Set the **Month** to May and the **Day** to 23.

- Keep the **Repeating Event** and **Every Year** check boxes turned on, because Uncle Zeke has a birthday practically every year. (Let's do the old guy a favor and leave the **Until** option turned off.)

- Click **OK**, and you'll see Uncle Zeke's Birthday (May 23) in the Events window.

- Click **OK** to close the Calendar preferences. The May 23 cell now lists Uncle Zeke's Birthday in green, as I've circled in Figure 1-42.

Figure 1-41.

Figure 1-42.

Unlike most settings in the Organizer, custom events are *not* stored in the current catalog file. They are stored in a special file buried on your hard drive called *customevents.dat*. This allows Elements to include your custom events in all catalogs that you create, not just the current catalog. You may not want to be reminded of the imaginary Uncle Zeke's birthday from now to eternity, so when you've finished working through this lesson, you'll probably want to revisit Edit→Preferences→Calendar, select his birthday from the Events window, and click the handy Delete button. Or you could just send me a present every year, and I'll make sure it gets to him.

13. *Change the cell icon for May 21.* Now let's turn our attention to May 21. By default, the cell for that date shows the first photo I shot. But you can change that. First, I need you to leave the month view and enter the day view. Click the **May 21** cell to select it, and then click the **Day** button at the bottom of the screen. Or just double-click the May 21 cell. This switches to the day view, which is essentially an expanded version of the right side of the month view (see Figure 1-43). The Daily Note section appears larger and the slide show expands to fill the window. Click the big blue ▶ button to watch the slide show, or click one of the flanking buttons (◀ or ▶) to step through the images manually. You can also click a thumbnail in the column to see the image in the large preview.

To change which photograph serves as the date icon in the month view, right-click the last of the five thumbnails—the one of the sleepy guy—and choose the only option, **Set as Top of Day**. The drowsy fellow immediately appears both in the preview and at the top of the thumbnail column, as in Figure 1-44 on the facing page. Now click the **Month** button at the bottom of the screen, and you'll see the new thumbnail in the calendar cell.

14. *Switch to the year view.* Finally, let's take a step back and look at the year in review. Click the **Year** button at the bottom of the screen to reveal the year view, pictured in Figure 1-45.

Figure 1-43.

Although the year view lacks thumbnails, it has everything else. Holiday dates are lavender, and custom events are green. Dates containing photos are shaded blue. The active date gets a dark outline, and you have access to the slide show and the Daily Note field. From here you can click a date cell to select it, double-click a date cell to open it in the day view, or double-click the name of a month to open that month in the month view.

The Organizer makes time-travel so easy, it makes H. G. Wells jealous. I know because he came forward in time and told me himself.

Figure 1-44.

Comparing Similar Photos

Digital photography encourages you to take a lot of pictures. After you finish paying for the camera, the memory card, and other equipment, snapping a digital photo is as close to free as anything the material world has to offer. But as you attempt to capture the perfect photo, you're liable to end up with piles of similar shots. It's possible to have so many similar shots, in fact, that you might want to see only the best one in the photo browser. But how do you choose which photograph is the best?

In this exercise, we'll look at two methods Elements offers for studying and comparing photos. You'll then learn how to create a *stack*, so that one shining image can serve as the representative for other similar photos in the photo browser.

1. *Go to October 18, 2004 in the day view.* In case you're not picking up this exercise from the point at which we left the last one, make sure the **Date**

Figure 1-45.

View icon is active at the top-right corner of the screen. Click the **Year** button at the bottom of the workspace and navigate to that bygone year, 2004. Then double-click the cell for **October 18** in the calendar. Your screen should look like the one in Figure 1-46.

Figure 1-46.

2. *Enter the full-screen view mode.* Notice the ⬜ icon below the large preview (which I've circled in the figure). This icon launches the Organizer's instant, full-screen slide show function. Photoshop Elements is big on slide shows, allowing you to create everything from inset slide shows in the date view to full-blown multimedia creations, deliverable in the PDF format (as I examine in Lesson 12, "Slide Shows and Other Creations"). This photo review function falls somewhere in between, making it a great way to create an impromptu slide show without a lick of preparation.

Click the ⬜ icon, press the F11 key, or choose View→View Photos in Full Screen. Your monitor switches to the full-screen view in the background, but first you have to contend with the **Full Screen View Options** dialog box. I want you to change three settings:

- You're about to hear one of those hidden audio files that we imported into the catalog at the beginning of the lesson. I'm not a big fan of the default choice. It's upbeat and cheerful to be sure, but it doesn't hold up well to repeated listenings. In other words, it will drive you nuts before this exercise is over. Set the **Background Music** option to something that wears better, namely, **Light_Jazz.mp3**.

- Turn off the **Include Captions** check box. Unless you have specifically taken the time to add your own captions in the Properties palette, this option will likely display a statement from the camera vendor that does nothing but obscure your view of the photographs.

- Turn on the **Show Filmstrip** check box. This adds a column of thumbnails known as the *filmstrip*, along the right side of the screen, great for navigation. Click a thumbnail to instantly see that image displayed large on the screen.

- Turn on the **Start Playing Automatically** check box. Users of Elements 3 will remember that it was necessary to use the play controls in the toolbar to start the slide show. This new option makes the slide show begin the moment you click OK.

When your Full Screen View Options dialog box looks like the one in Figure 1-47, click the **OK** button. Your screen switches to the one pictured in Figure 1-48 on the next page.

3. *Enjoy the slide show.* The mellow piano music plays as the six images fade gracefully from one to the next. After Elements displays the final image, the slide show stops. But the piano plays on. For a moment there, it seems as if it's going to stop too. But after a brief lull, it starts up again. Nice music and everything, but enough is enough. How in the world do you get it to stop?

4. *Make the music stop.* Move your cursor to the upper-left corner of the screen to summon the ghostly toolbar, and click the 👉 icon to the right of the trash can to display a menu of options. Then choose the final option, **Full Screen View Options**. Change the **Background Music** option to **None** and click **OK**. Ah, much better. Now I can hear myself type.

A few words about that toolbar, as labeled in Figure 1-48:

- Use the play controls to stop and restart the slide show. Or better yet, press the spacebar to play and pause; once you've paused, you can use the ← and → keys to advance from one slide to the next.

Figure 1-47.

- The edit controls let you rotate and delete photos. The final edit control displays a pop-up menu of commands for tagging photos and adding them to collections.

- The next pair of icons let you switch between the full-screen slide show and the related-yet-altogether-different photo comparison mode, which I explain in Step 5.

- The zoom controls let you define how the images appear on the screen. By default, Elements scales an image to fit the screen size. If the image looks jagged, click the second zoom icon or press Ctrl+Alt+0 (that's the zero key) to view the image at its smoothest size. You can also monkey around with the zoom slider (or press Ctrl+⊟ or Ctrl+⊞) to make the image shrink and grow.

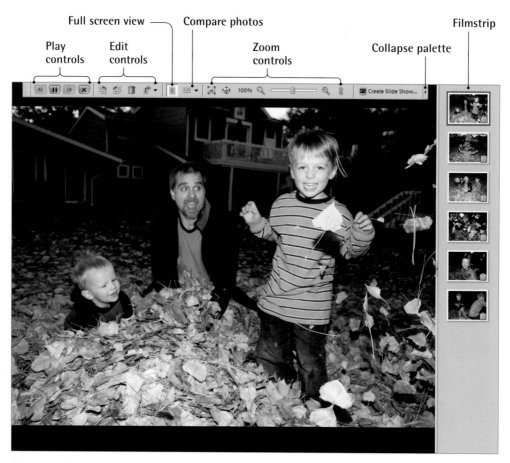

Figure 1-48.

In addition to playing slide shows, the full-screen view mode invites you to view single images with its great zoom capabilities. For example, suppose that you're trying to inspect an image in the photo browser, but you just can't get in close enough, even at the highest level of magnification. Select the photo and choose View→View Photos in Full Screen or press the F11 key. Then press Ctrl+⊡ to zoom in as close as you want.

5. *Enter the photo comparison mode.* In addition to the full-screen slide show, Photoshop Elements provides a mode for comparing photos, which splits the screen so that you can view two photos side by side (good for vertical, portrait-style shots) or top and bottom (better for horizontal photos like these). To enter the photo comparison mode, do like so:

   • Click the first photo at the top of the filmstrip. Once again, you should see me with my boys and my mouth wide open in an expression of manic joy.

   • Click the light blue ▉▉ icon in the toolbar (labeled *Compare photos* in Figure 1-48). Then choose the **Above and Below** command from the menu immediately to the right.

   Elements divides the screen into two horizontal sections, with the first image at the top and the second at the bottom, as in Figure 1-49. Notice that Elements has numbered the corresponding thumbnails in the filmstrip 1 and 2.

   As you might guess, the photo comparison mode is great for comparing photos. So let's compare the images of me and my kids, choose the best one, and stack the other five under our favorite in the photo browser.

6. *Swap the second image for the third.* The top half of the screen is currently selected; you can tell because it's outlined in blue. I like this photo, so let's leave it on the screen. I'm less pleased with the second photo. I like the pillar of leaves, but we're missing the faces. To select it, click in the bottom half of the screen so the blue outline surrounds the photo.

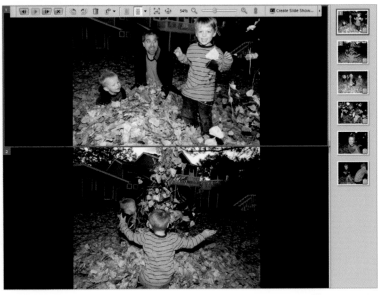

Figure 1-49.

Now click the third thumbnail in the filmstrip or press the ↓ key. The image loads into the bottom half of the screen and receives the number 2.

7. *Examine the two images.* To examine the two images and choose the best, we need to increase their magnification.

   - In the toolbar, click ⊕ or press Ctrl+⊡. Elements zooms in on the lower image because it's selected.

   - Now click the ⊗ button on the far right side of the toolbar. This links the upper image to the lower one, so that the two zoom and pan together.

   - Continue clicking ⊕ or pressing Ctrl+⊡ until you reach the 200 percent zoom level (as identified in the toolbar).

   - Drag inside either image with the hand-shaped cursor until my face is visible in both images, as in Figure 1-50.

At this magnification level, my face is in sharper focus in the bottom image. Furthermore, the bottom image features the endearing sight of my little Sammy shoving a handful of leaves and twigs into my eye. How can you top that? Clearly, the bottom image is superior. Let's mark it as such by right-clicking the image and choosing **Attach Tag**→**5 Stars**. Or you can press Ctrl+5. As rated by me, this is now a five-star photograph.

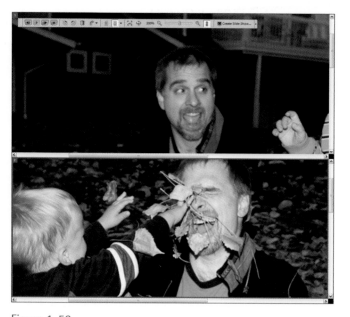

Figure 1-50.

8. *View the first six thumbnails in the photo browser.* Now that we know which photo is the best (okay, we didn't look at all six photos, but we saw enough), it's time to return to the photo browser.

- Click the ✪ button in the toolbar or press the Esc key to exit the photo comparison mode.

- With the top thumbnail selected in the day view, click the Byzantine little 📚 button to the right of the full-screen view button under the large preview. The Organizer cancels all filters left over from the previous exercises and displays the image of me with the gaping maw in the photo browser.

9. *Stack the six leaves photos.* Adjust the zoom setting in the photo browser so you can see all six leaves images. Then select all six by clicking the first photo and Shift-clicking the last, as in Figure 1-51. Next, choose **Edit→Stack→Stack Selected Photos** or press Ctrl+Alt+S. All but the newest of the six photographs disappear. As shown in the magnified Figure 1-52, the remaining photo appears to be stacked in front of some other photos and bears a special 📚 icon, circled in yellow in the figure. This thumbnail indicates the existence of a *stack*.

10. *View all six photos in the stack.* Although the stacked photos are currently invisible, they're still part of the catalog. Let's view them: Choose **Edit→Stack** to display a submenu of commands.

Figure 1-51.

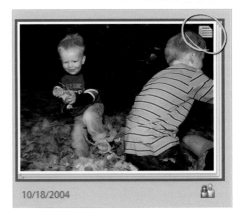

Figure 1-52.

Notice that you can choose Unstack Photos to undo the stacking, or Flatten Stack to delete all stacked images from the catalog except the one that's visible. I want you to choose **Reveal Photos in Stack** or press the keyboard shortcut Ctrl+Alt+R. As shown in Figure 1-53, the Organizer hides all the photos except the six inside the selected stack.

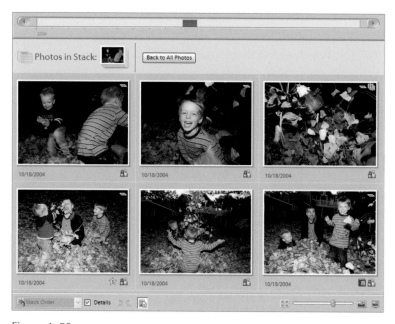

Figure 1-53.

11. *Place the fourth thumbnail at the top of the stack.* Right-click the leaves-in-the-eye thumbnail—the one marked with the yellow ☆ that we assigned in Step 7—and choose **Stack→Set as Top Photo**. The five-star image becomes the first thumbnail in the browser window.

12. *View all photos.* Click the **Back to All Photos** button. As shown in the magnified Figure 1-54, the new thumbnail assumes its place of honor as the representative photo in the stack.

Now you have an idea of what the Organizer can do and what you can do with it. In the next lesson, we move on to the Editor. But never fear, we will revisit the Organizer on a regular basis in the forthcoming lessons, and eventually settle back inside it in Lessons 11 and 12. By any measure, this is an extraordinary and highly practical workspace.

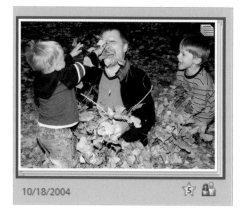

Figure 1-54.

WHAT DID YOU LEARN?

Match the key concept in the numbered list below with the letter
of the phrase that best describes it. Answers appear upside-down
at the bottom of the page.

Key Concepts

1. Welcome screen
2. The Editor
3. The Organizer
4. Catalog
5. Photo browser
6. Timeline
7. Tags
8. Collections
9. Date view
10. EXIF metadata
11. Stack
12. Full-screen view

Descriptions

A. A feature of the photo browser, this charts the number of images that you captured on a month-by-month basis in the form of a column graph.

B. The Organizer houses image thumbnails inside this kind of file, which remembers the links to the images on your hard drive and stores any information that you might want to associate with those images.

C. These minicatalogs let you group images that share a common destination, such as a slide show; you also have the option to manually sort the order of images inside these groups.

D. When you assemble thumbnails into one of these, a single thumbnail serves as the representative for the other photos in the group.

E. Strictly speaking, these are descriptive keywords that you can associate with one or more images.

F. This Organizer view shows a collection of thumbnails in the order defined by the sort order pop-up menu.

G. This Organizer view sorts thumbnails into calendars, either by year, month, or day.

H. This introductory workspace explains some of the tasks the program can accomplish and provides direct links to the most essential features.

I. A method for studying images in slide show format, with accompanying music (to drive you insane).

J. This exceptional workspace serves as a file browser and lets you import images from a digital camera as well as a hard drive or CD.

K. Photoshop Elements' main workspace, this program lets you open and make changes to photos, such as adjusting brightness and contrast and retouching details.

L. Embedded in digital photographs, this special information describes the time the photo was taken and the make and model of the camera.

Answers

1H, 2K, 3J, 4B, 5F, 6A, 7E, 8C, 9G, 10L, 11D, 12I

QUICK FIX AND SAVE

WHILE THE ORGANIZER workspace is great for acquiring, managing, and comparing your photographs, its ability to change an image file is limited. You can rotate a digital photo that was captured on its side. You can add keywords in the form of tags. You can automatically reverse the effects of red eye. You can even adjust the colors in an image by choosing Edit→Auto Smart Fix (which just so happens to duplicate a function that we examine in this lesson). But when it comes time to really roll up your sleeves and improve the appearance of an image—whether to correct its brightness, sharpen its focus, or apply a few cool effects—you need the other great workspace included with Photoshop Elements 4, the Editor.

The Editor workspace comes in two flavors. The first, the Standard Edit mode, is so capable and complex that I devote more than half of this book to it (see Lessons 3 through 10). The second, the Quick Fix mode, lets you apply a variety of corrections quickly and with little effort. As illustrated in Figure 2-1, Quick Fix relies on a series of buttons and slider bars along with original and corrected previews of the image. Happily, Quick Fix is simple enough to cover in a single lesson, and this lesson is it.

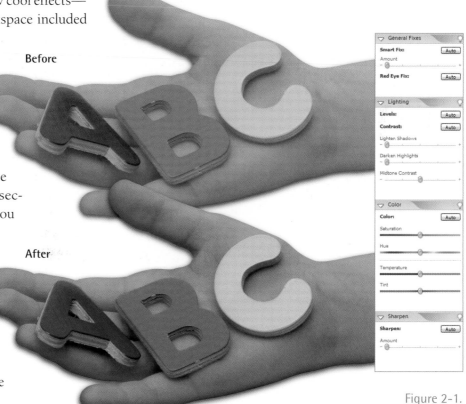

Before

After

Figure 2-1.

ABOUT THIS LESSON

This lesson examines the Quick Fix mode, which lets you correct the colors in an image by clicking buttons and adjusting slider bars. Over the course of the lesson, you'll learn how to:

Project Files

Before beginning the exercises, make sure you've installed the lesson files from the DVD, as explained in Step 5 on page xv of the Preface. This should result in a folder of images called *Lesson Files-PE4 1on1* on your desktop. We'll be working with the files inside the *Lesson 02* subfolder.

Video Lesson 2: Introducing Quick Fix

The Organizer is great for acquiring and managing photos. But if you want to modify an image, whether to correct its colors or apply a special effect, you need to turn to the Editor. This workspace provides two modes, Quick Fix and Standard Edit. Although Quick Fix is far and away the simpler of the two, a treasure trove of hidden features slumber within.

To learn how to use the Quick Fix mode, as well as navigate inside the Editor workspace, watch the second video lesson on the DVD. To view this lesson, insert the DVD, click the **Start** button, and then select **Lesson 2, Introducing Quick Fix** from the second pop-up menu. In just 9 minutes and 15 seconds, I explain the following operations and shortcuts:

Operation	Keyboard equivalent or shortcut
Scroll with the hand tool	spacebar-drag inside image
Zoom in or out	Ctrl+⊕ (plus) or Ctrl+⊖ (minus)
Fit the image on screen or view actual pixels	Ctrl+⊙ (zero) or Ctrl+Alt+⊙ (zero)
Deactivate an option name	Esc
Scroll up or down	Page Up or Page Down
Scroll to the right or left	Ctrl+Page Up or Ctrl+Page Down
Undo or redo an operation	Ctrl+Z or Ctrl+Y

Quick Fix Pros and Cons

To get to the Quick Fix mode, select one or more pictures that you want to edit inside the Organizer, and then choose Edit→Go to Quick Fix. (Alternatively, you can click the button labeled Quickly Fix Photos in the Welcome screen.) If the Editor workspace is not yet running, you'll have to wait a few moments for Photoshop Elements to start this independent program. You'll know that the Quick Fix mode is ready to go when you see a column of palettes headed by General Fixes (see Figure 2-2) on the right side of the screen. You should also see one or two large previews of your image; if not, open an image file from your hard drive by choosing File→Open.

The purpose of the Quick Fix mode is to address, as simply and efficiently as possible, the most common problems that might face an image. To its credit, the program does an admirable job of matching a quick solution with a common problem. But I wouldn't go so far as to call the Quick Fix interface easy to use. The order in which options are presented is confusing and suggests relationships that don't exist. Among the Lighting controls, for example, the three slider bars have nothing to do with the Levels and Contrast options above them. Meanwhile, four of the six Auto buttons are mutually exclusive. If you don't like the results of clicking one, choose Edit→Undo before trying another. Of the six Auto buttons, only Red Eye Fix and Sharpen should be combined with the others (see Figure 2-2).

Figure 2-2.

If I'm starting to sound a bit critical, I beg your pardon, for I have one more cautionary note to share: Don't place much faith in the Auto buttons. Like all automated functions, these buttons trade control and predictability for ease of use. Given the current state of artificial intelligence—which is to say, pretty rudimentary—an Auto button is every bit as likely to produce a bad result as a good one.

All I'm saying is, the Quick Fix mode is no image magician. Like most computer software, it's a collection of useful controls that respond well to the reasoned input of an educated user. Fortunately, that's all right with you, because an educated user is precisely what you'll be when you finish this lesson. In the next several pages, I'll explain how the various palette settings work, what kind of color problems they're designed to fix, and when you can expect the best results. I'll also show you how to save your changes to disk, and how to use version sets to track the changes you've made to an image. By the end of this lesson, you'll not only have a sense of how the Quick Fix mode works, but also be ready to take on the more capable color adjustments that I cover in Lesson 3.

Automatic Color Correction

The Auto buttons couldn't be easier to use. Click a button and watch it do its thing. You don't need my help to figure that out. The problem is, what "thing" is the Auto button doing? And is that thing going to benefit your image or make it worse? To answer these questions, we have to dig a bit deeper, which is the purpose of this first exercise.

The following steps examine the behavior of the first, third, fourth, and fifth Auto buttons, which let you modify the brightness and contrast of the colors in your image. We're going to skip that second button, Red Eye Fix, because it's identical to the automatic red-eye fix you performed on the images in the preceding lesson. And yes, I am well aware that you never actually saw the before-and-after results of that fix; to introduce a note of drama into these pages, I'm saving that unveiling for the very end of this lesson, where I talk about version sets.

One of the buttons, Smart Fix, comes with a slider bar that lets you specify the amount of correction you want to apply. The rest are one-shot wonders. Each button is meant to be used independently of the others. Click a button. If you like the result, great. If not, undo and try another. Here's an example:

1. *Start the Quick Fix mode.* To start things off, I want you to enter the Quick Fix mode without opening an image. You can do this in one of two ways:

   • Click the **Quickly Fix Photos** button at the top of the Welcome screen.

   • In the Organizer, choose **Edit→Deselect** to turn off all the thumbnails. Then choose **Edit→Go to Quick Fix** (also available from the shortcuts bar).

Photoshop Elements launches the Editor workspace and displays the Quick Fix interface. To confirm, check the upper-right corner of the screen and make sure that the Quick Fix button is active, as labeled in Figure 2-3.

2. *Open an image.* Click the yellow folder icon, labeled on the left side of Figure 2-3. Alternately, you can choose **File→Open** or press the keyboard shortcut Ctrl+O. However you go about it, the **Open** dialog box is sure to appear on the screen. Make your way to the *Lesson 02* folder inside the *Lesson Files-PE4 1on1* folder that you installed from the DVD. Then select the file called *Low contrast skull.jpg* and click the **Open** button.

Quick Fix mode is active

Open an image file

Figure 2-3.

3. *Assign the Adobe RGB profile to the image.* If you followed my advice in the Preface and picked Allow Me to Choose from the Color Settings dialog box (see Step 10, page xvi), you'll be greeted by the alert message pictured in Figure 2-4, which tells you that the image lacks a *color profile*. Without this little bit of code, Photoshop Elements can't tell where the image came from or how its colors should really look. Click the third option, **Optimize colors for Print output (use AdobeRGB)**, to bring *Low contrast skull.jpg* into the professional-standard Adobe RGB color space. Then click **OK**. The dull and lifeless photo of a saber-toothed tiger skull appears on screen.

Figure 2-4.

PEARL OF WISDOM

If you encounter this message when opening your own images, I recommend that you follow the same instructions outlined above. While you're at it, you might as well bypass future alerts and open images in the Adobe RGB space automatically by turning on the **Always take this action, and don't show me again** check box. By bringing the image into the Adobe RGB color space, you ensure that your image will display and print correctly, even on a different computer. Getting consistent color from one device to the next is one of the most vexing parts of dealing with digital images, and color profiles help enormously.

The Editor Interface

The Editor workspace divides into two parts: the Quick Fix mode, shown on this page, and the Standard Edit mode, pictured on the next. Labeled in the figures in the bottom half of this two-page spread, the key elements of the Editor interface are as follows, in alphabetical order. (The orange labels indicate items that I discuss in the context of other interface elements; for a discussion of the small italic items, see pages 12 and 13 of the previous lesson.)

- **Editor modes:** Click a button in the top-right corner of the workspace to switch between the Quick Fix and Standard Edit modes. Pictured below, the Quick Fix mode lets you correct the colors in an image with relatively little effort. All other edits—from touch-up tools to filters, from layers to effects—are the domain of the Standard Edit mode, pictured on the facing page.

- **Image previews:** The Quick Fix mode presents you with one or two image previews. To determine how many previews appear, as well as their orientation, select an option from the View pop-up menu in the lower-left corner of the interface.

- **Image window:** In the Standard Edit mode, each open image appears inside a separate window, thus permitting you to open multiple images at once. The figure on the facing page shows five images open, but I've minimized all except one to keep the screen moderately tidy.

- **Options bar:** The settings here modify the behavior of the active tool. The options bar is *context sensitive*, so you see a different set of options each time you switch to a different tool.

- **Palettes:** A *palette* is a window of options that remains on screen regardless of what you're doing. Most palettes reside in the palette bin, which is permanently affixed to the right side of the interface. But in the Standard Edit mode, palettes can float independently in front of the image window. To move a floating palette, drag the gray title bar at the top of the palette. To add a floating palette to the palette bin, click the More button and choose Place in Palette Bin when Closed, and then click the ✖ button in the palette's title bar.

- **Photo bin:** The photo bin lets you browse through all images that are open in the Editor. In the figure below, I have a total of five images open, all provided by the good people at iStockphoto.com. Click ◐ or ◑ to cycle from one image to the next. You can show or hide the photo

pin by clicking either the ▼ or ▼ icon, labeled *Photo bin display* in the annotated screen shot below.

- **Toolbox:** The toolbox provides access to the Editor's drawing, editing, and selection tools. Click an icon to select a tool, and then use the tool in the image preview or window. A small wedge (as in ◢) shows that multiple tools share a single box, or *slot*. Click and hold a slot to display a flyout menu of alternate tools. Or press the Alt key and click a slot to cycle between tools.

- **Zoom control:** Use the zoom control under the image preview in the Quick Fix window (see the facing page) to change the magnification of the image previews. You can also press the keyboard shortcuts Ctrl+⊡ or Ctrl+⊟ to zoom in or out, regardless of the mode.

Standard Edit

Shortcuts bar Image window Options bar Free-floating palette

Menu bar Window controls

Editor modes

Toolbox Palettes

Photo Bin

Photo bin display Palette display

If you don't get the error message, and you want to get in sync with the rest of the book, here's how: Click the lower of the two ✕ buttons in the upper-right corner of the screen to close the skull image. Next, choose Edit→Color Settings, select the Allow Me to Choose option, and click OK. Now reopen the skull image and change its color space, as directed on page 55.

4. *Switch to a before-and-after view.* Given that you're not sure how best to go about correcting this image, you may find it helpful to compare the altered image to its original state. Go to the **View** menu in the lower-left corner of the window and choose **Before and After (Portrait)**. The view shifts so that the portrait-oriented (that is to say, vertical) photo is displayed in two side-by-side previews, as in Figure 2-5. The Before view shows the image as it looked when you first entered the Quick Fix mode; the After view will show the results of your edits.

Figure 2-5.

5. *Apply Auto Contrast.* The skull image suffers from both low contrast and a slightly purple cast. Because the word contrast figures into the title of the image, let's try to fix that problem first. Go to the **Lighting** palette and click the **Auto** button to the right of the word **Contrast**. True to its name, the Quick Fix mode quickly fixes the image. As witnessed in Figure 2-6, the contrast improves dramatically, but the purplish cast lives on.

It's okay, but I have a sneaking suspicion that a different Auto button might serve us better.

6. *Undo the last adjustment.* Before you can apply a new color adjustment, you need to "unapply" the preceding one in one of the following ways:

- Click the blue ⟲ icon in the shortcuts bar.

- Choose **Edit→Undo Auto Contrast**.

- Press Ctrl+Z.

However you undo, Elements restores the right-hand preview to the original version of the image.

Figure 2-6.

7. *Apply Auto Levels.* Click the **Auto** button to the right of the word **Levels**. This time, Elements produces the effect shown in Figure 2-7. It is a better correction than the last one, almost entirely removing the purple cast. But is it the best the Quick Fix options can do? After all, the skull now looks a bit too brown, and other Auto color correction functions remain untested.

The only way to know whether the other Auto buttons can do better is to try them out, which means undoing Auto Levels. At the same time, I want to reserve the right to come back to this edit. The next step explains a hidden method for doing just that.

Figure 2-7.

8. *Switch to Standard Edit, then back to Quick Fix.* Without undoing or resetting the image, click the **Standard Edit** button in the upper-right corner of the screen. Photoshop Elements displays the corrected skull in an independent image window. Then click the **Quick Fix** button to return to the Quick Fix mode. Now both the Before and After views show the results of the Auto Levels adjustment.

9. *Undo the last adjustment.* Now here's the remarkable part: Click the blue ↻ icon in the shortcuts bar or press Ctrl+Z. Elements undoes the effects of the Auto Levels function and restores the original, low-contrast image to the After view. In two easy steps, we've managed to swap the Before and After views, as in Figure 2-8. This permits us to keep the Auto Levels adjustment while trying out new ones.

Figure 2-8.

10. *Apply Auto Color.* Click the **Auto** button at the top of the **Color** palette. Shown in Figure 2-9 on the facing page, the result comes close to accurately representing the original scene. But the real question is, do I like it the best? The greenish cast gives it a hospital flavor that I'm not too crazy about—and not just because this particular animal is beyond the help of modern medicine.

11. *Undo the correction.* Click the ↻ icon at the top of the screen or press Ctrl+Z to undo the operation.

Normally, you also have the option of clicking the Reset button to restore the image as it first appeared when you entered the Quick Fix mode. But in our case, this would reset the After view so it matches the present Before view (the post-Auto Levels state), and we don't want that. To step backward a single operation, undo is the way to go.

Figure 2-9.

12. *Apply Auto Smart Fix.* Click the very first **Auto** button, the one to the right of the words **Smart Fix**. Photoshop Elements applies the most complex of its automatic adjustments. Pictured in Figure 2-10, the result bears a strong resemblance to the Auto Levels adjustment that you applied in Step 7. But if you look closely, you'll notice two important differences: First, the contrast of the Smart Fix image is more subtle, with lighter, more detailed shadows. Second, the Smart Fix image hangs on to some residual purple, in contrast to the strong orange cast of the Auto Levels correction. (If you're having problems seeing the differences on your screen, try flipping between Figure 2-10 on the right and Figure 2-7 on page 59. The figures are located in the same positions on their respective pages, so you can move back and forth between them like frames in a flip book.)

EXTRA ⭐ CREDIT

The Smart Fix adjustment happens to be my favorite of the bunch, but it's still slightly more purple than I'd like. If it's good enough for you, feel free to skip to the next exercise, "Saving Your Changes," which begins on page 64. Or stick with me here and, in a few brief steps, learn how you can adjust the performance of the Smart Fix function using a slider bar. It's subtle stuff but worthy of a quick look.

Figure 2-10.

13. *Undo the Smart Fix adjustment.* To see the results of the Smart Fix slider bar, you need to first cancel the effects of the previous adjustment. So as you've done so often in the past, click the blue ↩ icon in the shortcuts bar or press Ctrl+Z.

14. *Adjust the Smart Fix Amount slider.* The Amount slider bar in the top palette permits you to vary the intensity of the Smart Fix operation. The middle

Figure 2-11.

setting is equivalent to clicking the Auto button. Experiment with moving the slider tab back and forth. Moving the slider to the right trends the image toward yellow, and yellow is just what this photo needs. So drag the slider option all the way to the right, as in Figure 2-11.

15. *Commit the Smart Fix adjustment.* Elements doesn't apply the slider setting until you request it to do so in one of the following ways:

- Click the ✔ icon to the right of the General Fixes tab (just left of the light bulb).

- Press the Enter key.

- Apply a different color adjustment.

For now, just press the Enter key. For the sake of comparison, the final image appears beside the original in Figure 2-12. Keep this image open; we'll save it in the very next exercise.

Uncorrected skull

Figure 2-12.

Smart Fix, cranked up to full volume

By definition, an Auto button adjusts an image without troubling you with the details. But that doesn't mean it applies the same level of correction to one photograph as it does to another. Quite the contrary—each Auto button analyzes an image and corrects it accordingly. A dark image receives different correction than a light one, a yellowish image receives different correction than a bluish one, and so on.

Although every image gets individualized attention, the Auto buttons modify it according to consistent sets of rules. The following list explains how each function works:

- **Auto Contrast** locates the darkest color in an image and makes it as dark as it can be without changing its color. It then makes the lightest color as light as possible. For example, if the darkest color is blue and the lightest color yellow, the blue becomes a darker blue and the yellow a lighter yellow. The color balance remains unchanged— just what you want when an image is properly colored, but not at all what you want when it's not.

- **Auto Levels** makes no attempt to preserve colors. Instead, it makes the darkest color a neutral black and the lightest color a neutral white. The result is more often than not a shift in color balance. This can be a good thing if the color balance needs fixing. But Auto Levels may go too far, replacing one color cast with another. In the example below, the color cast shifts from pink to blue.

- **Auto Color** can be a bit slower because it tries to do more. Like Auto Levels, it deepens shadows and lightens highlights with the intention of creating neutral blacks and whites. But where Auto Levels may shift the intermediate shades from one color to another, Auto Color tries to pinpoint brightness ranges and keep them neutral as well. Among these are the middle colors in an image, known as the *midtones*. Auto Color finds the midtones that are closest to gray and then leeches away the color. By sheer coincidence, this happens to be the best method for automatically correcting the colors in the image below.

- Unique to Photoshop Elements, **Auto Smart Fix** is the most complex of the automatic color correction functions. Like Auto Contrast, it expands the contrast of an image without changing the lightest and darkest colors. It then brings out details by lightening the shadows and darkening the highlights. And finally, it evaluates the color cast and shifts the colors in the opposite direction. For the photo below, the result is a shift toward green.

Because it attempts to balance shadows, highlights, and colors, the Smart Fix function frequently outperforms the rest of the Auto pack. But it's by no means foolproof, as illustrated below. That's why I recommend that you test each of the Quick Fix mode's Auto functions and decide for yourself which one delivers the most desirable results.

Original image

Auto Contrast

Auto Levels

Auto Color

Auto Smart Fix

Figure 2-13.

Saving Your Changes

Permit me to relate a rather sad but illustrative story. Back in March of 1994, I got my hands on my first digital camera, a QuickTake 100 from Apple. By modern standards, the images were tiny, measuring a scant 640 by 480 pixels. But at the time, the QuickTake was the height of cool technology. I knew Photoshop quite well by then, so I didn't hesitate to edit the photos and save the changes. In other words, I saved over the originals.

To understand the significance of this rash act, consider the photo in Figure 2-13. After shooting this image, I increased the brightness and contrast, rotated it, exaggerated the sharpness, and cropped it to a heartbreaking 409 by 634 pixels (reproduced here at a mere 140 pixels per inch). These days, I regard this image with a combination of horror and dismay. Garish and noisy, it leans slightly to the left and drunkenly into the pinks. If I had the original, I could reapply my edits with the subtlety and savvy born of more than another decade of experience, not to mention the accuracy afforded by a more sophisticated screen display. But alas, I was so liberal with confidence and conservative with disk space that the edited file is all that remains.

Fortunately, Photoshop Elements prevents you from making such mistakes. The first time you choose File→Save when working with an original image, Elements asks you to save the image under a new name or in a different location so that the original file—the one captured by the digital camera or scanner—will remain intact. And it's a good thing too. As your image-editing acumen grows, you will probably grow dissatisfied with your early efforts, just as I have. With the original images at hand, you can take a fresh crack at improving those old photos.

This exercise explains how to save your changes to an image with the future in mind.

1. *Start with the corrected skull.* If you closed this photo, take heart; it's quick work to replay the last exercise. Open the file *Low contrast skull.jpg* in the *Lesson 02* folder. Then crank the Smart Fix slider all the way to the right and press the Enter key. Who knew I could summarize seven pages in a single paragraph?

2. *Choose the Save command.* Choose **File→Save** or press Ctrl+S to display the **Save As** dialog box. Most likely, Elements automatically takes you to the *Lesson 02* folder, which contains the original skull photo. If not, make your way to the *Lesson Files-PE4 1on1* folder and then enter the *Lesson 02* folder.

To see thumbnail previews of your saved images, click the ⊞ icon in the upper-right corner of the Save As dialog box and choose the thumbnails option, as illustrated in **Figure 2-14**.

---

3. *Rename the edited image.* The existing occupant of the **File name** option box hardly fits your newly edited image, does it? So change the name to "STT skull.jpg" or something similar. (STT stands for saber-toothed tiger, in case you're wondering.)

4. *Leave the other settings unchanged.* Pictured in Figure 2-14, these settings include the following:

   • The Format option determines how a file is saved and how it can be used in the future. The most common format for digital images is JPEG (pronounced *jay-peg*), which makes files small and portable. For higher quality images, you can choose TIFF, the format used to print all the images in this book. Or you can select Elements' native PSD (Photoshop Document), which lets you save your images with all the program's advanced features intact, including selections, layers, and editable text. For this exercise, leave the **Format** option set to **JPEG (*.JPG; *.JPEG; *.JPE)**.

   • Turn on the **Include in the Organizer** check box to automatically list the saved image inside the catalog that you last opened in the Organizer workspace. Assuming you haven't switched catalogs since you completed the last lesson (if you did, please take a moment now to switch it back), Photoshop Elements will add the corrected skull to the *PE4 1on1.psa* catalog.

   • Turn on the **ICC Profile: Adobe RGB (1998)** check box to embed a color profile into your image, which identifies how Elements last displayed the colors. If you later open the image on another computer using an application that recognizes color profiles (such as Photoshop Elements,

Figure 2-14.

Photoshop CS2, and most other Adobe applications), there's a good chance the image will look approximately the same as it does on your computer.

- For compatibility with all varieties of computer systems—Windows, Macintosh, or otherwise—leave the **Use Lower Case Extension** check box turned on. This way, the filename will end in *.jpg* and not *.JPG*.

5. *Click the Save button.* Click **Save** to accept your filename and other settings and exit the Save As dialog box. Elements next displays the **JPEG Options** dialog box, which asks you to specify how you want the JPEG file to be saved.

6. *Confirm the JPEG settings.* The JPEG file format reduces the size of a file by compromising the quality of the image using what's known as *lossy compression*. Less quality means a smaller file on disk; more quality means a larger file. For the best balance, I recommend that you adjust the settings in the JPEG Options dialog box as follows:

- Use the Quality setting to define the amount of compression applied to an image. You can adjust this value from as high as 12 to as low as 0. To see the effect of the Quality setting on the image, leave the Preview check box turned on and watch the After image in the Quick Fix mode. Elements also estimates the resulting file size at the bottom of the dialog box. For instance, a Quality setting of 12 results in a file size of about 750K, but a Quality of 0 takes the file size down to a mere 50K. For a decent looking image that's light on your hard drive, set the **Quality** option to 10.

- The remaining options control how your JPEG image loads in a Web page. To ensure compatibility with other software, select the first option, **Baseline ("Standard")**.

7. *Save the image.* Click the **OK** button to save the image to disk. A second or two later, Photoshop Elements displays the new name of the image, *STT skull.jpg,* in the top-left corner of the Quick Fix mode window.

Congratulations, you've managed to save your corrected image and maintain the original digital photograph for posterity. Click the second of the two × icons in the upper-right corner of the screen or choose **File**→**Close** to close the skull image. (The first × quits the program.)

Lighting, Color, and Focus

There's more to Quick Fix than a bunch of one-shot Auto buttons. You can achieve greater control—and make dramatic improvements to an image—using the slider bars. In this exercise we'll explore the sliders in the Lighting, Color, and Sharpen palettes. And rather than opening an image directly into the Editor, as we did at the beginning of the lesson, we'll try out a different scenario: importing an image into the Organizer and then handing it off to the Quick Fix mode. These steps will also set the foundation for the final exercise in this lesson, in which you'll learn about the Organizer's unique version sets.

1. *Open the Organizer.* Assuming you're still in the Quick Fix mode from the preceding exercise, click the **Photo Browser** button in the shortcuts bar, as in Figure 2-15. (Depending on the size of your screen, you may see just the ⟳⊞ icon without the text. That's the Photo Browser button, so go ahead and click it.) A few moments later, Elements loads the Organizer workspace and displays the photo browser.

Figure 2-15.

2. *View all the thumbnails.* If necessary, open the *PE4 1on1.psa* catalog using File→Catalog. Scroll to the bottom of the photo browser and you'll find the corrected version of the saber-toothed tiger photograph, which Elements loaded into the Organizer per your instructions in the Save As dialog box (see Step 4, page 65). I shot the photo during a visit to the La Brea Tar Pits on February 22, 2003, making this the earliest image in the catalog. So it appears last in the sort order, as highlighted in Figure 2-16 on the next page.

3. *Import an image into the catalog.* Click the camera icon in the shortcuts bar and choose **From Files and Folders**, or just press Ctrl+Shift+G. Use the **Look in** pop-up menu at the top of the dialog box to switch to the *Lesson 02* folder inside *Lesson Files-PE4 1on1*. Select the file named *London Elle.jpg* and then click the **Get Photos** button. After the Organizer displays the imported image in the photo browser window, click the **Back to All Photos** button or click the Backspace key to see the image in context with the other photos in the catalog. I captured this photo of my wife drinking tea on May 19, 2004, just a couple of days before I shot the V&A busts. (As usual with these London photos, the time is off by several hours.)

Figure 2-16.

4. *Open the image in the Quick Fix mode.* Scroll to the imported image, the eighth from the end in the Organizer. Click to select it. Then click the **Edit** button in the shortcuts bar and choose the **Go to Quick Fix** command. A few moments later, Elements switches to the Quick Fix mode and inserts the photo in the Before and After previews.

If you want to see something interesting, press Alt+Tab or go to your Windows task bar and switch back to the Organizer for a moment. The thumbnail for *London Elle.jpg* now sports a red band and a lock icon (see **Figure 2-17**), signifying that it's open inside the Editor. The result: You can't tinker with it inside the Organizer. Who says the left hand doesn't know what the right hand is doing? Press Alt+Tab to switch back to the Editor and continue.

Figure 2-17.

5. *Experiment with the Smart Fix option.* While Elle is brightly illuminated, her background is the fabulous, formless darkness of a dimly lit pub during morning rush hour. Much is hidden in the shadows. As a lark, click the **Auto** button to the right of **Smart Fix** in the top-right corner of the screen. In a flash, Elements exposes a world of detail in the shadows. But it also creates a weird bluish-green haloing, most evident on and around the right side of the image. Plus, it makes the light areas of the image pink. Nice try, Elements, but no cigar. Press Ctrl+Z to undo the operation and restore the original image.

Figure 2-18.

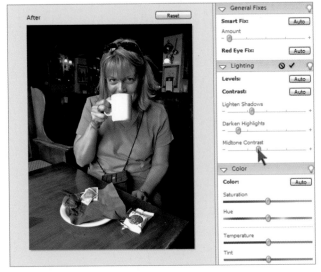

Figure 2-19.

6. *Lighten the shadows.* Now suppose you try a hand at drawing out the details in the shadows. Drag the **Lighten Shadows** slider until it's just a little to the right of the second tick mark (or more precisely, under the *d* in *Shadows*), as in Figure 2-18. This pulls a lot of detail from the background, but it doesn't have the same detrimental effect on the foreground as the Smart Fix option had. Sure enough, you also draw out some of those nasty green edges, but don't fret; we'll take care of those in a few steps.

7. *Darken the highlights.* To offset the overly light areas in the foreground, drag the **Darken Highlights** slider to the right until it's under the letter *n* in the word *Darken*. Elements darkens the areas around the mug and the white objects on the table.

This helps to balance the extreme difference between the lighting of the foreground and the background objects. But to my way of thinking, the contrast remains a bit too hot, so a little more balancing is in order.

8. *Adjust the contrast in the midtones.* Reduce the contrast slightly by dragging the **Midtone Contrast** slider a smidgen to the left, so it's under the *a* in *Contrast*, as in Figure 2-19. The resulting image is a bit softer, a bit more subtle, a bit more representative of what I meant to shoot in the first place.

9. *Experiment with the Hue control.* We need to somehow offset the olive-green cast of the image. The **Color** palette gives us several ways to accomplish this, so let's

turn our collective attention to it. If you're working on a small screen, click the ▽'s in front of General Fixes and Lighting to twirl those palettes closed.

We'll start with the Hue option, which lets you spin colors around the rainbow. Drag the **Hue** slider tab back and forth and see what happens. You can make my wife lime green, blueberry blue, and a host of other fruity flavors. But never better. A slight tweak left of center eliminates the green of the background, but it also makes Elle a hot pink. (That tea she's drinking can't be *that* hot.) As we'll see in Lesson 3, Hue adjustments have lots of uses, but this isn't one of them. Click the ⊘ at the top of the palette or press Esc to return the Hue slider to its default position.

10. *Adjust the Temperature and Tint settings.* Having witnessed the results of the Hue slider, it's obvious we don't really want to rotate *all* the colors in the image around the rainbow. We just want to peel away some of the greens. The Quick Fix mode offers two ways to remove a predominant color:

   • The job of the Temperature slider bar is to make colors cooler (that is, more blue) or warmer (more red). This image could use a little warming up, so drag the **Temperature** slider tab *very* slightly to the right, to the point just before you reveal the seam between blue and red in the slider bar.

   • The Tint slider moves colors along a different axis, namely green to magenta. In our case, we want to do whatever it takes to move away from green. So drag the **Tint** slider a tab width to the right to urge those greens into remission without adding too much magenta, as in Figure 2-20.

11. *Boost the saturation.* Now that we have some good colors to work with, let's intensify them. Drag the **Saturation** slider a couple of tab widths to the right until Elle's T-shirt is a vivid orange, as in Figure 2-21. The effect is a bit much, but it serves to demonstrate the big difference a few tiny adjustments to a few slider bars can make.

Figure 2-20.

Figure 2-21.

These steps provide a basic introduction to color correction. Rest assured, we'll deal with shadows, highlights, contrast, and the others at greater length in Lesson 3, "Correcting Colors." But before we leave the Quick Fix mode, there's one more aspect to this photograph that I want to improve: the focus.

12. *Zoom the image to 100 percent.* Look closely at the Before and After previews. Notice how jagged the transitions are, especially around the edges of my wife's shirt and in her hair. Because we're zoomed out from the image, Elements is having to perform some rough approximations. This jaggedness isn't a big deal when you're trying to adjust a photograph's colors, but if you want to concentrate on the focus, you need a smoother, more accurate view of the image.

    Click the **Actual Pixels** button in the top-left portion of the screen. This enlarges the image to the 100-percent view, so that every pixel in the image is matched to a pixel on your monitor's display. Get the hand tool from the toolbox on the left side of the screen (the one that looks like 🖑) and drag inside one of the image previews so that you can see Elle's face. The strands of her hair are now smoothly rendered. The 100 percent view is better for gauging the focus of an image, but you can't see as much of the image on-screen at any one time.

13. *Maximize your view of the image.* If you want to see more of the photograph, expand the amount of room devoted to the image previews:

    • First make sure the Editor workspace is taking up the entire screen. If it isn't, click the maximize button (☐) in the upper-right corner of the interface.

    • Second, hide the thumbnails at the bottom of the screen by clicking the ▼ **Photo Bin** button in the bottom-left corner of the screen.

    Figure 2-22 atop the facing page shows a detail from my expanded preview area, complete with larger and more magnified Before and After images.

14. *Try out Auto Sharpen.* If you need still more room in the palettes, twirl closed the Color palette by clicking its ▽. Then click the **Auto** button in the **Sharpen** palette. Elements applies what it considers to be an ideal amount of image sharpening, but in my opinion, it's too much. Assuming you agree with me, click the ↶ icon in the shortcuts bar or press Ctrl+Z to remove the effects of the Auto button. Let's try the slider instead.

Figure 2-22.

15. *Sharpen the image manually.* In the Sharpen palette, drag the **Amount** slider tab so the tab appears under the *n* in the word *Amount.* As Figure 2-23 shows, this provides us with a more subtle sharpening effect that better outlines the important details in the image. Go ahead and click the ✔ or press the Enter key to accept this final adjustment.

Now that you've corrected the image, keep it open and continue directly into the next brief exercise, in which I show you how to save the edited image along with the original in the Organizer.

Saving in a Version Set

Now that you have this wonderfully improved version of *London Elle.jpg*, you'll naturally want to save and manage it in the Organizer just like the *STT skull.jpg* image. The difference this time is that the original version of *London Elle.jpg* is already in the Organizer. One solution is to change the name of the edited version to keep it from overwriting the original. But then you'd end up with two versions of the same photo in the Organizer. And is that what you really want?

Figure 2-23.

For example, suppose that you want access to all incarnations of an image, but you want to see just one thumbnail preview. And you want that one thumbnail to show the image at its best. As luck would have it, Elements provides the answer. You can save both the edited and original versions of the image in a version set. When you ran the auto red-eye correction in the last lesson, the two photos that Elements corrected were saved in version sets along with their corresponding originals. In general, a *version set* behaves like the stack of playing-in-the-leaves photographs that you created at the end of the last lesson (see Step 9, page 47). However, stacks are useful for manually consolidating similar photos in the Organizer, but version sets are created to consolidate photos that are *identical* except for color adjustments and other modifications.

In the next steps, you'll save the edited version of my wife drinking tea in a version set along with the original image. You'll then see how the version set looks in the Organizer's photo browser. And finally, I *promise*, we'll check out those two version sets that we created in the last lesson, and see how well Elements did at automatically finding and fixing red eye.

Figure 2-24.

1. *Open the Save As dialog box.* Make sure the edited version of *London Elle.jpg* remains open inside the Quick Fix mode. (If the image is not open, follow the steps in the preceding exercise, "Lighting, Color, and Focus," which begins on page 67.) Then choose **File→Save** or press Ctrl+S to display the **Save As** dialog box.

2. *Turn on the Version Set option.* If it isn't on already, turn on the **Save in Version Set with Original** check box, highlighted with an orange arrow in Figure 2-24. The Editor automatically suggests a new name for the file, *London Elle_edited-1.jpg.* This keeps the edited file from overwriting the original; plus, it initiates a numbering scheme, in the event you decide to save other edited versions of the image.

3. *Save the edited image.* Make sure the Save As dialog box is trained on the *Lesson 02* folder. Then confirm that all available check boxes except As a Copy are turned on (as you can see in Figure 2-24) and click the **Save** button.

4. *Dismiss the Version Set message.* Elements greets you with a long but helpful message that explains the nature and purpose of version sets. After you've read and thoroughly digested the information, turn on the **Don't show again** check box and then click the **OK** button.

5. *Confirm the JPEG settings.* Next comes the familiar **JPEG Options** dialog box. Set the **Quality** value to 10 if necessary, keep **Baseline ("Standard")** selected, and click **OK**.

6. *Close the image.* To best view the image in the Organizer, close it and free it from the Editor workspace. Choose **File→Close** or click the second × in the upper-right corner of the interface.

7. *View the version set in the Organizer.* After closing the photograph in the Editor, Elements should automatically switch you to the Organizer workspace. If not, press Alt+Tab or click the **Photo Browser** button in the shortcuts bar at the top of the screen. If necessary, scroll to the eighth thumbnail from the end of the catalog, where you'll find *London Elle_edited-1.jpg*, elaborately highlighted in Figure 2-25. The version set icon (▣) appears in the upper-right corner of the thumbnail.

Figure 2-25.

8. *View the two photos in the version set.* Right-click the version set thumbnail and choose **Version Set** to display a submenu that makes available four commands:

- Choose Reveal Items in Version Set to display just those images contained in the version set.

- The Flatten Version Set command disbands the version set and deletes all photos except the top thumbnail photo (by default, the edited version) from the catalog.

- The Convert Version Set to Individual Items command also disbands the version set, but keeps all the included photos in the catalog, displaying them side by side in the browser.

- The fourth command, Revert to Original, disbands the version set and deletes all photos except the original.

Choose **Reveal Items in Version Set** to view just two images in the photo browser, as in Figure 2-26. In case you don't recognize them, that's the edited version on the left and the original on the right.

Figure 2-26.

Organizer assumes by default that you want the edited version of the image to be the one that appears in the photo browser, but this doesn't have to be the case. While viewing all photos in the version set (as I presume you are doing now), right-click the original image and choose Version Set→Set as Top Item. The original photo will now represent the version stack in the photo browser, with the edited version stacked beneath it.

9. *Examine a red-eye set.* Now let's check out the two version sets that we created in the preceding lesson, when we let the Organizer automatically search and destroy red-eye problems (see "Getting Photos into Elements," Step 8, page 9).

   • Press the Backspace key or click the **Back to All Photos** button above the images to close the version set and return to the full catalog.

   • Scroll down to the fourth thumbnail from the last, *Downtown Max_edited-1.jpg*. Like *London Elle*, it bears the telltale mark of the version set (📖) in its upper-right corner.

   • Right-click the image and choose **Version Set→Reveal Items in Version Set.**

Figure 2-27 reveals that Elements did a commendable job of pinpointing Max's glowing red eyes in the original photo and fixing them in the edited version, on left. (If you can't quite make it out on your screen, press the ⊞ key to zoom in.) Now that's some useful automation for you.

Figure 2-27.

Figure 2-28.

Figure 2-29.

10. *Check out the other, supposed red-eye set.* Click **Back to All Photos** above the image thumbnails to see the entire catalog view. Then scroll up to the very first thumbnail.

   • The second red-eye set is nestled inside the stack of playing-in-the-leaves photos we made in the preceding lesson. So right-click the *Leaves Max & Sam-3.jpg* image and choose **Stack→Reveal Photos in Stack**.

   • The fourth image, *Leaves Max & Sam_edited-1.jpg*, sports the familiar 🔖 icon. Right-click this thumbnail and choose **Version Set→Reveal Items in Version Set**.

All eyes are closed, so there is no chance of a successful red-eye correction. And a quick comparison of the photos suggests no difference between the two whatsoever. But if you look closely, you might notice that Elements has darkened what was formerly the faintly reddish spot on a leaf. I take that back; there's no way you'll notice it. Highlighted in Figure 2-28, this spot may qualify as the tiniest, most insignificant spot on the face of the planet. Sorry, Elements; potatoes may have eyes, but leaves don't.

11. *Undo what Elements has done.* Right-click either image and choose **Version Set→Revert to Original**. As shown in Figure 2-29, Elements responds with a warning that all but the original thumbnail for this version set will go away. Turn on the **Also delete items from the hard disk** check box to move the *Leaves Max & Sam-6_edited-1.jpg* file from the *Lesson 01* folder to your computer's Recycle Bin. Click **OK**. Another message tells you that the version set is going away. This is to be expected; click **OK** to show you understand. Finally, click **Back to All Photos** at the top of the screen to again see all images in the catalog.

The moral of the story is, automation is all very well and good, but it doesn't always work. One automatic function turns your prehistoric skull into a work of art fit for a museum; another finds eyes in your leaves. And that's an excellent lesson to bear in mind as we move on to Lesson 3, where you'll learn how to apply more methodical and more precise color adjustments. Albeit, these commands are a bit harder to use, but they provide infinitely greater control.

WHAT DID YOU LEARN?

Match the key concept in the numbered list below with the letter
of the phrase that best describes it. Answers appear upside-down
at the bottom of the page.

Key Concepts

1. Quick Fix
2. Standard Edit
3. Color profile
4. Photo Bin
5. Auto Contrast
6. Auto Levels
7. Auto Color
8. Auto Smart Fix
9. JPEG
10. Temperature
11. Tint
12. Version set

Descriptions

A. This file format reduces the size of a file by compromising the quality of the image to the extent that you specify.

B. Deepens shadows and lightens highlights in an image, while changing them to neutral grays. It also leeches away the color from the midtones that are closest to gray.

C. This Editor mode lets you apply a variety of corrections to an image with only small investments of time and effort.

D. The most powerful of the Auto functions, this button expands an image's contrast, lightens the shadows, darkens the highlights, and attempts to correct the color cast—all with varying degrees of success.

E. Adjusts colors along a strictly green-to-magenta axis.

F. Makes the darkest color in an image neutral black and the lightest color neutral white, usually creating a shift in color balance.

G. This Editor mode offers the most capable and complex image-editing tools in Photoshop Elements.

H. Makes the darkest color in an image as dark as possible and the lightest color as light as possible, without actually changing the colors.

I. Similar to a stack, this type of image group pairs all edited versions of a photo with the untouched original.

J. This component of the Editor interface features clickable thumbnails that allow you to browse through all the images you have open.

K. Makes colors cooler (more blue) or warmer (more red).

L. Embedded in an image file, this information helps maintain the image's consistent appearance from one computer screen to another, or from the computer screen to a printer or another device.

Answers

1C, 2G, 3L, 4J, 5H, 6F, 7B, 8D, 9A, 10K, 11E, 12I

I ADMIRE the Quick Fix mode. It really does try like crazy to automatically address some of the most common problems that afflict digital images. But it is not what I would call predictable. Even if you know exactly what a specific Auto button is supposed to do, clicking it is as likely to mess up an image as make it better. Photoshop Elements' brand of artificial intelligence is no substitution for the real thing.

Which brings us to the more complex but likewise more powerful Standard Edit mode. Once upon a time, Standard Edit was all there was to Photoshop Elements, and it remains the program's nucleus. As you'll experience in this and the next seven lessons, Standard Edit is far and away Elements' most capable, versatile, and practical workspace.

At heart, the Standard Edit mode is nothing more or less than an image cobbler. Its primary mission is to take a worn photograph, with the pixel-based equivalent of sagging arches and worn heels, and make it better. As with shoes, not all images can be repaired; some are hopelessly defective from the moment they leave the factory. But most images have more life left in them than you might suspect. And if anyone can fix them, you and the Standard Edit mode can (see Figure 3-1).

Over the next several lessons, I'll show you many ways to correct a photograph—and the order in which these corrections are best applied. In addition to explaining how to use Photoshop Elements' tools and commands to their utmost ability, I'll answer

Uncorrected shoe

Corrected automatically (with Smart Fix) in the Quick Fix mode

Corrected in the Standard Edit mode
(could still use a real cobbler)

Figure 3-1.

ABOUT THIS LESSON

This lesson introduces you to the program's most capable color adjustment commands. We'll also explore such concepts as white balance, color temperature, and Camera Raw. You'll learn how to:

Project Files

Before beginning the exercises, make sure you've installed the lesson files from the DVD, as explained in Step 5 on page xv of the Preface. This should result in a folder of images called *Lesson Files-PE4 1on1* on your desktop. We'll be working with the files inside the *Lesson 03* subfolder.

Video Lesson 3: The Standard Edit Mode

The Quick Fix mode is great at performing simple color manipulations. But when it comes time to roll up your sleeves and do some real work, there's no substitute for the Standard Edit mode. This is where the real power of Photoshop Elements resides, so much so that it fully occupies our attention for eight of the twelve lessons in this book.

To get acquainted with the Standard Edit mode, watch the third video lesson on the DVD. To view the video, insert the DVD, click **Start**, and then select **Lesson 3, The Standard Edit Mode** from the second pop-up menu. This 13-minute 10-second movie shows you how to get around inside the Standard Edit mode, and introduces these shortcuts:

Tool or operation	Keyboard equivalent or shortcut
Open an image from the Organizer in the Standard Edit mode	Ctrl+I
Advance to the next or previous open image	Ctrl+Tab or Ctrl+Shift+Tab
Hide or show any free-floating palettes	Tab
Fit the image on screen or view actual pixels	Double-click hand or zoom tool icon
Zoom in or out with the magnifying glass	Ctrl+spacebar-click or Alt+spacebar-click
Scroll with the hand tool	spacebar-drag in image window

a rarely addressed question: When should you do what? Sequence makes a difference because every change you make to an image builds on the previous adjustment.

In this lesson, you'll learn how to correct the colors in an image. In the next lesson, you'll use selections to isolate your corrections. And after that, we'll move on to cropping, sharpening, and more. Amend each attribute of your troubled photograph in the order suggested by these lessons and you can rest assured that the results will look as good as they possibly can. This is how the pros do it.

Figure 3-2.

Hue, Saturation, and Brightness

Before we set about correcting the colors in an image, it may help to know what the term *color* means. As it just so happens, it means a lot. Color is too complex to define with a single set of names or numerical values. For example, if I describe a color as orange, you don't know if it's yellowish or reddish; vivid or drab; dark, light, or somewhere in between. To give you a better sense of what a color looks like, Photoshop Elements divides it into three properties called *hue*, *saturation*, and *brightness*:

- Sometimes called the *tint*, the hue is the core color—red, yellow, green, and so on. When you see a rainbow, you're looking at pure, unmitigated hue.

- Known variously as *chroma* and *purity*, saturation measures the intensity of a color. By way of example, compare Figure 3-2, which shows a sampling of hues at their highest possible saturation values, to Figure 3-3, which shows the same hues with much of the saturation removed.

Figure 3-3.

- Also known as *luminosity*, the brightness of a color describes how light or dark it is.

The contrast between Figures 3-2 and 3-3 may lead you to conclude that bright, vivid hues make for better colors. Although this may be true for fruit and candy, most of the real world is painted in more muted hues, including many of the colors we know by name. Pink is a light, low-saturation variation of red; brown encompasses a range of dark, low-saturation reds and oranges. Figure 3-4 shows a collection of browns at normal and elevated saturation levels. Which would you prefer to eat: the yummy low-saturation morsel on the left or the vivid science experiment on the right?

Figure 3-4.

Photoshop Elements provides a wealth of commands for correcting the colors in an image. The best of these—that is to say, the ones we'll be looking at—provide you with *selective control*, meaning that the commands let you adjust one color property independently of another. For example, you might change the brightness without affecting the hue or saturation. Armed with these amazingly capable commands, you have all the tools you need to get the color just right. Be it red or blue, night or day, the sky's the limit.

Eliminating a Color Cast

One of the most common color problems associated with digital images and photographs in general is color cast, a malady in which one color permeates an image to an unrealistic or undesirable degree. For example, an old photograph that has yellowed over the years has a yellow cast. A snapshot captured outdoors using the wrong light setting may suffer from a blue cast.

Of course, Photoshop Elements offers a solution. Designed to restore a photograph's natural color balance, Enhance→Adjust Color→Remove Color Cast is superb at combining ease of use with great results. In fact, I might go so far as to call Remove Color Cast Elements' most successful consumer-level color correction function. As it just so happens, the command is available from both the Quick Fix and Standard Edit modes. We'll invoke the command from the Standard Edit mode, if for no other reason than Standard Edit is where we'll be spending the next eight lessons of the book.

1. *Open an image.* Make sure you're inside the Editor workspace. Then open the image called *Museum of the dead.jpg*, included in the *Lesson 03* folder inside *Lesson Files-PE4 1on1*. I captured this photograph of a deceased bighorn sheep through a plate of glass in the superb Denver Museum of Nature and Science. Thanks to the creature's willingness to remain still, the image is perfectly composed and focused. But my failure to account for the warm lighting of the diorama makes for an unnaturally yellow image. As a result, the saturation's okay but the *ewe* is all wrong. (Har-de-har.)

2. *Switch to the Standard Edit mode.* Click the **Standard Edit** button in the upper-right corner of the application window, labeled in Figure 3-5 on the facing page. Elements populates the toolbox, switches out the palettes along the right side of the screen, and relegates the image to a free-floating window.

Click the
Standard Edit
button...

to see new
palettes...

not to mention,
a free-floating
image window

Figure 3-5.

If you prefer that the image fill the interface the way it does in
the Quick Fix mode, choose Window→Images→Maximize Mode or
click the ☐ icon in the upper-right corner of the image window.
To reinstate the free-floating image window, choose the Maximize
Mode command again or click the ⬚ icon immediately above the
Standard Edit button, in the upper-right corner of the screen.

3. *Choose the Remove Color Cast command.* Choose **En-
hance→Adjust Color→Remove Color Cast** to display the
wordy dialog box pictured in Figure 3-6, which serves little
purpose except to explain how the command works. No
sense in reading Adobe's prose; you'll experience the feature for yourself a few short steps from now. But it is important to leave the dialog box on screen. In other words,
don't click the OK button until I tell you to.

Unlike some color correction commands, Remove Color Cast does
not list a shortcut. But if you like choosing commands from the
keyboard, there is a way. Press the Alt key and type the letters
N-C-T (as in No Color casT). Alt+N displays the Enhance menu, C
selects Color, and T selects Remove Color Cast. It's not the simplest
keyboard trick, but I reckon I'd be remiss if I didn't pass it along.

Figure 3-6.

Figure 3-7.

4. *Magnify the image.* To see more detail and better evaluate the image, choose **View→Actual Pixels** or press Ctrl+Alt+⓪ (zero). This magnifies the image to the 100-percent zoom ratio. Amazingly, Elements lets you navigate inside the image window even when a color correction dialog box is on screen.

5. *Click inside the image.* Move the cursor out of the dialog box and into the photograph. Notice that the cursor changes to an eyedropper, which is Elements' way of showing you that you're about to read, or *sample*, a color. Now click. Assuming that the Preview check box is on, the image updates immediately.

What's happening? When you click a color in the image, Photoshop Elements leeches away its saturation, making it *neutral*. This neutral color creates a kind of vacuum, one that Remove Color Cast fills by shifting neighboring colors. The trick, then, is to click a color that ought to be colorless—black, white, or gray—so that other colors can emerge in its place.

Feel free to click at different points inside the image. The changes are not cumulative—each click references the original image—so you can click as many times as you like. Figure 3-7 shows the results of clicking at four points inside the photo. (I added the yellow circles for emphasis.) Note that the lower-left corner of the cursor is the "hot spot," meaning that it defines the color that Elements neutralizes.

6. *Click the OK button to accept your changes.* After you arrive at a group of colors you like—for my part, I like the final image in Figure 3-7—click the **OK** button in the dialog box.

7. *Apply the Auto Levels command.* The corrected image is a tremendous improvement over the original, but it's not perfect. My biggest complaint: a slight lilac color cast remains. To get rid of it, choose **Enhance→Auto Levels** or press Ctrl+Shift+L. Yes, the Auto Levels function is available inside the Standard Edit mode, and yes, it helps. The final image appears below the original in Figure 3-8 on the facing page.

You are now finished with this image. Close the file by choosing File→Close or clicking the × icon in the upper-right corner of the image window. When asked whether you want to save the image, click the Yes or No button depending on your personal whims. Either choice is okay; we won't be revisiting this image later. Incidentally, from this point on, I'll instruct you to save changes only when a subsequent technique or exercise demands it. Otherwise, when you arrive at the end of an exercise, feel free to close any images you may have open, abandon the changes, and move on.

Adjusting for Skin Tones

Unless you're a zoologist, you probably don't have an innate feel for the authentic colors of a bighorn sheep. But when it comes to human skin tones, you're a natural-born authority. Which is fortunate, because when people appear in a photograph, they seize our attention. Capturing the precise blue of the sky or green of the grass isn't nearly as important as seeing your clients and loved ones in their true colors.

This makes Photoshop Elements 4's new Adjust Color for Skin Tone command a welcome addition to the toolkit. Like the Remove Color Cast command, Adjust Color for Skin Tone lets you fix an image by clicking in it with an eyedropper. Only now, instead of clicking a neutral color, you are invited to click a representative bit of skin. In theory, this should bring the rest of the image's colors in line. But even when that theory doesn't quite work out, your audience is likely to forgive you. When the skin looks good, the photo looks good.

Before

After Remove Color Cast and Auto Levels

Figure 3-8.

1. *Open an image.* Open the file *Goat grooming.jpg*, included in the *Lesson 03* folder inside *Lesson Files-PE4 1on1*. Co-author Galen Fott captured this photo of his son Burton on an excursion to a petting farm. As witnessed in Figure 3-9, the image is a bit too blue and a lot too pink. The resulting magenta color cast is most obvious in young Burton's skin.

2. *Choose the Adjust Color for Skin Tone command.* Choose **Enhance→Adjust Color→Adjust Color for Skin Tone** to display the dialog box pictured in Figure 3-10 on the following page.

To access this command from the keyboard, press the Alt key and type N-C-S (as in Naturally Colored Skin).

---

3. *Adjust the skin tones.* Move your cursor into the image window. Then click the eyedropper on the right lobe of Burton's upper lip, as indicated by the position of the eyedropper in Figure 3-9. Immediately, you should see a dramatic change in the image as the colors shift toward yellow

Figure 3-9.

Figure 3-10.

and orange. The dialog box also changes as the three slider bars sprout knobs. The final slider knob appears somewhere below the letters *era* in the word *Temperature*, cooling down the image to balance out the newly warmed skin tones.

In this context, *temperature* refers to the color of the lighting source. Low-temperature lighting produces a yellowish cast, which you can offset by sliding the Temperature knob toward blue. Higher temperature lighting such as shaded daylight produces bluish casts; dragging the slider knob toward red warms the image.

4. ***Sample some more skin tones.*** Unlike the eyedropper in Remove Color Cast, your current eyedropper produces a cumulative effect. So the more you click, the more changes you make. Try clicking a few more times in Burton's lips, as well as inside his ear. These are the rosiest areas of his flesh and therefore the most likely to make a difference. The image preview and the Temperature knob react to your clicks.

5. ***Adjust the Tan and Blush sliders.*** The two Skin sliders define the color of skin along two axes. Tan adds or subtracts a yellowish orange; Blush adds or subtracts red. Neither control changes skin brightness, so light and dark flesh tones are served equally well. Here's what I suggest for Burton:

   - Drag the **Tan** control until it's about 80 percent of the way to the right side of the slider.

   - Burton's cheeks and lips already enjoy a naturally rosy red quality, but they could use a boost. So drag the **Blush** slider almost all the way to the right.

   Figure 3-11 shows my recommended settings. Throughout, Elements moves the Temperature knob to the right, thereby warming the skin tones while reducing the saturation of Burton's shirt. But skin is more important than fabric, so I deem the muted blues acceptable.

Figure 3-11.

6. ***Click the OK button.*** Turn the Preview check box off and on to compare the old image to the new one. Assuming you like the changes, click **OK**.

7. ***Apply the Auto Contrast command.*** This fixes the color cast, but the image remains a bit washed out. To correct the brightness without affecting the colors, choose **Enhance→ Auto Contrast** or press Ctrl+Shift+Alt+L. Figure 3-12 shows the final image, complete with healthier skin tones and rich brown fence.

Balancing the Colors

The Remove Color Cast command is swell as long as your image contains a color that should be gray. Adjust Color for Skin Tone is just peachy, provided your image contains natural skin tones. What do you do if there are no obvious grays or well-lit flesh tones? In those circumstances, you should take advantage of Photoshop Elements' all-purpose color-balance command, Enhance→Adjust Color→Color Variations.

Like the two previous functions, Color Variations takes a straightforward approach to color restoration. But rather than previewing your corrections in the main image window, Color Variations presents you with a collection of tiny thumbnail previews. Your job is to click the one thumbnail that looks better than the others. You can click as many thumbnails as you like and in any order. The following exercise walks you through a typical use for the Color Variations command.

1. *Open an image.* Open the file *Color science.jpg*, included in the *Lesson 03* folder inside *Lesson Files-PE4 1on1*. Captured without a flash under colored lights on the set of one of my Photoshop Elements video series for Total Training—in which I played one of those kooky chemists whose specialty is dry ice—this image suffers from what I like to call "A Nutty Preponderance of Red" (see Figure 3-13).

   To look at it, you might assume that this image would be well suited to one of the previous commands. After all, the bottled smoke contains gobs of what ought to be neutral colors, and I'm showing plenty of skin. Two problems: Both commands apply wholesale changes, thus affecting all colors in an image by roughly equal amounts. And the red lighting is too extreme for either command to correct. This photo requires a more nuanced approach.

2. *Choose the Variations command.* Choose **Enhance→ Adjust Color→Color Variations** to display the **Color Variations** dialog box, as shown in Figure 3-14 on the next page.

   Once again, Elements fails to provide a shortcut for Color Variations. But you can choose the command using Windows-imposed hot keys. To do so, press the Alt key and type N-C-N (Nuanced Color Neutralizer).

Figure 3-12.

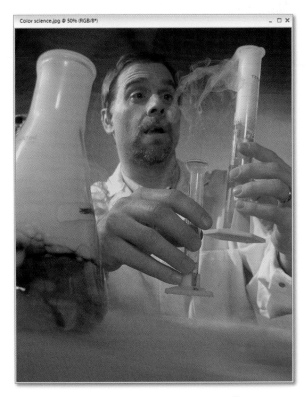

Color science.jpg @ 50% (RGB/8*)

Figure 3-13.

Figure 3-14.

3. *Select the Midtones option.* The Color Variations command lets you modify certain color ranges independently of others. It does so by subdividing the brightness of an image into three tiers—shadows, highlights, and midtones, or what the uninitiated might call dark colors, light colors, and everything in between. To specify the desired range, select one of the first three items in the lower-left portion of the Color Variations dialog box. Of the three, Shadows is sometimes useful, and Highlights is almost never. That leaves Midtones as the option of choice. (As for Saturation, we'll come to it in a moment.) If it isn't already selected, give **Midtones** a click.

4. *Set the intensity slider to the middle.* The slider bar labeled **Adjust Color** lets you modify the intensity of your edits. Set the triangle to the exact middle of the slider, as it is by default.

5. *Click the Decrease Red thumbnail twice.* When Shadows, Midtones, or Highlights is active, the bottom portion of the dialog box contains a total of eight thumbnails: six hue and two brightness variations. Click any hue variation thumbnail to nudge the colors in the image toward or away from a range of hues. For example, Increase Blue represents not only blue but a whole range of hues—violet, cobalt, and so on—that have blue at their center. (For more information about these and other hues, refer to the sidebar "The Visible-Color Spectrum Wheel," which appears on the facing page.)

Our problem color is red, so click the **Decrease Red** thumbnail twice in a row. (Be sure you get both clicks in; if you click too fast, Elements has a tendency to ignore one.) All hue thumbnails update to reflect the change, as illustrated in Figure 3-15.

6. *Decrease the intensity setting.* The remaining problems with the image are more subtle. To prepare for the subtle solutions, move the **Adjust Color** slider triangle two notches to the left. The triangle should now appear as shown in the diminutive Figure 3-16. This setting will reduce the intensity of the next steps.

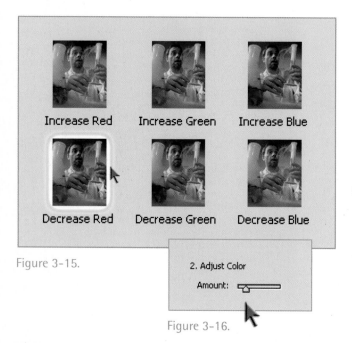

Figure 3-15.

Figure 3-16.

To feel comfortable working in the Color Variations dialog box, it helps to understand the composition of a little thing called the *visible-color spectrum wheel*. Pictured below, the wheel contains a continuous sequence of hues in the visible spectrum, the saturation of which ranges from vivid along the perimeter to drab gray at the center.

The colors along the outside of the circle match those that appear in a rainbow. But as the labels in the circle imply, the colors don't really fit the childhood mnemonic Roy G. Biv, short for red, orange, yellow, green, blue, indigo, and violet. An absolutely equal division of colors in the rainbow tosses out orange, indigo, and violet and recruits cyan and magenta, producing Ry G. Cbm (with the last name, I suppose, pronounced *seebim*). Printed in large colorful type, these six even divisions correspond to the three primary colors of light—red, green, and blue—alternating with the three primary pigments of print—cyan, magenta, and yellow.

In theory, cyan ink absorbs red light and reflects the remaining primaries, which is why cyan appears a bluish green. Cyan and red represent *complementary colors*, meaning that they form neutral gray when mixed together. The Color Variations dialog box treats complementary colors as opposites. For example, clicking the Decrease Red thumbnail not only reduces the amount of red in the image but also adds cyan. Similarly, Decrease Green adds magenta and Decrease Blue adds yellow.

Of course Ry G. Cbm is just a small part of the story. The color spectrum is continuous, with countless nameable (and unnameable) colors in between. I've taken the liberty of naming secondary and tertiary colors in the wheel. Because there are no industry standards for these colors, I took my names from other sources, including art supply houses and consumer paint vendors. I offer them merely for reference, so you have a name to go with the color.

The practical benefit is that you can use this wheel to better predict a required adjustment in the Color Variations dialog box. For example, the color orange is located midway between red and yellow. Therefore, if you recognize that an image has an orange cast, you can remove it by clicking red's opposite, Decrease Red, and then clicking yellow's opposite, Increase Blue.

The other color-wheel-savvy command, Adjust Hue/Saturation (see the "Tint and Color" exercise on page 92), tracks colors numerically. A circle measures 360 degrees, so the Hue value places each of the six primary colors 60 degrees from its neighbor. Secondary colors appear at every other multiple of 30 degrees, with tertiary colors at odd multiples of 15 degrees. To track the difference a Hue adjustment will make, just follow along the wheel. Positive adjustments run counterclockwise; negative adjustments run clockwise. So if you enter a Hue value of 60 degrees, yellow becomes green, ultramarine becomes purple, indigo becomes lavender, and so on. It may take a little time to make complete sense of the wheel, but once it sinks in, you'll want to rip it out of the book and paste it to your wall. Trust me, it's that useful.

Figure 3-17.

7. *Click the Lighten thumbnail.* At this point, the photo strikes me as a wee bit dark. So click the **Lighten** thumbnail to make the image lighter. Because the Midtones button is active (Step 3), clicking the Lighten thumbnail affects only the medium colors in the image. The darkest and lightest colors remain untouched.

8. *Click the Increase Green thumbnail.* After all these wonderful changes, the image remains a bit too purple. There is no Decrease Purple thumbnail. But by referring to "The Visible-Color Spectrum Wheel" chart on the preceding page, we find that purple's closest complement is green. So click the **Increase Green** thumbnail to infuse the image with green and reduce the amount of purple.

9. *Select the Saturation option.* So much for the brightness and hue, now on to saturation. To display the saturation controls, select **Saturation** in the lower-left portion of the dialog box. Color Variations swaps in two new thumbnails, which let you add or delete saturation.

10. *Click the Less Saturation thumbnail.* The colors in the photograph are a bit too vivid. Click **Less Saturation** to leech away colors and make them more neutral.

11. *Click the OK button.* It's hard to judge for sure from a bunch of dinky thumbnails, but the After image in the upper-right portion of the dialog box appears more or less on target. Click **OK** or press the Enter key to exit the Color Variations dialog box and apply your changes.

Figure 3-17 shows the finished image, unencumbered by color cast, with my natural pale skin tone restored to all its pasty glory. We dry-ice chemists don't get out much.

Tint and Color

Like the Color Variations command, Enhance→Adjust Colors→ Adjust Hue/Saturation lets you edit a range of colors independently from or in combination with luminosity values. But where Color Variations permits you to limit your adjustments to brightness ranges (highlights, shadows, and midtones), Adjust Hue/Saturation lets you modify specific hues. This means you can adjust the hue, saturation, and luminosity of an entire photograph or constrain your changes to, say, just the blue areas. The following exercise provides an example.

1. *Open an image.* Open the file *Helicopter & hotel.jpg* in the *Lesson 03* folder inside *Lesson Files-PE4 1on1*. Having awoken one downtown Los Angeles morning to the unrelenting thrashing of a circling helicopter, I snapped this photo from the window of my hotel room. As shown in Figure 3-18, I pointed my camera into the sun, so reflected light obscures the view and washes out the image.

2. *Apply the Auto Smart Fix command.* The photo obviously suffers from low contrast and pale shadows. To right these wrongs, choose **Enhance→Auto Smart Fix** (yet another function available in both the Quick Fix and Standard Edit modes) or press Ctrl+Alt+M. The result appears in Figure 3-19.

3. *Choose the Hue/Saturation command.* Choose **Enhance→ Adjust Colors→Adjust Hue/Saturation** or press the keyboard shortcut Ctrl+U to display the **Hue/Saturation** dialog box, as shown in Figure 3-20.

4. *Raise the Saturation value.* Click the word **Saturation** to select the numerical value and change it to +60 percent. This radically increases the intensity of colors throughout the image. (Unlike the Color Variations dialog box, Hue/Saturation updates the appearance of the image dynamically.)

Figure 3-18.

Figure 3-19.

Figure 3-20.

Figure 3-21.

You can change the Saturation value by entering 60 into the option box (the + sign is not necessary) or by dragging the corresponding slider control. Alternatively, you can press Shift+↑ to raise the value in increments of 10. Or, weirdest of all, you can *scrub* the value by dragging directly on the word **Saturation**. Press Shift while scrubbing to adjust the value in increments of 10.

5. *Lower the Hue value.* The sky and mirrored windows of the building are trending distinctly toward purple. My sense is that they would look better if they trended toward blue. According to the color wheel ("The Visible-Color Spectrum Wheel," page 91), shifting the hues from purple to blue is a clockwise rotation, which means a negative value. Press Shift+Tab to select the **Hue** value. Then press Shift+↓ to reduce the value to −10 degrees, which removes the slight purple tint, as in Figure 3-21.

Generally speaking, the dramatic boost to the Saturation value holds up nicely. The red brick of the building looks terrific, as do the yellow reflections and some of the other touches. But the blue sky is just too much. In a lesser piece of software, we'd have to split the difference—that is, come up with a Saturation value high enough to boost the brick but low enough to avoid overemphasizing the sky. Fortunately, Elements lets us work on the sky and brick independently.

6. *Isolate the blues.* The Edit pop-up menu at the top of the Hue/Saturation dialog box is set to Master. This setting tells Elements to transform all colors in an image by an equal amount. To limit your changes to just the sky colors, select **Blues** from the **Edit** menu instead. This appears to wipe out your previous values. But don't worry: they remain in force. They're just hidden so we can work on new values.

Now just because you select Blues doesn't mean you've isolated the *right* blues. The blues in this particular photograph could exactly match Elements' definition of blue, but just as likely they could lean toward ultramarine, indigo, cobalt, or sky (again, see page 91). Although the Edit pop-up menu doesn't provide access to these colors, it does permit you to nail a range of hues by moving your cursor into the image window and clicking on the precise color you want to identify. The following step explains how.

7. *Confirm the colors in the image window.* The numerical values at the bottom of the dialog box read 195°/225° and 255°\285°. According to the color wheel chart, this tells you

that Photoshop Elements is prepared to modify the colors between ultramarine (225°) and indigo (255°), centered at blue. The change will taper off as the colors decline to sky (195°) and purple (285°).

Change your cursor to an eyedropper by moving it outside the Hue/Saturation dialog box. Then click near the moon in the upper-left region of the image. The numbers at the bottom of the dialog box should shift to something in the neighborhood of 180°/210° and 240°\270°, as in Figure 3-22. (If your numbers differ by more than 5 degrees, move your cursor slightly and click again.) These values describe a range of cobalt (210°) to blue (240°), with a softening as far away as cyan (180°) and violet (270°). In other words, Elements has shifted the focus of the adjustment by −15 degrees; so instead of changing the blues in the image, you're all set to change the slightly greener ultramarines.

Figure 3-22.

Admittedly, the theory is dense, but one click is all it takes to translate the theory into action. Having isolated the colors in the sky, you're ready to make your changes.

8. *Lower the Saturation value.* Reduce the **Saturation** value to −40 percent to take some of the intensity out of the sky. This large Saturation shift may seem to make only a modest difference. But the sky no longer overwhelms other elements of the image, so all is well.

9. *Click OK.* Or press the Enter key to accept your changes and exit the Hue/Saturation dialog box.

The final image (Figure 3-23) is both more accurate and more dramatic than the original. One might argue that, of the two attributes, drama is given the edge. Well for crying out loud, the photograph has a helicopter in it. If that doesn't call for drama, I don't know what does.

PEARL OF WISDOM

You may have noticed that throughout the entire exercise, I never once touched the Lightness value. And for good reason—it's rarely useful. The Lightness value changes the brightness of highlights, shadows, and midtones by compressing the luminosity range. Raising the value makes black lighter while fixing white in place; lowering it affects white without harming black. It's not the worst luminosity modifier I've ever seen, but other commands—most notably Levels and Shadows/Highlights—provide much better control. Happily, these very commands are the topics of the next exercises.

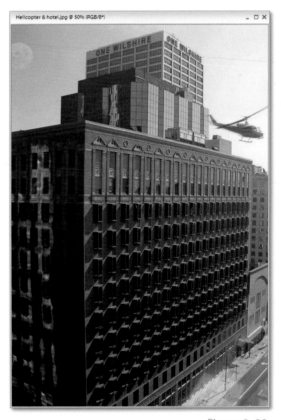

Figure 3-23.

Adjusting Brightness Levels

Thus far, we've looked at four commands that permit you to adjust colors inside Photoshop Elements. But what happens if your image problems have less to do with color and more to do with luminosity? You most often hear such problems characterized as issues of brightness and contrast, where *brightness* indicates the prevailing lightness or darkness of an image and *contrast* denotes the degree of difference between light and dark colors.

Photoshop Elements pays lip service to this colloquialism with a little ditty known as Enhance→Adjust Lighting→Brightness/Contrast. Although exceedingly easy to use, this command lacks what I would describe as a reasonable degree of predictability and control. Simply put, Brightness/Contrast leaves you shooting in the dark; it is every bit as likely to damage an image as it is to make it better.

Figure 3-24.

Which is why we turn our collective attention to a better command, Enhance→Adjust Lighting→Levels. Although a bit harder to use—this command isn't shy about asking you to roll up your shirtsleeves and smear on the elbow grease—Levels provides a perfect marriage of form and function. It lets you tweak highlights, midtones, and shadows predictably and with authority while maintaining smooth transitions between the three. In other words, it makes an image look its absolute best.

PEARL OF ● WISDOM

The Levels command is better at increasing contrast than decreasing it. To decrease the contrast of an image—particularly one with overly harsh shadows and highlights—see the exercise "Compensating for Flash and Backlighting," which begins on page 102.

The following exercise explains how to correct the brightness and contrast of an image with the Levels command.

1. *Open an image.* Open *End of rail.jpg*, found in the *Lesson 03* folder inside *Lesson Files-PE4 1on1*. Captured with an Olympus C-5050 at the top of Pikes Peak—right at the point where the cog railway drops into the abyss—this image features some atrocious light metering (see Figure 3-24). But don't blame the camera; I dropped it and broke off an important dial hours before I shot the photo. Fortunately, even though the camera was damaged, it captured enough color information so I could repair the photo in Photoshop Elements.

2. *Choose the Levels command.* Choose **Enhance→Adjust Lighting→Levels** or press Ctrl+L. Pictured in Figure 3-25, the stark and technical dialog box that follows may seem like something of a cold slap in the face, especially when compared with its user-friendly counterparts from previous exercises. And so I feel it incumbent to provide an option-by-option introduction. If you don't care to be introduced, skip to the next step—it won't affect your ability to follow along with the steps one iota. Then again, you may find that you understand what you're doing a little better if you take a few moments to read the following:

Figure 3-25.

- In the word of digital photography, an image is expressed as a combination of three primary colors: red, green, and blue. Each of the three primary colors resides in an independent reservoir called a *channel*. Located at the top of the Levels dialog box, the Channel pop-up menu lets you edit the contents of each primary channel independently. To edit the entire image at once, choose RGB, which just so happens to be the default setting.

- The three Input Levels values list the amount of adjustment applied to the shadows, midtones, and highlights, respectively. The default values—0, 1.00, and 255—indicate no change. More about these in a moment.

- The black blob in the middle is the *histogram*, which is a graph of the brightness values in your image. For more information on this item, read the sidebar, "How to Read and Respond to a Histogram," which begins on page 100.)

- The two Output Levels values let you lighten the darkest color in the image and darken the lightest color. In other words, they let you reduce the contrast. Although useful for dimming and fading, they rarely come into play when correcting an image.

- The Auto button applies the equivalent of the Auto Levels command, which you can then modify as needed.

- See the three eyedropper tools above the Preview check box? Select an eyedropper and then click in the image window to modify the clicked color. The black eyedropper makes the clicked color black; the white one makes it white; and the gray one robs it of color, leaving it a shade of gray.

Figure 3-26.

Figure 3-27.

- Turn on the Preview check box to see your changes applied dynamically to the active image.

This check box is great for before-and-after comparisons. So useful, in fact, that you have a shortcut: Alt+P.

3. **Click the Auto button.** Click the **Auto** button to apply the Auto Levels function. The histogram stretches to fill the center portion of the dialog box, but the numerical Input Levels values stay the same, as in Figure 3-26. (You'll see why in the next step.) As in the previous lesson, Photoshop Elements' automated adjustment isn't perfect, but it's a good place to start. Now, however, we can use Levels to tweak the adjustment.

4. **Switch to the Red channel.** Choose **Red** from the **Channel** pop-up menu or press Ctrl+1. You now see the histogram for the Red channel, complete with adjusted Input Levels values, as shown in Figure 3-27.

PEARL OF WISDOM

Clicking Auto in Step 3 changed the Input Levels settings on a channel-by-channel basis. So even though you see an altered histogram in the composite view (as in Figure 3-26), you have to visit the individual channels to see the numerical changes.

5. **Nudge the shadows and highlights.** Notice the black and white slider triangles directly below the histogram (highlighted red in Figure 3-27). They correspond to the first and last Input Levels values, respectively. In my case, the black slider tells me that any pixel with a brightness of 20 or less will be made black in the Red channel; the white slider says any pixel 198 or brighter will be made white. (Remember, 0 is absolute black and 255 is absolute white.) Those values are okay, but I recommend you tighten them up a little—that is, send a few more colors to black or white. Nudge the black value from 20 to 30; nudge the white value from 198 to 168.

By *nudge*, I mean use the arrow keys on the keyboard. Highlight the 20 and press Shift+↑ to raise it to 30. Highlight 198 and press Shift+↓ three times to lower the value to 168. Together, these adjustments make the image slightly redder.

6. **Raise the midtones value.** Increase the middle **Input Levels** value to 1.23, thus increasing the brightness of the midtones in the Red channel. The result appears in Figure 3-28.

Figure 3-28.

7. *Switch to the Green channel.* Choose **Green** from the **Channel** pop-up menu or press Ctrl+2.

8. *Adjust the shadows, midtones, and highlights.* Change the three **Input Levels** values to 36, 1.25, and 205. This brightens the green values, as in Figure 3-29.

9. *Switch to the Blue channel.* Choose **Blue** from the **Channel** pop-up menu or press Ctrl+3.

10. *Adjust the shadows, midtones, and highlights.* This time, change the three **Input Levels** values to 50, 1.26, and 187. The changes to the black and white values darken the Blue channel, while the change to the gamma value lightens the midtones. The result is a slight shift in colors in the evergreens in the background and the dirt beneath the track.

11. *Switch to the RGB composite image.* Choose **RGB** from the **Channel** pop-up menu or press Ctrl+☐. The ☐ key is the ~ to the left of the 1.

12. *Raise the gamma value.* Advance to the second **Input Levels** value. (If this value was last active in the Blue channel, it remains active in the composite image.) Then press Shift+↑ twice to raise the value to 1.2. This lightens the midtones across all color channels, as shown in Figure 3-30 on page 102.

13. *Click OK.* Or press the Enter key to accept your changes and exit the Levels dialog box.

The resulting image is significantly brighter than the original photograph, especially where the midtones are concerned. One of the downsides of lightening midtones is that it tends to bleed some of the color out of an image. Fortunately, you can restore color using Adjust Hue/Saturation, as explained in the next step.

Figure 3-29.

How to Read and Respond to a Histogram

In the world of statistics, a *histogram* is a kind of bar graph in which the bars vary in both height and width to show the distribution of data. In the Levels dialog box, it's a bit simpler. The central histogram contains exactly 256 vertical bars, each only one pixel wide. Each bar represents one brightness value, from black (on the far left) to white (on the far right). The height of each bar indicates how many pixels correspond to that particular brightness value. The result is an alternative view of your image, one that focuses exclusively on the distribution of colors.

Consider the annotated histogram below. I've taken the liberty of dividing it into four quadrants. If you think of the histogram as a series of steep sand dunes, a scant 5 percent of that sand spills over into the far left quadrant; thus, only 5 percent of the pixels in the image are dark. Meanwhile, fully 25 percent of the sand resides in the big peak in the right quadrant, so 25 percent of the pixels are light. The image represented by this histogram contains more highlights than shadows.

One glance at the image itself (opposite page, top) confirms that the histogram is accurate. The photo so obviously contains more highlights than shadows that the histogram may

seem downright redundant. But the truth is, it provides another and very helpful glimpse into the image. Namely, we see where the darkest colors start, where the lightest colors drop off, and how the rest of the image is weighted.

With that in mind, here are a few ways to work with the histogram in the Levels dialog box:

- **Black and white points:** Bearing in mind the sand dune analogy, move the black slider triangle below the histogram to the point at which the dunes begin on the left. Then move the white triangle to the point at which the dunes end on the right. (See the green graph below.) These adjustments make the darkest colors in the image black and the lightest colors white, which maximizes contrast without harming shadow and highlight detail.

- **Clipping:** Take care not to make too many colors black or white. If you do, you'll get *clipping*, an effect in which Photoshop Elements renders entire regions of your image flat black or white. Clipping is fine for graphic art but bad for photography, where you need continuous color transitions to convey depth and realism.

To preview exactly which pixels will go to black or white, press the Alt key as you drag a slider triangle. When dragging the black triangle, any pixels that appear black or any color *except* white (as in the example at the bottom of this page) are clipped. When dragging the white triangle, Photoshop Elements clips the nonblack pixels.

- **Balance the histogram on the gamma:** When positioning the gray gamma triangle, think "center of gravity." Imagine that you have to balance all that sand in the histogram on a teetering board poised on this single gray triangle. If you position the gamma properly, you can distribute the luminosity values evenly across the brightness spectrum, which generally produces the most natural results.

Bear in mind that these are suggestions, not rules. For example, clipped colors can result in interesting effects. Meanwhile, an overly dark image may look great set behind white type. These suggestions are meant to guide your experimentation so you can work more quickly and effectively inside the Levels dialog box.

Figure 3-30.

Figure 3-31.

14. *Choose the Hue/Saturation command.* Choose **Enhance→Adjust Color→Adjust Hue/Saturation** or press Ctrl+U. As we saw in the "Tint and Color" exercise that began on page 92, the Hue/Saturation dialog box is especially adept at modifying the intensity of colors in an image.

15. *Raise the Saturation value.* Press Tab until you advance to the **Saturation** value. Press Shift+↑ three times to raise the value to +30 percent. Then click **OK** or press the Enter key. The once drab image is now brimming with color, as shown in Figure 3-31.

The final image is a resounding success. But you may wonder how in the world I arrived at the specific values that you entered into the various Input Levels option boxes. The answer, of course, is trial and error. I spent a bit more time flitting back and forth between the channels and nudging values than the exercise implies, just as you will when correcting your own images. But as long as you keep the Preview check box turned on, you can see the effect of each and every modification as you apply it.

That said, my approach wasn't entirely random. Back in Step 8, I didn't know that 36 was the magic shadow value, but I suspected it was somewhere in that neighborhood. The trick is knowing how to read and respond to a histogram, as I explain in the aptly named sidebar "How to Read and Respond to a Histogram" on page 100.

Compensating for Flash and Backlighting

Photography is all about lighting—specifically, how light reflects off a surface and into the camera lens. So things tend to turn ugly when the lighting is wrong. One classic example of bad lighting is *backlighting*, in which the background is bright and the foreground subject is in shadow. Experienced photographers know that you adjust for backlighting by adding a fill flash, but even the best of us forget. An opposite problem occurs when shooting photos at night or in a dimly lit room using a consumer-grade flash. You end up with unnaturally bright foreground subjects set against dark backgrounds.

Whether your image is underexposed or overexposed, the solution is Enhance→Adjust Lighting→Shadows/Highlights. This marvelous function lets you radically transform shadows and highlights while maintaining reasonably smooth transitions between the two. Here's how it works:

Figure 3-32.

1. *Open an image.* Open *Sammy in snow.jpg* from the *Lesson 03* folder inside *Lesson Files-PE4 1on1*. Having set my youngest against such a bright background (see Figure 3-32), I should have known better than to shoot a picture without a flash. But if, indeed, even the best of us forget, it's a wonder I remember anything at all. The result of my inattention is a photograph that casts Sammy in deep gloom, quite out of keeping with his sunny personality. Fortunately, Elements lets me fix that.

2. *Open the Histogram palette.* Shadows/Highlights lets you modify the contrast of an image in ways that the Levels command simply can't match. But as we'll see, it lacks the Levels command's most prominent feature, the histogram. Fortunately, Photoshop Elements lets you display the histogram as a separate palette any time you need it. Choose **Window→Histogram** to display the **Histogram** palette, which shows you the same histogram you see in the Levels dialog box. As you might expect, the histogram includes peaks on the left and right with a valley in the center, indicating lots of shadows and highlights separated by scarce midtones.

3. *Refresh the histogram.* Most likely, you'll see a tiny caution icon (⚠) in the upper-right corner of the histogram, which means you're viewing a cached (that is, old and inaccurate) version of the histogram. Caching saves Elements some computational effort, but it proves a hindrance when you're trying to gauge the colors in an image. To update the histogram based on the latest and greatest information, click the circular ↻ arrows or the yellow ⚠ icon, as in Figure 3-33. And incidentally, go ahead and leave the Histogram palette open. You may find it helpful to keep an eye on it in future steps.

Figure 3-33.

Figure 3-34.

Figure 3-35.

4. *Choose the Shadows/Highlights command.* Again visit the **Enhance** menu and this time choose **Adjust Lighting→ Shadows/Highlights**. The resulting **Shadows/Highlights** dialog box (see Figure 3-34) contains just three slider bars:

- The Lighten Shadows option lets you lighten the darkest colors in the photo—i.e., Sammy.

- The Darken Highlights option darkens the lightest colors, which would be the snowy background.

- The Midtone Contrast expands or contracts the midtones in the image to increase or reduce, respectively, the amount of contrast between light and dark pixels.

No Ctrl-key shortcut exists for Shadows/Highlights. To choose the command using Windows-imposed hot keys, press the Alt key and type N-L-W. Again, it isn't memorable, but it's an option.

---

5. *Adjust the shadows and highlights.* By default, Elements is too conservative about both lightening the shadows and darkening the highlights. To temper the dark colors, raise the **Lighten Shadows** value to 40 percent. Then raise the **Darken Highlights** value to 60 percent. Assuming the Preview check box is on (as by default), Elements updates both the image and the histogram. As Figure 3-35 shows, the black portion of the histogram is the updated view; the gray portion is the original.

6. *Reduce the contrast.* In the process of lightening the shadows and darkening the highlights, the Shadows/Highlights command effectively reduces the contrast of the image. Elements provides the Midtone Contrast option so you can restore the contrast. But we have the opposite problem. This photograph exhibited such radical contrast in the first place that, if anything, we need to remove more. So press the Tab key to advance to the **Midtone Contrast** value, and reduce the value to −40 percent.

7. *Apply your changes.* Click **OK** or press the Enter key to accept your changes and exit the Shadows/Highlights dialog box.

The result, which appears in Figure 3-36, is an improvement over the original, but it still needs some help. The shadows are now a bit too light; the midtones are a bit too dark. There's not much I can do about this with the Shadows/Highlights command—not without compromising the integrity of the image, anyway. But I can easily fix both problems with Levels.

8. *Choose the Levels command.* Go to the **Enhance** menu and choose **Adjust Lighting→Levels** or press Ctrl+L. The **Levels** dialog box appears on the screen.

9. *Change the shadows and midtones values.* Darken the shadows by changing the first **Input Levels** option to 20. Then lighten the midtones by tabbing to the gamma value and changing it to 1.3. When you arrive at the effect pictured in Figure 3-37, click the **OK** button.

Shadows/Highlights is an amazing command, capable of reconstructing image detail captured under some of the worst lighting conditions imaginable. But it may produce some undesirable effects. Witness the almost greenish glow of Sammy's face. Using Adjust Color for Skin Tone to increase the blush in Sammy's face helps, but just a bit. In the course of exacting its radical brightness adjustments, the Shadows/Highlights command tends to flatten or exaggerate color transitions in ways that may compromise the credibility of surfaces and textures. The upshot is that even an inexperienced viewer might look at the photo and wonder, "Did you do something to this?"

Still, I regard these issues as acceptable casualties of correction. The lighting is now significantly more balanced than it was in the original photograph. Sammy no longer appears shrouded in silhouette. Heck, if you look closely, you can make out that he has brown eyes, compared with nearly solid black in the original. Despite its occasional compromises, Shadows/Highlights is Photoshop Elements' best tool for correcting extremely high-contrast images.

Figure 3-36.

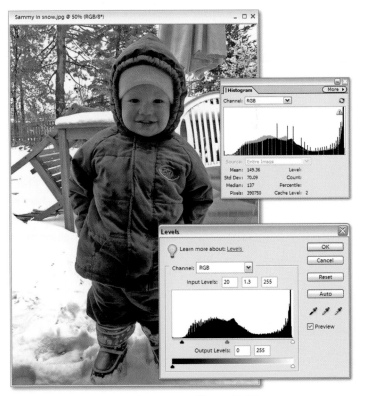

Figure 3-37.

Correcting Camera Raw

The final method for correcting colors with Photoshop Elements applies to photographs captured by a midrange or professional-level digital camera and saved in the camera's *raw* format. This raw file represents the unprocessed data captured by the camera's image sensor. Such a file is typically several times larger than an equivalent JPEG file that digital cameras would normally use for saving images because it also contains more information. This means you can shoot fewer pictures at a time, but you capture a wider range of colors and more accurate image detail. Plus, in Photoshop Elements, you can open a raw image and correct its colors and luminosity values in a single operation.

PEARL OF WISDOM

At present, Photoshop Elements supports raw files from a select group of digital cameras sold by Olympus, Canon, Nikon, Minolta, and others. If you purchased a new camera for less than $500, chances are it does not qualify (that is to say, it shoots only JPEG images, which you can open and modify using the techniques outlined in all the exercises *except* this one). Note: TIFF files are not considered raw files. If your camera supports both raw and TIFF, raw is the better choice; the images contain more data and the file sizes are smaller. Check your camera's documentation for more information.

1. *Open a raw image.* Open the file *Daniel balloons.dng* in the *Lesson 03* folder inside *Lesson Files-PE4 1on1*. I captured this photo with an Olympus E-1 and saved it as an ORF (Olympus Raw Format) file. Then I converted the image to the more universal DNG (Digital Negative) format using Adobe's Digital Negative Converter software, which you can download for free from *www.adobe.com/dng*.

   Rather than opening the photograph in a new image window, Elements displays the Camera Raw window pictured in Figure 3-38 on the facing page. The window includes a high-resolution preview of the image and a full-color histogram, both of which update as you adjust the color settings. Use the zoom and hand tools in the upper-left corner of the window to magnify and scroll the preview, respectively.

   The title bar lists the model of camera used to shoot the photo as well as the light sensitivity (ISO), shutter speed, aperture, and focal length in use when the photo was captured. Elements uses this information to automatically process the image in case you decide to skip the manual adjustments and go straight for the Open button.

2. *Rotate the image upright.* Click the second rotate icon (↻) in the upper-left corner of the image preview to rotate the photo 90 degrees clockwise. Or you can press the R key (short for rotate right).

Figure 3-38.

3. *Set the White Balance controls.* The color cast of highlights in a photograph is commonly known as the *white balance*. Because of the trickle-down nature of white balance, you can neutralize a color cast throughout an image using the White Balance controls in the Adjust panel. Here's how:

   • By default, the White Balance option is set to As Shot, which refers to the default calibration settings for this specific model of camera. To override this setting, select a lighting condition from the White Balance pop-up menu or dial in your own Temperature and Tint values, as follows.

   • This marks our third encounter with a Temperature option in this book, but this time, we have a numerical value, which compensates for the color of the lighting source, measured in degrees Kelvin. Low-temperature lighting produces a yellowish cast, and higher temperature lighting produces bluish casts. The closest thing to neutral is direct sunlight, which hovers around 5500 degrees.

- Tint compensates for Temperature by letting you further adjust the colors in your image along a different color axis. Positive values introduce a magenta cast (or remove a green one); negative values do just the opposite.

This particular image was shot outdoors with moderate cloud cover and no flash. So set the **White Balance** to **Shade**, which results in a **Temperature** of 7500 degrees and a **Tint** of 10, as shown in Figure 3-39. This setting makes the photograph a little warmer than it probably ought to be, but I like it that way.

Another way to set the white balance is to use the eyedropper tool in the upper-left corner of the Camera Raw window. Select the eyedropper and click a color in the image that should be white or neutral gray. Elements sets the Temperature and Tint values as needed. If you don't like the results, try again. Double-click the eyedropper icon to restore the As Shot values.

Figure 3-39.

4. *Adjust the highlights and shadows.* The Exposure and Shadows values are analogous to the white and black slider triangles, respectively, inside the Levels dialog box (see "Adjusting Brightness Levels," Step 5, page 98). The main difference is that Exposure is computed in f-stops. For example, raising the Exposure to +0.50 simulates opening the lens aperture of the camera a half stop wider.

I recommend raising the **Exposure** value to –1.10, a slight adjustment from the automatic setting but sufficient to help elevate the whites. Because the image contains plenty of black pixels, lower the **Shadows** value to 0.

Press the Alt key and drag the Exposure or Shadows slider triangle to preview clipped pixels. When you adjust the Exposure, nonblack pixels indicate clipped highlights; for Shadows, nonwhite pixels represent clipped shadows.

---

5. *Lower the Brightness setting.* The closest thing to a gamma control in the Camera Raw window is the Brightness setting. It's not an exact match, but it does let you adjust midtones using a rough percentage system. Values below 50 compress shadows and expand highlights, thereby lightening an image; values above 50 do the opposite. In this example, change the **Brightness** value to 125 to lighten what was previously an overly dark photograph.

6. *Adjust the Contrast and Saturation values.* The rest of the slider bars have no equivalents in the Levels dialog box, but I wish they did. The Contrast slider expands or compresses the histogram to increase or decrease the contrast between pixels, respectively. As always, the Saturation value increases or decreases color purity. Enter a **Contrast** value of –10 and a **Saturation** value of +20.

7. *Zoom in on the image.* The next set of options we'll look at let you sharpen the focus of a photo and smooth away noise artifacts. To best judge the details in your image, double-click the zoom tool icon in the upper-left corner to zoom in to 100 percent. Then press the spacebar to access the hand tool and drag the image so you can see the look of abject terror in my brother's face, so very evident in Figure 3-40 on the next page.

8. *Set the Sharpness, Smoothing, and Noise values.* Click the **Detail** tab to access the remaining three slider bars. Here's how they work:

   - Raise the Sharpness value to increase the amount of contrast between neighboring pixels. Unlike Contrast, Sharpness doesn't affect the overall histogram; rather, it compares adjacent pixels and increases their difference from one another. (Lesson 7, "Filters and Distortions," contains lots more information.) The result is increased edge definition, which gives the appearance of sharper focus.

- If you increase the Sharpness value too much, you'll increase the contrast between pixels that should be smooth. The result is randomly colored pixels, or *noise*. To soften areas of noise that are the result of variations in lightness and darkness, increase the Luminance Smoothing value.

- To soften noise that results from variations in hue or saturation, increase the Color Noise Reduction value.

Figure 3-40.

If you don't anticipate any major edits to a photograph, I advise that you crank the Sharpness up to 100 so you can see the image noise at full volume. Then use Luminance Smoothing and Color Noise Reduction to smooth out the rough patches. And finally, revisit the Sharpness option and adjust it to taste.

For this image, my preferred settings are **Sharpness**: 50, **Luminance Smoothing**: 20, and **Color Noise Reduction**: 50, as pictured in Figure 3-41.

9. *Leave the Depth setting unchanged.* Now turn your attention to the bottom-left corner of the window, where you'll find an option called Depth. At the risk of overloading your brain—trust me, I wouldn't do it if I didn't have to—Photoshop Elements supports two varieties of full-color images. One contains 8 bits of data per channel, which works out to a maximum of 16.8 million potential colors. The other contains 16 bits of data per channel, which works out to as many as 281.5 *trillion* colors.

This particular raw image contains slightly more than a billion possible colors. In other words, Elements needs to convert it. You have two options for this conversion: reduce the colors by a factor of 64 to the 16.8 million-color space, or preserve all billion colors inside the gargantuan 281.5 trillion-color space.

Figure 3-41.

The latter option might sound more logical, but it comes at a price: 16-bit images are demanding, so much so that most of Elements' editing functions don't work in the 16-bit color mode. Furthermore, no monitor or printer supports the 16-bit space, so all but a fraction of those trillions of colors are wasted.

My advice: Make sure **Depth** is set to **8 Bits/Channel**, as by default. Otherwise, you'll slow down the performance of the software, sacrifice much of the program's functionality, and gain almost nothing in return.

10. *Click Open.* Confirm that your values match those pictured in Figures 3-40 and 3-41. Then click the **Open** button. After you do, Photoshop Elements imports the image from the raw DNG format and applies the color and focus corrections that you specified in the previous steps. Note that the program does not save the zoom information; the image will appear zoomed out, so that it fits on the screen.

The corrected photograph appears on the left side of Figure 3-42. For the sake of comparison, I include, on the right, the same photo subject to the default settings defined by the camera. (To see the image on your screen in this same condition, open the file again and choose Camera Raw Defaults from the Settings pop-up menu in the Camera Raw window.) Obviously, the camera's default suggestions were off, as were the automatic guesses made by Elements' Camera Raw function. It just goes to show you that taking the time to assign your own deliberate and carefully considered color corrections makes all the difference in the world.

Final color-corrected raw photograph

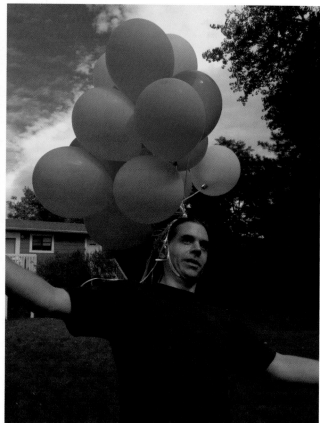

Same photo according to the camera's default settings

Figure 3-42.

WHAT DID YOU LEARN?

Match the key concept in the numbered list below with the letter of the phrase that best describes it. Answers appear upside-down at the bottom of the page.

Key Concepts

1. Hue
2. Saturation
3. Brightness
4. Shadows
5. Highlights
6. Midtones
7. Complementary colors
8. Contrast
9. Temperature
10. Histogram
11. Gamma value
12. Camera Raw

Descriptions

A. The darkest range of colors in an image.

B. Known variously as *chroma* and *purity*, this property measures the intensity of a color.

C. A bar graph in which each bar represents one brightness value in an image, from black (on the far left) to white (on the far right).

D. Located on opposite sides of the visible-color spectrum wheel, these form neutral gray when mixed together.

E. This type of file format preserves the unprocessed data captured by a camera's image sensor.

F. Sometimes referred to as *tint*, this property defines a color's core value—red, yellow, green, and so on.

G. This is generally the most useful range of colors to adjust with the Color Variations command.

H. The lightest range of colors in an image.

I. This refers to the warmth or coolness of the color of the lighting source.

J. Also known as *luminosity*, this color property describes how light or dark the color is.

K. The degree of difference between an image's light and dark colors.

L. Known as the Levels command's "center of gravity," adjusting this setting modifies the midtones in an image independently of the shadows or highlights.

Answers

1F, 2B, 3J, 4A, 5H, 6G, 7D, 8K, 9I, 10C, 11L, 12E

MAKING SELECTIONS

MANY COMPUTER PROGRAMS allow you to manipulate elements on a page as objects. That is to say, you click or double-click an object to select it, and then you modify the object in any of several ways permitted by the program. For example, if you go to the Windows desktop and double-click the Recycle Bin icon, your PC shows you a window full of files that you've thrown away. To make a word bold in Microsoft Word, you double-click the word and then click the Bold button. Every object is a unique, selectable thing.

The real world harbors a similar affinity for objects. Consider the three sunflowers pictured in Figure 4-1. In life, those flowers are objects. You can reach out and touch them. You can even cut them and put them in a vase.

But although Photoshop Elements lets you modify snapshots taken from the world around you, it doesn't behave like that world. And it bears only a passing resemblance to other computer programs. You can't select a sunflower by clicking it because Elements doesn't perceive the flower as an independent object. Instead, the program sees pixels. And as the magnified view in Figure 4-1 shows, every pixel looks a lot like its neighbor. In other words, where you and I see three sunflowers, Photoshop Elements sees a blur of subtle transitions, without form or substance.

Where you see flowers...

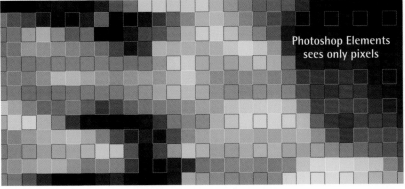

Photoshop Elements sees only pixels

Figure 4-1.

ABOUT THIS LESSON

Project Files

Before beginning the exercises, make sure you've installed the lesson files from the DVD, as explained in Step 5 on page xv of the Preface. This should result in a folder of images called *Lesson Files-PE4 1on1* on your desktop. We'll be working with the files inside the *Lesson 04* subfolder.

This lesson examines ways to select a region of an image and edit it independently of other regions using the various selection tools along with a few menu commands. You'll learn how to:

Video Lesson 4: Selection Tools

Elements' selection tools rank among its most essential capabilities. Unless you want to apply an operation to an entire image or layer, you have to first define the area that you want to affect by dragging or clicking with a selection tool.

To see an overview of Elements' selection tools, as well as a few of the most common selection-editing commands, watch the fourth video lesson on the DVD. To view this video, insert the DVD, click **Start**, select **Set 2: Select, Crop, and Edit** from the first pop-up menu, and then select **Lesson 4: The Selection Tools** from the second pop-up menu. The movie lasts 18 minutes and 37 seconds, during which you'll learn about the following shortcuts:

Command or operation	Keyboard equivalent or shortcut
Fill selection with foreground color	Alt+Backspace
Deselect image	Ctrl+D (or click outside selection)
Add to selection	Shift-click or drag with selection tool
Subtract from a selection	Alt-click or drag with selection tool
Hide selection outline	Ctrl+H
Move marquee as you draw it	press and hold the spacebar
Inverse (reverse selection)	Ctrl+Shift+I

So rather than approaching an image in terms of its sunflowers or other objects, you have to approach it in terms of pixels. This means specifying which pixels you want to affect and which you do not using *selections*.

Isolating an Image Element

Let's say you want to change the color of the umbrella shown in Figure 4-2. As you'll learn in the exercise "Colorizing an Image with Adjustment Layers" (Lesson 10, page 313), you can colorize an object using the Gradient Map function. But to colorize the umbrella and only the umbrella, you must first select it. Never mind that the umbrella is so obviously an independent object that even an infant could pick it out. For all its power, Photoshop Elements is no infant. If you want to select the umbrella, you must tell the program exactly which group of pixels you want to modify.

Fortunately, Elements provides a wealth of selection functions to help you do just that. Some functions select regions of colors automatically, others require you to painstakingly define the selection by hand. Still others, like the tools I used to describe the bluish regions in Figure 4-3, select geometric regions. All the tools can be used together to forge the perfect outline, one that exactly describes the perimeter of the element or area that you want to select.

As if to make up for its inability to immediately perceive image elements such as umbrellas and sunflowers, Photoshop Elements treats *selection outlines*—those dotted lines that mark the borders of a selection—as independent objects. You can move selection outlines independently of an image. You can combine them or subtract from them. You can undo and redo selection modifications. You can even save selection outlines for later use.

Selected umbrella

Colorized using Gradient Map

Figure 4-2.

Figure 4-3.

Figure 4-4.

Furthermore, a selection can be every bit as incremental and precise as the image that houses it. Not only can you select each and every pixel inside an image—as a group or independently—you can also specify the degree to which you want to select a pixel—all the way, not at all, or in any of a couple of hundred levels of translucency in between.

This means you can match the subtle transitions between neighboring pixels by creating smooth, soft, or fuzzy selection outlines. In Figure 4-4, I selected the umbrella and the man holding it and transferred the two to a different backdrop. Not only was I able to maintain the subtle edges between the man and his environment, I was also able to make the darkest portions of his coat translucent so they would blend with the backdrop. Selections take work, but they also deliver the goods.

Selecting Colored Areas with the Magic Wand

We'll start things off with one of the most automated tools in all of Photoshop Elements, the magic wand. A fixture of the program since way back when it was called Photoshop LE, the magic wand lets you select an area of color with a single click. It works especially well for removing skies and other relatively solid backgrounds, as the following exercise explains.

1. *Open two images.* Make sure the Editor workspace is running. Then open the *PhotoSpin giraffe.jpg* and *Bolivian backdrop.jpg* files, located in the *Lesson 04* folder inside *Lesson Files-PE4 1on1.* (You can select two images at a time in the Open dialog box by clicking one and Ctrl-clicking the other.) Press Ctrl+⊟ a couple of times to zoom out from both images, and then move the image windows on screen so you can see most of both of them. Click the title bar for *PhotoSpin giraffe.jpg* to bring it to the front, as illustrated in Figure 4-5 on the facing page. Our goal during this exercise is to use the magic wand tool to select the giraffe and then bring it into the *Bolivian backdrop.jpg* image. The fact that the two images come from different continents doesn't bother Photoshop Elements one bit.

Figure 4–5.

2. *Select the magic wand tool in the toolbox.* Click the magic wand tool in the toolbox along the left side of the Editor screen (see Figure 4-6) or press the W key.

3. *Confirm the options bar settings.* Pictured in Figure 4-7, the options bar displays a series of settings for the magic wand. Confirm that they are set as follows:

- The **Tolerance** value defines how many pixels the wand selects at a time. I discuss this very important option in Step 5. In the meantime, leave it set to its default, 32.

- Turn on the **Anti-alias** check box to soften the selection outline just enough to make it look like an organic, photographic boundary. I talk more about this option in Step 13 on page 123.

- Turn on **Contiguous** to make sure that the magic wand selects only uninterrupted regions of color. We'll get a sense of how contiguous selections work in Step 6.

Figure 4-6.

Because this image does not include layers, the Sample All Layers check box has no effect.

Figure 4-7.

4. *Click anywhere in the sky.* For the record, I happened to click at the location illustrated by the cursor in Figure 4-8. But if my experimentations are any indication, you can click just about anywhere and you won't select the entire sky. That may seem like an odd thing. Here's this tool that selects regions of color, and it can't select what may be the most consistently colored cloudless sky ever photographed. What good is it?

PEARL OF WISDOM

What looks to you like a field of homogeneous blue that lightens a bit as it travels from top to bottom is in fact a collection of roughly 500,000 independent colors. Given current settings, the wand can select at most half that number, so some pixels are bound to get left out.

Figure 4-8.

5. *Raise the Tolerance value.* The Tolerance setting determines how many colors are selected at a time, as measured in luminosity values. By default, Photoshop Elements selects colors that are 32 luminosity values lighter and darker than the click point. After that, the selection drops off. Given that Elements did not select the entire sky, the Tolerance must be too low.

I suggest raising the value to 50. The easiest way is to click the word **Tolerance** in the options bar to highlight the value, type 50, and press the Enter key. Note that this has no immediate effect on the selection. Tolerance is a *static* setting, meaning that it affects the next operation you apply, as Step 6 explains.

6. *Expand the selection using the Similar command.* The Select menu provides two commands that let you expand the range of a selection based on the Tolerance setting. They both affect any kind of selection, but they were created with the wand tool in mind:

- Select→Grow reapplies the magic wand as if we had clicked all the pixels at once inside the selection with the magic wand tool. In other words, it uses the selection as a base for a larger selection. The Grow command selects only contiguous pixels—pixels adjacent to the selected pixels.

- Select→Similar is almost identical to Grow, except that it selects both adjacent and non-adjacent pixels. So where Grow would select blue sky pixels up to the point where it encounters nonblue pixels, such as the giraffe's mane, Similar selects all blue pixels within the Tolerance range regardless of where they lie, including those deep inside the mane.

For our purposes, we want to get all the blue pixels, wherever they may reside, so choose **Select→Similar**, as shown in Figure 4-9.

7. *Fill out the selection.* With a modicum of luck, you should have selected the entire sky. But if you miss a spot, press the Shift key and click that spot in the image window. Shift-clicking with the magic wand adds to a selection.

8. *Reverse the selection.* You may wonder if this approach makes sense. You want to select the giraffe, and yet you've gone and selected the sky. As it turns out, this is by design. It's easier to select a solid-colored sky than a spotty-colored giraffe, and you can always reverse the selection. Choose **Select→Inverse** or press Ctrl+Shift+I to select those pixels that are not selected and deselect those that are. In this case, now the giraffe is selected and the sky is not (see Figure 4-10).

Figure 4-9.

Figure 4-10.

Figure 4-11.

9. *Select the move tool in the toolbox.* Click the move tool in the toolbox (see Figure 4-11) or press the V key (as in mooV). The move tool lets you move selected pixels within an image or from one image to another.

10. *Drag the giraffe into the Bolivian backdrop.* This operation is a little tricky, so I recommend you read the following paragraph before you begin.

   Position your move tool cursor inside the giraffe so the cursor appears as a plain arrowhead. Then drag the giraffe from the *PhotoSpin giraffe.jpg* image window into the *Bolivian backdrop.jpg* image window. Before you release the mouse button, press and hold the Shift key. Finally, release the mouse button and then release the Shift key.

   By pressing Shift on the drop, you instructed Photoshop Elements to *register* the giraffe inside its new background, so that it lands in the same spot relative to the new background as it enjoyed in the old background, as shown in Figure 4-12. Had you not pressed Shift, the giraffe would have landed wherever you dropped it. (If you didn't get it quite right, press Ctrl+Z to undo the operation and try again.)

Figure 4-12.

At this point, you have successfully used the magic wand tool to transfer the giraffe into a new habitat. The only problem is, it doesn't look particularly realistic. In fact, it looks like what it is—a digital montage. If that's good enough for you, skip ahead to the next exercise, "Using the Marquee Tools," which begins on page 125. But if you want to make this giraffe look like it's really at home, we have a few steps to go.

11. *Select the Background layer in the Layers palette.* The **Layers** palette most likely appears in the bottom-right corner of your screen, in the Palette Bin. If not, choose **Window→Layers** or press the F11 key to open it. You should see two layers, one for the giraffe—an imported selection always appears on a new layer—and another for the background. Click the **Background** layer to make it active, as shown in Figure 4-13.

Figure 4-13.

12. *Apply the Gaussian Blur filter.* To create a more realistic depth-of-field effect, blur the background. The best command for this purpose is **Filter→Blur→Gaussian Blur**. Choose this command, change the **Radius** value to 12 pixels, and click the **OK** button, as demonstrated in Figure 4-14.

13. *Zoom in on a few details.* Use the zoom tool at the top of the toolbox to zero in on the giraffe's horns and mane and gauge how well Elements selected the image. As you can see in Figure 4-15 on the next page, the selection has some slight problems:

Figure 4-14.

- The horns look a little jagged. More careful inspection reveals that the jagged edges are mitigated by a slight softening effect. Known in technical circles as *antialiasing*, this softening is a function of the Anti-alias check box that you turned on back in Step 3. The check box instructed the magic wand to partially select a thin line of pixels around the perimeter of the selection, thus creating a slight fade between the giraffe and its new background. Had you turned Anti-alias off, the edges of the horns would appear even more jagged.

Figure 4-15.

• Pictured in the bottom half of Figure 4-15, the mane exhibits a problem called *haloing* (also called *fringing*), where a foreground image is outlined with a fringe of background color, in this case blue.

The jagged edges aren't perfect, but they look fine when we're zoomed out and are likely to print fine as well. The haloing is another matter. That you should fix. And although Elements 4 introduces a new command designed specifically for this purpose (Enhance→Adjust Color→Defringe Layer), it's something of a dog, in my humble opinion. We'll fix this problem with the help of a better tool, a predefined layer style.

14. *Select the giraffe layer in the Layers palette.* Click the **Layer 1** item to make it active.

15. *Bring up the Deke Edges styles.* Directly above the Layers palette, you should see a palette called **Styles and Effects**. If not, choose **Window**→**Styles and Effects** or press the F7 key to open it. The palette begins with two side-by-side pop-up menus:

• Choose **Layer Styles** from the first pop-up menu to gain access to a series of drop shadows, glows, and other methods for tracing the perimeter of a layer.

• Click the second pop-up menu to unfurl it. In the second section, you should see a collection of options that begin with the word *Deke*, as in Figure 4-16. (The Deke libraries appear only if you installed my presets, as directed in Step 5 on page xv of the Preface.) Choose **Deke Edges** to trace the inside edge of a layer with any of ten colors.

16. *Apply the Orange Edge Tint style.* Of all the hues represented by the Deke Edges styles, orange is the one that best matches the yellowish brown of the animal's mane, spots, and horns. So click the thumbnail named **Orange Edge Tint** in the Styles and Effects palette. Elements traces a subtle corona of orange around the inside perimeter of the giraffe's head and neck.

Figure 4-16.

17. *Adjust the layer style settings.* Currently, the inner glow effect is too thick, meaning that it doesn't merely tint the edges but seeps into the giraffe's face as well. Fortunately, you can change this. Notice the ⦿ to the far right of Layer 1 in the Layers palette? This symbol indicates that a style has been applied to the layer. Double-click the ⦿ to display the **Style Settings** dialog box, as illustrated in Figure 4-17. Then reduce the **Inner Glow Size** value to 40 pixels, so the glow just covers the mane, and click the **OK** button.

The Orange Edge Tint style ably corrects the blue haloing, as demonstrated in Figure 4-18. To learn more about layer styles and their many practical and creative uses, read Lesson 10, "Styles and Adjustment Layers."

Using the Marquee Tools

After seeing the magic wand and its ability to select irregular regions of color, you may question the usefulness of a geometric selection tool such as the rectangular or elliptical marquee. After all, how many image elements are precisely rectangular or elliptical? The answer is: plenty. Every image begins life as a rectangle, and ellipses are as common as, well, our own Mother Earth.

Figure 4-17.

Figure 4-18.

But it goes beyond that. Both tools are great for selecting general regions to be used for a wide variety of purposes, as the following exercise makes clear:

1. *Open three images.* Open the *PhotoSpin moon.jpg,* *PhotoSpin red sky.jpg,* and *PhotoSpin road.jpg* files, all of which appear in Figure 4-19. These files are located in the *Lesson 04* folder inside *Lesson Files-PE4 1on1.* In the following steps, we'll combine these images in a complex composition using the undeniably simple rectangular and elliptical marquee tools. We'll also add a dynamic fill layer to make the colors of the road and moon conform to those of the vivid red sky.

2. *Select the rectangular marquee tool in the toolbox.* Bring the *PhotoSpin road.jpg* image to the front and click the rectangular marquee tool in the toolbox (see Figure 4-20) or press the M key. (If you get the elliptical marquee tool instead, press the M key again.) The rectangular marquee tool lets you select rectangular portions of an image.

Figure 4-19.

Figure 4-20.

3. *Confirm the options bar settings.* In the options bar, make sure that the **Feather** value is set to 0 and the **Mode** is set to **Normal**. These default settings ensure that the marquee tool draws hard-edged rectangles of unconstrained height and width. In other words, they cause the tool to behave normally.

4. *Select the bottom portion of the image.* Drag with the rectangular marquee tool to select the bottom portion of the *PhotoSpin road.jpg* image shown in Figure 4-21. Make sure you select all the way to the edges.

If you miss a bit of an edge, press the spacebar (while keeping the mouse button down) to temporarily stop drawing the marquee and instead adjust its position. When the spacebar is down, the marquee moves; release the spacebar to continue drawing.

---

5. *Choose the Feather command.* Choose **Select→Feather** or press Ctrl+Alt+D to display the **Feather Selection** dialog box, which allows you to blur the boundaries of a selection outline. Enter a relatively enormous **Feather Radius** value such as 120 pixels, and click **OK** (see Figure 4-22). Although the selection outline does not appear to change, have faith: This creates a gradual transition between selected and deselected pixels, as we'll see in the next step.

Figure 4-21.

PEARL OF WISDOM

If Feather is so deft at creating gradual transitions, why didn't we use it to fix the edges of the giraffe? The purpose of the Feather command is to blur the edges of a selection so that it has an indistinct boundary. A blurry boundary around a sharply focused giraffe would have looked all wrong. But a road that fades gradually into its background will look great.

---

6. *Drag the selected road and drop it into the red sky image.* You could use the move tool at the top of the toolbox, as in Steps 9 and 10 of the preceding exercise (see page 122), but this time I'd like you to try something different.

Press and hold the Ctrl key to temporarily switch to the move tool. With Ctrl down, drag the selected part of the road from *PhotoSpin road.jpg* into the *PhotoSpin red sky.jpg* image window. Before you drop the selection, press and hold the Shift key to register the selection inside its new home. Release the mouse button, and then release both keys. You should get the result shown in **Figure 4-23** on the next page.

Figure 4-22.

7. *Bring the moon image to the front.* Click the title bar for *PhotoSpin moon.jpg* to bring it to the front.

8. *Select the elliptical marquee tool.* Go to the toolbox and choose the elliptical marquee tool from the marquee tool flyout menu. Or press the M key (or Shift+M, depending on how you set your preferences).

9. *Select the moon (and then some).* Drag with the elliptical marquee tool to select an area well outside the moon, as illustrated in Figure 4-24.

Here are three keyboard tricks that can help you define your selection while dragging with the elliptical marquee tool. Press the Alt key to draw from the center of the image out; this may help you align the selection outline evenly around the moon. Press the Shift key to constrain the ellipse to a circle. (The moon is not quite circular, but you still may find Shift helpful.) Press the spacebar to move the ellipse on-the-fly.

Figure 4-24.

Figure 4-23.

10. *Feather the edges of the selection.* Choose **Select→Feather** or press Ctrl+Alt+D. Enter a **Feather Radius** value of 12 pixels and click **OK**. Although you can't tell yet, this value blurs the outline around the moon. Granted, it's not as blurry as the super-gradual transition we assigned to the road, but it's blurry nonetheless.

11. *Drag the moon into the red sky image.* Press Ctrl and drag the moon into the *PhotoSpin red sky.jpg* image window. This time, instead of pressing the Shift key to center the moon, just drop it in front of the sun over the road, as pictured in Figure 4-25.

To move an image element after you drop it, press the Ctrl key and drag it to the desired location. You can also press the Ctrl key and nudge the image using the four arrow keys (↑, ↓, ←, →).

12. *Invert the colors in the moon.* Choose **Filter**→**Adjustments**→ **Invert** or press Ctrl+I to invert the light and dark colors in the moon. The moon turns a deep blue, as in Figure 4-26. I like the luminosity values, but I want the colors to match the rest of the image.

Figure 4-25.

Figure 4-26.

13. *Add a layer of vermilion.* We'll colorize the image in an unusual but highly effective way. Go to the **Layers** palette and click the ⬤ symbol in the top row of icons. This displays a pop-up menu of specialty layers. Choose **Solid Color**, which creates a layer filled with a single color. To find out what color you'd like, Elements displays the **Color Picker** dialog box. The first three values—**H**, **S**, and **B**—stand for Hue, Saturation, and Brightness. Change them to 20, 100, and 100, respectively, as in Figure 4-27. Then click **OK** to create a new layer, completely filled with vermilion. This probably seems like a weird step—after all, you just blotted out your entire image! But suspend your disbelief for a moment and trust me, your devoted trainer: it'll look great.

Figure 4-27.

Figure 4-28.

14. Change the blend mode to Color. Now to mix the vermilion with the layers below it. Click the word **Normal** at the top of the **Layers** palette and choose **Color** from the pop-up menu that appears. This retains the hue and saturation of the vermilion layer and mixes them with the luminosity values of the moon, road, and sky below it. See? All better. The colorized result appears in Figure 4-28.

EXTRA ★ CREDIT

If you like, you can stop now. After all, you've used the rectangular and elliptical marquee tools to great effect, merging three images from different photographs into a seamless whole. But the marquee tools can also be used to paint color into an image. In the remaining steps, I explain how to add a jet of white descending from the moon to the road and how to lift color from an image using the eyedropper tool. If you don't feel like following along, skip to the next exercise, "Lassoing an Irregular Image" on the facing page. Otherwise, we've just six more steps.

15. Create a new layer in front of the road. Click the **Layer 1** item in the Layers palette. If you accurately followed the steps, Layer 1 contains the image of the road. Click the 🖼 icon at the top of the palette to create a new layer in front of the road.

16. Draw a new marquee. Get the rectangular marquee tool by pressing M, pressing Shift+M, or selecting it from the toolbox. Then draw a marquee that connects the moon to the road. It should be slightly narrower than the moon and descend slightly into the road, as shown in Figure 4-29.

17. Feather the selection. Choose **Select→Feather**, and note that the Feather Radius value is still set to 12 pixels, as you specified back in Step 10. This continues to be a wonderful setting. To accept it and move on, click **OK**. The corners of the rectangular marquee appear to round off slightly.

Figure 4-29.

18. Hide the selection outline. The selection outline is a bit intrusive for my taste, so let's hide it. Choose **View→Selection** or press Ctrl+H to hide the animated dotted outline—AKA, "marching ants"—around the marquee.

Note that the selection outline is still there; the animated outline is hidden merely so you see the results of your changes better. To redisplay the marching ants, press Ctrl+H again.

19. *Fill the selection with white.* Press the D key to switch to the default foreground and background colors, black and white. Then press Ctrl+Backspace to fill the selection with the background color. Even though the selection is invisible, Elements goes ahead and colors it white.

20. *Reduce the Opacity setting.* The white rectangle is too opaque. I suggest we make it more translucent. Select the **Opacity** value in the Layers palette and change it to 40 percent. Or forget about selecting the value and just press the 4 key. (If pressing 4 doesn't work, press the Esc key to deactivate the Color blend mode from Step 14, and then press 4 again.) So long as the marquee tool is still active, the column of white turns translucent, as shown in Figure 4-30.

PEARL OF WISDOM

The Opacity value acts as an ingredient mixer. If you think of the white rectangle as one ingredient and the road below it as another, Opacity determines how much of each image is used to create the final blend. A value of 100 percent favors the rectangle. So 40 percent makes the rectangle quite translucent, with 60 percent of the road showing through.

Figure 4-30.

The most amazing aspect of this otherworldly composition is that we managed to pull it off using Elements' simplest selection tools, the rectangular and elliptical marquees. Of course, it didn't hurt to soften the transitions with the Feather command. I sincerely hope that the exercise leaves you with a sense of the many and varied applications for geometric selection outlines in Photoshop Elements.

Lassoing an Irregular Image

The lasso tools let you select irregular portions of an image. The primary lasso tool invites you to drag around an image to trace it freehand. But like freehand tools in all graphics programs, the lasso is haphazard and hard to control, at least when using a mouse. That's why Photoshop Elements also includes a polygonal lasso, which allows you to select straight-edged areas inside an image. Admittedly, the polygonal lasso tool doesn't suit all images, particularly those that contain rounded or curved objects. But as you'll see, the tool is easy to control and precise to boot.

Figure 4–31.

Figure 4–32.

In the following exercise, you'll experiment with both the standard and polygonal lasso tools, and get a feel for why the latter is typically more useful. You'll also get the opportunity to play with a couple of special effects commands from Elements' Filter menu.

1. *Open an image.* Open the *Denver Public Library.jpg* file located in the *Lesson 04* folder inside *Lesson Files-PE4 1on1.* This image captures an amazing work of architecture with a terribly dull backdrop, as shown in Figure 4-31. It seems to me that a structure like this should be paired with a dramatic sky. Fortunately, Photoshop Elements excels at dark and stormy nights.

2. *Click the lasso tool in the toolbox.* It's the one that looks like a Wild-West-style lariat. Alternatively, you can press the L key. (The tool icon should look like ⌒. If it includes a magnet or it has spikes, press L until you see ⌒.) The lasso tool can be difficult to control, but I want you to experience the tool for yourself so you can decide what you think of it firsthand.

3. *Try dragging around the library building.* The portion of the building I'd like you to select appears highlighted in Figure 4-32. Trace along the red line to select the area inside the building. (The green area represents the region outside the selection.) Feel free to occasionally drag outside the boundaries of the image window.

   The lasso is flexible, scrolling the image window to keep up with your movements and permitting you to drag outside the image to select the extreme edges. But if you're anything like me, you'll have a heck of a time getting halfway decent results out of it.

4. *Deselect the image.* Assuming your selection looks like complete and utter garbage, choose **Select→Deselect** or press Ctrl+D to throw it away and start over. If, on the other hand, your selection outline looks great, give yourself a gold star and skip to Step 7.

5. *Select the polygonal lasso tool in the toolbox.* Click and hold the lasso icon to display a flyout menu of additional tools, and then choose the polygonal lasso (see Figure 4-33). Or just press L or Shift+L a couple of times. However you select it, the polygonal lasso lets you select straight-sided areas inside an image.

6. *Click around the roof of the library.* I added the yellow arrowheads in Figure 4-34 to point to the eight corners at which you need to click. Start by clicking at the corner labeled ❶. (There's no special reason to start at this particular corner; it's just as good a point of reference as any of the others.) Then move the cursor down to corner ❷. As you do so, a straight line connects the cursor to ❶. Make sure this line follows the line of the roof, and then click to set the corner in place. Keep clicking the corners in the order indicated in the figure.

If you have problems, some words of advice. First, take your time. Click deliberately and take care not to double-click, because the latter completes the selection. Second, if you make a mistake, press the Backspace key to delete the last click point. Or press Ctrl+D to abandon the selection and try again. And third, hang in there; you'll get it.

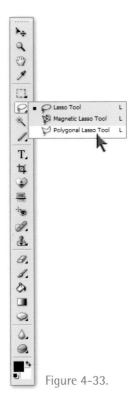

Figure 4-33.

After you click at corner ❽, you have two options for completing the selection:

- Click corner ❶ to come full circle and close the selection outline.

- Double-click at point ❽ to end the selection and connect points ❶ and ❽ with a straight segment. Or click at ❽ and press Enter.

7. *Select the elliptical marquee tool.* The central tower of the building is a cylinder, and the top of a cylinder is elliptical. You could try to select the rounded edges using the lasso. Or you could use a tool better suited to ellipses. Press M (or Shift+M) a couple of times or select the elliptical marquee from the toolbox flyout menu.

8. *Select the cylindrical top of the building.* This is another tricky step, so read the following paragraph before you begin.

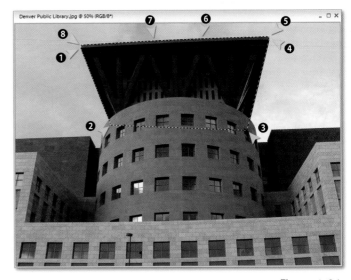

Figure 4-34.

Press and hold the Shift key. Then drag with the elliptical marquee tool to add the ellipse to the existing straight-sided selection. After you begin your drag, you can release the Shift key.

Figure 4-35.

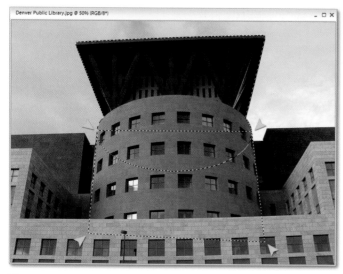

Figure 4-36.

As you drag, remember that you can press the spacebar to move the ellipse on-the-fly. When you get the ellipse into position, release the spacebar and continue dragging. When the ellipse is properly sized (as in **Figure 4-35**), release the mouse button.

9. *Select the polygonal lasso.* Click the lasso icon in the toolbox and then select the polygonal lasso tool from the flyout menu. Or press the L key or Shift+L to return to the tool.

10. *Select the lower portion of the cylinder.* Press the Shift key and click the perimeter of the central building. It should take you just four clicks (see Figure 4-36). Remember to double-click or press Enter to close the selection.

So far, everything we've drawn has been a crisp-edged selection. The only softening is due to antialiasing, which minimizes jagged transitions. But let's say you want all future edges to be fuzzy. For example, in this image, we have yet to select the portion of the building at the bottom of the photo. For purely aesthetic reasons, I think it'd be terrific if this area sported a blurry selection outline. This requires adjusting the polygonal lasso tool's Feather value, as follows.

11. *Raise the Feather value in the options bar.* Click the **Feather** item in the options bar to highlight the value. Then type 6 and press Enter. Like most of the values in the options bar, this one has no influence over the existing selection; instead, it affects the next selection outline you create.

12. *Increase the size of the image window.* Size the window so that you can see a generous amount of light gray pasteboard around all sides of the image. (The dark gray background of the application window doesn't count.) The easiest way to see the pasteboard is to maximize the image window by clicking the ☐ icon in the top-right corner of the window. If necessary, you can also press Ctrl+⊟ to zoom out.

13. *Select the main building with the polygonal lasso tool.* Press the Shift key and click around the lowest elements of the building. To make sure you select everything, click outside the image in the light gray pasteboard, as illustrated in Figure 4-37.

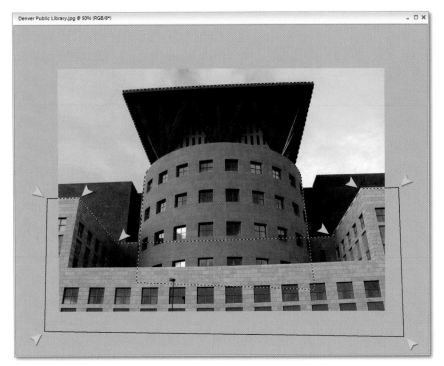

Figure 4-37.

14. *Send the selection to its own layer.* Now let's set about transforming the background into the dark and stormy night that I promised at the outset of the exercise. With the entire building now selected, choose **Layer→New→Layer via Copy**, or press Ctrl+J to send it to its own layer.

15. *Select the Background layer in the Layers palette.* Make sure the **Layers** palette is visible on the right side of the screen. (If it isn't, press the F11 key.) Then click the **Background** layer in the palette to make the lowest layer active.

16. *Lift some dark blue from the windows.* To make the dark and stormy night, we'll be using a filter that relies on the active foreground color. This means changing the foreground color to something dark and stormy, such as deep blue. Begin by selecting the eyedropper tool in the toolbox or pressing the I key. Then click a dark blue pixel in one of the center windows in the cylindrical portion of the library. Elements updates the foreground color at the bottom of the toolbox; for now, nothing else changes.

Figure 4-38.

17. *Apply the Fibers filter.* Choose **Filter→Render→Fibers** to open the **Fibers** dialog box. The Fibers filter draws rough vertical lines of color in the foreground and background colors. In our case, the dark blue and white create an effect similar to rain. The default values shown in Figure 4-38 are fine, so click **OK** to accept.

18. *Apply the Difference Clouds filter.* Choose **Filter→Render→Difference Clouds** to merge a cloud pattern into the Fibers rain and create a dark, nasty storm.

19. *Repeat Difference Clouds a few times.* Pressing Ctrl+F repeats the most recently applied filter. Each additional application of Difference Clouds inverts the background and applies more clouds. To achieve the effect pictured in Figure 4-39, I pressed Ctrl+F five times in a row. Given the random nature of this filter, your results will look slightly different.

Rain rarely falls strictly in back of a building. But frankly, I like the look of the stormy sky when isolated to the background. I think it makes the library seem safer—more like a cozy, kooky, mad-scientist's hangout—the kind of place where you can curl up and read a scary book.

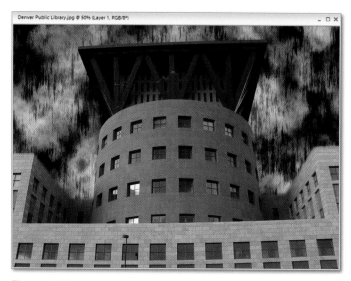

Figure 4-39.

The final lasso tool, the magnetic lasso, is one of the most amazing selection tools in Photoshop Elements' arsenal. No kidding, this tool can actually sense the edge of an object and trace it automatically, even when the contrast is low and the background colors vary. But as miraculous as this sounds, the magnetic lasso has never won the hearts and minds of Photoshop Elements users the way, say, the magic wand has. Why? Part of the reason is that it requires you to work too hard for your automation. Perhaps worse, the tool makes a lot of irritating mistakes, thereby requiring you to work *even harder* for your automation. Even so, the magnetic lasso can work wonders, especially when tracing highly complex edges set against evenly colored backgrounds.

To give it a whirl, select the magnetic lasso from the lasso tool flyout menu. As when using the polygonal lasso, click along the edge of the image element that you want to select to set a point. Next, move the cursor—no need to drag, the mouse button does not have to be pressed—around the image element. As you move, Elements automatically traces what it determines is the best edge and lays down square *anchor points*, which lock the line in place. In the figure below, I clicked the bottom-left corner of the library's trapezoidal roof and then moved the cursor up and around to the right.

Some other techniques:

- If the magnetic lasso traces an area incorrectly, trace back over the offending portion of the line to erase it. Again, just move your mouse; no need to press any buttons.

- Anchor points remain locked down even if you trace back over them. To remove the last anchor point—at any stage in the game—press the Backspace key.

- Elements continuously updates the magnetic lasso line until it lays down a point. To lock down the line manually, just click to create your own anchor point.

- Of the various options bar settings, the most useful is Width, which adjusts how close your cursor has to be to an edge to "see" it. Large values allow you to be sloppy; small values are great for working inside tight, highly detailed areas.

The best thing about the Width setting is you can change it by pressing one of the bracket keys. While working with the magnetic lasso, press [to make the Width value smaller; press] to make it larger.

- Double-click or press Enter to complete the selection. You can also click the first point in the shape. Press the Esc key to cancel the selection.

Photoshop Elements' smartest lasso tool is clearly the most challenging to use. But it's usually worth the effort. And remember, you can always combine it with other tools.

Painting a Free-Form Selection

The next selection tool, the selection brush, offers two advantages over the ones we've looked at so far. First, for many of us, painting with a brush is easier than dragging with, say, a lasso. Painting gives you unique control over your selection outline, particularly if you're using a drawing tablet from Wacom or some other manufacturer.

The second advantage of the selection brush is that it simulates the more sophisticated *masking* functions of Photoshop CS2. Remember when we feathered the selection outline around the moon back in the "Using the Marquee Tools" exercise (see Step 10, page 128)? As you may recall, the marching ants were incapable of accurately representing the soft-edged selection. Masking eschews marching ants for a translucent overlay; the overlay shows you varying degrees of selection by equating them to levels of transparency. If a pixel is completely selected, the overlay is transparent. Otherwise, the overlay becomes murkier and murkier as the selection fades away.

In this exercise you'll use the selection brush both in the standard marching ants selection mode and in the mask mode to select a couple of objects in a layered image. You'll also see how Elements lets you save and load selection outlines, a tremendous time-saver should you ever need to select a complex object more than once.

Figure 4-40.

1. *Open a layered image.* Open the file named *My someday prince.psd*, which is located in the *Lesson 04* folder inside *Lesson Files-PE4 1on1.* Figure 4-40 shows a lovely, blue poison arrow frog captured by Terry McGleish for iStockphoto. This document contains two layers. We'll begin with the image of the frog set against white on the top layer. You'll select this frog with the selection brush.

2. *Load a selection outline.* I've already selected part of the frog to get you started. To load this selection, choose **Select→Load Selection** to display the dialog box in Figure 4-41. Make sure that **Frog** is active in the **Selection** pop-up menu. Also confirm that the **Invert** check box (which reverses the selection) is turned off, and then click **OK**. Elements draws marching ants around one front leg and one rear leg. Your task is to complete the job.

3. *Choose the selection brush.* Press the A key to choose the selection brush, which shares a flyout menu in the toolbox with the magic selection brush. You can also select the tool from a flyout menu (see Figure 4-42), but that invokes an irritating message that we'll address in the next exercise.

Figure 4-41.

4. *Adjust the brush size.* You'll begin your frog selection by roughing in the frog's body. But you need a nice big brush. As Figure 4-43 shows, the selection brush offers its share of unique options in the options bar:

Figure 4-42.

- Click the ▾ arrow on the left side of the options bar to display a pop-up menu that lets you choose from a vast library of brush shapes and sizes. These options can be quite useful when painting (as you'll learn in Lesson 6, "Paint, Edit, and Heal"), but basic is better when creating selections. Look at the menu if you like, but leave the default setting as is.

- The Size option changes the diameter of the brush. Increase the **Size** to 40 pixels to get that nice big brush I alluded to a moment ago.

- The Mode pop-up menu offers two options, Selection and Mask. Make sure it's set to **Selection**.

- The Hardness value sets the sharpness of the brush. Make sure **Hardness** is set to 100 percent, which results in an antialiased brush. Like a roll of cheap toilet paper, it retains only the barest hint of softness.

Figure 4-43.

You can resize the selection brush using the bracket keys. Press [to shrink the brush or] to make it bigger. Press Shift+[to make the brush softer; press Shift+] to make it harder. These shortcuts might seem odd, but they can be big time-savers.

5. *Rough in the middle of the frog.* Press Ctrl+Alt+⊡ to zoom in to the 100 percent view size. Spacebar-drag to center the frog in the image window. Then paint a selection well inside the central portion of the frog's body, as in Figure 4-44. Right away, the selection brush behaves differently from the other selection tools. Even though you already have an active selection (the one you loaded in Step 2), there's no need to press the Shift key to add to it. The brush automatically operates in add mode.

Figure 4-44.

If you accidentally paint outside the edges of the frog, you have two options for getting back inside the lines:

- Click the button in the shortcuts bar or press Ctrl+Z to undo the last brushstroke.

- Press the Alt key and paint over the mistake. Alt puts the selection brush in subtract mode. So rather than painting over the area you want to select, Alt-drag to paint over the area you want to deselect.

6. *Paint around the edges of the amphibian's body.* Now to home in and select those pesky edges. For that, you'll want to be closer. Press Ctrl+⊡ to magnify the image to 200 percent. Then press the ⊡ key twice to reduce the brush diameter to 20 pixels. Because the edges of the frog aren't razor-sharp, we need to soften the brush. Pressing Shift+⊡ would lower the Hardness value in 25 percent increments, taking it down to 75 percent. That's too soft for these edges, so I recommend you click **Hardness** in the options bar and change the value to 90 percent.

Paint around the perimeter of the frog. Don't leave any gaps between the already selected middle of the animal and its meandering edges. Leave the front leg deselected for now. And don't obsess about getting the outline super-smooth. He's a frog, after all; what do a few warts matter? When you finish, your selection should look something like the one pictured in Figure 4-45.

Figure 4-45.

7. *Select the frog's leg.* Because the sides of the frog's foreleg—oh heck, let's call it a *forearm*—are reasonably straight, I'll teach you a trick for selecting them.

- First, press the ⬚ key to reduce the diameter of the brush to 10 pixels.

- Position your cursor as shown in the top window in Figure 4-46, making sure the edge of the cursor is along the upper edge of the frog's forearm. Click once to create a small circle of selection.

- Move your cursor to the location indicated by the bottom window in the figure and Shift-click.

Photoshop Elements paints a straight stripe of selection. Shift-clicking always connects the last click point to the next one, so it's an easy way to create straight-edged selections. Repeat this trick along the lower edge of the frog's forearm.

To paint the details of the frog's fingers, shrink the brush size to 6 pixels or so. Then continue painting until the entire outline of the frog is filled in. And don't forget to Shift-click like crazy. This guy's fingers are rife with straight segments.

8. *Save the selection.* After all the time you spent painting the frog selection, you owe it to yourself to save it. Choose **Select→Save Selection**. In the **Save Selection** dialog box, set the **Selection** option to **Frog**. Leave the **Replace Selection** option turned on and click **OK**. Elements replaces the partial selection that I drew for you with the full frog outline.

9. *Delete the frog's background.* The frog is selected. So to get rid of the background, we need to reverse the selection. Choose **Select→Inverse** or press Ctrl+Shift+I. If you're zoomed in on a detail of the frog, you'll swear nothing happened. But press Ctrl+⬚ to zoom all the way out and you'll see those ants marching around the entire perimeter of the image. The frog outline now represents a hole in the selection.

Press the Backspace key to reveal the background beneath the Frog layer. Wishing and hoping below the blue critter is a dreamy-looking little girl photographed by Gisele Wright, once again available from iStockphoto.

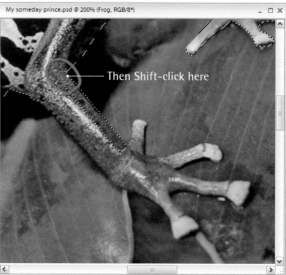

Figure 4-46.

10. *Give the frog a shadow.* Let's add a layer style to the frog to help it stand out from its brand-new, off-white background. Choose **Select→Deselect** or press Ctrl+D to deselect the animal's empty background. Next, do the following:

    • Go to the **Styles and Effects** palette on the right side of the screen. (If the palette is missing, press the F7 key.)

    • Choose **Layer Styles** from the upper-left pop-up menu and **Drop Shadows** from the right menu.

    • Finally, click the third thumbnail, **Noisy**.

    The result appears in Figure 4-47.

11. *Switch to the Mask mode.* Now let's shift to the Background layer and complete the design. Click the **Background** layer in the **Layers** palette or press Alt+⬚. Next, change the **Mode** setting in the options bar to **Mask**. Although there's no immediate change to the image, the options bar gets two new options:

    • The Overlay Opacity setting determines the translucency of the masked areas. Unless you have some reason for changing it, I'd leave this option set to 50 percent.

    • The next option, Overlay Color, defines the color of the mask. The default color is red, harkening back to the precomputer days of publishing, when you masked photographs and other artwork by cutting red plastic sheets called *rubylith*. Thing is, if you're trying to select a maraschino cherry sitting on top of a red-frosted cake, a ruby red overlay wouldn't do you much good. (To change the overlay color, click the color swatch and select another color.) For our purposes, however, red will do just fine.

12. *Paint inside the girl's outline.* Change the **Size** of the selection brush to 150 pixels. Then paint inside the girl's face and body, taking care to stay well within the lines. As you do so, you lay down a translucent coating of red. Fair enough, but what the heck is going on?

Figure 4-47.

In the Selection mode, you paint to select; in the Mask mode, you paint to deselect. So the red coating indicates an area that is not selected. The area outside the coating—where the rubylith is transparent—is selected. True to its name, a mask protects an image from harm and leaves the rest of the image vulnerable to edits.

As in the Selection mode, holding down the Alt key reverses the tool. Therefore, if you find yourself painting outside the boundary of the girl, you can Alt-drag with the brush to erase the mask.

13. *Paint around the perimeter of the girl.* Now to get in and brush those edges. I won't lie to you, this takes some skill and determination, and your mask may come out looking a little different than mine. But I can offer some pointers:

- When filling in the girl's arms and shoulders, I recommend shifting to a smaller, softer brush. Press the ⬚ key several times to reduce the diameter of the brush to 50 pixels or so. The focus on the girl is pretty soft, so press Shift+⬚ once to lower the **Hardness** value to 75 percent.

- Before tracing her ears, decrease the **Size** value even further, to about 20 pixels.

- We want a nice soft outline around the girl's scalp. So for her hair, decrease the **Hardness** value another notch to 50 percent.

As you'll no doubt be happy to hear, you can skip the tendrils of hair sticking up from the top of her head because the next step eliminates any need to accurately select them. So when you finish your mask, it should look vaguely similar to the one in Figure 4-48.

14. *Paint a thought balloon.* The next step is to use the Mask mode's unique selection-display ability to paint a dreamy thought balloon behind the girl's head. In the options bar, take the **Hardness** value all the way down to 0 and increase the brush **Size** to 300 pixels.

Figure 4-48.

Figure 4-49.

Scrub over the frog and the protruding strands of the girl's hair to mask those areas completely. Then paint a cloud-like balloon over and behind the girl's head, as in Figure 4-49. Yours doesn't have to look exactly like mine; let your artistic muse be your guide.

15. *Hide the overlay.* Choose **View→Selection** or press Ctrl+H to hide the red overlay so you can better see the results of the next step.

16. *Fill the selection with blue.* Choose **Edit→Fill Selection** or press Shift+Backspace to display the **Fill Layer** dialog box. Then do the following:

    - Choose **Color** from the **Use** pop-up menu. Change the **H**, **S**, and **B** values to 220, 50, and 90, respectively. Then click **OK**.

    - Set the **Mode** option to **Multiply**. Then click **OK**. The blue merges with the background inside the selected portions of the Background layer, as in Figure 4-50.

17. *Save your newest selection.* Now that you've spent all that time working on this wonderful mask, you might as well save it. Choose **Select→ Save Selection**, which lets you save a selection, regardless of what form it's in. Leave the **Selection** option set to **New**, enter "Girl and balloon" in the **Name** field, and click **OK**. This image now has two saved selection outlines, which you can load and use again at any time simply by choosing **Select→Load Selection**.

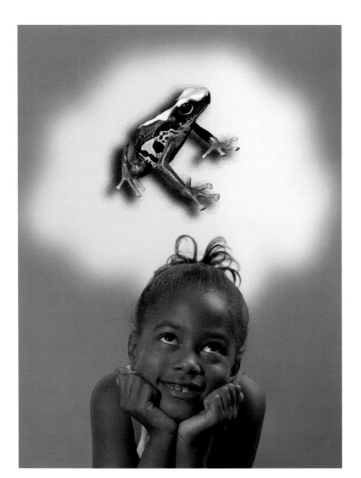

Figure 4-50.

Separating Foreground from Background

I devote the final two exercises in this lesson to brand-new selection functions inside Photoshop Elements 4. These are the magic selection brush and the Magic Extractor command. Both allow you to paint in selections. But they work more like the magic wand tool than the selection brush, intelligently detecting edges and hunting down areas of continuous color.

Both functions ask you to identify an image's foreground (the thing you want to select) independently of its background (the stuff you don't want to select). The tool's big selling point is that it's not necessary to painstakingly trace all the way around the edges. Instead, you paint with one color to indicate the foreground and another color to indicate the background. The tool does the rest automatically—for better or for worse.

Figure 4-51.

The magic selection brush and Magic Extractor command are as close as Elements comes to "seeing" the sunflowers back in Figure 4-1 (page 115). That's why I elected to start things out by using the magic selection brush to select a different sunflower image and move it from one home into another—all while maintaining a seamless transition between foreground and background.

1. *Open two images.* Open the files named *Sunflowers.tif* and *Storm clouds.psd*, both of which are located in the *Lesson 04* folder inside *Lesson Files-PE4 1on1*. Figure 4-51 shows the photographs captured by Lee Pettet (flowers) and Kevin Russ (clouds), again care of iStockphoto.

2. *Choose the magic selection brush in the toolbox.* Thanks to the wispy clouds and sliver of ground, the magic wand is poorly suited to selecting the sunflowers. So choose the more powerful magic selection brush from the selection brush flyout menu. Or press the F key.

Figure 4-52.

3. *Dismiss the message.* This tool offers an explanatory message, shown in Figure 4-52. By default, Elements regards the message as so helpful that it sees fit to show it to you every time you access the tool. Phooey on that. Select the **Don't show again** check box and then click **OK**.

Figure 4-53.

Add to foreground

New selection   Paint away background

Figure 4-54.

4. *Click in the image.* Let's start out simply. Click once at the position in the larger sunflower illustrated in the left half of Figure 4-53. Bear in mind that the bottom-left corner of the cursor is the "business end" of the tool. A translucent red dot momentarily appears where you click. This is soon replaced by a selection outline, complete with marching ants, as in the right half of the figure. (If your selection looks different than mine, it's because you clicked in a slightly different location. In any case, don't worry about it. We'll all achieve the same results before the exercise is over.) The selection is very similar, if not identical, to what you would get had you clicked with the magic wand tool. Not bad for a start, but let's educate Elements a little further.

5. *Paint inside the sunflowers.* Notice that your cursor now includes a little plus sign in its bottom-right corner. After you use the magic selection brush to make a selection, the tool automatically switches to the *add mode*, meaning that more brushing adds to the foreground calculation. This is confirmed by a glance at the options bar, which shows the ✎ icon to be active (labeled *Add to foreground* in Figure 4-54).

Press the ⬜ key a couple of times to increase the size of the magic selection brush to 30 pixels. (Or change the Size value in the options bar.) Then paint a squiggly brushstroke inside the yellow parts of the two sunflowers. The stroke appears translucent red; the red dot from the previous step also appears on screen. When your scribble covers roughly the same area as the one in Figure 4-55 on the facing page, release the mouse button. Depending on the speed of your machine, you may see a progress bar. But in a moment, Elements generates a new, larger selection.

6. *Paint in the stalks and leaves.* By now, you should have selected all the yellow areas of the flowers. Now to select the green areas. Press the ⬜ key a few times to shrink the size of the brush so you can get to the slender areas. Some of the stems require a brush as small as 3 pixels. For delicate details like these, it's best to paint several short strokes rather than attempt to hit everything in one pass.

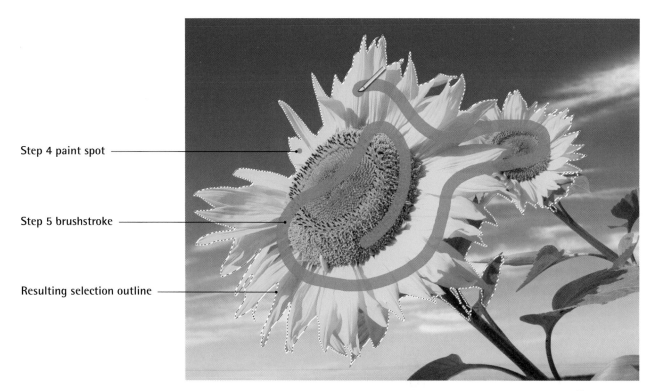

Step 4 paint spot

Step 5 brushstroke

Resulting selection outline

Figure 4-55.

Frankly, it's a bit of a bummer that the magic selection brush cursor gives you no idea of how big an area you're about to paint. To help center your strokes, press the Caps Lock key, which changes the cursor to a crosshair, known as the *precise cursor*. (Just be sure to turn off Caps Lock when you're finished because it affects *all* cursors.) If you accidentally paint into the blue sky, press Ctrl+Z to undo the last stroke. Ctrl+Z is also useful for undoing a stroke that mysteriously subtracts from the selection, as sometimes happens with this unpredictable tool.

I managed to get by with just three brushstrokes, which I've itemized in Figure 4-56 on the next page. (I added the rectangular highlights for emphasis.) However you get there, keep painting until all the yellow and green areas of the flowers appear inside the selection. Don't fret that you select some sky in the process; we'll address that in the next step.

7. *Paint away the sky.* With any luck, the main region of the sky that surrounds the flowers and stalks remains deselected, and that's a good thing. But lots of little patches of blue are peeking out between the various leaves and stems, and those need to be deselected too. Thus far, the magic selection brush can't tell the difference between those blue sky patches and the green stalks, so you'll have to show it.

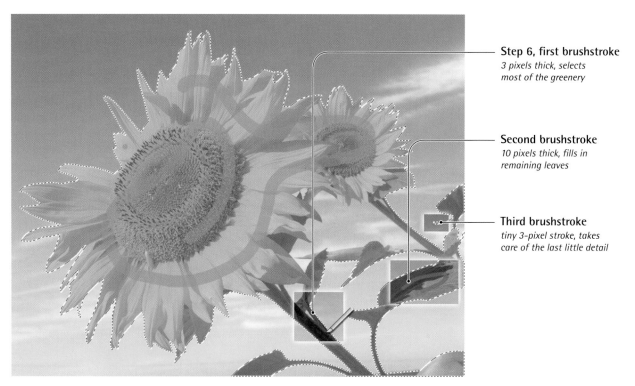

Step 6, first brushstroke
*3 pixels thick, selects
most of the greenery*

Second brushstroke
*10 pixels thick, fills in
remaining leaves*

Third brushstroke
*tiny 3-pixel stroke, takes
care of the last little detail*

Figure 4-56.

To paint away the background, click the ✎ icon in the options bar (labeled *Paint away background* in Figure 4-54 on page 146). Then click and scribble in the selected pockets of sky to deselect them. (The default color for background brushstrokes is blue, but you can change them to a color that better contrasts with the sky using the Color swatch in the options bar. I changed mine to black.) Every click you make with the magic selection brush, whether in the foreground or background mode, gives the tool more information from which to refine its overall selection outline.

Deselecting one area can cause an unexpected change in another, so you'll probably need to do a bit of switching between the foreground and background modes. If you tire of returning to the options bar over and over again, try switching modes from the keyboard. Press and hold the Shift key to add to the foreground; press and hold the Alt key to paint away the background.

There are more than a dozen little patches of sky, including a couple near the top of the image between the yellow petals, so take care to get them all. In the end, your selection outline should look like the one in Figure 4-57. For reference, I also include foreground brushstrokes in red and background brushstrokes

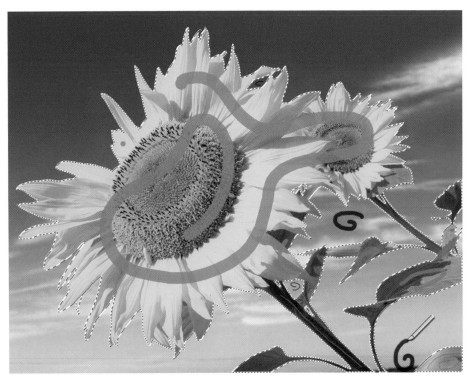

Figure 4-57.

in black (a bit of trickery because, quite unfortunately, the two are never visible at the same time). It might be a chore to decipher, but I wanted to show you my work in case you run into trouble.

8. *Drag the sunflowers into the storm clouds image.* Make sure you can see both image windows. Then press the Ctrl key and drag the selected flowers into the *Storm clouds.psd* image window. No need to press the Shift key this time; just drop them any old place. Then Ctrl-drag the sunflowers so the bottom-right corner of the flowers snap into alignment with the bottom-right corner of the clouds, as in Figure 4-58.

9. *Paint the stalks with a gradients.* The lighting of the flowers is all wrong. But we can make it better, and eliminate the slight blue edges around the stalks, by adding a gradient. Illustrated by the numbered items in Figure 4-59 on the next page, here's how the process works:

Figure 4-58.

- Go to the **Layers** palette and click the ⊞ icon to the right of the word **Lock** (labeled ❶ on the right side of Figure 4-59). This locks the transparency of the layer, which prevents you from painting outside the edges of the flowers. (You can also press the ⫾ key.)

- Select the gradient tool from the toolbox (❷). The shortcut for the gradient tool is G.

- Press the D key or click the ❧ icon (❸) to restore the default foreground and background colors, black and white. (These are the global foreground and background colors, not the ones that govern the magic selection brush.)

- Go to the options bar and click the ▾ arrow to the left of the Edit button to display a pop-up palette of gradient styles. Select the second thumbnail, the one that flows from black to a checkerboard pattern (❹). This loads the gradient tool with a black-to-transparent gradient.

Figure 4-59.

- Press Enter to hide the palette. Press the 8 key to lower the **Opacity** setting for the gradient tool to 80 percent (❺).

- Drag from the bottom-right corner of the *Storm clouds.jpg* image window up and to the left, until you reach the right-hand petals of the large flower (labeled ❻ in the figure).

The stalks are now shaded to match their stormy backdrop. But the bright yellow flowers still look out of place. Rather miraculously, you'll fix this problem with one click.

10. ***Turn on the Colorize layer.*** See that top layer in the Layers palette? Click in the box to the left of the layer name to display the 👁 icon and reveal the contents of the **Colorize** layer in the image window. This special adjustment layer colorizes the contents of all layers below it, thereby binding sunflowers and clouds with a common color scheme. (For more information on these amazing layers, read "Colorizing an Image with Adjustment Layers," which begins on page 313 of Lesson 10.)

Displayed in Figure 4-60, the effect is fairly spectacular. But lest you get the wrong impression about the magic selection brush, I hasten to note that the *Sunflower.tif* image is just about as perfect a subject for the tool as one could hope for: A well-defined foreground set against a smoothly transitioning, differently colored background. With less ideal photos, I suggest you try out the Magic Extractor command instead, as you will in the next section.

Figure 4-60.

Extracting a Photographic Element

Justifiably proud of its new "magic" selection technology, Adobe has assigned it to a second function in Photoshop Elements 4, the Magic Extractor. Like the magic selection brush, the Magic Extractor command asks you to paint independently inside the foreground and background of an image. But it provides a unique twist.

One of the biggest problem that arises when transferring an image from one background to another is haloing. The edges of every element in a photo incorporate ambient colors from the photo's background. So when you replace or recolor the background, as in Figure 4-61 on the next page, the edges have an alarming habit of retaining their original coloring.

A buffalo in its native habitat

When the background is replaced, the ambient color survives

Figure 4-61.

Figure 4-62.

Elements' solution is the Magic Extractor. Strictly speaking, this command is not a selection function. When you *extract* an image, you promote it to a floating layer and erase the background pixels, leaving the foreground image adrift in a checkerboard sea of transparency. The advantage of extraction is that it enables Elements to leech away fringe colors from the old background, something it can't currently do with a selection. The disadvantage is that it permanently erases pixels, giving you fewer options for adjustments. In my experience, the Magic Extractor command is the more successful incarnation of Adobe's magic selection technology, if only because it tends to produce the best results.

In the following exercise, we'll extract a buffalo from a predominantly green environment and place it into a multicolored china shop. Along the way, you'll not only learn how to use the Magic Extractor but also increase your experience with layers.

1. *Open an image and a background.* This time, the files are *PhotoSpin buffalo.jpg* and *China shop.jpg,* located in the *Lesson 04* folder inside *Lesson Files-PE4 1on1.* (Jan Tyler captured the shop window for iStockphoto.) Observe that the animal pictured in Figure 4-62 is set against a smooth background. Like the magic selection brush, the Magic Extractor command functions best when removing smooth backgrounds; busy textures tend to mix it up.

2. *Summon the Magic Extractor.* Make sure that the *PhotoSpin buffalo.jpg* window is in front, and then choose **Image→Magic Extractor**. Elements displays the **Magic Extractor** window, which behaves like a separate utility, complete with its own tools and options, as in Figure 4-63.

To display the Magic Extractor window from the keyboard, press the Alt key and type I-X (for Image eXtractor).

Figure 4-63.

If you sneak a peek at the Layers palette, you'll notice that Elements renamed the one layer in the image from Background to Layer 0. Extractions leave behind transparency, but the Background layer can't accommodate transparency; hence the upgrade to a full-fledged floating layer.

The center of the window features a large preview of the image. You can zoom it or scroll it using the standard navigation tricks introduced in Video Lesson 3, "The Standard Edit Mode" (see page 82). Strangely, however, the window lacks scroll bars or any mention of a zoom ratio percentage. So it's difficult to know if you're seeing all the image or how many pixels are being interpolated away. Fortunately, you can always double-click the zoom tool icon on the left side of the dialog box to switch to the 100 percent view. Then spacebar-drag the preview to scroll it. Also note that you can scale the window by dragging its bottom-right corner.

3. *Identify the foreground of the image.* Click the top tool in the column along the left side of the window, or press the B key to select the foreground brush. This tool is basically just the magic selection brush but with a welcome addition: The circular cursor changes to reflect your brush size.

Drag within the buffalo to paint translucent red brushstrokes, which represent the general areas of color, brightness, and detail you want to keep. The Magic Extractor can be a calculation-intensive command, meaning that the more information you give it, the longer it will take to make a selection. So for the sake of speed, fewer brushstrokes are better. In Figure 4-64, for example, I drew just three.

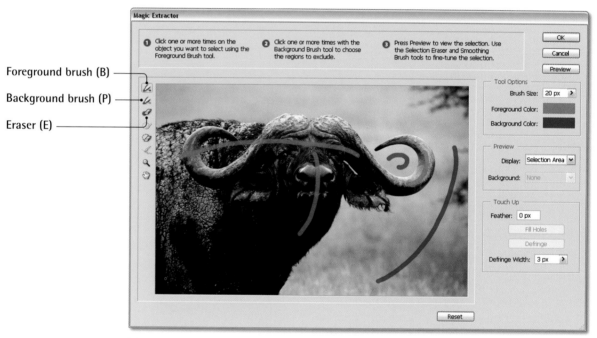

Foreground brush (B)

Background brush (P)

Eraser (E)

Figure 4-64.

If you make a mistake and paint outside the buffalo, press Ctrl+Z to undo and try again. You get just one undo, so if you don't like a couple of brushstrokes, use the eraser tool (labeled in Figure 4-64) to erase them. To select the eraser from the keyboard, press the E key.

---

4. *Identify the background.* Now click the second tool icon or press the P key to select the background brush. Paint one vertical line to the right of the buffalo to sample the many shades of green in the background. Then paint a swirl inside the horn, as indicated by the blue brushstrokes in Figure 4-64.

5. *Preview the extraction.* To see whether your extraction is going to work or not, click the **Preview** button in the top-right corner of the interface. Elements thinks for a few seconds and displays something along the lines of Figure 4-65. The checkerboard pattern represents the transparent pixels—that is, those that will be erased.

6. *Erase the grassy wedge.* Zoom in so that you can clearly see the sliver of green grass under the right horn (the beast's left). The default 20-pixel brush is far too large to fit in this area, so change the **Brush Size** value to 4 pixels. Then click one time each at the top and bottom of the sliver. Click the **Preview** button again and the sliver goes away.

Figure 4-65.

At this point, you might want to scroll around the image and see how it looks. But if you press the spacebar, you'll notice some strange behavior. In this particular dialog box, the spacebar activates the last button you clicked. So pressing the spacebar now reruns the Preview button. The simplest way to avoid this problem is to press the H key to switch to the hand tool. Then just drag to scroll as much as you want.

The extraction looks pretty good, huh? But looks can be deceiving. The gray-and-white transparency checkerboard isn't a particularly helpful backdrop for judging the edges of the extraction. So let's change it.

7. *Switch out the backdrop.* In the Preview area of the magic extractor controls, change the **Background** option from the default **None** to **Black Matte**. Or just press the F key. Now scroll around the image and check out the unsightly green halo that surrounds our bovine friend. You may also come across some ragged edges, such as the notches along the top of the horns.

8. *Defringe the halo.* Change the **Defringe Width** value in the lower-left corner of the window from the default 3 pixels to 6. Then click the **Defringe** button. As Figure 4-66 shows, the verdant halo is mostly gone. A few places under the ear still need touching up, but bear in mind that the china shop image is busier than the plain black backdrop and therefore infinitely more forgiving.

Figure 4-66.

If you scroll to the top of the image—by dragging with the hand tool, don't press that spacebar!—you'll notice that the defringing process exaggerated the notches along the top of the creature's head. Plus, a hairline of green still exists along the inside edge of the curly horn. We'll fix these problems in the next two steps.

9. *Smooth out the rough patches.* Click the tool icon directly above the magnifying glass or press the J key to select the smoothing brush (labeled in Figure 4-66), which lets you smooth out

rough edges in an extraction. Increase the Brush Size value to 40 pixels. Then drag along the mass of keratin and bone along the top of the buffalo's head. As you paint, Elements smooths out the jagged bumps. I recommend you paint in short strokes, remembering that you have just one level of undo. If you find yourself bringing back too much green, immediately press Ctrl+Z and try again. Also paint along the top of the curly horn (labeled *Stray pixels* in Figure 4-66) to whisk away the stray pixels that tend to collect in this area.

10. *Erase away the horn fringe.* To erase the hairline fringe inside the curly horn, click the next icon up, which Elements calls the remove-from-selection tool, but which I'll call the remove tool. You can also get to it by pressing the D key. Then manually paint away any areas of green above the head and inside the curly horn, just as you would paint with an eraser. I achieved the best results using a 100-pixel brush, the largest the Magic Extractor function permits. Then lower the brush size as you come closer to the animal's face.

You can decrease or increase the brush size on-the-fly by pressing the bracket keys, ⬚ and ⬚. It's so dynamic, you can tap the keys while you're in the process of painting.

If you erase too much, hold down the Alt key and paint the details back in. Pressing Alt provides temporary access to the add-to-selection tool, located just above the remove tool.

11. *Fix the ear.* Scroll down so you can see the green haloing that hangs off the buffalo's ear, as well as the little patches along its chest. We could erase these with the remove tool, but that would take more effort than I care to expend. Let's automate it. Press the P key to select the background brush. Then paint a short 20-pixel brushstroke along the bottom edge of the ear. Don't worry that you're painting over brown hair and green background alike; better to sacrifice some hairs in the name of completely eliminating the green. Then click the Preview button to see the results of this brushstroke.

12. *Smooth out any lost details in the horns.* The ear haloing disappears. You might also notice that the updated extraction messes up some (though by no means all) of the adjustments you made in Steps 9 and 10. If so, feel free to revisit some areas with the smoothing brush and the remove tool. But the area in greatest danger from the last edit is the curly horn. To better

Figure 4-67.

judge the horn's condition, press the F key to switch to the **White Matte** view. Then use the smoothing tool to heal the gaps. The final horn should appear picture perfect, as in Figure 4-67.

13. *Accept the extraction.* Click the **OK** button to extract the buffalo from its erstwhile background. The program reduces the image to buffalo and checkerboard.

14. *Relocate the buffalo.* This photograph features a buffalo, and that's no bull. But we're still going to place it in close proximity to a china shop and hope for the best. Arrange your image windows so that you can see a bit of both photographs. Then hold down the Ctrl key and drag the buffalo into the *China shop.jpg* image window. After dropping him into his new home, Ctrl-drag the buffalo until he snaps to the bottom-left corner of the image. As Figure 4-68 shows, our woolly friend is ready to wreak havoc. Or maybe he's just looking for a teacup to complete a place setting. Either way, he's come to the right place, all thanks to extraction in Photoshop Elements 4.

Figure 4-68.

WHAT DID YOU LEARN?

Match the key concept in the numbered list below with the letter
of the phrase that best describes it. Answers appear upside-down
at the bottom of the page.

Key Concepts

1. Magic wand
2. Tolerance
3. Grow
4. Similar
5. Haloing
6. Antialiasing
7. Inverse
8. Feather
9. Polygonal lasso
10. Mask
11. Lock transparency
12. Magic Extractor

Descriptions

A. In addition to isolating a foreground subject by erasing any and all pixels associated with the background, this command tries to eliminate fringes of ambient color associated with the erased background.

B. This command selects currently deselected pixels and deselects currently selected pixels.

C. This term describes a fringe of background color around a selected object; the Magic Extractor command's Defringe option helps eliminate the problem.

D. This command expands the range of a selection to include additional adjacent pixels.

E. Click the ▩ icon near the top of the Layers palette to protect the transparent pixels in a layer, thus ensuring that you paint and modify only those pixels that fall inside the edges of the layered element.

F. Use this tool to select free-form, straight-sided areas in an image.

G. This command blurs the edges of a selection outline to create fuzzy transitions.

H. A setting in the options bar that determines how many colors the magic wand selects at a time, as measured in luminosity values.

I. Click with this tool to select regions of color inside an image.

J. This command expands the range of a selection to include additional nonadjacent pixels.

K. A very slight softening effect applied to selection outlines to simulate smooth transitions.

L. This selection brush mode uses a translucent overlay to show you varying degrees of selection by equating them to levels of transparency.

Answers

1I, 2H, 3D, 4J, 5C, 6K, 7B, 8G, 9F, 10L, 11E, 12A

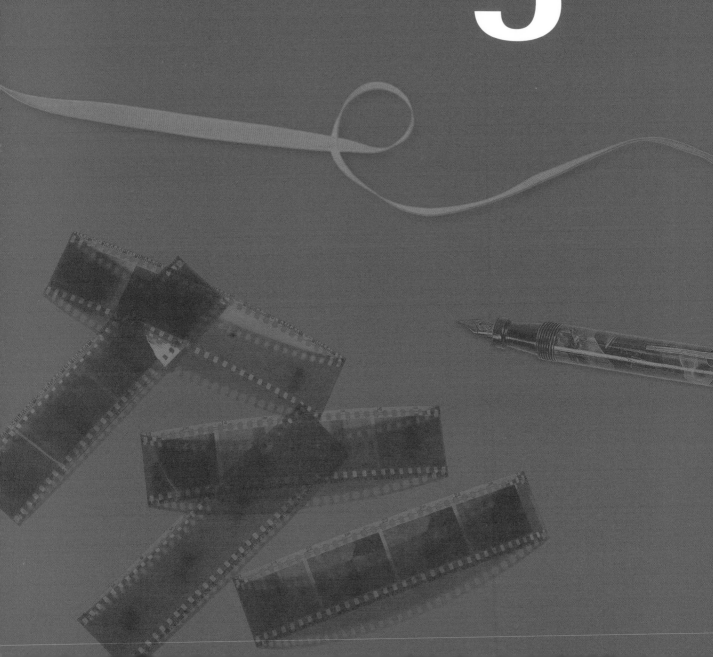

CROP, STRAIGHTEN, AND SIZE

I SUPPOSE IT'S possible that some people, on some remote planet, believe that the perfect photograph is one that needs no editing. On this far-flung world, programs such as Photoshop Elements are tools of last resort. The very act of opening a photograph in an image editor is a tacit declaration that the photo is a failure. Every command, tool, or option applied is regarded as a mark of flimflam or forgery.

But that's hardly the case here on Earth. Despite oft-voiced (and occasionally reasonable) concerns that modern image editing is distorting our perception of places and events, image manipulation has always been part and parcel of the photographic process. And there's no better example of this than cropping.

Since long before computers were widely available and eons before Elements and its older sibling Photoshop hit the market, it has been common practice among professional photographers to frame a shot and then back up a step or two before snapping the picture. This way, they have more options when it comes time to crop. Of course, nothing says you have to crop the image the way you first framed it; as illustrated in Figure 5-1, you can crop it any way you want to. And that's precisely the point. Even back in the old days, photographers shot their pictures with editing in mind because doing so ensured a wider range of post-photography options.

Whole-Image Transformations

If image editing is the norm, the norm for image editing is whole-image transformations. This includes operations such as scale and rotate applied to an entire image all at once. Although whole-image transformations may sound like a dry topic, they can produce dramatic and surprising effects.

Figure 5-1.

ABOUT THIS LESSON

Project Files

Before beginning the exercises, make sure you've installed the lesson files from the DVD, as explained in Step 5 on page xv of the Preface. This should result in a folder of images called *Lesson Files-PE4 1on1* on your desktop. We'll be working with the files inside the *Lesson 05* subfolder.

In this lesson, we explore ways to crop, straighten, and resize digital photographs using a small but essential collection of tools and commands. You'll learn how to:

- Automatically crop and straighten one or more images scanned to a single file . . . . page 164

- Use the straighten and crop tools to straighten an image and crop to a specific aspect ratio . . . . . page 168

- Cut an image into a custom shape and set it against a new background . . . . page 173

- Adjust the resolution of an image and select the best interpolation setting . . . . page 179

Video Lesson 5: Image and Canvas Size

This lesson addresses one of the most fundamental topics in Photoshop Elements: changing and managing the number of pixels in an image. To fully understand this topic, you must come to terms with the concepts of *image size* and *canvas size*. The two describe the number of pixels in an image in different ways.

For an introduction to these key concepts, watch the fifth video lesson on the DVD. To view this video, insert the DVD, click **Start**, select **Set 2: Select, Crop, and Edit** from the first pop-up menu, and then select **Lesson 5, Image and Canvas Size** from the second pop-up menu. The movie lasts 14 minutes and 28 seconds, during which time you'll learn about the following commands and shortcuts:

Command or operation	Keyboard equivalent or shortcut
Show or hide Info palette	F8
Image Size	Ctrl+Alt+I
Scrub a numerical value	Drag back and forth on option name
Scrub in 10× increments	Shift-drag on option name
Highlight Resolution value in Image Size dialog box	Alt+R
Change unit of measurement from Info palette	Click ✛ icon, next to X, Y coordinates
Advance to the next or previous option	Tab or Shift+Tab

More important, whole-image transformation forces you to think about basic image composition and ponder some important questions:

- The photo in Figure 5-2 is clearly at an angle, but just what angle is it? Photoshop Elements gives you ways to discover that angle (47.7 degrees), but it also gives you a new tool that does the job automatically with no messy math required.

- After you rotate the image, you have to crop it. Never content to limit you to a single approach, Elements dedicates no fewer than three tools, five commands, and a score of options to the task (symbolically illustrated in Figure 5-3). Variety is the spice of life, but which method do you use when?

- After the crop is complete, there's the problem of scale. Should you reduce or increase the number of pixels? Or should you merely reduce the resolution to print the image larger, as in Figure 5-4?

I provide these questions merely to whet your appetite for the morsels of knowledge that follow. If they seem like a lot to ponder, never fear; the forthcoming lesson makes the answers perfectly clear.

Figure 5-2.

Figure 5-3.

Figure 5-4.

The Order in Which We Work

At this point, you may wonder why I've waited until Lesson 5 to talk about such a fundamental topic as cropping. Bearing in mind that I'm addressing topics in the order you actually apply them, wouldn't it make more sense to first crop an image and then correct its colors, as discussed in Lesson 3? The answer is in some cases yes, but in more cases no.

PEARL OF WISDOM

Scaling an image changes the number of pixels. Straightening an image changes the orientation of pixels. Both operations throw away pixels and make up new ones—a process called *interpolation*—which is best performed after you correct the colors. In fact, interpolation can actually help a color correction by smoothing out the rough transitions sometimes produced by commands such as Shadows/Highlights and Adjust Hue/Saturation.

On its own, cropping does not require interpolation and may therefore be applied before color adjustments. However, Elements offers a few functions that crop and interpolate an image all at once, in which case you're better off correcting the colors first.

So by way of general advice, fix the colors to the best of your ability up front, and then set about cropping and straightening the image.

Auto Crop and Straighten

The best straightening and cropping commands are designed to accommodate scanned images, particularly those captured by a flatbed scanner. Photoshop Elements can open a crooked image, rotate it upright, and crop away the area outside the image—all automatically, without so much as batting an eye. Better yet, the program can work this magic on multiple images at the same time.

We'll begin by investigating the way Adobe recommends you rotate and crop a scanned photograph. Then we'll look at a better way, one that not only is more accurate but also offers the benefit of rotating and cropping several pictures at a time. Prepare to be amazed.

1. *Open the scanned image.* Open *Me at 21.jpg* in the *Lesson 05* folder inside *Lesson Files-PE4 1on1*. It features a photo of me in a Paris subway back when I was a twig of a lad (see Figure 5-5). Diet secret: split a loaf of bread with your travelling buddy every day for two weeks and save the rest for beer. Forget Atkins, forget South Beach; a pure carb diet works wonders.

2. *Choose the Straighten and Crop Image command.* Conventional wisdom (as well as Adobe's documentation) holds that the best way to fix a crooked scan is to choose a command called Straighten and Crop Image. But there's one tiny problem: it works only occasionally. The command performs well when a photo is set against a squeaky clean white background. But any amount of dust, hair, or color variation throws it off.

To see the command in action, choose **Image→Rotate→Straighten and Crop Image** and watch what happens. Thanks to the deep blue color of the background and a smattering of dust, Elements incorrectly evaluates the image and rotates it nearly 45 degrees clockwise, or about six times as far as it should. Worse, the program chops off the corners of the photo, leaving us with less information than we started with. Just for laughs, the astonishingly wrong result appears in Figure 5-6.

3. *Undo the last operation.* Clearly, we can't leave the image the way it is. So choose **Edit→Undo Straighten and Crop Image** or press Ctrl+Z to restore the image file to its previous canvas size and orientation.

Fair enough. At least where this image is concerned, Straighten and Crop Image is an unqualified failure. Fortunately, a much better solution is close at hand.

4. *Choose the Divide Scanned Photos command.* To straighten and crop a scanned photo set against even a dusty, colored background, choose **Image→Divide Scanned Photos**. Then sit back and watch the fireworks. As if on autopilot, Photoshop Elements duplicates the image and then runs a sequence of operations that culminate with the expertly corrected

Figure 5-5.

Figure 5-6.

Figure 5-7.

Figure 5-8.

photograph shown in Figure 5-7. And because the revised photo appears in its own image window, the original scan remains unscathed, just in case you want to take another swing at it later.

Wonderful feature, right? But what's with the name? Why in the world is a command that straightens and crops snapshots called Divide Scanned Photos? Divide them from *what*, exactly? Well, from each other, as it turns out. Although Divide Scanned Photos is just the ticket for straightening and cropping a single photo, its true strong suit is addressing multiple photos at a time, as the next steps explain.

5. *Open another scan.* Close the *Me at 21.jpg* image without saving it. Then open the file called *The gang.jpg*, also included in the *Lesson 05* folder. Therein, you'll find a collection of seven images of various shapes and sizes—some photographs, some printed artwork, all witnessed in Figure 5-8. I created this file by taking the seven pictures and throwing them down on a flatbed scanner. Then, rather than using the scanner's software to assign each image to a separate file, I captured them all to one file. Called *gang scanning*, this previously ill-advised technique works wonders when combined with Photoshop Elements.

6. *Choose the Divide Scanned Photos command.* Amazingly, that's all there is to it. The moment you choose **Image→Divide Scanned Photos**, the windows start flying as the program duplicates, rotates, and crops each image. Honestly, if all of Photoshop Elements was this easy, I'd be out of a job.

7. *Review the cropped images.* In less than a minute on most systems, the Divide Scanned Photos command makes order from chaos. In all, the command generates seven separate images, each named *The gang copy* followed by a number, in the order shown in Figure 5-9. (To create the figure, I chose Window→ Images→Cascade and dragged each window to a separate location.) Note that Elements analyzes the pictures from top to bottom. This is why the photo of my son Sammy—which is slightly higher than that of my late, lamented tabby—comes up first.

The Divide Scanned Photos command does a swell job of straightening the images, even managing to accurately evaluate pictures with irregular edges, such as the perforated special delivery stamp and the clipped magazine photo of the hard drive. But it doesn't know when an image is on its side. That means the snapshot of the late, lamented tabby still needs our assistance.

8. *Rotate the cat photo.* Click the title bar for the cat photo, which Elements has named *The gang copy 3*. (Oh, heartless program!) Then choose **Image→Rotate→90° Right**, which rotates both image and window one-quarter turn clockwise. Alternatively, you can hold down the Alt key and type I-E-0. (That last character is the zero key, [0].) This rotates the entire image, changing it from vertical to horizontal, as in Figure 5-10.

9. *Save the images.* Elements does not automatically save the images it generates; you have to do that manually. So if you want to keep any of these images, you have to save them. (Where this book is concerned, we're through with these files, so trash them at will. But for the sake of background, I'll continue.) When saving a photograph, the JPEG format with a high Quality setting is your best bet. But because JPEG modifies image details in its attempt to minimize the file size, it is not well suited to high-contrast artwork, such as the stamps. You may prefer to save these images as TIFF files. Then again, you may prefer not to save the images at all. I leave that decision up to you.

If an image (such as the hard drive) requires further cropping, or the *contents* of a photo are crooked (from, for example, having shot the image with a nonlevel camera), you can take advantage of the straighten and crop tools, as discussed in the next exercise.

Figure 5-9.

Figure 5-10.

Using the Straighten and Crop Tools

The Divide Scanned Photos command works wonders on crooked images captured with a scanner, but it doesn't work worth a hill of beans on crooked images shot with a digital camera. Consider the image in Figure 5-11. The photo of a granary near Perry, Oklahoma was snapped by Laura Bigbee-Fott, wife of co-author Galen. The sun was setting, the son Burton was definitely *not* setting, so Laura had just a few seconds to snap the photo before heading home. It's a peaceful, lonesome shot, but Laura wasn't exactly holding the camera level when it was taken. Without an obvious rectangle to work with, neither of the commands we've seen so far does any good. Luckily, Photoshop Elements 4 introduces a new tool that makes straightening images a breeze.

Let's imagine our goals for this exercise are to both straighten the image and crop it to make a 4 by 6-inch print. Were you to scale the image to 6 inches wide in its current state, it would measure 4½ inches tall. This means we have to adjust the *aspect ratio*—the relationship between the height and width of the image—by trimming away half an inch of image. Deciding which half inch to trim is an aesthetic decision that might actually help us improve the appearance of the photo.

Figure 5-11.

1. *Open a crooked photograph.* Open the file named *Granary.jpg*, located in the *Lesson 05* folder inside *Lesson Files-PE4 1on1*. Of the two tasks we have to perform—straightening and cropping—straightening needs to come first. Straightening necessitates cropping, so you might as well do all the cropping in one pass.

2. *Select the straighten tool in the toolbox.* Click the straighten tool, as illustrated in Figure 5-12. Or press P for *plumb*.

3. *Confirm the options bar settings.* The humble straighten tool offers just two settings in the options bar. Both should be set to their defaults:

   • The **Canvas Options** setting determines whether and how Elements resizes the canvas to accommodate the rotated image. Make sure it's set to **Grow Canvas to Fit**.

   • Leave **Rotate All Layers** turned on. (Turn this option off only when you want to rotate one layer in a composition independently of others.)

   Also press D or click the tiny ◧ icon at the bottom of the toolbox to restore the default foreground and background colors—black and white, respectively.

Figure 5-12.

4. *Straighten the image.* If you're looking for perpendicular lines in the image—lines that ought to be vertical or horizontal—you'll probably first notice the vertical sides of the granary. However, the straighten tool works only on horizontal lines. Use it on the side of the granary and the entire image will be turned on its ear. That pretty much leaves us with the horizon as our sole reference guide. There's a bit of a crest in the land to the left of the granary, so let's concentrate on the horizon on the right.

   Drag along the horizon from the right side of the granary all the way to the right side of the image, as in Figure 5-13. Take a moment to check that the line

Figure 5-13.

accurately reflects the angle of the horizon before releasing the mouse button. A split second later, Elements rotates the image to make the horizon absolutely flat.

Your image should now be upright. But in expanding the boundaries of the image to include the rotated photograph, the straighten tool exposed empty wedges around the corners, as in Figure 5-14. The wedges appear in the background color, which you set to white in Step 3. You need to crop away the wedges, but how? Using the crop tool, of course.

Figure 5-14.

Figure 5-15.

As it turns out, Elements can automatically delete the wedges for you. Before using the straighten tool, set Canvas Options to Crop to Remove Background. Then drag with the tool. The program automatically removes any hint of wedges without cropping any more than it absolutely has to. The other setting, Crop to Original Size, maintains the image's original pixel dimensions, which results in slimmer wedges. We opted for Grow Canvas to Fit because it preserves the most information for our manual crop, coming up next.

5. *Select the crop tool in the toolbox.* Click the crop tool icon in the toolbox (see Figure 5-15) or press C for *crop*, not to mention *clip*, *cut*, and *curtail*.

6. *Draw a crop boundary.* Drag inside the image window to draw a rectangle around the approximate portion of the image you want to keep, as demonstrated in Figure 5-16. As you do so, you enter the *crop mode*. From this point until you press Enter or Esc, most of Elements' commands and palettes are unavailable. You have now made a commitment—albeit a short-term one—to cropping.

As with the marquee tools, you can adjust the position of the crop boundary while drawing it by pressing and holding the spacebar. But don't get too hung up on getting things exactly right. You can move, resize, and even rotate the crop boundary after you draw it, as I examine in Step 8.

Granary.jpg @ 33.3% (RGB/8*)

33.33%   7.007 inches x 5.363 inches (300 ppi)

Figure 5-16.

7. *Change the Aspect Ratio attribute in the options bar.* We want this image to measure 4 by 6 inches—half again as wide as it is tall—and it's all but certain that the crop boundary you drew doesn't exactly conform to that aspect ratio. So go to the options bar and change the **Aspect Ratio** setting to **4 x 6 in**. Your crop boundary snaps to the desired proportions.

8. *Move and scale the crop boundary.* I suggest you make the boundary as large as you can without including any of the background wedges. Drag the dotted outline or one of the eight square handles surrounding the boundary to scale it. Drag inside the crop boundary to move it. Also worth noting:

   • Press Alt while dragging to scale with respect to the center of the boundary. In other words, the corners move but the center stays in place.

   • Inasmuch as the straighten tool can crop, it stands to reason that the crop tool can straighten. While this technique is not necessary in our case, I pass it along for your future reference: To rotate the crop boundary, move your cursor outside the boundary and drag.

However you get there, try to make your crop boundary look like the one pictured in Figure 5-17 on the next page.

Granary.jpg @ 33.3% (RGB/8*)

33.33%   7.007 inches x 5.363 inches (300 ppi) ▶ ◁

Figure 5-17.

9. ***Apply your changes.*** Click the green check mark (✔) that appears in the tab below the bottom-right corner of the crop boundary. Or just press the Enter key. Elements crops away everything outside the boundary. The result is the more compelling shot featured in Figure 5-18. The slightly panoramic 4-by-6 aspect ratio lends a widescreen feeling to the image, better capturing the desolation of the Oklahoma plains.

In addition to changing the aspect ratio, the crop tool changed the resolution of the image so that it will print at precisely 4 by 6 inches, as illustrated in the figure. (For more information on resolution and print dimensions, see the final exercise in this lesson, "Resizing an Image," which begins on page 179.)

— 6 inches —

4 inches

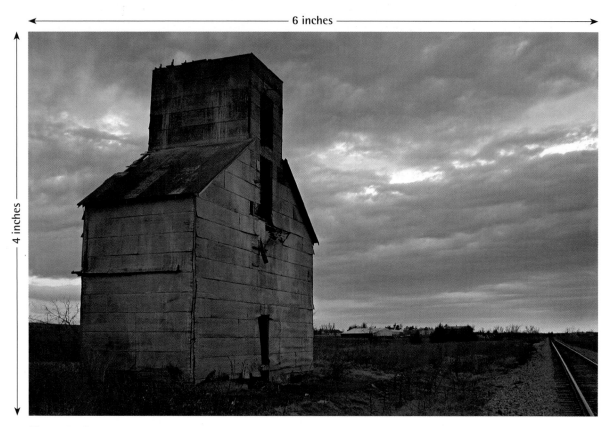

Figure 5-18.

Cropping with the Cookie Cutter

Photoshop Elements provides a second cropping tool, the cookie cutter tool, which looks like a valentine with a simplified image of a person in it. But although the cookie cutter icon immediately follows the crop tool in the toolbox and features a cropping mode that works a lot like the crop tool, that's not really its main purpose. Just as a real-world cookie cutter stamps shapes from rolled-out cookie dough, the cookie cutter tool stamps shapes out of images, discarding the excess pixels that lie outside the shape. (Unfortunately, you can't lump the excess pixels into a ball and roll them out again.) Cookie cutting is ideal for scrapbooking—say, when you want to crop a wedding photo into the shape of a heart and place it against another background. But the tool has other practical and creative uses, as you'll discover in this exercise.

1. *Open two images.* Go to the *Lesson 05 folder* inside *Lesson Files-PE4 1on1* and open *Gold metal.jpg* and *Sheep.jpg*. Arrange the image windows in the Editor workspace so that *Gold metal.jpg* is in front, as in Figure 5-19. Because both are JPEG images, they are flat files that contain one Background layer apiece and nothing more.

2. *Select the cookie cutter tool.* Click the cookie cutter tool in the toolbox, as in Figure 5-20, or press Q.

Figure 5-19.

3. *Select a frame shape.* But first, let's take a moment to review the settings available in the options bar at the top of the screen:

   • Click the icon next to Shape (❤ by default) to see a pop-up palette of shapes that you can draw with the cookie cutter tool. You'll see quite a few, but that ain't all of them. Click the ⊙ arrow to display several libraries of additional shapes. Choose the first library option, All Elements Shapes, to gain instant access to a jaw-dropping 569 predefined shapes.

   • The Shape Options pop-up menu features options for constraining the cookie cutter to a specific aspect or size.

   • The Feather option gives the shape a fuzzy outline.

   • By default, the cookie cutter crops a shape out of an image but leaves the canvas size unchanged. If you turn on the Crop check box, the tool crops the canvas to fit the shape.

Figure 5-20.

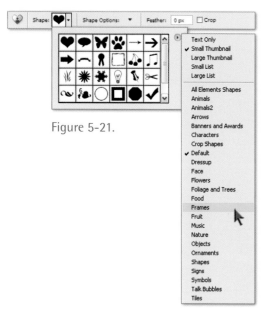

Figure 5-21.

Click the ▾ arrow to open the **Shape** pop-up palette. Then click the ⊙ arrow on the right side of the palette. Choose **Frames** (see Figure 5-21) to load a library of predrawn frame outlines. If you hover the cursor over a shape, a tool tip reveals the name of the shape. But to expedite things, click ⊙ again and choose **Large List** from the top of the submenu. The palette now displays a thumbnail along with the name of the shape. Scroll down to **Frame 14** and double-click it.

4. *Crop the frame.* Armed with the cookie cutter tool, drag from the upper-left region of photographer Yohan Juliardi's *Gold metal.jpg* image to the lower-right region, as in Figure 5-22. Several things happen. Most obviously, a frame appears in the image, surrounded by a cropping marquee. Behind the frame you see a gray-and-white checkerboard pattern; this is how Elements represents transparency, which is what the cookie cutter leaves outside the cropped shape. Meanwhile, if you take a peek at the Layers palette, you'll see that the Background layer has turned into a full-fledged layer called Layer 0.

Figure 5-22.

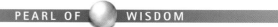

PEARL OF WISDOM

The cookie cutter stamps shapes out of layers and makes any pixel that falls outside the shape transparent. Background layers can't contain transparency, so if you use the image on a Background layer, the tool has no choice but to promote the Background to a full-fledged layer. If you're concerned about losing the rest of the image, duplicate the Background layer by pressing Ctrl+J and then use the cookie cutter on the duplicate.

Just as with the crop tool, the cookie cutter tool lets you tweak your cropping before making it final. Drag the corners of the crop marquee to the corners of the image window. Assuming that View→Snap to Grid is turned on, the marquee will snap to the perimeter of the canvas size. Click the ✔ icon in the options bar or press the Enter key, and you have a new frame shape.

5. *Restore the Background layer.* We're going to build a layered composition inside this image. And for the best results, we need a Background layer. Click the ⬚ icon in the upper-left corner of the **Layers** palette to create a transparent Layer 1 on top of Layer 0. Then choose **Layer→New→Background From Layer**. Assuming the background color is white, Elements converts Layer 1 into a white Background layer.

6. *Crop a shape.* Now bring the *Sheep.jpg* image forward. Captured by Tobias Ott, this photo (like the others in this exercise) comes to us from the good people at iStockphoto. Click the ⯆ arrow in the options bar to open the **Shape** pop-up palette. Then click the ⯈ arrow and choose the **Crop Shapes** library. Finally, double-click the shape called **Crop Shape 12** to select it. Drag from one corner to the opposite corner in the photo to frame it, more or less as you see in Figure 5-23. For compositional reasons, we don't want the marquee to align with the extreme edges of the image. Remember, after you drag out the shape, you can adjust it as you see fit. Click ✔ or press Enter to accept the shape. The sheep appears cropped inside an artful, brushstroke shape.

Figure 5-23.

7. *Drag and drop the sheep.* Press the V key to get the move tool. Then drag the sheep, hold down the Shift key, and drop the shape into the *Gold metal.jpg* window. Shift centers the shape.

Note that you *have* to use the move tool. When using the cookie cutter, you can't move images by Ctrl-dragging them, the way you can when using the selection tools (see Step 6, page 127). So I'll give you a new tip instead: If your screen is too crowded to get to the *Gold metal.jpg* image, no problem. Just drag the sheep from its image window into the thumbnail of the gold metal image in the Photo Bin along the bottom of the screen, as illustrated in **Figure 5-24**. Elements automatically centers the sheep shape, without the help of the Shift key.

Figure 5-24.

8. *Add some dimension to the shapes.* Make sure that the *Gold metal.jpg* image window is in front. Now that we have this wonderful sheep-in-a-frame composition, let's add a couple of layer styles to the mix:

Figure 5-25.

- Go to the **Styles and Effects** palette and choose **Layer Styles** from the left pop-up menu and **Drop Shadows** from the right. With the sheep layer (Layer 1) selected in the Layers palette, click the **Low** drop shadow thumbnail in the Styles and Effects palette to add a subtle drop shadow behind the wool-bearing animal.

- Next, click **Layer 0** in the Layers palette or press Alt+⬚ (assuming that Layer 0 is at the top of the stack). Then click the **High** item in the Styles and Effects palette.

- Finally, switch the pop-up menu in the top-right corner of the Styles and Effects palette to **Bevels**, and then click the **Inner Ridge** thumbnail. Your image should now look like Figure 5-25.

One problem: the High drop shadow that you added to the frame extends beyond the boundaries of the image. Easily remedied. Choose **Image**→**Resize**→**Reveal All** and the canvas grows to the minimum size needed to fully accommodate the shadow.

EXTRA ★ CREDIT

You've managed to clip a couple of cookie cutter shapes and imbue them with layer styles to create a distinctive photo frame. So you might very well consider the image complete, and bask in the glow of the sheep's gentle majesty. Or you can follow along with the remaining steps and turn the whole thing into a cheap visual joke, totally robbing the animal of its last vestige of dignity. And who knows? Along the way, you might even learn a few more things about the cookie cutter tool.

9. *Open a few more images.* Close *Sheep.jpg* if you like but leave the layered *Gold metal.jpg* composition open. Then open three more photos from iStockphoto.com, also found in the *Lesson 05* folder. These are *Fairgrounds.jpg*, *Shell.jpg*, and *Text.jpg*. Make sure *Fairgrounds.jpg* is in the front.

10. *Select a wig shape.* Press Q to get the cookie cutter tool. Display the **Shape** pop-up menu, click the ⊙ arrow, and select the **Dressup** library. Then double-click the first shape, **Wig 1**.

11. *Cut a shape out of the cotton candy.* Photographer Ginger Garvey might have had something different in mind when she shot this image. But my take is this: That cotton candy would make a great sheep's wig. And for the optimal effect, I reckon the edges should be a bit fuzzy. Click the word **Feather** in the options bar, change the value to 4 pixels, and press the Enter key. Then constrain the proportions of the wig by Shift-dragging with the cookie cutter tool.

While Shift-dragging, you can also press the spacebar to reposition the shape on-the-fly. When you're happy with the location of the wig relative to the cotton candy, release the spacebar. But keep the Shift key down until you've finished drawing.

Encircle as much cotton candy as the wig shape will hold. When the shape looks like the one in Figure 5-26, release the mouse button, release Shift, and press the Enter key.

Figure 5-26.

12. *Put the wig on the sheep.* Press V for the move tool and drag the wig shape into *Gold metal.jpg.* (If your screen is a jumble, drop the wig onto the *Gold metal.jpg* thumbnail in the Photo Bin.) Then position the wig on the sheep's head, as in Figure 5-27. The humiliation has just begun.

13. *Cut out some glasses.* Our farmyard friend could use some stylish glasses, and what better substance for the frames than tortoise shell? Bring *Shell.jpg* (care of Angelika Stern) to the front and press Q for the cookie cutter tool. Click the **Shape** pop-up palette, scroll to the bottom of the list, and double-click **Glasses 2**. You don't want fuzzy glasses, so reduce the **Feather** value to 0 pixels.

Try to position your cursor as close to the center of the tortoise shell image as possible, and begin dragging. While pressing the mouse button, hold down both the Shift and Alt keys. Shift constrains the proportions; Alt draws the shape from the center out. When you've drawn the shape about as large as the image accommodates (see the tiny but powerful Figure 5-28), release the mouse and then release the keys. Press Enter to accept the new shape.

Figure 5-27.

14. *Put the glasses on the sheep.* Press the V key to slip back into the move tool. Drag the glasses by whatever means necessary into the increasingly elaborate *Gold metal.jpg* composition, and move the glasses over the sheep's eyes.

Figure 5-28.

Figure 5-29.

15. ***Put words in the sheep's mouth.*** To give the sheep something to say, switch to the *Text.jpg* image. Press Q for the cookie cutter. Then do the following:

    • Display the **Shape** pop-up palette, click the ⊙ arrow, and load **Talk Bubbles**. Then double-click the first one, which looks like ●, known as Talk 1.

    • Draw the talk balloon shape inside *Text.jpg* (photographed by Marcie Cheatham). For now, keep the shape small; we need some wiggle room for our edits.

    • The balloon's tail should point in the other direction. After you release the mouse button, drag the left handle of the cropping marquee all the way to the other side of the shape to flip it. (If it's easier to drag the right handle, or both the left and right, fine.)

    • Then drag the corner handles and stretch the bubble until it nicely frames the text. You should end up with a talk balloon like the one in Figure 5-29.

    • Press Enter to accept the shape.

16. ***Move the balloon.*** For the last time, press the V key for the move tool. Then drag the talk bubble into *Gold metal.jpg*. Inside the multilayer composition, move the talk balloon so that it overlaps the top of the frame. (If your talk balloon is behind the frame, choose Layer→Arrange→Bring to Front or press Ctrl+Shift+⌷ to move it to the front.) Match the location pictured in Figure 5-30. For now, that means your balloon will extend beyond the top of the canvas. Don't worry; we'll fix that problem in a jiffy.

17. ***Apply the finishing touches.*** Set the right pop-up menu in the **Styles and Effects** palette to **Drop Shadows** and click the **High** style. Then choose **Image→Resize→Reveal All** to expose every nook and cranny of the final masterpiece. As witnessed in the terribly tasteful Figure 5-30, this is one piece of cookie cutter art that's anything but.

Figure 5-30.

Resizing an Image

Now we leave the world of rotations and canvas manipulations in favor of what may be the single most essential command in all of Photoshop Elements: Image→Image Size. Designed to resize an entire image all at once—canvas, pixels, the whole shebang—Image Size lets you scale your artwork in two very different ways. First, you can change the physical dimensions of an image by adding or deleting pixels, a process called *resampling*. Second, you can leave the quantity of pixels unchanged and instead focus on the *print resolution*, which is the number of pixels that print within an inch or a millimeter of page space.

Whether you resample an image or change its resolution depends on the setting of a check box called Resample Image. As we'll see, this one option has such a profound effect on Image Size that it essentially divides the command into two separate functions. In the following steps, we explore how and why you might resample an image. To learn about print resolution, read the "Changing the Print Size" sidebar on page 182.

1. *Open the image you want to resize.* Open the file named *Enormous chair.jpg*, included in the *Lesson 05* folder inside *Lesson Files-PE4 1on1*. Shown in Figure 5-31, this 21-foot tall rocking chair is not only enormous in real life but also contains the most pixels of any file we've seen so far (not including layers).

2. *Check the existing image size.* To see just how many pixels make up this image, click and hold the box in the bottom-left corner of the image window that reads **7.5 inches × 9.067 inches (300 ppi)**. (If you see something different here, click the ▶ to the right of the box and choose **Document Dimensions**. That will put us in agreement, but it won't affect the outcome of this step.)

Figure 5-31.

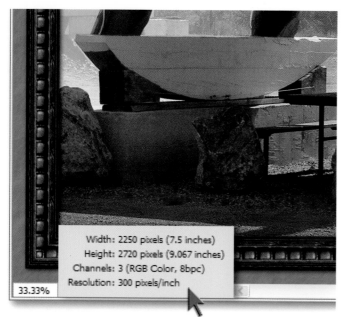

Figure 5-32.

As Figure 5-32 shows, clicking on the box reveals a pop-up window that lists the size of the image in pixels, along with its resolution. This particular image measures 2250 pixels wide by 2720 pixels tall, for a total of 2250 × 2720 = 6.12 million pixels. When printed at 300 ppi, the image will measure 7.5 inches wide by a little more than 9 inches tall.

3. *Magnify the image to 100 percent.* Double-click the zoom tool icon in the toolbox. Then scroll around the photograph until you can see the sign tacked to the front of the chair. Pictured in Figure 5-33, the text on the sign is perfectly legible, a testament to the high resolution of the photograph. But there's also a lot of noise (see the midsection of Step 8 of "Correcting Camera Raw," Lesson 3, page 110). So even though we have scads of pixels, they aren't necessarily in great shape.

4. *Decide whether you need all these pixels.* This may seem like a cerebral step, but it's an important one. Resampling amounts to rewriting every pixel in your image, so weigh your options before you plow ahead.

Let's say you want to email this image to a couple of friends. If your friends want to print the photo, they can print it smaller or at a lower resolution. But chances are they won't print it at all; they'll just view it on screen. A typical high-resolution monitor can display at most 1600 by 1200 pixels, a mere 30 percent of the pixels in this photo.

Conclusion: Resampling is warranted. This is a job for the Image Size command.

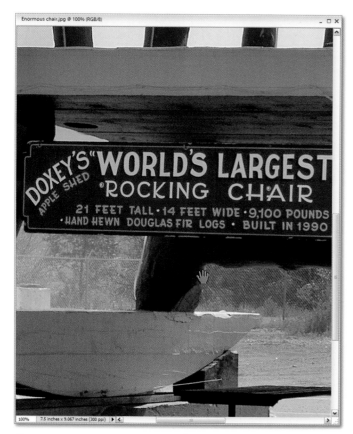

Figure 5-33.

5. *Choose the Image Size command.* Choose **Image→Resize→ Image Size**, or press Ctrl+Alt+I. Photoshop Elements displays the **Image Size** dialog box (see Figure 5-34), which is divided into two parts:

Figure 5-34.

- The options in the Pixel Dimensions area let you change the width and height of the image in pixels. Lowering the number of pixels is called *downsampling*; increasing the pixel count is called *upsampling*. We'll be downsampling, which is by far the more common practice.

- The Document Size options control the size of the printed image. They have no effect on the size of the image on the screen or on the Web.

6. *Turn on the Resample Image check box.* Located at the bottom of the dialog box, this option permits you to change the number of pixels in an image.

7. *Select an interpolation setting.* To the right of the Resample Image check box is a pop-up menu of interpolation options, which determine how Photoshop Elements blends the existing pixels in your image to create new ones. When downsampling an image, only three options matter:

- When in doubt, select Bicubic, which calculates the color of every resampled pixel by averaging the original image in 16-pixel blocks. It is slower than either Nearest Neighbor or Bilinear (neither of which should be used when resampling photographs), but it does a far better job as well.

- Bicubic Smoother compounds the effects of the interpolation to soften color transitions between neighboring pixels. This helps suppress film grain and noise.

- Bicubic Sharper results in crisp edge transitions. Use it when the details in your image are impeccable and you want to preserve every nuance.

Because this particular image contains so much noise, **Bicubic Smoother** is the best choice.

8. *Turn on the Constrain Proportions check box.* Unless you want to stretch or squish your image, leave this option turned on. That way, the relationship between the width and height of the image—known as the *aspect ratio*—will remain constant.

Changing the Print Size

As often as not, you'll have no desire to change the number of pixels in an image; you'll just want to change how it looks on the printed page. By focusing exclusively on the resolution, you can print an image larger or smaller without adding or subtracting so much as a single pixel.

For example, let's say you want to scale the original *Enormous chair.jpg* image so that it prints 10 inches wide by 12 inches tall. Would you upsample the image and thereby add pixels to it? Absolutely not. The Image Size command can't add detail to an image; it just averages existing pixels. So upsampling adds complexity without improving the quality. Upsampling can be helpful—when matching the resolution of one image to another, for example—but these occurrences are few and far between.

The better solution is to modify the print resolution. Try this: Open the original *Enormous chair.jpg*. (This assumes that you have completed the "Resizing an Image" exercise and saved the results of that exercise under a different filename, as directed by Step 14 on page 184.) Then choose Image→Resize→Image Size and turn off the Resample Image check box.

Note that the Pixel Dimensions options are now dimmed and a link icon (🔗) joins the three Document Size values, as in the screen shot below. This icon tells you that it doesn't matter which value you edit or in what order. Any change you make to one value affects the other two, so you can't help but edit all three values at once. For example, change the Width value to 10 inches. As you do, Elements automatically updates the Height and Resolution values to 12.089 inches and 225 ppi, respectively. So there's no need to calculate the resolution value that will get you a desired set of dimensions; just enter one of the dimensions and Elements does the math for you.

Click OK to accept your changes. The image looks exactly the same as it did before you entered the Image Size dialog box. This is because you changed the way the image prints, which has nothing to do with the way it looks on screen. If you like, feel free to save over the original file. You haven't changed the structure of the image; you just added a bit of sizing data.

To learn more about printing—including how you can further modify the print resolution from the Print Preview dialog box—read the first exercise in Lesson 11, "Printing to an Inkjet Printer."

9. *Specify a Resolution value.* When Resample Image is turned on (Step 6), any change made to the Resolution value affects the Pixel Dimensions values as well. So if you intend to print the image, it's a good idea to get the Resolution setting out of the way first. Given that we are emailing the image and are not sure whether it will ever see a printer, a **Resolution** of 200 ppi should work well enough.

10. *Adjust the Width value.* The Pixel Dimensions values have dropped to 1500 by 1813 pixels. But given that most screens top out at 1600 by 1200 pixels, that's still too big. Under **Pixel Dimensions**, reduce the **Width** value to 900 pixels, which changes the Height value to 1088 pixels. This also reduces the Document Size to 4.5 by 5.44 inches (see Figure 5-35), plenty big for an email picture.

Figure 5-35.

11. *Take notice of the new file size.* The Pixel Dimensions header should now read *2.80M (was 17.5M)*, where the *M* stands for *megabytes*. This value represents the size of the image in your computer's memory. The resampled image will measure 900 × 1088 = 979,200 pixels, a mere 16 percent of its previous size. Not coincidentally, 2.8M is precisely 16 percent of 17.5M. The complexity of a file is directly related to its image size, so this downsampled version will load, save, print, and email much more quickly.

12. *Click OK.* Photoshop Elements reduces the size of the image on-screen and in memory. As verified by Figure 5-36, the result continues to look great when printed, but that's partly because it's printed so small. The real test is how it looks on your screen.

Figure 5-36.

13. *Magnify the image to the 300 percent zoom ratio.* Use the zoom tool to zoom in on the sign, as in Figure 5-37. The letters are rougher—no surprise given the lower number of pixels—but they remain legible. And the photo overall is less grainy. Downsampling with the Bicubic Smoother setting (see Step 7, page 181) goes a long way toward smoothing away the noise.

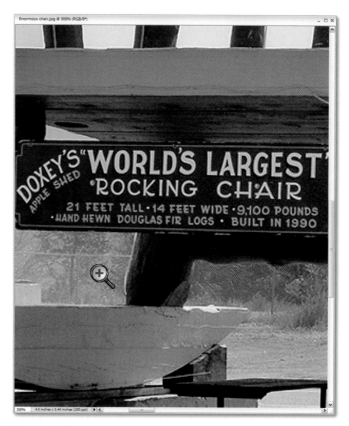

Figure 5-37.

14. *Choose the Save As command.* Choose **File→Save As**, or press Ctrl+Shift+S. Then give the file a new name. Don't fret about the JPEG settings; just go ahead and accept the defaults. The reason I have you do this is to emphasize the following very important point.

WHAT DID YOU LEARN?

Match the key concept in the numbered list below with the letter
of the phrase that best describes it. Answers appear upside-down
at the bottom of the page.

Key Concepts

1. Cropping
2. Whole-image transformations
3. Interpolation
4. Divide Scanned Photos
5. Gang scanning
6. Shield
7. Origin point
8. Reveal All
9. Print resolution
10. Downsampling
11. Bicubic Smoother
12. Resample Image

Descriptions

A. A means of cutting away the extraneous portions of an image to focus the viewer's attention on the subject of the photo.

B. To change the physical dimensions of an image by reducing the number of pixels.

C. A quick-and-dirty method of capturing several images with a flatbed scanner to a single image file, which you crop later.

D. The number of pixels that will print within a linear inch or millimeter of page space.

E. The translucent film of color that covers the portions of an image that will be deleted after you apply the crop tool.

F. The process of throwing away pixels and making up new ones by averaging the existing pixels in an image.

G. Operations such as Image Size and the Rotate commands that affect an entire image, including any and all layers.

H. The center of a rotation or another transformation.

I. Turning off this check box keeps the Image Size command from interpolating the pixels in an image.

J. Although designed to accommodate multiple images, this command is Elements' best method for cropping and straightening a single image.

K. This command enlarges the size of a layered image to display any hidden pixels that lie outside the image boundaries.

L. An interpolation setting that makes a special effort to suppress film grain, noise, and other artifacts.

Answers

1A, 2G 3F, 4J, 5C, 6E, 7H, 8K, 9D, 10B, 11L, 12I

LESSON

6

PAINT, EDIT, AND HEAL

SO FAR, WE'VE seen a wealth of commands that correct the appearance of an image based on a few specifications and a bit of numerical input. On balance, nothing's wrong with these commands, and many are extraordinarily useful. But all the automation in the world can't eliminate the need for some occasional old-fashioned, hard-fought, wrist-breaking, sometimes-toilsome-but-always-rewarding artistic labor.

Such is the case with painting and retouching in Photoshop Elements. Whether you want to augment a piece of artwork or adjust the details in a photograph, it's time to give the commands a slip and turn your attention to the toolbox. Elements devotes nearly half its tools—including all those pictured in Figure 6-1—to the tasks of applying and modifying colors in an image. The idea of learning so many tools and putting them to use may seem intimidating. And because they require you to paint freehand in the image window, they respond directly to your talents and dexterity—or your lack thereof. Fortunately, despite their numbers, the tools are a lot of fun. And even if your fine motor skills aren't everything you wish they were, there's no need to fret. I'll show you all kinds of ways to constrain and articulate your brushstrokes in the following exercises.

The Necessary Nine, Plus Two

Of the tools shown in Figure 6-1, seven include flyout menus of additional tools. In all, these ten let you access twenty tools. Of those, sixteen are *brush-based*; select such a tool and drag in the image window to create a brushstroke of colored or modified pixels. The remaining four tools are modeled after the selection tools discussed in Lesson 4. You either click to replace a colored region, as with the magic wand, or drag to change a free-form area, as with the lasso.

Figure 6-1.

ABOUT THIS LESSON

Project Files

Before beginning the exercises, make sure you've installed the lesson files from the DVD, as explained in Step 5 on page xv of the Preface. This should result in a folder of images called *Lesson Files-PE4 1on1* on your desktop. We'll be working with the files inside the *Lesson 06* subfolder.

The exercises in this lesson explain how to use Photoshop Elements' paint, edit, and healing tools to brush color and effects into an image. You'll learn how to:

Video Lesson 6: Brush Options

Many of the paint, edit, and heal tools rely on a common group of options and settings that Adobe calls the *brush engine*. These options dictate the thickness, fuzziness, and scatter pattern of a brushstroke.

You can adjust brush engine settings from the options bar and keyboard, as well as from the Tablet Options and More Options palettes. To get a feel for how these settings work, watch the sixth video lesson on the DVD. Insert the DVD, click **Start**, select **Set 2: Select, Crop, and Edit** from the first pop-up menu, and then select **Lesson 6, Brush Options** from the second pop-up menu. Clocking in at 15 minutes and 29 seconds, this video introduces you to the following tools and operations:

Tool or operation	Keyboard equivalent or shortcut
Brush tool (paintbrush)	B
Incrementally enlarge or reduce brush diameter	] (right bracket) or [(left bracket)
Make the brush harder or softer	Shift+] or Shift+[
Change the Opacity setting of the active brush	1, 2, 3, . . . , 0
Change the Flow setting of the active brush	Shift+1, 2, 3, . . . , 0
DIsplay brush palette	Right-click with paintbrush in image window
Lift color with eyedropper	Alt-click with paintbrush in image window

Brush-based or otherwise, you don't need to learn every one of these tools. As with everything in Photoshop Elements, some tools are good, some tools are bad. In this lesson we'll focus on what I consider to be the Necessary Nine brush-based tools: the paintbrush (which Adobe calls the brush tool); the dodge, burn, sponge, smudge, color replacement, and clone stamp tools; and the spot and standard healing brushes. We'll also look at two selection-type tools: the paint bucket and the red-eye removal tool.

This emphasis on brushes may lead you to think that tools such as the paintbrush and sponge are best suited to creating original artwork. Although you *can* create artwork from scratch in Elements, it's not what the program's designers had in mind. The purpose of these tools is to help you edit photographic images or scanned artwork, and that's how we'll use them in this lesson.

Figure 6-2.

The Three Editing Styles

Photoshop Elements lets you use tools—brush-based or otherwise—to apply and modify colors in three ways:

- The first group of tools, the *painting tools*, comprises the paintbrush, the paint bucket, and others. They permit you to paint lines and fill shapes with the foreground color. I drew the lines in Figure 6-2 with the paintbrush while switching the foreground color between black and white.

- *Editing tools* is a catchall category for any tool that modifies rather than replaces the existing color or luminosity of a pixel. The burn tool darkens pixels, the smudge tool smears them, and the color replacement tool swaps out hue and saturation values, as demonstrated in Figure 6-3.

Figure 6-3.

Figure 6-4.

- The *cloning and healing tools* permit you to clone elements from one portion of an image to another. Using a sophisticated color-matching algorithm, the healing tools are capable of merging the cloned details with their new backgrounds to create seamless transitions, as illustrated in Figure 6-4.

Coloring Scanned Line Art

Photoshop Elements is great at manipulating digital photographs. But it's also a capable program for coloring scanned line drawings and otherwise enhancing original artwork. This means you can exploit the best aspects of traditional and digital media:

- It's easier to draw on paper with a pencil and pen than it is to sketch on screen, if only because you can see the entire sheet of paper all at once without zooming or panning.

- Meanwhile, it's easier to add colors in Photoshop Elements than hassle with conventional paints.

Skeptical about that last point? Fair enough. In this exercise, you'll take a hand-drawn illustration and apply colors to it using just two tools: the paint bucket and paintbrush. Not only will you learn how to paint *precisely* inside the lines—and without exercising the least bit of care—but you'll also do so without harming so much as a single stroke in the original drawing. Elements really is the best of all worlds.

1. *Open the scanned artwork.* Starting in the Editor workspace, go to the *Lesson 06* folder inside *Lesson Files-PE4 1on1* and open *Butterfly.tif.* Pictured in Figure 6-5 on the facing page, this artwork is part traditional and part digital. It started as a sketch that I drew with a common, run-of-the-mill Sharpie on a piece of cheap copier paper. While these are admittedly low-tech art tools, I prefer them to anything Elements has to offer. But my original sketch included just the left half of the butterfly. To create the entire insect, I copied the sketch, flipped it, and joined the two halves, all inside Photoshop Elements.

Your job is to color the butterfly. In this case, that means painting the black lines and leaving the white background alone. One way to approach this task is to select the lines using, say, the magic wand, and then paint the selected area. But while the wand does a terrific job of selecting the blacks, it isn't so hot at capturing the transitions between blacks and whites around the edges. That's why we're going to take advantage of an easier technique that involves painting on an independent layer.

2. *Make a new layer.* Choose **Layer→New→ Layer** or press Ctrl+Shift+N to add a layer to your image. In the **New Layer** dialog box, name the layer "Color." Then click the word **Normal** and choose **Screen** from the **Mode** pop-up menu, as in Figure 6-6. Click the **OK** button to add the new layer to the top of the Layers palette.

Figure 6-5.

3. *Change the foreground color to red.* Let's start by coloring the butterfly red. Choose **Window→Color Swatches** to display the **Color Swatches** palette, which contains a collection of predefined colors. Make sure the pop-up menu at the top of the palette is set to **Default**. Then click the very first color swatch, red, to make it the active foreground color, as in Figure 6-7.

Figure 6-6.

Figure 6-7.

Figure 6-8.

Figure 6-9.

4. *Select the paint bucket tool.* Click the paint bucket icon in the toolbox, as in Figure 6-8. Or press the K key.

5. *Click inside the image window.* To fill the entire butterfly with the foreground color, click anywhere inside the image window. The Screen mode that you assigned in Step 2 ensures that only the black lines are affected. But hey, what gives? Instead of filling lines with red, the paint bucket colors them gray. The problem: This is a grayscale image. Ideally suited to black-and-white line art, a grayscale file is simple and small. This is because each pixel is permitted a luminosity value and nothing more; hue and saturation are out of the picture. One look at Figure 6-8 confirms that the foreground color swatch at the bottom of the toolbox is not the red we clicked but a grayscale version of it. To add color to the image, you must first convert it.

6. *Convert the image to RGB.* To open up the color spectrum, choose **Image→Mode→RGB Color**. A highly misleading alert message prompts you to flatten your artwork and get rid of the layer you created in Step 2. This inane suggestion is intended to avoid the color shifts that sometimes result when recalculating blend modes. The problem is, these shifts are *not even possible* when converting from grayscale to RGB. In other words, there's no reason on Earth to flatten. Sadly, there is no Heck No! or Are You Crazy? button. So you'll have to satisfy yourself by clicking the **Don't Flatten** button, as in Figure 6-9.

To choose the RGB Color command from the keyboard, press and hold the Alt key and type I-M-R. Then press the D key to activate the Don't Flatten button.

---

7. *Fill the layer again.* Again click inside the image window with the paint bucket tool. Now that the image is set to accommodate color, the black lines of the butterfly turn red.

To color the butterfly from the keyboard, press Alt+Backspace. This handy shortcut fills the entire layer with the foreground color.

---

8. *Select the paintbrush tool.* Photoshop Elements supplies you with two painting tools, the paintbrush (AKA, the brush tool) and the pencil. The pencil paints jagged lines, making it most useful for changing individual pixels. The paintbrush

is more versatile, permitting you to modify the sharpness of a line and tap into a wealth of controls that the pencil can't touch. Conclusion: when you want to paint, get the paintbrush. To do exactly that, click the paintbrush icon in the toolbox (see Figure 6-10) or press the B key.

9. *Change the foreground color to blue.* Click the fifth swatch in the top row of the Color Swatches palette (the swatch displays the hint *RGB Blue* when you hover over it) to change the foreground color to blue.

10. *Select the soft 300-pixel brush.* Go to the options bar at the top of the screen and click the ⬘ arrow to the right of the brush preview (just to the left of the word Size) to bring up a pop-up palette of predefined brush settings. Scroll down the list and click the first brush labeled **300**. (When you hover over the brush setting, you should see the hint *Soft Round 300 pixels*, as in Figure 6-11.) This selects a circular brush with a diameter of 300 pixels and a hardness of 0. That is to say, the brush is big and fuzzy. To hide the pop-up palette and accept your changes, press the Enter key. Or just start painting in the image window. (The other way to hide the pop-up palette is to press the Esc key, but that also abandons your changes.)

Figure 6-10.

Figure 6-11.

To incrementally change the size of the brush, raise or lower the Size value in the options bar. You can also change the brush attributes from the keyboard using, of all things, the bracket keys. Press the ⬚ key to reduce the brush diameter; press ⬚ to raise it. Press Shift+⬚ to make the brush softer; press Shift+⬚ to make it harder. These shortcuts may seem weird, but once you come to terms with them, they're a heck of a lot easier than hunting around for the corresponding options.

---

11. *Paint inside the butterfly.* Paint as much of the butterfly as you like, wherever you like. As you do, Photoshop Elements confines your brushstrokes to the line art, as shown in Figure 6-12 on the next page.

Figure 6-12.

12. *Adjust the Scatter and Fade values.* If you're hungry for more brush options, click the ✐ icon to the right of More Options on the far right side of the options bar. This displays the pop-up palette pictured in Figure 6-13, which includes many of the options that I discussed in Video Lesson 6, "Brush Options." Then do the following:

- Increase the fifth value, **Scatter**, to 25 percent. This separates the spots of color laid down by the paintbrush, as you can see previewed on the left side of the options bar (labeled in Figure 6-13).

- Increase the **Fade** value to 150. This tells Photoshop Elements to gradually fade the brushstroke to transparent over the course of 150 spots of color. This ensures that you don't obliterate one color as you lay on another.

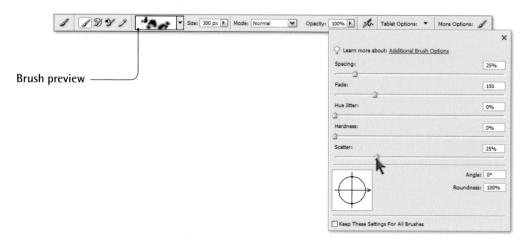

Brush preview

Figure 6-13.

When you finish, press the Enter key to accept your changes and hide the palette. If the palette remains visible, press Enter again.

13. *Switch colors and paint.* Select a color that strikes your fancy and paint inside the butterfly. When the paint runs out (according to the Fade value), switch colors and paint some more. To achieve the result pictured in

Figure 6-14, I painted one brushstroke in yellow, a second in green, and a third in a color called Pure Yellow Orange (which is swatch number 61 in the Color Swatches palette). The colors go a long way toward offsetting the rigid symmetry of the insect. Naturally, I'm all for that. The only reason the butterfly is symmetrical in the first place is because I was too lazy to draw the other half.

14. *Enter 0 for the Fade and Scatter values.* Click the ✒ icon on the far right side of the options bar. Then restore the **Fade** and **Scatter** values to their default settings of 0 and press Enter.

15. *Switch to black and choose the Overlay mode.* Press the D key to restore black as the foreground color. Then choose **Overlay** from the **Mode** pop-up menu in the options bar. The Overlay mode will paint with black while maintaining some of the most vivid colors that you added in previous steps.

16. *Paint inside the bug's body.* Paint the body and the two antennae. If the effect is too light, paint a second brushstroke. Each stroke results in a progressively darker effect.

17. *Paint the tips of the wings.* Press the right bracket key (⌗) twice to increase the diameter of the brush to 500 pixels. Paint along the top and bottom edges to give the wings a bit of a toasting, as shown in Figure 6-15. Again, feel free to paint in multiple strokes.

18. *Save your artwork.* If you want to keep your artwork, choose **File→Save As** or press Ctrl+Shift+S. Inside the **Save As** dialog box, choose **Photoshop (*.PSD; *.PDD)** from the **Format** pop-up menu. Then click the **Save** button.

Figure 6-14.

Figure 6-15.

Dodge, Burn, Sponge, and Smudge

We now move from painting to editing. And by *editing*, I mean using Photoshop Elements' tools to modify the saturation values, brightness levels, and color transitions in a photographic image. We start with Elements' core editing tools:

- The dodge tool lightens pixels as you paint over them.

- The burn tool darkens pixels as you paint over them. If you're having problems keeping the dodge and burn tools straight, just think of toast—the more you burn it, the darker it gets.

- The sponge tool adjusts the saturation of colors, making them either duller or more vivid.

- The smudge tool smears colors. Used in moderation, it can be useful for smoothing out harsh transitions.

Elements provides other edit tools, but the ones I listed are the most useful. The following exercise explains how to use these four edit tools to solve some common retouching problems.

My apologies in advance.jpg @ 50% (RGB/8*)

Figure 6-16.

1. *Open the photo of some poor sap who requires an emergency makeover.* Open the image titled *My apologies in advance.jpg* in the *Lesson 06* folder inside *Lesson Files-PE4 1on1*. The file features an all too accurate head shot of me, your gruesome-looking author, pictured in horrifying detail in Figure 6-16. In his *Maxims for the Use of the Overeducated*, Oscar Wilde wrote, "A subject that is beautiful in itself gives no suggestion to the artist. It lacks imperfection." That said, my face is extremely suggestive. In that same volume, Wilde wrote, "Those whom the gods love grow young." Well, the gods may not love me in real life, but they're going to fawn all over me in Photoshop Elements. *The Picture of Dorian Gray* has nothing on this program.

If you don't want to use my face—and really, who can blame you?—use a picture of yourself, a loved one, or a dire enemy. The specific concerns may be different, but the general approach will be the same. One potential difference: Because my flesh tones trend toward glow-in-the-dark white boy, my face needs a little dodging and a whole lot of burning. If the face you're working on is rich in melanin, it may require just the opposite.

---

2. *Click the dodge tool in the toolbox.* At the end of the toolbox (see Figure 6-17), possibly nestled behind the sponge tool, the dodge tool is one of the *toning tools*. To get the dodge tool from the keyboard, press the O key. (That's the letter, not zero.) If another tool appears at the bottom of the toolbox, keep pressing O until you get the lollipop-looking dodge tool.

3. *Reduce the Exposure value to 30 percent.* Located in the options bar, the **Exposure** value controls the intensity of edits applied by the dodge tool. In my experience, the default value of 50 percent is too extreme for most editing work. Just press the 3 key. Or select the value and change it to 30 percent.

4. *Drag over the image details you want to lighten.* In my case, I started with my nose—my big, splotchy, freckly nose. I reduced the brush diameter a few notches (to 40 pixels) and dragged inside the eyes, teeth, and eyelids. I also dragged over the smile lines trailing away from my nose. In Figure 6-18, the areas that received my attention appear in color. (Unaffected areas are overlaid in blue-gray stripes.) Feel free to follow my lead or go your own way.

Figure 6-17.

Figure 6-18.

The biggest mistake people make when working with the edit tools is to push things too far. For example, it's tempting to take my coffee-stained teeth (positive note: no spinach stuck between them) and scrub them until they're pearly white. But if you do that, my newly brilliant smile will look ridiculous compared with the rest of me. Better to make small adjustments—one or two passes at most—so that you leave the shadows intact. We'll get rid of the yellow in Step 10.

5. *Select the burn tool in the toolbox.* Click and hold the dodge tool icon to display a flyout menu, and then choose the little hand icon that represents the burn tool, as in Figure 6-19. Or if you prefer, press the Alt key and click the dodge icon to advance to the next tool. Or just press the O key.

6. *Reduce the Exposure value to 20 percent.* Again, the default **Exposure** value is 50 percent, far too radical for burning. Press the 2 key to permit yourself more subtlety and flexibility.

Figure 6-19.

Figure 6-20.

7. *Drag over the image details that you want to darken.* The burn tool adds shadows, and shadows give an image volume, depth, and form. I started by increasing the brush diameter several notches (to something in the 250- to 300-pixel range) and dragging up and down both sides of my face, including over the ears. Then I reduced the brush to around 80 pixels and painted under my eyebrows, nose, cheekbones, and chin, along the sides of my nose, and over my thinning hair, as indicated by the full-color areas in Figure 6-20. Basically, use the burn tool anywhere you would apply makeup—assuming of course that you feel comfortable applying makeup to a manly, he-man bucko of virile potency like myself.

Don't worry about dragging over the same spots with the burn tool as you did with the dodge tool. If they require burning, edit away. About the worst that can happen is you undersaturate color values, but that's something you can remedy later with the sponge tool.

Attention Caucasians: The burn tool can serve as a nifty tanning aid, but don't overdo it. A few brushstrokes are all that stand between plausibly augmented skin tones and surreal George Hamilton territory, as in **Figure 6-21**.

---

8. *Select the sponge tool in the toolbox.* Now to modify the saturation levels. Press Alt and click the burn tool icon in the toolbox to advance to the next toning tool, the sponge. Or press the O key.

9. *Reduce the Flow value to 30 percent.* Although it's calculated differently, the **Flow** value in the options bar serves the same purpose as the dodge and burn tools' Exposure value—it modifies the intensity of your brushstrokes. In my experience, the default value of 50 percent is too much. Press the 3 key to knock it down to 30 percent.

10. *Drag in the image to leech away aberrant colors.* Make sure the **Mode** option in the options bar is set to **Desaturate**. Then drag inside the teeth. A couple of passes gets rid of most of the yellow and leaves the teeth a more neutral white. (Be sure to leave behind some yellow. Gray teeth won't look right.) I also dragged over some of the more lurid pinks in the eyelids, ears, and lips, as well as some unusually orange patches in the forehead, as indicated by the colored areas in Figure 6-22.

11. *Switch the Mode setting to Saturate.* You can also increase the saturation of colors using the sponge tool. After choosing **Saturate** from the **Mode** pop-up menu in the options bar, click a few times inside each iris. This brings out both the olive-green of the iris and the red eye. We'll remedy the latter in the next exercise.

Healthy glow   Not even remotely possible

Figure 6-21.

Figure 6-22.

12. *Select the smudge tool in the toolbox.* Click and hold the blur tool icon—the one that looks like a drop of water—to display a flyout menu of *focus tools*. Then choose the smudge tool, as in Figure 6-23. Or press the R key one or more times to cycle between the focus tools until you see the smudge tool icon.

13. *Reduce the Strength value and change the Mode setting.* The smudge tool's default settings are designed to create painterly effects. If you want to use it to edit an image, you need to rein the tool in a bit. Press the 2 key to reduce the **Strength** value in the options bar to 20 percent. Then choose **Lighten** from the **Mode** pop-up menu (see Figure 6-24). Now the tool will smear light colors into dark ones and not the other way around.

Figure 6-24.

Figure 6-23.

Figure 6-25.

14. *Drag in the image to smear colors.* Press the ⎡ key a couple of times to increase the brush diameter to 30 pixels. (If nothing happens, press Esc to deactivate the Mode option, and then press the ⎡ key again.) Drag across my bottom lip to smooth over the grooves and make the skin look more hydrated. Be sure to trace along the lip, as demonstrated by the area highlighted in color in Figure 6-25. (Dragging across recruits colors from the teeth and whiskers.) You may have to smudge the lip multiple times to give it that "just ChapStick'ed" look. I also painted over some of the more pitted portions of my skin. That doesn't narrow it down too much, so look to the highlighted areas in Figure 6-25 for the specifics.

To limit the area affected by the smudge tool, draw a selection outline. For example, if you lasso the lower lip, you can drag anywhere you please inside the image but affect only the lower lip. This technique works for all the paint and edit tools, including the paintbrush. But it's especially useful when using the smudge tool, which is unique in that it can smear colors from deselected pixels even as it modifies selected ones.

15. *Save your image.* The photo suffers a few remaining problems, which we'll do our utmost to resolve in the next exercise. As a precaution, choose **File→Save As** or press Ctrl+Shift+S and rename the image "Partially fixed.jpg" or words to that effect. In the **JPEG Options** dialog box, leave the **Quality** set to 10 and click **OK**. And leave the image open.

Red Eye and Other Color Errors

Red eye is a common by-product of consumer cameras. Because the strobe is mounted so close to the lens element on a point-and-shoot camera, the flash has a tendency to pass through a moderately dilated iris and bounce off the back of the retina, as illustrated in Figure 6-26. And when you view the well-lit interior of an eye from a few feet away, it looks red.

Although red eye can occur in real life—when you catch a pedestrian in the beams of your car headlights, for example—the effect is fleeting and rare. As a result, red eye in a photograph looks weird—so weird, in fact, that Photoshop Elements 4 provides three ways to eliminate it:

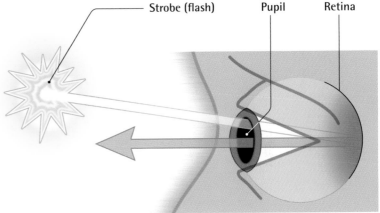

Figure 6-26.

- As we learned way back in Lesson 1, the Organizer automatically checks for red eye when adding images to a catalog. This same function is available in the Editor by choosing Enhance→ Auto Red Eye Fix. Only problem: It frequently doesn't work. In the case of the photo of my face, for example, it fixes one eye and ignores the other. (Feel free to try it out if you like.)

- The second red-eye fix, the Editor's red-eye removal tool, can correct pupils with a single click. It's easy-to-use, it's well-implemented, it's the perfect tool.

- The third, the color replacement tool, is the more versatile. Originally designed to fix red eye, it can correct a variety of color problems, including pet eyes and skin blotches.

In this exercise, we'll use both the red-eye removal and color replacement tools to fix the red of my pupils and the splotchy colors in my uniquely imperfect face. But first, let's fix my thinning hair with a more familiar tool, the paintbrush.

1. *Open my face.* If your *Partially fixed.jpg* photograph has remained on-screen, you're ready to go. Otherwise, please locate and open it now. If you can't find it, or you'd prefer to work from my edited version of the photo, open the file called *Pupil problems.jpg* contained in the *Lesson 06* folder inside *Lesson Files-PE4 1on1*.

2. *Click the paintbrush in the toolbox.* Or press B. We'll use this tool to fill in my fine hair.

3. *Eyedrop a representative hair color.* With the paintbrush active, press the Alt key to temporarily access the eyedropper, and then click a shade of brown in one of the rare full portions of my hair. To see what color you lifted, click the brown foreground color swatch at the bottom of the toolbox to bring up the **Color Picker** dialog box. My color was in the neighborhood of **R**: 100, **G**: 90, **B**: 80. You may end up with something different because my hair has a lot of variation, especially depending on how much you burned it back in Step 7 in the preceding exercise. Feel free to use the color you eyedropped or dial in my numbers—either should work fine.

Figure 6-27.

4. *Paint the scalp using the Color mode.* Change the **Mode** setting in the options bar to **Color**. Or press the keyboard shortcut, Shift+Alt+C. Change the brush diameter to 125 pixels. Then paint the top of my scalp to get the effect shown in Figure 6-27.

5. *Paint some more using the Multiply mode.* Choose **Multiply** from the **Mode** menu, or press Shift+Alt+M. Press 2 to lower the **Opacity** value to 20 percent. (If Elements ignores you, press Esc to deactivate the blend mode option and then press 2 again.) Then paint short strokes in the light areas of the scalp to darken them, as in Figure 6-28.

6. *Select the red-eye removal tool in the toolbox.* Your next task is to remove the red eye caused by the camera's flash. Click the eyeball icon in the toolbox, as in Figure 6-29. Or press the Y key.

7. *Click near one of the pupils.* Just so we're on the same page, zoom in on the left pupil (my right). Then click up and to the left of the eye, at

Figure 6-28.

the approximate position indicated by the yellow arrow in Figure 6-30. So long as you click on or even *near* the pupil, Elements replaces the red eye with black.

Figure 6-29.

PEARL OF WISDOM

What makes the red-eye removal tool so smart that it can find a pupil in the vicinity of your click point? First, it finds the nearest area of red or pink in the image. Second, it confirms that an ellipse will fit inside that area and paints the ellipse black, making sure to preserve all the highlights. To get a sense of what the tool does when there's no pupil to be seen, click in my mouth. True to form, Elements draws a black oval inside the pink of the tongue or lips.

If you have a sharp eye—the one in your head, not in the image—you may notice that the red-eye removal tool darkens a bit more than the pupil. In my case, the tool ever-so-slightly darkened my upper eyelid and eyelashes. If you find that bothersome, you can modify the behavior of the tool using a few values in the options bar:

- Use the first option, Pupil Size, to expand or reduce the area affected by the tool. Virtually any value results in the pupil getting colored. But a lower value—such as 20 percent—prevents the eyelashes from being affected.

- If the pupil ends up looking gray instead of black, undo the operation, raise the Darken Amount value, and try again. If you discover that you're losing highlights, lower the value.

Well, that's how the options are supposed to work anyway. In my experience, even radical adjustments—a Pupil Size of 1 percent and a Darken Amount of 100 percent, for example—produce such subtle changes that you can barely see the difference. (The final option, Auto, applies the hit-or-miss Auto Red Eye Fix command.)

8. *Drag around the other pupil.* Here's another way to use the tool: Still armed with the red-eye removal tool, draw a rectangular marquee around the other eye. For the best results, your marquee should enclose the entire eye, as illustrated in Figure 6-31. Assuming everything goes according to plan, Elements blackens the pupil to match the other perfectly. It also darkens the eyelashes above my eye, removing some pink from the skin.

Figure 6-30.

Figure 6-31.

Figure 6-32.

9. *Select the color replacement tool.* Straightforward and fast, the red-eye removal tool is one of the shining stars of the Elements toolbox. But it is also the program's most narrowly focused tool—it fixes red eye and nothing else. If you want to remove other kinds of color aberrations—such as the ruddy patches in my skin—it's time to take up the more sophisticated color replacement tool. To get it, click and hold the paintbrush icon in the toolbox. Then choose the color replacement tool from the flyout menu, as in Figure 6-32.

If you start right in painting, you'll make my face and everything else with which you come in contact gray. This is because the foreground color is set to a grayish brown and the options bar settings are too aggressive. In other words, a few preliminary adjustments are in order.

10. *Eyedrop a flesh tone.* Press the Alt key and click one of the areas of my skin that trends toward orange as opposed to pink. A good color to match is **R**: 205, **G**: 165, **B**: 150 (which you can confirm from the Info palette, if it's open, or by clicking the tan foreground color icon at the bottom of the toolbox).

11. *Adjust the option bar settings.* Increase the brush size to 60 pixels and reduce the **Hardness** setting in the **More Options** area to 0 percent. (Remember, you can use ⬚ and Shift+⬚ from the keyboard.) Then do the following:

- Set the **Mode** option to **Hue**, which replaces the core hues while leaving the saturation values intact.

- To the right of Mode, click the second eyedropper, the one that looks like ✐, as in Figure 6-33. This sets the *sampling*, which is the number of times Elements reads a color for replacement. By clicking ✐, you tell the tool to sample a color just once, at the beginning of your drag. The program replaces only those colors that match the starting pixel, which makes the tool much more precise.

- Reduce the **Tolerance** value to 20 percent by pressing 2. (As usual, if nothing happens, press Esc and press 2 again.) This setting limits the number of colors affected at a time.

Figure 6-33.

12. *Paint away the pinks in the skin.* Paint over the pink areas in the eyelids, cheeks, and nose, as well as the more understated pinks of the neck, ears, and forehead, all outlined in Figure 6-34. As you do, these areas will turn a uniform fleshy peach color, as if my face were coated in a subtle but forgiving layer of foundation.

13. *Continue to adjust details as needed.* Don't expect to be able to retouch an image in thirty or so tidy steps over the course of two exercises. After all, a change made with the color replacement tool might beg you to make another with the burn tool, which in turn requires you to take up the sponge tool, and so on. In short, expect to revisit all these tools as you create that near-perfect image.

As you switch between the various tools, here are a few techniques and words of advice:

Figure 6-34.

- The dodge and burn tools affect specific color ranges. By default, the Range menu in the options bar is set to Midtones, which changes the midtones and protects the highlights and shadows. If you prefer to adjust the lightest or darkest colors, choose Highlights or Shadows instead. In Figure 6-35 on the next page, I set the burn tool to Highlights and dragged around the perimeter of the background to create a slight vignette effect.

- The dodge and burn tools are interchangeable. Just press the Alt key to darken with the dodge tool or lighten with the burn tool. Pressing Alt is a great way to take the settings assigned to one tool—such as a brush diameter and Range setting—and apply them to the opposite function.

- The dodge, burn, sponge, and smudge tools work best when used with a soft brush (typically, a Hardness value of 50 percent or lower). The color replacement tool can go either way, hard or soft.

- Feel free to cheat. Just because you have all these edit tools doesn't mean you have to use them. For example, my lower lip was resolutely determined to remain a bright crimson despite my best efforts. So I selected the lip with the lasso tool. Then I used Enhance→Adjust Color→Adjust Hue/Saturation to nudge it more toward red and bring down the saturation. As long as you get results, it doesn't matter how you get there.

Figure 6-35 compares the original photograph to the edited version. Now you know why I never let a picture of me (or anyone else I care about) leave the house without a proper retouching.

Figure 6-35.

Healing a Damaged Image

The edit tools are well suited to a variety of retouching scenarios. But they can't create detail where none exists. To fix dust and scratches or cover up scars and wrinkles, you need tools that can paint imagery on top of imagery. Tools like the clone stamp tool and healing brushes:

- The clone stamp tool paints one section of an image onto another, a process called *cloning*. You identify the portion of the image that you want to clone, and then paint away.

- The healing brushes also clone. The big difference is that after you paint, Elements mixes the cloned pixels with the color and lighting that surrounds the brushstroke to create a seamless patch. The spot healing brush selects the area to clone automatically; the standard healing brush lets you decide.

This final exercise shows you how to use these powerful tools to fix a variety of photographic woes, ranging from rips and tears to blemishes and age spots.

1. *Open a broken image.* Open the file *PhotoSpin bluebeard.jpg* located in the *Lesson 06* folder inside *Lesson Files-PE4 1on1*. Available in perfect condition from PhotoSpin's Ed Simpson International People collection, this version of the photo appears so tragically scratched because, well, I scratched it. I printed the image to a continuous-tone Olympus P-400 image printer. Then I folded the output once vertically and again horizontally, scored the crease with a pair of scissors, pressed it flat, and scanned it. The result appears in Figure 6-36. The image is representative of the worst sorts of photographic wounds, found in both the subject of the photo and the medium.

Figure 6-36.

2. *Click the spot healing brush in the toolbox.* As witnessed in Figure 6-37, the spot healing brush looks like a band-aid with a handful of dots to the left of it (✎). Click the band-aid or press the J key. (If you don't see the dots, press J again.)

3. *Confirm the default settings.* In the options bar, make sure **Type** is set to **Proximity Match**. This setting uses the pixels around the perimeter of a brushstroke to determine how the painted area is healed. (The other option, Create Texture, averages the colors inside the brushstroke. Although this may sound okay, it usually results in an unacceptably blurry patch.) Also confirm that the brush preview on the left side of the options bar has a hard edge. If in doubt, press Shift+▯ a few times to be sure.

Figure 6-37.

4. *Click the lesser mole below the giant mole.* Increase the brush diameter a couple of notches, to 30 pixels. Then click the little mole below the great mole on the left cheek (his right), which appears circled in yellow in Figure 6-38. In one operation, Elements selects the area you clicked, looks for a close equivalent elsewhere in the image, clones from the equivalent area, and blends it with the surrounding image data. Upshot: the mole disappears, as witnessed in the right half of the figure.

Click   Heal

Figure 6-38.

If Elements replaces the unsightly mole with some other unsightly defect, don't fret. Just press Ctrl+Z and try again.

5. *Heal the giant mole.* Now for something more challenging—and less predictable. Drag over the giant mole on the left cheek. As you drag, Elements paints a translucent milky brushstroke. When you release, the program hunts down what it regards as a near match—usually something quite close by—and merges it with the area around the mole.

PEARL OF WISDOM

The good news: No matter what, the mole goes away. The bad news: Elements may very well replace it with something just as bad or worse. To give you an idea of what I mean, **Figure 6-39** shows the area of the mole I painted followed by three different outcomes. (In each case, I undid the previous operation before trying again.) In the final case, I painted over the area multiple times to get it just right. In other words, be prepared to undo a few operations, fuss with the tool, and sigh with exasperation before achieving a credible patch.

Figure 6-39.

At this point you may be wondering, what good is an automated tool if it requires this much effort to make it function properly? My answer: not much. In my none-too-humble opinion, the spot healing brush is a failed solution to a problem that doesn't exist. It was designed to simplify the performance of the standard healing brush, which hails from the full version of Photoshop (version 7, to be exact). But between you and me, the standard healing brush doesn't require simplification. What Adobe regards as the more complex tool, I see as the more capable, more expedient, and ultimately easier to use too. So use it we shall in the remaining steps.

6. *Select the standard healing brush.* Click and hold the band-aid icon in the toolbox and then choose the second tool, which is the standard variety of the healing brush, as in Figure 6-40. Alternatively, you can Alt-click the band-aid icon or press the J key.

7. *Confirm the default settings.* Again consult the options bar and confirm that the default settings are in play. Specifically, check that **Source** is set to **Sampled** and the **Aligned** check box is off. The Sampled setting tells Elements to clone pixels from a spot inside an image (as you'll specify in the next step); turning off Aligned lets you clone repeatedly from that one pristine spot.

If these options are not set properly, you can restore all default settings in one operation by clicking the band-aid (⊘) icon on the far left side of the options bar and choosing the **Reset Tool** command.

---

8. *Set the source point for the healing.* The healing brush uses a source point to identify which portion of the image you want to clone. To set the source point, press the Alt key and click at the spot below the left cheek indicated by the crosshairs in Figure 6-41.

9. *Heal the left part of the scratch.* Check the options bar to make sure the brush diameter is set to 19 pixels. Then do the following:

   • Drag over the top-right fragment of the left scratch, indicated by the yellow brushstroke in the first example in Figure 6-42. (Note that the brushstroke colors in this figure are for illustration purposes only; your brushstrokes will be normal.)

Figure 6-40.

Figure 6-41.

Figure 6-42.

- Press the ⬜ key to reduce the brush diameter to 10 pixels. Then drag along the bottom fragment, as indicated in cyan in the figure.

- In a separate brushstroke, drag along the remaining portion of the left scratch, indicated in purple.

- Finally, paint the area pictured in green.

In each case, I started my brushstroke on the right and dragged to the left. If you're right-handed, this may seem backward. But it's important to follow my lead in this case; if you drag from left to right, you will clone the vertical scratch and mar your image.

Alas, as powerful as the healing brush is, it may produce less than perfect results. For my part, I can clearly see rows of inconsistent pixels running through the old man's cheek and ear (see the spotlighted example in Figure 6-43). Known as *scarring*, these bad seams tell the world that your image has been modified. Fortunately, you can re-heal an area by painting over it once, twice, or as many times as you like.

10. *Move the source and paint short strokes.* Using the healing brush effectively is all about selecting a good source point. The previous source worked well across the forward portion of the cheek, but then we ran into a bad spot. Thankfully, when one source fails, you can switch to another. Sources generally work best when set in an area that closely resembles the *destination* (the area you want to heal).

- To heal inside the ear, for example, Alt-click in the top part of the ear and then drag over the scarred section.

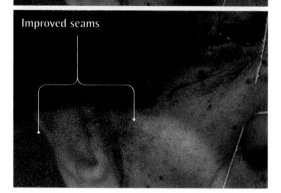

Digital scarring

Improved seams

Figure 6-43.

- To heal in the face, set the source point in the lower area of the cheek, where the flesh is relatively smooth.

- To heal the shadows in the hat, Alt-click somewhere in those shadows. If you get some haloing along the edge of the ear—a function of Elements recruiting ear colors into its healing algorithm—Alt-click along the edge of the ear and paint again.

Keep your brushstrokes short. When using larger brushes, individual clicks can be very effective. I finally arrived at the revised cheek and ear shown in the bottom image in Figure 6-43.

11. *Set a new source.* Now to fix the nearly vertical scratch in the bottom half of the image. Scroll down. Then press Alt and click just to the left of the scratch along the red hat strap, as shown on the left side of Figure 6-44.

12. *Click and Shift-click to draw straight lines.* Set the brush diameter to 20 pixels. Click at the point where the scratch intersects the red strap, indicated by the yellow target in the right half of Figure 6-44. Then press the Shift key and click midway up the scratch, at the point indicated by the cyan target in the figure. Photoshop Elements connects the two points with a straight line of healing, which I've colorized in orange. Finish off the scratch by Shift-clicking just to the left of the nose, indicated by the purple target.

13. *Heal the bottom of the scratch.* That still leaves an inch or so of scratch at the bottom of the image. Once again, click where the strap intersects the scratch (the yellow target in Figure 6-44) to reset the relationship between the source and destination points. Then press Shift and click down and to the left to heal away the scratch.

Figure 6-44.

Figure 6-45.

Telltale white wedge

Healing brush results in pale ghosting

Figure 6-46.

14. *Fix scars and repeated details.* If you look closely enough, you can make out repeated details around the nose and mouth. But the bigger problems occur near the collar and among the whiskers, as highlighted on the left side of Figure 6-45. To fix these, you'll need to source very similar areas—meaning collar-to-neck transitions and whiskers at similar angles—and paint them in using very small brushes, as small as 6 or 7 pixels in diameter. To build up the two horizontal whiskers, I sourced what little remained of one, clicked to double its width, sourced that, clicked again, and so on. It takes a little patience, but in the end, you can build something out of almost nothing (shown in the right half of the figure).

15. *Clean up the remaining scratches.* From here on out, it's more of the same. You can fix the remaining scratches—those in the top and right portions of the image—by setting new source points and using the Shift-clicking technique laid out in Step 12. If you're looking for additional practice, use the healing brush for cleaning up blemishes. For my part, I went ahead and painted over most of the moles and age spots. But I left the wrinkles. Wrinkles add character, and this particular gentleman wears them well.

16. *Select the clone stamp tool.* This photo suffers one final flaw. The bottom-left corner exhibits a telltale wedge of white that lets you know the image has been straightened. You could of course crop the wedge away, as we did in "Using the Straighten and Crop Tools" in Lesson 5. But that would rob the image of a lot of really great detail, and no one wants to do that. The solution: Rebuild the corner with cloning.

PEARL OF   WISDOM

Your inclination might be to start painting away with the healing brush. But as **Figure 6-46** shows, the healing brush is the wrong tool for this particular job. Its specialized pixel-mending technology, which so often leads to flawless patches, fails here because the far edges of the corner are populated by white pixels. The healing brush thus merges with white, resulting in an unrealistic ghosting effect.

It's time to switch to the original cloning tool, the clone stamp tool. Select the clone stamp tool from the toolbox (see Figure 6-47) or press the S key. Much simpler than the healing brush, the clone stamp tool lifts details from the source and paints them into the destination, with no fancy blending in between. Even so, it's sometimes the best tool for the job.

17. *Remove the corner wedge.* You already know how to use the clone stamp tool, because it handles just like the standard healing brush. Here's what I want you to do:

- Press the ⬛ key a few times to raise the brush diameter to 50 pixels.

- The brush preview in the options bar should show a soft brush. Because there is no special blending, the logic is simple—soft brushes ensure soft transitions. If in doubt, make the brush its absolute softest by pressing Shift+⬛ four times.

- Check to see that the Aligned check box is turned on (as by default). This ensures that you continually clone from a relatively common point, so that one brushstroke aligns with another.

- Press the Alt key and click in the middle of the edge of the man's shoulder, as indicated by the crosshairs in the left example of Figure 6-48. Be sure that the center of the crosshairs lands directly on the border between shoulder and sky.

- Start painting at the three-way intersection of shoulder, sky, and wedge, as indicated by the yellow target in the figure. If you want help getting the cursor exactly aligned, press the Caps Lock key to get the precise cursor.

- Paint the edge of the shoulder out to the side of the image, and then paint downward to fill in the rest of the man's garment.

Figure 6-47.

Figure 6-48.

- To fill in the hat and the triangle of sky, you'll need a new source point. Alt-click at the base of the hat, near the left edge, as indicated by the crosshairs in the right example of Figure 6-48.

- Begin painting at the point indicated by the magenta target in the figure. Then paint down into the sky and up into the hat.

When you're finished, you may want to switch back to the healing brush to smooth over any awkward transitions in the sky. The clone stamp tool and the healing brush make a great team: Use the clone stamp tool to make big changes in the image, and then use the healing brush to smooth over the problematic transitions.

Figure 6-49 compares the original version of the image—that is, the one I purposely damaged—to the photograph as it appears after I repaired it inside Photoshop Elements. If you search hard enough, you can find a few scars and flaws. But I suspect most folks would have no idea this image has been tampered with at all—not once but twice.

Figure 6-49.

WHAT DID YOU LEARN?

Match the key concept in the numbered list below with the letter of the phrase that best describes it. Answers appear upside-down at the bottom of the page.

Key Concepts

1. Painting tools
2. Editing tools
3. Healing tools
4. Screen
5. Bracket keys (□ and □)
6. Scatter
7. Dodge tool
8. Burn tool
9. Sponge tool
10. Exposure
11. Cloning
12. Aligned

Descriptions

A. This tool darkens pixels as you paint over them.

B. Available from the options bar, this value controls the intensity of the edits applied with the dodge and burn tools.

C. This clone stamp tool and healing brush option preserves the physical relationship between the source and destination points (the point where you Alt-click and the point where you begin painting, respectively).

D. These are the most convenient way to change the diameter of a brush; adding Shift changes the hardness of the brush.

E. This tool adjusts the saturation of colors, making them either duller or more vivid.

F. Available from the More Options pop-up palette, this slider bar separates the spots of color laid down by the paintbrush.

G. These tools modify (rather than replace) the existing color or luminosity of a pixel; examples include the burn and smudge tools.

H. The process of painting one section of an image onto another.

I. This tool lightens pixels as you paint over them.

J. These tools permit you to create lines and to fill shapes with the foreground color; the brush and pencil tools belong to this category.

K. If you paint on a layer that has this blend mode applied to it, your painting will lighten everything beneath it.

L. These tools permit you to clone photographic details from one portion of an image to another.

Answers

1J, 2G, 3L, 4K, 5D, 6F, 7I, 8A, 9E, 10B, 11H, 12C

FILTERS AND DISTORTIONS

PHOTOSHOP ELEMENTS offers more than a hundred *filters*. Named for the interchangeable camera lenses once commonly used to adjust and tint a scene before it was captured on film, Elements' filters permit you to modify the focus, color, and overall appearance of an image long after it is captured.

But while this group of commands derives its moniker from traditional filters, one bears little if any resemblance to the other. In fact, comparing Elements' filters to *anything* is an exercise in futility. Some filters modify the contrast of neighboring pixels, others trace the contours of a photograph, and still others deform an image by moving pixels to new locations. (See Figure 7-1 for examples.) And that's just some of them. If I had to come up with a definition for filters, I would call them a loosely associated collection of commands—some easy to use,

Original image   Filter→Blur→Motion Blur Filter→Artistic→Colored Pencil Filter→Distort→Wave

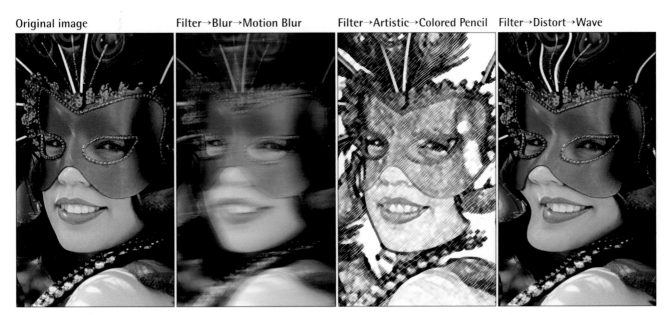

Figure 7-1.

ABOUT THIS LESSON

Project Files

Before beginning the exercises, make sure you've installed the lesson files from the DVD, as explained in Step 5 on page xv of the Preface. This should result in a folder of images called *Lesson Files-PE4 1on1* on your desktop. We'll be working with the files inside the *Lesson 07* subfolder.

In this lesson, I explain how to modify the perceived focus of a photograph, apply effects filters, and apply free-form distortions. You'll learn how to:

- Amplify the edge detail in an image using the Unsharp Mask filter . . . . .page 221

- Use the Radius value and High Pass filter to achieve the best possible sharpening effect. . . . . .page 226

- Experiment with multiple effects filters in the Filter Gallery dialog box. . . . . .page 229

- Change the shape of eyes, jaw lines, and other facial features using the Liquify command . . . . .page 235

Video Lesson 7: Filtering Basics

The Filter menu offers access to just over one hundred commands. Known generically as *filters*, these commands range from extremely practical to wonderfully frivolous. This lesson is about some of the best of the filters, including those that let you sharpen an image, add special effects, and apply complex, transformative distortions.

To get a sense for how these filters work, watch the seventh video lesson on the DVD. Insert the DVD, click **Start**, select **Set 3: Filters, Layers, and Vectors** from the first pop-up menu, and then select **Lesson 7, Filtering Basics** from the second pop-up menu. The 15-minute, 19-second movie contains information about the following commands and shortcuts:

Command or operation	Keyboard equivalent or shortcut
Hide or display the Styles and Effects palette	F7
Hide or show the thumbnails in the Filter Gallery	click ⊗ or ⊗ button
Add effect inside Filter Gallery window	click ⬓ icon in bottom-right corner
Adjust selected value incrementally	↑ or ↓
Adjust selected value by 10x the increment	Shift+↑ or ↓
Duplicate (jump) image to an independent layer	Ctrl+J
Reapply last-applied filter (with different settings)	Ctrl+F (Ctrl+Alt+F)
Change the Opacity setting of the active layer	1, 2, 3, . . . , 0

others quite complex—that apply effects to an image and reside in both the Filter menu and the Filters section of the Styles and Effects palette. Otherwise, filters are as varied as they are abundant.

This lesson makes no attempt to introduce you to all the filters in Photoshop Elements or even a broad cross section of them. Either task would consume an entire book—and not a particularly helpful one at that. For one thing, filters are too unpredictable in approach, implementation, and quality to warrant that sort of attention. More to the point, you can learn most of what you need through experimentation. Choose a command, adjust a few slider bars, apply the filter, and see how it looks.

Filter→Distort→Pinch, Amount: 50%   Undo, Pinch again: −30%

Figure 7-2.

For example, try this: Open a picture of a person's face. Choose Filter→Distort→ Pinch. Set the Amount value to 50 percent and click OK. Admire the goofy effect for a moment or two. Then press Ctrl+Z to undo the filter. Suddenly, the original face (which once looked fine) appears downright swollen. For extra fun, reapply Pinch with a negative value to bulge the face further (see Figure 7-2).

As parlor tricks, filters rate high marks. But as a rule, they tend to be better time-wasters than tools. So for the sake of expediency, I'll spend this lesson homing in on a handful of representative filters that serve a practical or creative purpose. Before you read on, take a few minutes to watch Video Lesson 7, "Filtering Basics" (as explained on the facing page). It'll give you a sense of how filters work and how to make the most of your experimentation.

The Subterfuge of Sharpness

The most useful filters in Photoshop Elements are devoted to the task of adjusting focus. If you think that sounds a bit far-fetched, you're right. After all, the focus of an image is defined when it is formed by the camera lens. The moment you press the shutter release, you accept that focus and store it as a permanent attribute of the photograph. If the photograph is slightly out of focus, it stays out of focus. No post-processing solution can build more clearly defined edges than what the camera actually captured, or fill in missing or murky detail.

So how does Elements adjust focus? It fakes it. Although the program can't reach back into your camera and modify the lens element for a better shot, it can simulate worse or better focus. It can compare neighboring pixels to enhance or impair the edges inside an image. Your eyes think they see a differently focused image, but really they see an exaggerated version of the focus that was already there.

Consider the photos in Figure 7-3. The first is a detail from a high-resolution image that was shot to film and then scanned. The focus is impeccable, but even so, you can make out film grain in the magnified inset. The second and third images show variations imposed by Photoshop Elements. Softening blurs the pixels together; sharpening exaggerates the edges. Softening bears a strong resemblance to what happens when an image is out of focus. Sharpening is a contrast trick that exploits the way our brains perceive definition, particularly with respect to distant or otherwise vague objects. A highly defined edge with sharp transitions between light and dark tells us where an object begins and ends.

This is not to impugn Elements' sharpening capabilities. Photography itself is a trick that simulates reality, specifically geared to the human eye and brain. If Elements' sharpening augments that trick, more power to it. I just want you to know what you're doing. After all, magicians who knows their bag of tricks are better equipped to perform magic.

Real focus | Elements-imposed softening | Elements-imposed sharpening

Figure 7-3.

Sharpening an Image

Of the four filters that reside in the Filters→Sharpen submenu, only one, Unsharp Mask, lets you control the amount of sharpening you apply to an image. As a result, it does everything the three fixed-settings filters do—which isn't much—plus a whole lot more.

Unsharp Mask derives its name from an old and largely abandoned traditional darkroom technique in which a photographic negative was sandwiched together with a blurred, low-contrast positive of itself and printed to photographic paper. This blurred positive (the "unsharp" mask) traced shadows around the dark edges and bright halos around the light edges. As a result, the process accentuated the edges in the original image, resulting in the perception of increased sharpness.

To see how Unsharp Mask's arcane origins translate to the way Elements' sophisticated sharpening functions work, read the upcoming sidebar "Using Blur to Sharpen" on page 226.

Having engaged in some traditional unsharp masking in my youth, I can attest that the Unsharp Mask filter is every bit as capable, far more forgiving, and several times easier to use. Although Unsharp Mask still lacks the power to generate detail that doesn't exist (for that, you'll have to wait for the Magical Fairy Sharpen filter), I regard it as the single most essential filter in Elements' far-flung and often indiscriminate arsenal. The goal of this exercise is to demonstrate how to put this wonderful filter to everyday use.

1. *Open a soft and a blurry image.* Go to the *Lesson 07* folder inside *Lesson Files-PE4 1on1* and you'll find two photos of an unconscious young tabby, *Sleepy kitten.jpg* and *Sloppy kitten.jpg* (see Figure 7-4). I shot both pictures at a nearby farm. The kitten slept in a pen, so I had to position the camera lens between links in the surrounding fence. Unfortunately, my companions included an army of enthusiastic preschoolers who would, without warning, grab the fence and shake it until their mothers made them stop. When I captured the first photo, *Sleepy kitten.jpg*, the fence was in between shakes. I was not so lucky on the second photo—I got smacked.

Figure 7-4.

The upshot: The first image is soft, meaning that it's a little off from its ideal focus, most likely a function of me moving the camera after focusing it. The second image looks blurred because the camera was moving when I took the shot. The kind of blur and degree of blurriness determine how we approach the images and just how much good we can do.

2. *Bring the soft image to the front.* We'll start with the soft, cuddly *Sleepy kitten.jpg*, so click its title bar to make sure the image is active and ready for edits.

3. *Choose the Unsharp Mask command.* Elements gives you two ways to access the Unsharp Mask dialog box. The method you employ is up to you:

   • Choose **Filter→Sharpen→Unsharp Mask**.

   • Display the **Styles and Effects** palette, which appears in the bottom-left in Figure 7-5. Set the first pop-up menu in the palette to **Filters**. Then scroll to the bottom of the list and double-click the item labeled **Unsharp Mask**.

Figure 7-5.

4. *Turn on the Preview check box.* Pictured in Figure 7-5, the **Unsharp Mask** dialog box supports all the previewing options that I demonstrated in Video Lesson 7. It includes a cropped preview of the effect inside the dialog box. When the **Preview** check box is on, Elements applies the effect in real time to the larger image window as well.

5. *Click in the image window.* Click the cat's forward-facing paw to center the preview inside the dialog box. You want to center on some detail that you'd like to bring into sharper focus. Drag inside the preview box to further adjust the view.

6. *Set the views to different zoom ratios.* Set the image window to the 100 percent view size and the preview to 50 percent, or vice versa. This way, you have two views into the results of your changes.

Why 100 and 50 percent? Because the first shows you every pixel in the image, and the other more closely represents the image as it appears when printed (which packs more pixels into a smaller space). Also worth noting, 50 percent is an interpolated zoom, meaning that Elements properly smooths over pixel transitions. By comparison, odd zooms such as 67 and 33 percent are jagged and misleading.

7. *Raise the value.* Raise the **Amount** value to 200 percent. This is a temporary value that merely exaggerates the effect and permits us to see what we're doing.

8. *Specify a Radius value of 2.5 pixels.* Even though **Radius** is the second value, I recommend you start with it because it's the hinge pin of the sharpening operation. Unsharp Mask simulates sharper edges by drawing halos around the edges (see "Using Blur to Sharpen," page 226). The Radius value defines the thickness of those halos. Thin halos result in a precise edge; thick halos result in a more generalized high-contrast effect. Figure 7-6 shows some examples.

For everyday sharpening, the best Radius value is the one you can barely see. This value varies depending on how your final image will be viewed:

- If you intend to display the image on-screen (say, for a Web page), enter a very small value, such as 0.5 pixel.

Figure 7-6.

- For medium-resolution printing, a Radius of 1.0 to 2.0 pixels tends to work best.

- For high-resolution printing, a Radius of 2.0 or higher results in sharp edges.

The examples in Figure 7-6 were printed at 280 pixels per inch, so the 2.5-pixel Radius delivers the best edges. A smaller Radius value most likely looks better on your screen, but for now, I'd like you to pretend you're going to print the image, so enter 2.5.

Use the ↑ and ↓ keys to nudge the value by its smallest increment, 0.1 in the case of Radius, 1 in the case of Amount and Threshold. Add Shift to nudge 10 times that increment.

---

9. *Lower the Amount value to 100 percent.* The **Amount** value controls the degree to which the image gets sharpened. Higher Amount values result in more crisply defined edges. The effects of the Amount value become more pronounced at higher Radius values as well. So where 200 percent may look dandy with a Radius of 1 pixel, the image may appear jagged and noisy at a Radius of 2.5. An image set to too high an Amount value is said to be *oversharpened*, as is presently the case for our tabby.

Press Shift+Tab to highlight the Amount value. Then press Shift+↓ a few times in a row to nudge the value down in increments of 10 percent. Figure 7-7 shows a few examples. For my money, the last setting (100 percent) is the best fit.

Figure 7-7.

10. *Leave the Threshold value set to 0.* The final value, **Threshold**, decides whether or not neighboring pixels are factored into the sharpening equation. Threshold is measured in luminosity levels. The default, 0, means that neighboring pixels have to be at least 0 levels different from each other to be considered a potential edge. In other words, all pixels are sharpened uniformly. Higher Threshold values rule out more and more pixels. For those who enjoy symmetry in their software, the Threshold value measures colors just like the magic wand's Tolerance setting (see Step 5, page 122). Only instead of including pixels, as Tolerance does, Threshold rules them out.

In theory, the Threshold value helps avoid sharpening grain and other artifacts. In practice, it just doesn't work. Because Threshold is an on or off proposition—pixels get sharpened or they don't—any value large enough to produce a visible effect does as much to create grain as defeat it. For example, a Threshold of 40 calls out random flecks in the kitten's fur, magnified to 100 and 200 percent in **Figure 7-8**. These awful flecks are why I prefer to leave this value set to 0 under all circumstances.

11. *Click the OK button.* Confirm that your values match those in Figure 7-9. Turn on and off the **Preview** check box to see how far you've come. And then click **OK** to apply the filter.

12. *Bring the blurry image to the front.* That pretty well fixes the first photograph. Now what can we do about the second? Well, sad to say, not a whole lot. To see for yourself, bring the *Sloppy kitten.jpg* image up front by clicking its title bar or choosing its name from the bottom of the **Window** menu.

13. *Again display the Unsharp Mask dialog box.* But don't choose Filter→Sharpen→Unsharp Mask. Instead, click the **Filter** menu and notice that the first command now reads Unsharp Mask, as in Figure 7-10. As I explained in Video Lesson 7, "Filtering Basics" (see page 218), choosing this command would reapply the filter with the same settings as before. However, don't do that. Instead, press and hold the Alt key and then choose **Filter→Unsharp Mask**. Or better yet, press the keyboard shortcut Ctrl+Alt+F. Elements revisits the dialog box, permitting you to apply the filter with different settings.

Figure 7-8.

14. *Raise the Amount value.* This image requires more sharpening than the first one. So click **Amount** in the **Unsharp Mask** dialog box and then press Shift+↑ several times to increase the value in 10 percent increments. This adds to the sharpness of the image, but it also brings out more of the diagonal lines of noise associated with the motion blur, as shown in Figure 7-11 on page 228.

Figure 7-9.

Figure 7-10.

Using Blur to Sharpen

The "unsharp" in Unsharp Mask is a function of the softly tapering halo applied by the Radius value. Understand this and you can master the art of focus in Photoshop Elements.

Consider the line art in the figure below. The top-left example features dark lines against a light background. The other three images are sharpened with increasingly higher Radius values. (Throughout, the Amount value is set to 200 percent.) In each case, the Unsharp Mask filter traces the dark areas inside the lines (the brown areas) with a blurry dark halo and the light areas outside the lines (the green areas) with a blurry light halo. The thickness of these halos conforms to the Radius value. So all Unsharp Mask does is increase the contrast by tracing halos around edges.

Given that the Radius value is all about blurring, it's no surprise that this option also appears in the Gaussian Blur dialog box (Filter→Blur→Gaussian Blur), where it once again generates halos around edges. In fact, if we were to trace the lineage of these filters, we would find that Gaussian Blur is Unsharp Mask's grandparent. The missing family member in between is an obscure command called High Pass.

Why should you care? Because Unsharp Mask's parent, High Pass, is a more flexible sharpening agent than its progeny.

Try this: Go ahead and open *Sleepy kitten.jpg*. (If it's still open from the "Sharpening an Image" exercise, choose Edit→Revert to revert the image to its original appearance.) Now press Ctrl+J to copy the image to an independent layer. Next, choose Filter→Other→High Pass. Pictured below, the High Pass dialog box contains a single option, Radius. Change this value to 2.5 pixels, the same Radius you applied in the exercise using Unsharp Mask. Then click OK.

Looks like a big mess of gray, right? But there are tenuous edges in there. To bring them out, press Ctrl+L or choose Enhance→Adjust Lighting→Levels to display the Levels dialog box. Change the first and third Input Levels values to 75 and 180, respectively, as in the figure below. Then click OK.

Still looks terrible. But what you're looking at are the very same light and dark halos that Unsharp Mask creates. To apply those halos to the original photograph, go to the Layers palette and choose Overlay from the top-left pop-up menu. Just like that, Photoshop Elements drops out the grays, blends in the edges, and makes it all better, as shown below. The result is almost exactly what you'd get if you applied Unsharp Mask with a Radius of 2.5 and an Amount of 200 percent. (In other words, the current High Pass layer is twice as strong as the equivalent Unsharp Mask.) This means that the photograph is oversharpened just as it was at the outset of Step 9 on page 224. To match the more pleasing Amount value of 100 percent that we eventually settled on in the exercise, reduce the layer's Opacity setting to 50 percent.

Why go through all this just to get the same effect we achieved in the exercise? Because now you have a floating layer of sharpness whose Amount you can change at any time just by modifying the layer's Opacity setting. This means you can change your mind well into the future, as opposed to being locked into the static result of Unsharp Mask. Sure, it's an unusual approach, and it takes a bit of experience to get it down pat. But the additional flexibility you gain is well worth the effort.

Figure 7-11.

Figure 7-12.

Figure 7-13.

For my money, an Amount of 200 percent gets the image as close to focused as we can reasonably expect. What about raising the Radius value? Doesn't really help. Where Unsharp Mask is concerned, this is as good as it gets.

15. *Cancel out of the dialog box.* But let's say this isn't good enough. Let's say this is your *only* picture of this cute little kitten sleeping on a pumpkin and you're bound and determined to make it the best you possibly can. In that case, press the Esc key and kiss Unsharp Mask goodbye. Turns out, there is another way.

16. *Duplicate the image to a new layer.* Press Ctrl+J to jump the image to a new layer.

17. *Choose the Emboss command.* Unsharp Mask has many relatives. For example, it has a close cousin that's adept at removing motion blur (though you wouldn't know it to look at it). To access this virtuous cousin, choose **Filter→Stylize→Emboss.**

18. *Adjust the settings and apply the filter.* As you'll see in the preview, the Emboss command etches an image in gray relief. It looks a bit ugly and anything but sharp. But suspend disbelief and imagine the grays dropping away. Then apply these settings:

   • Your first task is to match the angle of the motion blur inherent in the image. I found that an **Angle** value of 20 degrees came closest.

   • **Height** is analogous to the Unsharp Mask command's Radius value. Set it to 6 pixels.

   • **Amount** is Amount. Make it 200 percent.

   Click the **OK** button. The result appears in Figure 7-12. Looks awful. But as with the High Pass filter (see page 226), all we care about is how the edges look. And the edges look great.

19. *Set the blend mode to Overlay.* Go to the **Layers** palette and select **Overlay** from the first pop-up menu. Or press Shift+Alt+O. The grays drop away, leaving just the directional edges. Press the Esc key and then press 8 to reduce the **Opacity** value to 80 percent. The result appears in Figure 7-13.

To get a feel for the difference, turn on and off the ☻ in front of **Layer 1** in the Layers palette. Not satisfied? Then grab your camera, go back to that farm, and try your best to talk the kitten into sleeping on that pumpkin just one more time. And be quick about it because, no joke, those preschoolers are murder.

Playing with the Filter Gallery

The Filter Gallery is a cluster of special effects filters that you can mix and match inside a single dialog box before applying them. Fewer than half of the hundred or so filters in Elements qualify for inclusion in the Filter Gallery. Many of these effects are *media filters*, meaning they try to make your digital photos look like drawings and paintings created with traditional tools such as chalk, charcoal, or watercolor. But the best thing about the Filter Gallery is that it lets you apply multiple filters in sequence, and even juggle the order in which the filters are applied, all from a central location. The order in which you apply filters can make a big difference in the final result, and with the Filter Gallery, you can experiment until you're satisfied.

In this exercise, you're going to work on another orange kitty cat—this one a ferocious Bengal tiger. You'll maneuver through the Filter Gallery and combine its media filters to construct a unique and foreboding effect.

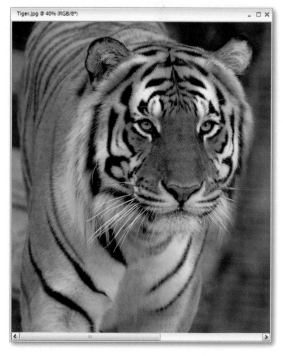

Figure 7-14.

1. *Open an image.* Go to the *Lesson 07* folder inside *Lesson Files-PE4 1on1* and open the file called *Tiger.jpg*, an iStockphoto image captured by Kitch Bain. Figure 7-14 shows a screen shot of the majestic feline.

2. *Prepare the interface.* Many of the filters in the Filter Gallery draw on the active foreground and background colors to work their magic. Press the D key to set the former to black and the latter to white. If your colors were previously set to something other than black and white, you'll see the change at the bottom of the toolbox.

3. *Open the Filter Gallery.* There are lots of ways to open the Filter Gallery. For example, you can choose any of the 47 filters that are members of the Gallery from either the Filter menu or the Styles and Effects palette. But the most straightforward method is to invoke the command with clear intent: Choose **Filter→Filter Gallery** to display a window like the one in Figure 7-15 on the next page.

Figure 7-15.

Figure 7-16.

4. *Zoom in on the image.* The left side
of the Filter Gallery features a generous
image preview that you can navigate
by clicking the ⊟ or ⊞ buttons in the
lower-left corner or by using familiar
keyboard equivalents.

Ctrl-click in the preview to zoom in; Alt-
click to zoom out. Alternatively, you can
press Ctrl+⊡ or Ctrl+⊟. To scroll the
image, just drag inside it.

Make sure the zoom ratio is set to 100
percent. Then drag the image so you
can see some portion of the tiger's face,
as in Figure 7-15.

5. *Tuck away the thumbnails.* The middle section of the Filter Gallery houses
filter thumbnails, arranged in folders
that correspond to the submenus found
in the Filter menu and the Styles and
Effects palette. To give yourself more
room to preview your edits, collapse
this section by clicking the ⊛ button
to the left of the OK button.

6. *Apply a filter.* We want to begin by applying an etched-line effect to the tiger.
And the best way to start things off is
with a filter that traces edges. Click the
⊡ icon in the lower-right corner of the
window to create the first filter in the
stack. Click the pop-up menu below
the Cancel button—which provides
access to all the Filter Gallery effects—
and choose the **Glowing Edges** filter.
You should see light edges against a
black background, as in Figure 7-16.

7. *Add a second filter.* Glowing Edges does a fine job of finding edges, but the result is more intricate than what I have in mind. I want to add another filter to simplify the edges. And that filter is Cutout. Problem is, if I were to select Cutout from the pop-up menu, I'd replace the Glowing Edges filter. I want to combine the effects of the two filters, so I need to add a filter to the stack. Click the ▣ icon at the bottom of the dialog box to add a new effect.

8. *Switch to the Cutout filter.* By default, the Filter Gallery adds another layer of Glowing Edges. Obviously, we don't need that. Click **Glowing Edges** in the pop-up menu up top and choose the **Cutout** filter in its place. The result is a dim series of chiselled polygons—interesting, I suppose, but not what I'm looking for. I want the Cutout filter to simplify the behavior of the Glowing Edges filter, so I need to reverse the order of the commands.

9. *Reorder the filters.* To hide the effects of a filter, click the ◉ icon beside its name in the lower-right region of the dialog box. For example, if you click the ◉ in front of Glowing Edges, you can observe the effect of the Cutout filter on its own. Cutout reduces an image to a few distinct fields of color, making it look like the image is clipped from construction paper. If this filter is to simplify the effects of Glowing Edges, it needs to be behind it. So turn the **Glowing Edges** filter back on. And then drag the word **Cutout** below Glowing Edges. When you see a heavy horizontal line below Glowing Edges, release your mouse button. Figure 7-17 shows the result.

Figure 7-17.

10. *Add a third filter.* Click the ▣ icon again to add another filter to the top of the stack, this time a copy of Cutout. Click **Cutout** in the pop-up menu and swap it for **Plaster**. The Filter Gallery converts the colors to grayscale and carves the lines into deep grooves against the black background. Now we're talking.

Figure 7-18.

11. *Adjust the filter settings.* Now that we have the correct filters in place—and in the desired order, no less—we just need to do a little noodling with the settings:

- Select the **Cutout** filter at the bottom of the stack to display its settings. The line effect is currently a little busy, so raise the **Edge Simplicity** value to 5 to have the filter ignore some of the more complex details.

- The result is still too complex, so let's take a more drastic plan of attack: Shift+Tab to select the **Number of Levels** value and press ↓ to lower the value to 3.

- Click the **Glowing Edges** item in the middle of the filter stack. I think the edges could be thicker in general, so raise the **Edge Brightness** value to 8. This gives the Plaster filter a better opportunity to carve into the edges.

We could spend all day goofing around with these settings. But let's not. Click **OK** to close the Filter Gallery and accept your changes. Figure 7-18 shows the etched-line effect.

12. *Undo and layer.* Let's say that I'm happy with the chiselled appearance of the image. But I'd like to retrieve the rich array of colors from the original. To do that, I need to restore my original image and add a layer. But if I undo the current effect, I lose it, right? Not quite. Here's what I want you to do:

- Click the ↺ icon in the shortcuts bar or press Ctrl+Z to undo the effects of the Filter Gallery.

- Press Ctrl+J to create a duplicate of the Background layer named Layer 1.

- Click the **Background** layer in the **Layers** palette or press Alt+□ to make the rear version of the tiger active.

Go to the **Filter** menu and notice that it now begins with two variations of the Filter Gallery command, the second with an ellipse (...) and the first without. The first command applies the most recent filter—or in our case, filters—subject to the same settings. The second one brings up the Filter Gallery dialog box so you can apply new settings.

13. *Reapply the three filters.* Choose the first **Filter→Filter Gallery** or press Ctrl+F to reapply the Cutout, Glowing Edges, and Plaster filters to the Background layer. You won't see any changes in the image window because Layer 1 is covering them. But you can see the filter combo applied to the Background thumbnail in the Layers palette. In other words, take heart—the filters were applied and everything is going according to plan.

14. *Apply a new filter.* Click **Layer 1** in the Layers palette or press Alt+☐ to make the top layer active. Then choose the second **Filter→Filter Gallery**, or press the shortcut for invoking the last-used filter with new settings, Ctrl+Alt+F. Once again, Photoshop Elements displays the **Filter Gallery** dialog box. Most likely, you'll see the same trio of filters—Cutout, Glowing Edges, and Plaster—in the stack at the bottom. If so, click the trash can icon in the bottom-right corner of the dialog box twice in a row to delete the Plaster and Glowing Edges filters. You should be left with a single application of Cutout.

Figure 7-19.

The Filter Gallery offers another technique that lets you wipe out all filters in one fell swoop. Hold down the Ctrl key and notice that the Cancel button changes to Default. With Ctrl still down, click that button. Elements removes all the filters and leaves you with nothing. Then click the ☐ icon in the bottom-right corner of the dialog box to add a brand-new filter to the stack.

---

15. *Apply the Palette Knife filter.* Click the pop-up menu below the Cancel button and choose the **Palette Knife** filter. Palette Knife tries to simulate the blotchy effect of oil paint applied to canvas with a knife, but a close inspection reveals that it leaves jagged edges. So raise the **Softness** slider all the way up to 10, as in Figure 7-19.

16. *Add one last filter.* Click the ☐ icon to add another filter to the stack. The Filter Gallery creates a copy of the Palette Knife filter. Click the pop-up menu at the top of the dialog box and choose the **Craquelure** filter instead. Named for the cracking that occurs in very old paintings (and which is often imitated

Figure 7-20.

by art forgers such as my Uncle Zeke to simulate age), Craquelure adds a cracked plaster surface to the face of the tiger. The problem is, the cracks go a little too deep. To soften things up a bit, reduce the **Crack Depth** value to 2. Then boost the **Crack Brightness** to 10 to take off that last bit of edge, as in Figure 7-20.

17. *Click the OK button.* Photoshop Elements applies the Palette Knife and Craquelure filters to Layer 1.

18. *Apply a blend mode.* We have an etched-line effect on one layer and a digital fresco effect on another. All that's left is to combine the two. See that option in the top-left corner of the **Layers** palette that says **Normal**? Click it to bring up a list of *blend modes* that let you mix the active layer with the ones below it using a variety of mathematical calculations. Choose the **Screen** option, which marries the painted tiger on Layer 1 with the black areas of the Background layer below. The result is a kind of deliciously retro textile art riddled with deeply etched seams, suitable for printing and display under black light. As witnessed in Figure 7-21, this particular cat looks infinitely more ominous after his trip through the Filter Gallery.

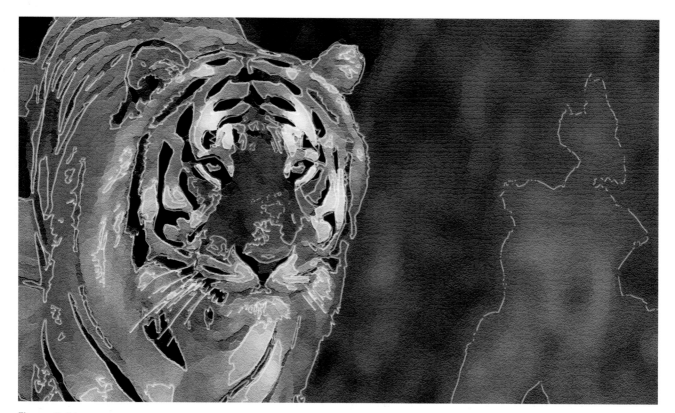

Figure 7-21.

Applying Free-Form Distortions

If Unsharp Mask is the most practical filter and Filter Gallery is the most fun, the award for the most powerful filter in Photoshop Elements goes to Liquify. Less a filter, it's more an independent program that happens to run in the Editor workspace. Liquify lets you distort an image by painting inside it using a collection of tools. One tool stretches pixels, another twists them into a spiral, and a third pinches them. These and other tools make Liquify ideally suited to cosmetic surgery. Whether you want to tuck a tummy, slim a limb, or nip a nose, Liquify gives you everything you need to get the job done.

In this exercise, we'll do something more radical. We'll take a photo of my mild-mannered, 2-year-old Sammy and morph him into a teenage superhero, complete with square chin, rugged jaw, cocky sneer, and eyes bright with righteous anger. In all Gotham City, only one filter can aid us in this goal, and that filter is Liquify.

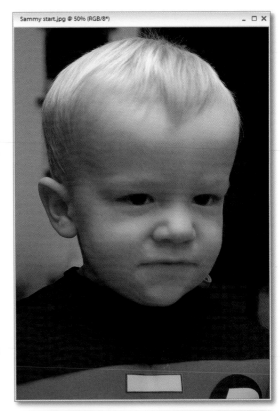

PEARL OF WISDOM

Be forewarned: Unlike other exercises, in which my instructions are concrete and easy to replicate, these next steps are subject to more interpretation. I'll be asking you to paint—not inside lines, as in Lesson 6, but free-form. You don't necessarily need heaps of artistic talent, but a little doesn't hurt. And regardless of how talented you are, your results and mine will be different. Don't sweat it. Even when all you're doing is making a big mess, this is one entertaining filter. In fact, I have never once demonstrated the Liquify filter—whether to a few family members or an audience of 500 professionals—that it doesn't inspire giddy laughter. So don't be frustrated; be amused.

1. *Open an image that you want to distort.* After capturing the very cute picture of Sammy dressed up for Halloween that appears at the top of Figure 7-22, it struck me that it might be fun to make him appear every bit the caped crusader that his outfit suggests. A couple of hours of dodging, burning, sponging, healing, and finally painting the snapshot eventually produced the bottom image in the figure. Although it possesses an undeniably graphic, surreal quality, my fair-haired boy continues to exude cuteness, the kind one associates less with a guardian angel and more with an excitable cherub. Few superheroes list "cute" or "cherubic" on their resumés, and so these attributes, however laudable, must be eradicated. To join me in my quest to convert child into champion, open the image titled *Gold hero.jpg*, included in the *Lesson 07* folder inside *Lesson Files-PE4 1on1*.

Figure 7-22.

2. *Choose the Liquify command.* Go to the **Filter** menu and choose **Distort→Liquify**. Photoshop Elements displays the **Liquify** window, which appears in Figure 7-23. This full-fledged, free-form distortion utility sports 11 tools on its left edge and several options on the right. The rest of the window is devoted to a comprehensive, accurate view of the image itself.

The same navigation techniques that work outside the Liquify window work inside it as well. You can zoom in or out by pressing Ctrl+⊡ or Ctrl+⊟, respectively. Press the spacebar and drag to pan the image.

Figure 7-23.

3. *Select the warp tool.* Click the topmost tool in the Liquify window or press the W key to select the warp tool, which lets you stretch or squish details in an image by dragging them. Of all Liquify's tools, this one is the most consistently useful.

4. *Increase the Brush Size value to 100 pixels.* Select the **Brush Size** value (or press Alt+S) and enter 100 in its stead.

5. *Arch the eyebrows.* Using the warp tool, drag the eyebrows to make them appear arched, as in Figure 7-24. This is an exaggerated effect, so if you try to pull it off in one or two brushstrokes, you'll smear the colors and wind up with digital stretch marks. Here's how to achieve more photo-realistic results:

   - Keep your strokes very short—just a few pixels at a time.

   - Because you're keeping your brushstroke short, you'll need a lot of them. I reckon I laid down about 20 strokes in all.

   - Drag *on* the detail you want to move. For example, to move an eyebrow, center your brush cursor on the eyebrow and then drag. If you drag next to the eyebrow (which, though it may sound weird, is the more natural tendency), you'll pinch the eyebrow and slim it down to a thin line.

Warp tool (W)

Adjust brush size

Drag directly on eyebrows

Figure 7-24.

For the present, be careful to avoid painting the eyes. We'll edit them in the next steps with a different tool.

6. *Switch to the pucker tool.* Click the fifth tool down or press the P key. This selects the pucker tool, which lets you pinch portions of an image, in much the same way as the Pinch filter, which I mentioned at the beginning of this lesson (see Figure 7-2 on page 219).

7. *Reduce the eyes.* Toddlers have lots of physical characteristics that distinguish them from adults. They're short, they have pudgy cheeks, and their skin is really smooth except for occasional patches of dried snot and spaghetti sauce. But if I had to choose their most unique feature, it'd be their eyes. Kids have adult-sized eyeballs packed inside pint-sized heads, which makes their eyes look enormous. Outside Japan, superheroes don't have big old baby eyes, and so Sammy's must be reduced.

   Raise the **Brush Size** value to 200 pixels. Then click each of Sammy's eyes. Click quickly and do not drag. If one click doesn't do the trick, click again. The finished eyes should look like those shown in Figure 7-25 on the facing page.

8. *Switch to the twirl clockwise tool.* To give my Sam a menacing appearance—so that he can more easily intimidate criminals and thwart their evil plans—I want to slant his eyes very slightly. Click the third tool on the left side of the window or press the R key to select the twirl clockwise tool.

9. *Slant the eyes.* Center the brush cursor on the iris of the left eye (his right). Then click. Again, click briefly; do not hold or drag. The eye spins a degree or two clockwise, raising the outside edge and lowering the inside.

Pucker tool (P) ———

——— Increase brush size

——— Click each eye

Figure 7-25.

Twirl clockwise (R) ———

Click the first eye ———

——— Alt-click second eye

Figure 7-26.

10. *Return to the warp tool.* I imagine Sammy to be the sort of edgy, cynical, postmodern superhero who openly sneers at his archenemies and lesser opponents. And there's no better tool for constructing sneers than the warp tool. Get it now by pressing the W key.

11. *Work the nose and mouth into a sneer.* Reduce the **Brush Size** to 120 pixels. Then drag downward on the nose, up on the nostrils, up on the left side of the mouth, and down on the right. You'll also want to drag that crease that connects the nose and mouth on the left side of the image. The results of my 30 or so brushstrokes appear in Figure 7-27.

12. *Switch to the bloat tool.* Okay, we've managed to outfit Sam with smaller eyes, arching eyebrows, and a tough-guy sneer. But he's still a little kid. It's time to bulk him out. Click the sixth tool on the left side of the window or press the B key to select the bloat tool.

13. *Bloat the chin and jaw.* Start by increasing the **Brush Size** value to 400 pixels. Then test the waters by clicking and holding for a brief moment on Sammy's chin. Also click a few times along the left and right sides of the jaw. I want you to really exaggerate the jaw line (see Figure 7-28), so feel free to hold the mouse button down for, say, a half second or so at a time. However, as when using the pinch and twirl tools, I recommend you refrain from dragging. (In other words, hold the mouse button down but keep the mouse still.)

14. *Pucker the forehead.* In real life, Sammy doesn't have much hair, but he has an ample forehead. That gives him a sort of Poindexter look that superheroes shun. Best way to get rid of it? Pinch it down to a more reasonable size. Which tool to use? You can use the one you already have, the bloat tool.

Center your brush cursor somewhere along the hairline. Then press the Alt key and click for a half second or more. Pressing Alt reverses the behavior of the tool, letting you swell with the pucker tool or, in our case, pinch with the bloat tool.

Continue to Alt-click along the hairline until you get an effect similar to the one pictured in Figure 7-28. For the best results, move the mouse at least slightly *between* (not during) clicks. This varies the center of the distortion and keeps your pinches from resulting in sharp points of converging color.

Warp tool (W) —

Reduce brush size

Drag on nose, mouth, and other details

Figure 7-27.

Bloat tool (B) —

Increase brush size

Click in chin and jaw

Alt-click in forehead

Figure 7-28.

15. *Apply your finishing touches.* Continue distorting my son's face as you see fit. (Naturally, I rely on you to apply your adjustments in good taste—he is my beloved progeny, after all.) For my part, I smoothed out the eyebrows, lifted the cheeks, tugged down the hairline, lifted the shoulders, and increased the size of the chest, all using the warp tool. When you arrive at an effect you like, click the **OK** button to accept your changes and return to the Standard Edit mode. Just for the sheer joy of it, Figure 7-29 shows my final effect incorporated into an elaborate poster treatment. Note that I used Image→Resize→Image Size to stretch the image vertically. This gives the head a less squat appearance. I also dodged and burned the chin to lend it more volume.

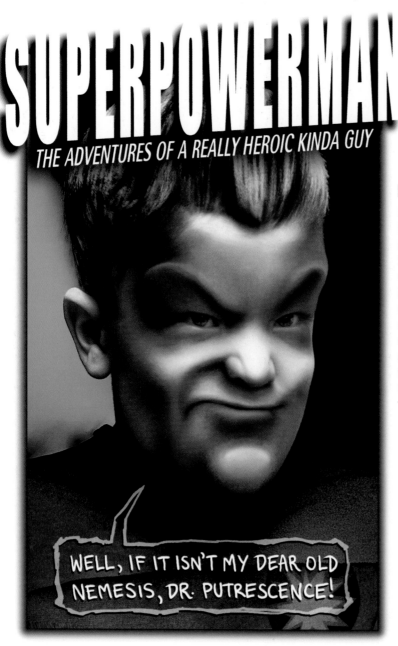

Figure 7-29.

WHAT DID YOU LEARN?

Match the key concept in the numbered list below with the letter
of the phrase that best describes it. Answers appear upside-down
at the bottom of the page.

Key Concepts

1. Focus
2. Filters
3. Edge
4. Unsharp Mask
5. Radius
6. Threshold
7. High Pass
8. Media filters
9. Blend modes
10. Warp tool
11. Pucker tool
12. Bloat tool

Descriptions

A. The most consistently useful of the Liquify functions, this lets you stretch or squish details in an image by dragging them.

B. This Liquify function lets you pinch selective portions of an image.

C. These are designed to make your digital photos look like drawings and paintings created with traditional tools.

D. A filter named for a traditional technique in which a photographic negative is combined with a blurred version of itself.

E. Unsharp Mask mimics the functionality of this filter by retaining areas of high contrast and sending low-contrast areas to gray.

F. Bulging and enlarging are the specialities of this function, available exclusively inside the Liquify dialog box.

G. Named for camera lenses once commonly used to adjust and tint a scene before it was captured on film, these permit you to modify the focus, color, and overall appearance of an image after it is captured.

H. The clarity of the image formed by the lens element and captured by the camera.

I. A ridge formed by areas of extreme contrast between adjacent pixels.

J. These let you mix the colors in the active layer with those in the layers beneath it using a variety of mathematical calculations.

K. This Unsharp Mask option decides whether or not neighboring pixels are factored into the sharpening equation, and is best left set to 0.

L. The thickness of the effect applied by a filter, often expressed as a softly tapering halo.

Answers

1H, 2G, 3I, 4D, 5L, 6K, 7E, 8C, 9J, 10A, 11B, 12F

BUILDING LAYERED COMPOSITIONS

EVERY IMAGE begins life as a few panes of primary color—most commonly, one each for red, green, and blue—fused into a single, continuous image (see Figure 8-1). Whether it comes from the least expensive digital camera or the most expensive drum scanner, the image exists entirely on one layer. One and only one full-color value exists for every pixel, and there is no such thing as transparency. Such an image is said to be *flat*.

But as soon as you begin combining images, you add layers. Each layer serves as an independent image, which you can stack, transform, or blend with other layers.

A document that contains two or more layers is called a *layered composition*. There's no need to wait until a specific point in the editing cycle to build such a composition. You can add layers to a document whenever you like, as we have several times over the course of the book so far. But layers have a way of becoming even more useful after some of the basic editing work is out of the way. That's why I've waited until now to show you the many ways to create and manage layers in Photoshop Elements.

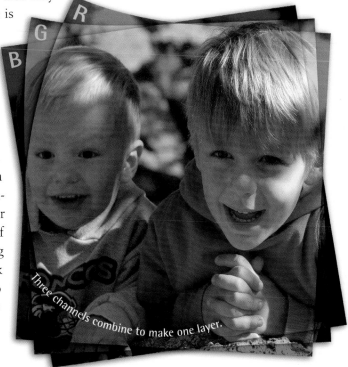

Figure 8-1.

The Benefits and Penalties of Layers

Photoshop Elements' reliance on layers makes for an exceedingly flexible (if sometimes confusing) working environment. As long as an image remains on a layer, you can move or edit it independently of other layers in the composition. Moreover, you can create relationships between neighboring layers using a wide variety of blending options,

ABOUT THIS LESSON

Project Files

Before beginning the exercises, make sure you've installed the lesson files from the DVD, as explained in Step 5 on page xv of the Preface. This should result in a folder of images called *Lesson Files-PE4 1on1* on your desktop. We'll be working with the files inside the *Lesson 08* subfolder.

In this lesson, we'll explore the many facets of building a layered composition in Photoshop Elements, from creation to navigation, from stroking to stacking order, from free-form transformations to four-point distortions, from applying blend modes to erasing backgrounds. You'll learn how to:

Video Lesson 8: Layers at Work

Layers are nothing more than independent images that you can set to interact with each other from the Layers palette. But what a difference they make. By relegating image elements and effects to independent layers, you give yourself the flexibility to adjust your artwork well into the future.

To get a sense of how layers work in Elements, watch the eighth video lesson on the DVD. To watch the video, insert the DVD, click **Start**, select **Set 3: Filters, Layers, and Vectors** from the first pop-up menu, and then select **Lesson 8, Layers at Work** from the second pop-up menu. The movie lasts 15 minutes and 59 seconds, during which time you'll learn about the following operations and shortcuts:

Operation	Keyboard equivalent or shortcut
Show or hide Layers palette	F11
Select move tool	V (or press Ctrl to access temporarily)
Exit transformation mode	Esc
Cut selection to independent layer	Ctrl+Shift+J
Deactivate highlighted option (such as blend mode)	Esc
Group active layer with layer below it	Ctrl+G
Create and name new layer	Ctrl+Shift+N

all of which work without changing the contents of the layers in the slightest.

But layers come at a price. Because they are actually independent images, each layer consumes space both in memory and on your hard drive. Consider the following example:

- I start with the image on the right, which measures 2100 by 2100 pixels, or 7 by 7 inches at 300 pixels per inch (see Figure 8-2). Each pixel takes up 3 bytes of data. The result is a total of 4.41 million pixels, which add up to 12.6MB in memory. Because the image is flat, I can save it to the JPEG format, which compresses the file down to 3.7MB at the highest quality setting.

- I introduce another image that measures the very same 2100 by 2100 pixels. Photoshop Elements puts the image on its own layer. I apply the Multiply blend mode to get the effect shown in Figure 8-3. The image size doubles to 25.2MB in memory. I can no longer save the layered composition in the JPEG format because JPEG doesn't permit layers. Thus, I save it in Photoshop's native PSD format instead. Although PSD is versatile, it lacks JPEG's exceptional compression capabilities, so the file on disk balloons to 25.7MB.

- I then add a series of image and text layers to fill out the composition, as pictured in Figure 8-4 on the next page. Because the layers are smaller, and the text layers are defined as more efficient vectors (see Lesson 9, "Text and Shapes"), the size of the image grows only moderately in memory (34.4MB) and barely at all on disk (26.2MB).

So as you add layers, your composition gets bigger. And as your composition gets bigger, Photoshop Elements requires more space in memory and on disk to manage the file. Generally speaking, you can let Elements worry about these sorts of nitty-gritty details. But bear in mind that no matter how sophisticated your computer, its memory and hard disk are finite. And if the memory or (worse) the hard disk fills up, your ability to edit your marvelous multilayer creations may come to a skidding halt.

Flat image, 2100 × 2100 pixels
12.6MB in memory, 3.7MB on disk (saved in JPEG format, Quality 12)

Figure 8-2.

Second layer, full 2100 × 2100 pixels
25.2MB in memory, 25.7MB on disk (saved in native PSD format)

Figure 8-3.

How to Manage Layers

Fortunately, a few precautions are all it takes to keep layered compositions on a diet and Photoshop Elements running in top form:

- First, don't let your hard disk get anywhere close to full. I recommend keeping at least 1GB available at all times, and more than that is always welcome. (Consult your computer's documentation to find out how to check this—or just hope and pray you're okay, like everyone else does.)

- Back up your Elements projects regularly to CD, DVD, or some other storage medium (which you can do by choosing File→Backup inside the Organizer workspace). This not only preserves your images but also permits you to delete files from your hard disk if you start running out of room.

- As you work in Photoshop Elements, you can keep an eye on the size of your image in memory by observing the document size values in the bottom-left corner of the image window. Click the ▶ arrow at the bottom of the window and choose Document Sizes. The value before the slash tells you the size of the image if flat; the value after the slash tells you the size of the composition with layers.

- You can reduce the size of an image on disk by *merging* two layers into one by choosing Layer→Merge Down or pressing Ctrl+E.

- To merge all layers and return to a flat image, choose Layer→Flatten Image. But be aware that this is a radical step. I usually flatten an image only as a preamble to printing it or placing it into another program. And even then, I make sure I save the flattened image under a different name to maintain my original layered file, using Organizer's version sets to keep track of everything. (See page 73 of Lesson 2 for the skinny on version sets.)

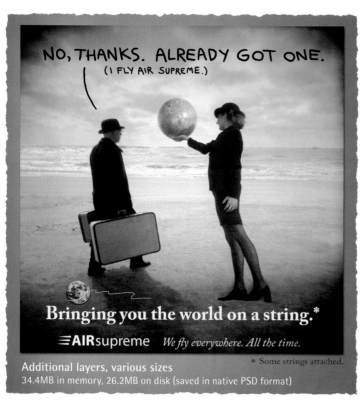

Additional layers, various sizes
34.4MB in memory, 26.2MB on disk (saved in native PSD format)

Figure 8-4.

Finally, when in doubt, err on the side of too many layers as opposed to too few. This may sound like strange advice, but it's better to push the limits and occasionally top out than unnecessarily constrain yourself and hobble your file. After all, you can always upgrade your computer to better accommodate your massive compositions. But you can never recover an unsaved layer (that is, one that you merged or flattened before saving and closing the file).

Arranging and Modifying Layers

The most basic use for layers is to keep objects separated from each other so you can modify their horizontal and vertical position as well as their front-to-back arrangement. Elements also permits you to transform layers by scaling, rotating, or even distorting them, as you'll see in the second of the upcoming exercises.

By way of demonstration, we'll take a cue from the classical artist I believe would have benefited most from layers, 16th-century imperial court painter Giuseppe Arcimboldo. Celebrated in his time as a master of the composite portrait, Arcimboldo rendered his subjects as fanciful collections of fruits, vegetables, flowers, trees, animals, meats—he even famously represented one fellow upside-down (right image, Figure 8-5). We'll embark on something infinitely simpler—Giuseppe had to thrill and delight Emperor Maximilian II, but we happily, do not. Even so, you'll get an ample sense of the pure imaging flexibility that layers afford.

In the following exercise, you'll begin the process of assembling a layered piece of artwork. You'll establish the content and order of the key layers in the composition and, in the process, learn how to select layers, modify their contents, change their order, and even rotate them.

Figure 8-5.

1. *Open a layered composition and some images to add to it.* We'll be looking at three files altogether, *Composite cowboy.psd*, *Cowboy hat.tif*, and *Eight ball.tif*, all included in the *Lesson 08* folder inside *Lesson Files-PE4 1on1*. At first glance, the layered image (shown on the left in Figure 8-6) looks like a football with flippers standing on a pile of towels. But as we'll see, there's so much more.

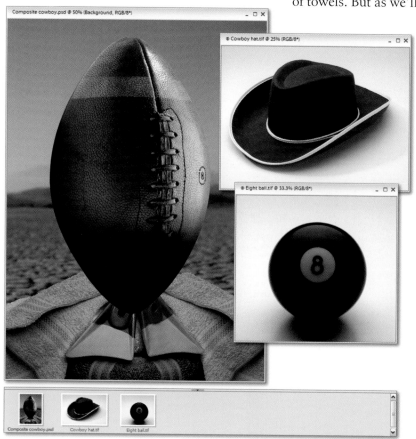

Figure 8-6.

2. *Bring up the Layers palette.* If it's on screen and expanded, fabulous. If not, choose **Window→Layers** or press the F11 key. The **Layers** palette shows thumbnails of every layer in the document, from the front layer at the top of the palette to the rear-most layer at the bottom. This arrangement of layers from front to back is called the *stacking order.*

3. *Make the multilayer file active.* Click the *Composite cowboy.psd* title bar to make that image active. If you take a peek at the Layers palette, you'll see that the file contains ten layers in all. And yet we can see just four items in the image window—football, flippers, towels, and background. (In case you're curious, the flippers are found on the Collar layer. More on that topic shortly.) The other layers are turned off or hidden by the football.

4. *Send the Football layer backward.* Click the **Football** layer in the Layers palette to make it active. Then drag it down the stack in this same palette to between the **Teeth** and **Collar** layers. You should now see all visible layers from the Teeth upward, as illustrated in Figure 8-7 on the facing page. Things don't look right, but they will soon.

5. *Load a selection outline.* The next step is to carve the football into the shape of a face, which we'll accomplish using a selection outline that I defined in advance and saved with this image. To access this selection, choose **Select→Load Selection**. With the **Selection** pop-up menu set to **face outline** (as in Figure 8-8), click the **OK** button.

6. *Reverse the selection.* Choose **Select→Inverse** or press Ctrl+Shift+I to reverse the selection and select the area outside the cowboy's face.

7. *Delete the selected pixels.* Make sure the Football layer is active (confirmed in the title bar by the word *Football* in parentheses). Then press the Backspace or Delete key to erase the selected pixels. Only the cowboy's silhouette remains, as shown in Figure 8-9.

8. *Restore the face selection.* Now let's add a cartoon outline around the cowboy's face. To restore the face outline from Step 5, again choose **Select→Inverse** or press Ctrl+Shift+I.

9. *Create a new layer.* Choose **Layer→New→Layer** or press the keyboard shortcut Ctrl+Shift+N to display the **New Layer** dialog box. Name the layer "Cowboy Outline" and click the **OK** button. Elements adds the new layer to the Layers palette.

Figure 8-7.

Figure 8-8.

Figure 8-9.

10. *Stroke the selection.* Choose **Edit→Stroke (Outline) Selection** to bring up the **Stroke** dialog box, which allows you to trace a colored outline around the contours of a selection outline. There is no shortcut for this command, but you can get to it from the keyboard by holding down the Alt key and then typing E and S.

11. *Specify the stroke settings.* Let's say you want to create a yellow outline that's 13 pixels thick. You do so by changing the numbered settings in Figure 8-10 as follows:

   • Change the **Width** value to 13 pixels (❶ in the figure).

   • Click the **Color** swatch (labeled ❷ in Figure 8-10) to display the **Color Picker** dialog box.

   • Change the **R**, **G**, and **B** values to 255, 240, and 180, respectively (see ❸ in the figure). The result is a pale yellow. Click the **OK** button to accept the new color.

   Check that the other options in the Stroke dialog box are set to their defaults (as they are in Figure 8-10). Then click the **OK** button to apply the stroke. Elements traces a 13-pixel yellow brushstroke around the perimeter of the face, as in Figure 8-11.

Figure 8-10.

Figure 8-11.

12. *Deselect the image.* We're finished with the selection outline. So choose **Select→Deselect** or press Ctrl+D to get rid of it.

13. *Click the Scruff layer.* Back in the **Layers** palette, find the layer called **Scruff** and select it. Then click the blank square next to the layer name to toggle the 👁 and reveal the layer. It looks like gray sandpaper, but it's actually our fellow's stubbly beard.

14. *Set the blend mode to Multiply.* Click the word **Normal** at the top of the Layers palette to display a list of blend modes. Then choose **Multiply** from the list. Or press the keyboard shortcut Shift+Alt+M. Multiply drops out the whites and preserves the dark colors, thus burning the stubble into the cowboy's football flesh, as in Figure 8-12.

Figure 8-12.

15. *Turn on the Hayseed layer.* This time, I want you to click not directly on the **Hayseed** layer but rather in front of it, in the column of 👁 icons. This shows the layer without activating it. The layer in question turns out to be a sliver of barley clasped tightly in the cowboy's teeth (the latter of which are actually seams in a baseball, for what it's worth). Shown in Figure 8-12, the look is interesting but inconsistent. The face outline should be in front of the teeth, hayseed, and scruff. The football flesh needs to be moved forward a couple of layers as well.

16. *Select the Cowboy Outline layer.* You might find it simplest to click the layer name. But I would be remiss in my duties if I didn't tell you how to select the layer from the keyboard.

You can cycle from one layer to the next by pressing Alt with a bracket key. First, press the Esc key to make sure no options are active. Then press Alt+⬚ to select down the layer stack; press Alt+⬚ to select up. In this case, pressing Alt+⬚ three times cycles from the Scruff layer down to Cowboy Outline.

---

17. *Bring the Cowboy Outline layer in front of Scruff.* You can accomplish this by choosing **Layer→Arrange→Bring Forward** three times in a row. But isn't life short enough without choosing inconveniently located commands multiple times in a row? Yes it is. Better to learn the shortcut.

To move a selected layer up or down the stack, press Ctrl with a bracket key. Ctrl+⬚ moves the layer behind the layer in back of it; Ctrl+⬚ moves it forward. To properly arrange the Cowboy Outline layer, press Ctrl+⬚ three times in a row.

---

18. *Select the Football layer.* Again, you can just click the layer name in the palette. But I have another technique for you to try. Press the V key to select the move tool. Then click an unobstructed portion of the hayseed in the image window. Elements automatically switches to the Hayseed layer. (If it doesn't, try clicking some other portion of the weed.) Then click inside the football to select that layer. The move tool's ability to switch layers is a function of the Auto Select Layer check box, which is active by default in the options bar.

PEARL OF WISDOM

In some cases, clicking with the move tool may grab the wrong layer. For example, if you click the lower portion of the fellow's face, you will most likely select the Scruff layer instead of the Football layer. Both layers share pixels at the click location and Scruff is in front. When beset by such troubles, try right-clicking instead, which displays a shortcut menu of possible layers. For example, if you right-click the bottom left tip of the hombre's mustache, the shortcut menu lists four layers—Chile, Scruff, Football, and Background (see Figure 8-13)—each of which contains an opaque pixel at the click point. Choose Football to go to that layer.

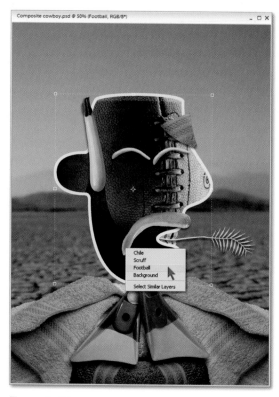

Figure 8-13.

19. *Bring the Football layer in front of Hayseed.* To make it happen, press Ctrl+⬚ twice. The properly arranged layer elements appear in Figure 8-13.

20. *Switch to the Collar layer.* Click the reddish snorkeling fins with the move tool to select the Collar layer. You may reckon those flippers look more like a dandy kerchief than a rugged collar, but that's just because they're upside-down. Let's remedy that, shall we?

21. *Rotate the flippers 180 degrees.* The best way to flip a layer upside-down—assuming that you don't want to create a mirror image of it—is to rotate it 180 degrees. To do so, choose **Image→Rotate→Layer 180°**. This command spins the fins so they look like a collar. To perform the operation from the keyboard, press Alt+I and then type E, 1 (⊡).

22. *Nudge the flippers upward.* Press Shift+↑ seven times in a row. Assuming the move tool is still active, each press of Shift+↑ nudges the layer up 10 pixels; so in all, you will have moved it 70 pixels, placing it as in Figure 8-14.

23. *Save your changes thus far.* It's always a good idea to save versions of a file as you go along. This way, you have the option of recovering elements from your original image later, if things go wrong. To save a new version, choose **File→Save As** or press Ctrl+Shift+S and give your file a new name, such as "Cowboy in progress." Then set the options as follows:

    - There's no need to manage this file in the Organizer workspace, so I recommend you turn off the **Include in the Organizer** check box.

    - Turn on both the **Layers** and **ICC Profile** check boxes to save all layers and color settings.

    - Set the **Format** option to **Photoshop (*.PSD; *.PDD)**.

    Finally, click the **Save** button to save the composition to your hard drive.

Figure 8-14.

Importing and Transforming Layers

Now that you've successfully arranged the layers in the composition, it's time to bring into the mix the rest of the elements, namely the eyes and the hat. In this exercise, you'll introduce portions of the *Cowboy hat.tif* and *Eight ball.tif* images into the composition that you've created so far (and saved in Step 23 of the preceding exercise). Then you'll scale and otherwise transform the layers so they fit into place. The result will be a fanciful cowboy face made of objects that you don't often see on cowboys—especially that hat.

1. *Bring the eight ball image to the front.* If you did not complete the preceding exercise, you need to do so now. Then make sure all the documents from that exercise remain open—namely, *Cowboy hat.tif*, *Eight ball.tif*, and the updated *Cowboy in progress.psd*. Click the title bar for *Eight ball.tif* to make the pool ball active.

2. *Select a central portion of the pool ball.* Use the elliptical marquee tool to select the circular area shown in Figure 8-15. Or, to guarantee that your circle exactly matches mine, load the one that I included in the image. How, you ask? Choose **Select→Load Selection**, confirm that the **Selection** option is set to **circle**, and click the **OK** button.

3. *Drag the eight ball into the cowboy composition.* Press the V key to make sure the move tool is active. Then drag the selection from *Eight ball.tif* into the *Cowboy in progress.psd* image window. Drop it near where one of the eyes should go. In all likelihood, you'll see the pool ball land in an undesirable position, behind the head, as in Figure 8-16. Photoshop Elements places the object in front of the previously selected layer, Collar. Looks like we'll need to rearrange.

Figure 8-15.

Figure 8-16.

4. *Rename the new layer.* In the **Layers** palette, double-click the current layer name, **Layer 1**, to highlight the letters. Then change the name to the more descriptive "Eyes."

5. *Bring the Eyes layer in front of Cowboy Outline.* Either drag the layer up the stack or press Ctrl+⬚ five times in a row.

6. *Choose the Auto Contrast command.* The eight ball is dimly lit with respect to its new surroundings. So choose **Enhance→ Auto Contrast** or press Ctrl+Shift+Alt+L to correct the brightness without upsetting the color balance.

7. *Scale the pool ball to 32 percent of its original size.* The pool ball is too big, so you need to scale it. To be precise, you need to reduce it to 32 percent of its current size. Armed with the move tool, you can pull this off in one of two ways:

   • Notice the dotted marquee with square handles that surrounds the pool ball. This is the *bounding box*, which allows you to scale, rotate, or otherwise transform a layer. (If you do not see the marquee, turn on the Show Bounding Box check box in the options bar.) To scale a layer uniformly— so that the width and height are affected equally—press the Shift key and drag a corner handle to constrain the proportions of the ball. As you drag, keep an eye on the scale values that appear in the options bar. When they reach 32 percent (or thereabouts), release the mouse button, and then release Shift.

   • For more precision, scale by the numbers. Move your cursor over the edge of the bounding box until it looks like ↕ or ↔, and then click to make the bounding box active and enter the *free transform mode*. Click the ⅊ between the W and H scale values in the options bar (which I circled in Figure 8-17) to constrain the proportions of the layer. Change either the **W** or **H** value to 32 (thanks to ⅊, both will update) and press Enter.

Figure 8-17.

To accept the scaled image and exit the free transform mode, press the Enter key (yes, again) or click the ✔ to the right of the numbers in the options bar.

8. *Move the eye into position.* For the sake of convenience, let's imagine that this pool ball is the left eye (which, to be fair to this fictitious person, is the cowboy's right). Drag the eye into the position shown in Figure 8-18.

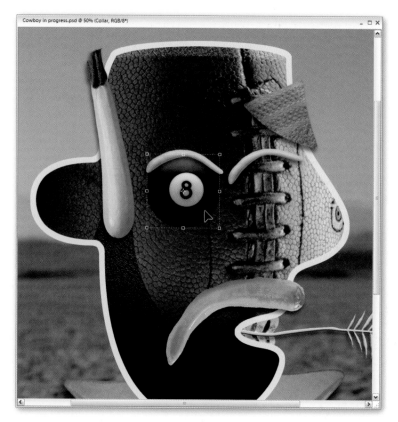

Figure 8-18.

9. *Add a drop shadow.* The interior of the layer exhibits the interplay of highlight and shadow that one typically associates with a real-world object. (Or as Giuseppe himself might have said, the pool ball possesses *chiaroscuro.*) But the layer fails to interact with its environment. Most obviously, the pool ball lacks a shadow. To remedy this gross oversight, do like so:

   • Bring up the **Styles and Effects** palette. (If the palette is not open already, choose **Window→Styles and Effects**.)

- Choose **Layer Styles** from the pop-up menu in the top-left corner of the palette. Then choose **Drop Shadows** from the top-right pop-up menu.

- Click the thumbnail labeled **Soft Edge**. This adds a fuzzy drop shadow positioned close to the object itself.

Elements casts a fuzzy black shadow behind the active layer.

10. *Add an inner shadow.* Now for some shadow along the inside edge of the layer. Choose **Inner Shadows** from the top-right pop-up menu in the Styles and Effects palette. Then click the first thumbnail, which goes by the name **Low**.

11. *Set the blend mode to Screen.* Return to the **Layers** palette and change the blend mode from **Normal** to **Screen**. You can also use the keyboard shortcut Shift+Alt+S. (If the shortcut doesn't work, press the Esc key and try again.) The opposite of the Multiply mode, Screen drops out the blacks and preserves the light colors, creating the appearance of a glass eyeball against the football background.

12. *Scale the shadows to 50 percent.* The transparent portions of the eye reveal the drop and inner shadows we applied in Steps 9 and 10. Only problem: the shadows are too big. To shrink them, choose **Layer→Layer Style→Scale Effects**. Change the **Scale** value to 50 percent and click **OK**. The glass eye and its more acceptable shadows appear in Figure 8-19.

13. *Select the eye and clone it.* Even a guy with a football for a head deserves depth perception. Therefore, I suggest we add a second eye. Of all the ways you can duplicate the eye, here's the easiest:

- Press the Ctrl key and click the **Eyes** layer thumbnail in the Layers palette. This traces a selection outline around the exact perimeter of the layer.

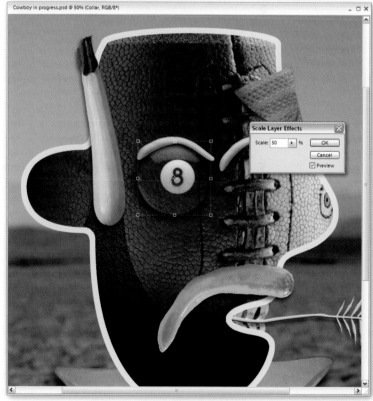

Figure 8-19.

- Check that the move tool is still active. Then hold down both the Shift and Alt keys, and drag the eye to the right. Pressing the Shift key constrains the movement along a horizontal axis. Pressing Alt creates a clone of the eye. After you get the pool ball into more or less the location pictured in Figure 8-20, release the mouse button and then release the Shift and Alt keys.

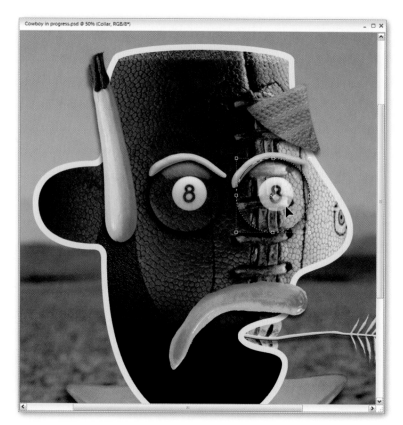

Figure 8-20.

14. *Deselect the image.* Press Ctrl+D to abandon the selection, which has now served us to its utmost capacity.

15. *Bring the cowboy hat image to the front.* The only thing missing in our strange and amazing composition is the hat. Let's go get it. Click the title bar for *Cowboy hat.tif.*

16. *Select the hat.* The hat is a little more difficult to select than the eight ball. So wouldn't you know it, this image contains a predefined selection outline to help you on your way. Choose **Select→Load Selection**. Verify that the **hat outline** selection is active and click **OK**. The selected hat appears in Figure 8-21.

An interesting thing to note: I did not create this particular selection outline. The image vendor, PhotoSpin, included it as part of the photograph. PhotoSpin provides selections with many of its "object" photographs, as do other full-service stock agencies.

Figure 8-21.

17. *Drag the hat into the cowboy composition.* Once again using the move tool, drag the selection from *Cowboy hat.tif* into the *Cowboy in progress.psd* image window. Drop the hat near the top of the head. Naturally, it comes in all wrong. The hat is too low on the head, too far down the stack, and *way* too big, as in Figure 8-22 on the next page. Such are the ways of the layered composition, and the reasons for the remaining steps.

18. *Rename the new layer.* Double-click the current layer name (as always, **Layer 1**) and change its name to "Hat."

19. *Bring the hat to the front of the composition.* Choose **Layer→Arrange→Bring to Front** or press Ctrl+Shift+⬚. The layer pops all the way to the top of the stack, where it rightly belongs.

Figure 8-22.

20. *Lower the Opacity value to 50 percent.* Change the **Opacity** value in the Layers palette. Or with the move tool active, you can bypass the option and just press the 5 key.

We'll want the final hat to be fully opaque. So why lower its opacity? By making the hat translucent in the short term, you can more easily align it with elements underneath. Note that it's essential that you perform this step now; you cannot modify the opacity or the blend mode when inside the free transform mode.

---

21. *Scale and rotate the layer.* Because the bounding box handles extend off-screen, I recommend that you start things off by scaling the hat numerically. Here's the wisest approach:

  • With the ↕ or ↔ cursor, click any side of the bounding box to enter the free transform mode.

- Click the 🔒 icon between the W and H values in the options bar. Then change either **W** or **H** to 62 percent (see the circled values in Figure 8-23).

- Having reduced the size of the hat so that it fits inside the image window, you can rotate the image in one of two ways. Move the cursor outside the bounding box and drag to spin the hat clockwise around its center until the rotate value in the options bar (△, to the right of H) reads 3.5 degrees. Or enter 3.5 into the △ option box and press Enter.

- Drag inside the boundary to move the hat as needed. You can also nudge the layer from the keyboard by pressing one or more arrow keys.

Don't press the Enter key yet—you want to remain in the free transform mode for the next step.

Figure 8-23.

22. *Distort the hat.* The one variety of transformation that you can't express entirely with numbers is the *four-point distortion*, which permits you to scale or slant one portion of a layer independently of another. To distort a layer in Elements, press the

Figure 8-24.

Ctrl key and drag a corner handle. The handle moves independently of the other handles, stretching the hat in that one direction. I ended up Ctrl-dragging all four corner handles to taper the top of the hat as shown in Figure 8-24. (Note that your scale and rotate values in the options bar will change as you perform the distortion. The values only partially track the transformation, so feel free to ignore them.)

23. *Accept the transformation.* Click the ✔ in the options bar or press the Enter key. Photoshop Elements applies the various transformations and exits the free transform mode.

24. *Restore the opacity to 100 percent.* Press the ⓪ key (that's zero, not the letter) or change the **Opacity** value in the Layers palette. The hat becomes opaque again.

EXTRA ⭐ CREDIT

Everything looks pretty good. But in my opinion, the Hat and Cowboy Outline layers are just begging for drop shadows. If you don't share that opinion, skip ahead to the next exercise, "Erasing a Background," on the facing page. But then you'll miss yet another new technique. For rather than define the shadows manually, as you did back in Steps 9 and 10 (see pages 260 and 261), we'll repurpose them from other layers.

25. *Copy the Collar layer's drop shadow.* Click the **Collar** layer in the Layers palette to make it active. Then choose **Layer→ Layer Style→Copy Layer Style**. This tells Elements to tag the layer and make a mental note of the shadows and other effects assigned to it.

26. *Paste the drop shadow on the Hat layer.* Click the **Hat** layer to make it active. Then choose **Layer→Layer Style→Paste Layer Style**. The cowboy hat receives a drop shadow that exactly matches the one applied to the flippers.

27. *Add a scaled drop shadow to the Cowboy Outline layer.* Click the **Cowboy Outline** layer and choose the **Paste Layer Style** command again. The shadow is way too big for the yellow

outline, so let's scale it. Choose **Layer→Layer Style→Scale Effects**. Change the **Scale** value to a mere 20 percent and click the **OK** button to accept your changes. The shadow slims down to a more reasonable size, as in Figure 8-25.

28. *Turn on the Arcimboldo layer.* Click the empty square to the left of the one remaining hidden layer to show its 👁 icon and display a frivolous caption that I drew by hand with a Wacom tablet.

29. *Save your composition.* So ends another jam-packed exercise. Choose **File→Save** to update the file on disk or choose **File→Save As** to save an independent version.

Erasing a Background

So far we've been talking about creating and managing the contents of layers. Now let's talk about ways to delete from layers and, paradoxically, create layers as we delete from them.

How is this possible? The answer resides with the Editor's trio of eraser tools. When used on any layer other than the Background, each of the eraser tools does just what you think it would do—it wipes away pixels from the layer, leaving transparency in its wake. However, when working on the Background layer, transparency is not an option. So the first of the three erasers, known simply as the eraser tool, paints with the background color, which is white by default. But the other two erasers—the background eraser and the magic eraser—do something extraordinary. They convert the Background layer to an independent layer and then set about erasing to transparency. When the eraser can't go to the mountain, Photoshop Elements brings the mountain to the eraser.

In this exercise, you'll use each of the erasers to eliminate the background from an image, thereby permitting you to combine the extracted foreground with an entirely different background and still maintain a photorealistic effect. You'll see that each eraser tool resembles one of Elements' selection tools. Indeed, you'll discover that erasing and selecting are closely related tasks.

Figure 8-25.

Zephyr.jpg @ 42% (RGB/8*)

Figure 8-26.

1. **Open a couple of flat images.** Open *Ruins.jpg* and *Zephyr.jpg*, both conveniently located within the *Lesson 08* folder inside *Lesson Files-PE4 1on1*. Make *Zephyr.jpg* the active image. And note that like all JPEG's, this photograph is flat, possessing a single Background layer and nothing more. This piece of sculpture happens to be Zephyr, the god of wind, which seems only appropriate to the topic of erasing. We're going to blow his background away.

Ruins.jpg @ 33.3% (RGB/8*)

Figure 8-27.

2. **Select the magic eraser in the toolbox.** The first eraser we'll explore is the enticingly named magic eraser. Like its mentor, the magic wand, the magic eraser identifies an area of homogeneous color. Unlike the wand, it then deletes that area. Click and hold the eraser tool to display a flyout menu of erasers; then select the magic eraser as in Figure 8-27. Alternatively, you can press the E key (or Shift+E) to switch between erasers until you get the one with the sparkle.

3. **Set the eraser tools back to their defaults.** To make sure your eraser tools work like mine, click the pink eraser icon on the far left side of the options bar, choose **Reset All Tools**, and click **OK**. (This may seem like overkill, but it's the easiest way to restore the default settings for all three erasers.)

PEARL OF WISDOM

The options bar settings are mostly identical to those that accompany the magic wand (see "Selecting Colored Areas with the Magic Wand," Step 3, page 119). The one addition is Opacity, which permits the tool to create translucent pixels. This option should be called Transparency because the default setting of 100 percent makes erased pixels 100 percent transparent.

4. **Magically erase part of the sky.** Click the wedge of cloudy sky to the right of Zephyr, as circled in Figure 8-28. In a heartbeat, the magic eraser blasts away the patch of sky that falls inside the Tolerance range, just as if you had clicked with the magic wand and then pressed Backspace. The difference is that the magic eraser has automatically turned the Background layer into a floating layer, giving it the name Layer 0. The gray checkerboard represents transparency, or nothingness.

5. **Switch out the checkerboard pattern.** The checkerboard isn't ideal for judging the outline of this particular layer. The checkers are too busy and too light. So let's change them:

   - Choose **Edit→Preferences→Transparency**, or press the shortcut Ctrl+K and then Ctrl+4.

   - Click each of the color swatches under the Grid Colors option and enter the **H**, **S**, and **B** values listed in Figure 8-29. The result is a vivid red pattern with little variation between one square and the next.

   - Click the **OK** button.

   Zoom in on the image. Examine the outline along the back of Zephyr's head now, and you'll see a thin but sharp line of light aqua fringe. Unacceptable; let's try again.

6. **Raise the Tolerance value.** Apparently, the magic eraser didn't erase enough pixels. So we need to incorporate more colors into the erasing equation. Click the word **Tolerance** in the options bar, raise the value to 75, and press Enter.

7. **Undo the magic eraser.** As was the case with the magic wand, the Tolerance value is static, affecting the next erased area, not the current one. So we have to run the operation again. Click the ↩ icon in the shortcuts bar or press Ctrl+Z. Happily, Elements undoes Step 4, not Step 5 or 6. Because the Undo command ignores the changing of preferences and other settings, the last thing it remembers is the magic eraser.

8. **Click again with the magic eraser tool.** Click again where you clicked in Step 4, behind the droopy-looking Zephyr's head. Thanks to the more liberal Tolerance setting, the magic eraser leaves only the slimmest hint of a gossamer fringe around the sculpted head. Indeed, as a bonus, the generous Tolerance value has permitted the tool to erase most of the blue area at the top of the sky as well. The much improved results appear in Figure 8-30.

Figure 8-28.

Figure 8-29.

Figure 8-30.

9. *Select the background eraser.* The remainder of the background is too complex for the simple but ultimately remedial magic eraser. So let's switch to a more powerful eraser. Click the background eraser tool in the options bar (as in Figure 8-31) or choose it from the flyout menu in the toolbox.

Figure 8-31.

Strictly speaking, the background eraser is a brush-based tool. Even so, it works a little like the magnetic lasso tool; you trace loosely around the perimeter of an object, and the tool does its best to accurately identify the edges (see "The Magnetic Lasso," page 137). But in my experience, the background eraser has a tendency to produce more desirable effects. In addition to evaluating edges, much as the magnetic lasso does, the background eraser reads which colors you want to erase as you drag over them. The trick is to keep the *sampling point*—identified by + in the center of the cursor—in the background, and move the outside of the brush over the object's edge and slightly into the foreground. It's tricky, but you'll soon get a sense of it.

10. *Adjust the options bar settings.* As seen in Figure 8-31, the background eraser offers three settings in the options bar. Here's how they should be set:

   • Click the **Brush** preview to see a pop-up palette of options that control the size and shape of the brush. For this exercise, I suggest you press the ⬚ key several times to increase the brush diameter to 60 or 70 pixels.

   • The **Limits** option determines which colors get erased inside the brush diameter. The default setting, Contiguous, erases only those colors that fall inside the Tolerance range *and* are adjacent to the sampling point; Discontiguous leaps over colors, sometimes into the foreground object. For most work, **Contiguous** is the better choice.

- The Tolerance (now measured as a percentage) defines how close a color has to be to the pixel under the + to be erased. We can't really evaluate this option until we try it, so leave the **Tolerance** set to 50 percent for now.

11. *Give the background eraser a try.* Position the background eraser as shown in the first example in Figure 8-32, with the cursor's central + inside the thin fringe of blue sky visible between the green of the tree and the red of the checkerboard. Drag around the perimeter of Zephyr until you are about level with his nose, as in the second example in the figure.

Figure 8-32.

Multiple brushstrokes are okay. For the best results, paint slowly so Elements has time to sample colors along the way. Keep the + outside Zephyr but overlap the outer edge of the brush into the sculpture.

The results are uneven. The tool did a pretty good job distinguishing the foliage from the sculpture when the + passed through the green of the trees. But when the + hit a blue patch of sky, the background eraser erased some of the sculpture as well.

12. *Adjust the tolerance and undo.* Reduce the **Tolerance** value to 30 percent, a little more than half its default setting. After all, it was working okay; no sense in being *too* conservative. Then press Ctrl+Z one or more times to undo the background eraser brushstrokes. (If you back up too far and undo the magic eraser operation, click the ↺ icon in the shortcuts bar or press Ctrl+Y to redo the operation.)

13. *Try painting again.* But with a few changes:

    - Position the brush just after the little patch of sky at the top of Zephyr's head, as indicated by the circled cursor in the first example in Figure 8-33. The sky is too complex for the background eraser to handle; we'll clean it up in a moment with the standard eraser tool.

Figure 8-33.

    - Click to set the initial spot that you want to erase. Then Shift-click at brief intervals along the perimeter of Zephyr's head, down to the fellow's chin. Take care to Shift-click often; each click samples a color, and it's important to have lots of them.

    - You'll have the best luck dragging in the neck region. If you see red creep into Zephyr's face, undo the brushstroke and try again. Keep dragging until you come up with something resembling the right image in Figure 8-33.

Figure 8-34.

Figure 8-35.

14. *Select the eraser tool.* We'll finish things off with the ordinary eraser tool, which is nothing more than a brush that paints transparency. Click the second of the four eraser icons in the options bar, labeled in Figure 8-34. Or press the E key (or Shift+E) a couple of times. Then press the] key four times to increase the brush size to 50 pixels.

15. *Finish erasing around Zephyr.* Use the eraser to complete the selection. You'll have to undo every once in a while, so minimize your pain by keeping your brushstrokes short. Note that the vertical aquamarine bar along the neck is the edge of a tile and belongs to the sculpture rather than the background; you can click at the top of the outside edge and then Shift-click at the bottom to erase in a straight line. Otherwise, reduce the brush diameter as you need to, and persevere. Eventually, you should get a nice edge, as in the left example in Figure 8-35. Finally, switch to a huge 200-pixel brush and erase the last of the background, leaving Zephyr awash in a red checkered sea, as in the right example in the figure.

16. *Relocate Zephyr to a new image.* Press the V key to get the move tool. Then drag Zephyr and drop it into the *Ruins.jpg* image. Move Zephyr to the lower-right corner of the ruins until it snaps into place. In Figure 8-36, I also switched to the **Background** layer and applied **Filter→Blur→Gaussian Blur** with a **Radius** of 8 pixels to create a quick depth-of-field effect. With a little help from the eraser tools, the god of wind has blown himself all the way from his original home of Nashville, Tennessee to the crumbled ruins in Antigua, Guatemala.

Figure 8-36.

WHAT DID YOU LEARN?

Match the key concept in the numbered list below with the letter
of the phrase that best describes it. Answers appear upside-down
at the bottom of the page.

Key Concepts

1. Flat
2. Layered composition
3. Stacking order
4. Free Transform
5. Photoshop (PSD) format
6. Merge Down
7. Bring Forward
8. Four-point distortion
9. Magic eraser
10. Background eraser
11. Sampling point
12. Eraser tool

Descriptions

A. The arrangement of layers in a composition, from front to back, which you can adjust by pressing Ctrl with the bracket keys, [and].

B. The ideal file format for saving all layers, blend modes, selections, layer styles, and anything else you can create in Photoshop Elements.

C. The original single-layer state of a digital photograph or scanned image.

D. Nothing more than a "dumb" brush, this tool paints in the background color (by default, white) on the Background layer or with transparency on any other layer.

E. This command moves a layer upwards in the stacking order.

F. This type of transformation permits you to scale or slant one portion of a layer independently of another.

G. The one command that enables you to scale, rotate, flip, skew, or distort layers.

H. When you click with this tool, it identifies an area of homogeneous color and then deletes that area.

I. Choose this command to combine the contents of the active layer with the layer beneath it.

J. A Photoshop Elements document that contains two or more images on independent layers.

K. When you trace loosely around the perimeter of an object with this tool, Elements tries to identify the edges and delete just those pixels that fall outside the edges.

L. Identified by a +, this component of the background eraser cursor reads colors from the image and decides which pixels to delete.

Answers

1C, 2J, 3A, 4G, 5B, 6I, 7E, 8F, 9H, 10K, 11L, 12D

TEXT AND SHAPES

AS YOU'VE NO doubt discerned by now, the overwhelming majority of features in the Editor workspace are devoted to the creation and manipulation of pixel-based images. The two exceptions are the subjects of this lesson. Known as text and shapes, they have nothing whatsoever to do with digital photography, scanned artwork, or pixels in general.

Where text and shapes are concerned, Photoshop Elements is more illustration program than image editor. You can create single lines of type or set longer passages. You can select text you created long ago and edit typos. You have access to a variety of common formatting attributes, including typeface, size, and style. You can even distort type along a curve. In addition to using type, you can augment your designs with rectangles, polygons, and custom predrawn symbols—the kinds of geometric shapes that you take for granted in a drawing program but rarely see in an image editor.

All this may seem like overkill, the sort of off-topic falderal that tends to burden every piece of consumer software these days. But while you may not need text and shapes for *all* your work, they're incredibly useful on those occasions when you do. Whether you want to prepare a bit of specialty type, mock up a commercial message (see Figure 9-1), or design a Web page, Elements' text and shape functions are precisely the tools you need.

This text acts as a label to the above graphic. Alas, if only I had something to say.

Figure 9-1.

ABOUT THIS LESSON

In this lesson, I show you how to use Photoshop Elements' text and shape tools, as well as ways to edit text and shapes by applying formatting attributes and transformations. You'll learn how to:

- Create a text layer and modify its appearance using typeface, size, and other formatting attributes. . . . . .page 276

- Apply transformations and filters to produce special text effects . . . . .page 282

- Draw, combine, transform, and duplicate scalable vector-based shapes . . . . .page 289

- Edit text on a path as well as warp text by bending and distorting it . . . . .page 297

Project Files

Before beginning the exercises, make sure you've installed the lesson files from the DVD, as explained in Step 5 on page xv of the Preface. This should result in a folder of images called *Lesson Files-PE4 1on1* on your desktop. We'll be working with the files inside the *Lesson 09* subfolder.

Video Lesson 9: Vector-Based Objects

Photoshop Elements treats text and shapes as special kinds of layers. Once created, they remain fully editable with the type and shape tools. And because they're vector-based, you can scale or otherwise transform the layers without degrading their quality.

To learn more about the incredible world of scalable vector art inside Photoshop Elements, watch the ninth video lesson, which I've included on the DVD. To watch the video, insert the DVD, click **Start**, select **Set 3: Filters, Layers, and Vectors** from the first pop-up menu, and then select **Lesson 9, Vector-Based Objects** from the second pop-up menu. Lasting 11 minutes and 36 seconds, this video introduces you to the following shortcuts:

Operation	Keyboard equivalent or shortcut
Preview font on selected type	↓ or ↑ when font option is active
Incrementally increase or reduce size of selected type	Ctrl+Shift+⊡ or Ctrl+Shift+⊡
Update text layer and return to the Standard Edit mode	Enter on keypad (or Ctrl+Enter)
Move text when type tool is active	Ctrl-drag text
Fill the text or shape layer with background color	Ctrl+Backspace
Position a shape on-the-fly as you draw it	spacebar
Cycle through custom shapes	⊡ or ⊡ (left or right bracket)

The Vector-Based Duo

Generally speaking, Photoshop Elements brokers in pixels, or *raster art*. But the subjects of this lesson are something altogether different. Elements treats both text and shapes as *vector-based objects* (or just plain *vectors*), meaning that they rely on mathematically defined outlines that can be scaled or otherwise transformed without degradation in quality.

For a demonstration of how vectors work in Elements, consider the composition shown in Figure 9-2. The Q is a text layer with a drop shadow. The black crown and the orange fire are shapes. The background is a pixel-based gradient. The reason the artwork appears so jagged is because it contains very few pixels. The image measures a scant 50 by 55 pixels (less than 2,800 pixels in all) and is printed at just 15 pixels per inch!

Clearly, you'd never create such low-resolution artwork in real life. I do it here to demonstrate a point: If this were an entirely pixel-based image, we'd be stuck forevermore with jagged, indistinct artwork. But because the Q, crown, and fire are vectors, they are scalable. And unlike pixel art, vectors grow smoother as you make them bigger.

The best way to scale vectors is to apply the Image Size command. To achieve the result pictured in Figure 9-3, I chose Image→Resize→Image Size and turned on the Resample Image check box. (Scale Styles and Constrain Proportions were also turned on.) Then I increased the Resolution value to a whopping 480 pixels per inch and clicked the OK button. The result is an amazing transformation, with vectors and drop shadow growing in picture-perfect form to fit the enhanced resolution. Only the pixel-based gradient remains jagged.

The upshot is that vectors are a world apart from anything else inside Photoshop Elements, always rendering at the full resolution of the image. To see more on this topic, watch Video Lesson 9, "Vector-Based Objects" (introduced on page 274).

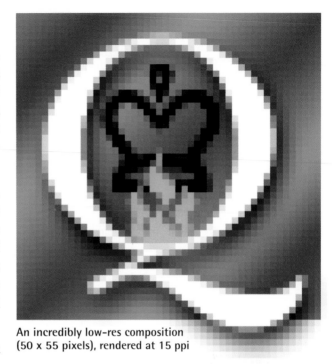

An incredibly low-res composition (50 x 55 pixels), rendered at 15 ppi

Figure 9-2.

The same image, scaled to 480 ppi (3200%) using the Image Size command

Figure 9-3.

Creating and Formatting Text

Text inside Photoshop Elements works just like it does inside your average publishing application. You can apply typefaces, scale characters, adjust line spacing, and so on. However, because Elements is first and foremost an image editor, it isn't particularly well suited to routine typesetting. So we won't belabor the routine typesetting functions. Instead, we'll take a look at some text treatments to which Photoshop Elements is well suited, as well as a few functions that are exceptional or even unique to the program.

In this exercise, we'll add text to an image and format the text to fit its background. In the next, we'll apply a few special effects.

1. *Open an image.* Not every image welcomes the addition of text. After all, text needs room to breathe. So your image should have ample dead space, the kind of empty background you might normally crop away. Such is the case with *Pumpkin light.psd* (see Figure 9-4). Found in the *Lesson 09* folder inside *Lesson Files-PE4 1on1*, this digital photo includes two strong foreground elements with lots of empty space below and above. These are perfect places for some relevant text.

Figure 9-4.

2. ***Click the type tool in the toolbox.*** Or press the T key. Elements provides four type tools, but the horizontal type tool—the one that looks like an unadorned T (see Figure 9-5)—is the only one you need. So press T to cycle to the horizontal type tool.

3. ***Establish a few formatting attributes in the options bar.*** When the type tool is active, the options bar provides access to *formatting attributes*, which are ways to modify the appearance of live text. Labeled in Figure 9-6, they include the following:

   - Click the first ☑ arrow to see a list of typefaces available to your system. I prefer the term *font families* (or just plain *font*) because most typefaces include multiple styles, such as bold and italic.

     To make the figures in this book look their best, I used **Adobe Caslon Pro**. (If it happens to be installed on your computer, you'll find it alphabetized under the C's.) Most likely, you don't have Caslon, in which case select **Times**, **Times New Roman**, or a similar font.

   - The type style pop-up menu lists all the stylistic alternatives available for the selected font. Set the style to read **Regular** or **Roman**. (All style icons toward the middle of the options bar should be off.)

Figure 9-5.

Font family · Antialiasing · Leading (line spacing) · Layer style

Type size · Alignment · Text color

Type style

Figure 9-6.

   - If using Caslon Pro, set the type size to 60 points. If using Times or Times New Roman, set the value to 68 points. Then press the Enter key to accept the new size value.

   - The [aa] icon determines whether Elements applies antialiasing (edge softening) to the text. Leave it turned on.

   - The alignment icons let you align rows of type to the left, center, or right of the point at which you click with the type tool. Leave the first icon set to ▤ for *flush left* text.

   - The distance between one line of type and another is called *leading*. By default, Elements' leading is set to Auto, which is 120 percent of the prevailing type size. This text will include just one line, so the leading is inconsequential.

- The color swatch determines the color of the type. By default, the swatch matches the foreground color. Press the D key followed by the X key to make the swatch white.

- The final option lets you apply a layer style to the text. For now, this option should be set to none, as in ◻.

You can change any of these formatting attributes after you create your text. Getting a few settings established up front merely saves a little time later.

4. **Click in the image window.** Click below the pumpkins in the lower-left portion of the image. Don't worry about the exact location. Better to get the text on the page and align it later.

PEARL OF WISDOM

When you click, Elements greets you with a square alignment point intersected by a vertical blinking insertion marker. You are now set to create *point text*, which is type that is unhampered by a maximum column width and aligned to the point at which you clicked, perfect for setting headlines and individual words or lines of type.

5. **Enter a line of text.** Turn on Caps Lock on your keyboard. Then type "fright lights." Be sure to turn off Caps Lock when you're finished. You should see white capital letters across the bottom of your image, as in Figure 9-7. If the **Layers** palette is visible, you'll also notice the appearance of a new layer marked by a **T** icon. This **T** indicates that the layer contains live text.

Figure 9-7.

> If you see a weird red pattern in the thumbnails in your Layers palette, it's because you changed the transparency pattern (albeit, per my instructions) in the preceding lesson. To restore the default gray, press Ctrl+K, press Ctrl+4, set the Grid Colors option to Light, and click OK.

6. *Accept your changes.* Press Enter on the keypad (not the Enter key above Shift) to exit the type mode and accept the new text layer. You can also press Ctrl+Enter. But don't press the standard Enter key on its own—doing so will add a carriage return.

> At this point, Elements changes the name of the new text layer in the Layers palette to FRIGHT LIGHTS. The program will even update the name if you make changes to the type. You can also rename the layer, but doing so prevents Elements from updating the layer name later.

7. *Drag the text to the lower-left portion of the image.* Press the Ctrl key and drag the text into the position illustrated in Figure 9-8. The text should be positioned slightly to the left of the large pumpkin and slightly below the little one.

Figure 9-8.

8. *Select and show the Body Copy layer.* Click the **Body Copy** layer, then click the empty box in front of it to make it visible. This layer contains a paragraph of type set in the world's ugliest font, Courier New. (For you, it may appear in some other Courier derivative, but rest assured, they're all dreadful.) The only reason the layer is here is to spare you the tedium of having to enter the type on your own. But that doesn't mean there's nothing for you to do. Much formatting is in order.

9. *Assign a better font.* As long as a text layer is active, you can format the entire layer by adjusting settings in the options bar. For starters, click the word **Courier**. This highlights the font name and provides you with a couple of options:

   - Press the ↑ or ↓ key to cycle to a previous or subsequent font in alphabetical order. This technique lets you preview your text as it appears when set in the various fonts installed on your system, handy if you want to see what fonts such as **CRITTER** or **CUTOUT** will look like. (Those are just examples; your strange fonts will vary.)

   - Enter the first few letters of the name of a font you'd like to use.

   For example, type V-e-r to switch to Verdana, which is included with Microsoft Windows. Then press the Enter key to apply the font and see how it looks. Figure 9-9 shows the result.

Figure 9-9.

10. *Make the first two words of the paragraph bold.* Zoom in on the words *Happy Jacks* at the beginning of the paragraph to better see what you're doing, either by pressing Ctrl+⊞ (plus) or by switching to the zoom tool. Then select the type tool again, if necessary, and follow these instructions:

    - Select both words by double-clicking *Happy* and, on the second click, dragging over *Jacks*.

    - Choose **Bold** from the type style menu in the options bar, as shown in Figure 9-10. You can do the same from the keyboard by pressing Ctrl+Shift+B.

11. *Make the word* clowns *italic.* Find *clowns*—the third-to-last word in the paragraph—and double-click it. Then choose **Italic** from the type style menu in the options bar or press the keyboard equivalent Ctrl+Shift+I.

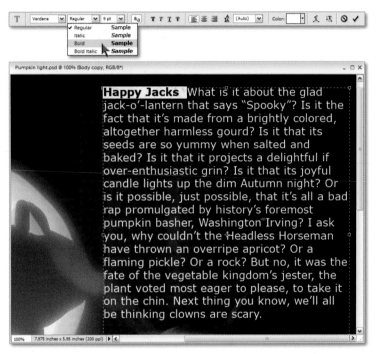

Figure 9-10.

12. *Select the entire paragraph, except the first two words.* Let's next change all but the first two words, *Happy Jacks*, to a yellowish orange to match the pumpkin. Start by double-clicking the third word, *What*. Then press the Shift key and click just after the period at the end of the paragraph.

13. *Change the color to a yellowish orange.* Click the white color swatch toward the right side of the options bar to display the **Color Picker** dialog box. Then move the cursor into the image window and click in one of the fleshy areas inside the big pumpkin's nose, as shown in Figure 9-11 on the next page. You should end up with a color in the vicinity of **H**: 40, **S**: 50, **B**: 90. (If you can't get a good match, go ahead and enter the values manually.) Then click the **OK** button to recolor the text. (Note that the text will appear blue on white because it's highlighted.)

14. *Accept your changes.* Press Enter on the keypad or press Ctrl+Enter to exit the type mode and accept the changes to the Body Copy layer. Then press Ctrl+⊡ to zoom back out a bit.

15. *Save your composition.* You're going to need this file to complete the next exercise. So choose **File→Save As**. Name your updated file "My pumpkin type.psd" and save it in the same *Lesson 09* folder inside *Lesson Files-PE4 1on1*. If you plan on moving on to the next exercise immediately, go ahead and leave the file open and skip to Step 2 on the facing page.

Figure 9-11.

Applying a Special Text Effect

All this editing and formatting is fine and dandy, but it's the kind of thing that you could accomplish in a layout program such as Adobe InDesign, which is better designed for composing and printing high-resolution text. In this exercise, however, you'll do something that's possible only in an image editor such as Photoshop Elements: apply some photographic depth and shadow treatments.

1. *Open the file you saved in the last exercise.* If the jack-o'-lanterns remain open, skip to the next step. Otherwise, find the file called *My pumpkin type.psd* in the *Lesson 09* folder inside *Lesson Files-PE4 1on1*. (Note that this is the file you created and saved in the last exercise. If you can't locate the file, you can create it by following the steps in the preceding section.)

2. *Show the Color Holder layer in the Layers palette.* Click in front of the **Color holder** layer to display the 👁 icon. A tiny brown pumpkin appears above the big pumpkin's head. This layer holds the color we'll apply to the FRIGHT LIGHTS text.

3. *Eyedrop the brown pumpkin.* Press the I key to select the eyedropper tool and then click the little pumpkin to make its brown the foreground color.

4. *Fill the Fright Lights layer with the sampled brown.* Click the **FRIGHT LIGHTS** layer in the **Layers** palette to make it active. Then press Alt+Backspace to fill the text with brown, as shown in Figure 9-12. When filling an entire text layer, this time-saving keystroke lets you recolor text without having to visit the Color Picker dialog box.

5. *Maximize the image window.* The next trick is to add a *cast shadow*, which is a shadow cast by the letters away from the light source. In this case, the light source is the pumpkin, so the shadow needs to extend toward the viewer in the area below the letters. To pull this off, you'll need some extra room. Click the ☐ icon in the top-right corner of the image window or choose **Window→Images→Maximize Mode** to surround the pumpkin artwork with gray pasteboard. To give yourself even more room, zoom out.

Figure 9-12.

6. *Duplicate and transform the text.* Press Ctrl+Alt+T. This does two things: It duplicates the layer and enters the free transform mode. But you'll have to take the duplication part on faith; the Layers palette doesn't show you the new layer until you edit it.

Ten More Ways to Edit Text

I couldn't begin to convey in one or two exercises all the wonderful ways Photoshop Elements permits you to edit and format text. So here are a few truly terrific tips and techniques to bear in mind when working on your own projects:

- Double-click a T thumbnail in the Layers palette to switch to the type tool and select all the text in the corresponding layer.

- Armed with the type tool, you can double-click a word to select it. Drag on the second click to select multiple words. Triple-click to select an entire line. To select all the text in a layer, press Ctrl+A when the text is active.

- To underline some type, press Ctrl+Shift+U. To draw a line through the type, press Ctrl+Shift+⎵. To restore the Regular or Roman style of a font, as well as turn off any underline or strikethrough style, press Ctrl+Shift+Y.

- To increase the size of selected characters in 2-point increments, press Ctrl+Shift+⎵. To reduce the type size, press Ctrl+Shift+⎵. To change the type size by 10 points, press Ctrl+Shift+Alt+⎵ or Ctrl+Shift+Alt+⎵.

- To override the default leading, click the ⁤A⁤ icon in the options bar to highlight the word (Auto) and then type a number. In the figure below, I changed the leading to 16 points. Note that the new leading value affects the distance between a selected letter and the line above it.

- To right-justify a layer of type, so the right edges are aligned and all text appears to the left of the alignment point, press Ctrl+Shift+R. To center the text, press Ctrl+Shift+C. To return the text to flush left (preferable for long passages), press Ctrl+Shift+L.

- To move text when it's active, press the Ctrl key and drag inside the text.

- The foreground color icon at the bottom of the toolbox does not always reflect the color of highlighted text. But if you change the foreground color, any highlighted text changes as well.

- Elements lets you change the formatting of multiple text layers at a time. Click one layer and Shift-click another to select a range of layers. Or press Ctrl and click to select multiple nonadjacent layers. Then select a font, style, size, or other formatting attribute from the options bar.

- When editing text, Edit→Undo is dimmed and Ctrl+Z is ineffective. Your only option for undoing a text edit or formatting adjustment is to press the Esc key. Problem is, this abandons *all* changes made since you entered the text edit mode. Furthermore, if you press the Esc key in the midst of creating a new text layer, you forfeit the entire layer. And because Esc can't be undone, there's no way to retrieve the layer. So be sure before you press Esc.

Happy Jacks What is it about the glad jack-o'-lantern that says "Spooky"? Is it the fact that it's made from a brightly colored, altogether harmless gourd? Is it that its seeds are so yummy when salted and baked? Is it that it projects a delightful if over-enthusiastic grin? Is it that its joyful candle lights up the dim Autumn night? Or is it possible, just possible, that it's all a

7. *Flip and scale the duplicate layer.* I have a few instructions for you here:

- Click in the center of the second icon in the options bar to make it look like ▦ (as circled red in Figure 9-13). This sets the transformation origin to the center of the boundary box for the text layer.

- Click the **H** in the options bar and change the value to −116 percent (circled blue in the figure). The negative value reverses the height of the layer, thus flipping it vertically. Press the Enter key to accept the value.

- Press Shift+↓ four times to scoot the text 40 pixels down from the bottom of the original upright text.

The final position is illustrated in Figure 9-13. Press Enter to apply the transformation and exit the free transform mode.

Figure 9-13.

 PEARL OF WISDOM

A couple of special benefits when transforming a text layer: The type remains live and editable, so you can add text or fix typos. And because Photoshop Elements is working from vectors, the transformation does not stretch pixels or otherwise reduce the quality of the graphic. This means you can transform the text in multiple sessions without fear of degrading the quality.

8. *Rename the layer.* Double-click the name of the new layer in the **Layers** palette and change it to "Cast Shadow." Press Enter twice to accept the new name and deactivate the font option. Then press Ctrl+⬚ to move the renamed layer behind the original Fright Lights letters, as you can see in the Layers palette.

9. *Set the blend mode to Multiply and reduce the opacity.* This layer is a shadow, so it must darken its background. Choose **Multiply** from the blend mode menu at the top of the Layers palette, or press Shift+Alt+M. Press Esc and then press the 9 key to reduce the **Opacity** to 90 percent.

Figure 9-14.

10. *Choose the Gaussian Blur filter.* To create a soft shadow, you need to apply one of the filters from the Filter→Blur submenu. But Elements' filters are applicable only to pixels; none of them can change live type. So when you choose **Filter→Blur→ Gaussian Blur**, the program alerts you that continuing requires you to "simplify" the type (see Figure 9-14), which is Elements' euphemism for converting the type to pixels. (After nearly 300 pages of steps, I ask you: What's so *simple* about pixels?) Click **OK** to confirm. From here on, you can no longer edit this particular layer with the type tool.

11. *Change the Radius value.* Enter a **Radius** value of 6 pixels and click **OK**. The blurred shadow type appears in Figure 9-15.

Figure 9-15.

12. *Again enter the free transform mode.* Now let's give the shadow some directional perspective so it looks like it extends out toward the viewer. Press Ctrl+T to enter the free transform mode, this time without creating a duplicate.

13. *Distort the shadow type.* The image in Figure 9-16 illustrates the two distortions I want you to apply, the first highlighted in the red options bar and the second in the blue one:

    - Once again, you need more room to work. So expand the width of the image window by dragging the right edge farther to the right.

    - Click the skew icon ($\angle$) in the options bar, which I've labeled in the figure.

    - Drag the handle in the lower-right corner of the transform boundary directly to the right. Keep dragging until the **W** value in the options bar reads 115 percent, as indicated by the red options bar and cursor (bottom-right) in Figure 9-16.

    - Drag the lower-left handle of the transform boundary to the left, this time until the **W** value reads 121.5 percent (blue in the figure).

Skew icon

Figure 9-16.

When you're satisfied that your shadow looks like mine—or, if you prefer, more to your liking than mine—press the Enter key to apply the perspective distortion.

PEARL OF WISDOM

You may wonder why two fundamentally opposite distortions were tracked by a single scale value. First, the W value reflected the amount of stretch applied to the bottom edge of the text only. So you stretched the bottom of the text independently of the top. Second, the value was cumulative, meaning that you added 15 percent (115) in one direction and 6.5 percent (121.5 – 115) in the other, thus resulting in a distortion.

You may also wonder why I had you wait until now to apply this distortion. Why didn't we do it when we were flipping and stretching the text back in Step 7? Although Elements lets you scale, rotate, and slant live type, you can't distort it. Therefore, this step had to wait until after the pixel conversion that took place in Step 10.

14. *Show the Style Holder layer.* Notice a hidden layer called **Style holder** at the top of the **Layers** palette? Click to the left of the layer name to reveal its 👁 icon. The layer is empty of pixels, so you won't see any change in the image window. But the empty layer includes a bevel style that will light up the type effect.

15. *Move Style Holder behind Fright Lights.* Either drag the layer behind **FRIGHT LIGHTS**, or click on **Style holder** and press Ctrl+⬚ three times to move it to the desired position.

16. *Merge the Fright Lights and Style Holder layers.* Click the **FRIGHT LIGHTS** layer to make it active. Then choose **Layer→ Merge Down** or press the keyboard shortcut Ctrl+E. Either way, Elements merges the two layers, converts the text to pixels, and applies the beveled edges associated with the Style Holder layer to the FRIGHT LIGHTS letters.

17. *Delete the Color Holder layer.* Drag the **Color holder** layer (the one that contains the brown pumpkin face) to the trash icon at the top of the Layers palette. The finished artwork appears in Figure 9-17.

18. *Save the file.* Choose **File→Save As**, give the file a different filename, such as "Happy Jacks.psd," and click **Save**. If you decide to revisit this file in the future, the Body Copy layer will remain editable with the type tool. As for the other layers, you can modify them as pixels.

Happy Jacks What is it about the glad jack-o'-lantern that says "Spooky"? Is it the fact that it's made from a brightly colored, altogether harmless gourd? Is it that its seeds are so yummy when salted and baked? Is it that it projects a delightful if over-enthusiastic grin? Is it that its joyful candle lights up the dim Autumn night? Or is it possible, just possible, that it's all a bad rap promulgated by history's foremost pumpkin basher, Washington Irving? I ask you, why couldn't the Headless Horseman have thrown an overripe apricot? Or a flaming pickle? Or a rock? But no, it was the fate of the vegetable kingdom's jester, the plant voted most eager to please, to take it on the chin. Next thing you know, we'll all be thinking *clowns* are scary.

Figure 9-17.

Drawing and Editing Shapes

Elements' shape tools allow you to draw rectangles, ellipses, polygons, and an assortment of prefab dingbats and symbols. On the surface, they're a pretty straightforward bunch. But when you delve into them a little more deeply, you quickly discover that the uses for shapes are every bit as wide-ranging and diverse as those for text.

You found out how to draw rectangles and ellipses back in "Using the Marquee Tools" (page 125). And you experimented with custom shapes in "Cropping with the Cookie Cutter" (page 173). The techniques you learned in those exercises apply to the rectangle, ellipse, and custom shape tools as well. So in the following exercise, we'll focus on shapes you haven't yet seen, namely polygons, stars, and lines.

1. *Open an image.* Open the file *Election.psd* located in the *Lesson 09* folder inside *Lesson Files-PE4 1on1*. You'll be greeted by what appears to be a couple of text layers set against a fabric background, as shown in Figure 9-18 on the next page. But in fact, the word *Election* is a shape layer. I originally set the text in Copperplate, a well-regarded typeface that you probably don't have on your system. To avoid having the letters change to a different font on your machine, I converted

them to shapes using the more expensive Photoshop CS2. This prevents you from editing the type, but you can scale or otherwise transform the vector-based shapes without any degradation in quality.

Figure 9-18.

Figure 9-19.

Figure 9-20.

2. *Convert the 2032 layer to pixels.* Let's say we want to similarly prevent the text 2032 from changing on another system. Unlike Photoshop CS2, Elements doesn't let you convert text to shapes. But you can convert text to pixels. Right-click the word **2032** in the **Layers** palette and choose **Simplify Layer** (see Figure 9-19). Elements converts the characters to pixels, which will easily survive the journey from one system to another.

3. *Select the polygon tool in the toolbox.* Click and hold the shape tool icon near the bottom of the toolbox to display the flyout menu pictured in Figure 9-20. Then choose the polygon tool, which lets you draw regular polygons—things like pentagons and hexagons—as well as stars.

4. *Change the foreground color to white.* Press the D key followed by X. Elements now knows to draw the shape in white.

5. *Copy the Election layer's drop shadow.* Right-click the **Election** layer and choose **Copy Layer Style** to copy the layer's drop shadow for later use. This action also selects the layer, thus ensuring that the next layer you draw appears at the top of the stack.

6. *Set the Polygon Options to Star.* Our image is a States-side election graphic, so naturally one feels compelled to wrap the composition in stars and stripes. Click the ⬇ arrow to the left of the **Sides** value in the options bar. This displays the **Polygon Options** pop-up menu pictured in Figure 9-21:

   - Turn on the **Star** check box to have the tool draw stars.

   - Make sure both **Smooth** check boxes are off so the corners are nice and sharp.

   - Set the **Indent Sides By** value to 50 percent (as by default). This ensures that opposite points align with each other, as is the rule for a 5-pointed star.

Figure 9-21.

7. *Set the Sides value to 5.* You can either select the **Sides** value and change it to 5, or you might try the following trick:

To raise the Sides value in increments of 1, press the ⎁ key. To lower the value, press the ⎀ key. Add the Shift key to raise or lower the value by 10. This tip holds true for any other value that may occupy this space in the options bar.

---

8. *Draw the first star.* The polygon tool draws shapes from the center out. To draw the star shown in Figure 9-22, drag from the location highlighted by the yellow ⊕ to the one highlighted by the dark green ⬤. The new star receives a white fill.

Figure 9-22.

9. *Paste the drop shadow.* Right-click the new **Shape 1** layer and choose **Paste Layer Style**. The star receives the drop shadow that you copied in Step 5.

10. *Carve a second star out of the first.* Hold down the Alt key and draw another star from the same starting point (the yellow ⊕ in Figure 9-23) to just inside the first star point (the dark green ⊕). Because the Alt key is down, Elements subtracts this shape from the last one. The result is a star-shaped white stroke.

Figure 9-23.

As you draw the inner star, you may find that your alignment is a wee bit off. If so, bear in mind that you can adjust the placement of a shape on-the-fly by pressing and holding the spacebar. When you get the star in the right position, release the spacebar and keep drawing.

11. *Click the arrow tool in the toolbox.* Or press the U key three times to advance to the arrow. Elements calls this the shape selection tool (see Figure 9-24) because it lets you select and modify individual *path outlines* in a shape layer.

12. *Select both inner and outer star paths.* Turn off the **Show Bounding Box** check box in the options bar. (The arrow tool behaves more predictably with this option off.) Click the inner star, and then press the Shift key and click the outside star. Or drag around any portion of the star outlines to surround them with a marquee. Either way, Elements selects both paths.

13. *Transform and duplicate the star.* Press Ctrl+Alt+T to duplicate the selected star paths and enter the free transform mode. As in the last exercise, you have to have faith that you've cloned the paths since they exactly overlap the original paths.

Figure 9-24.

14. *Scale, rotate, and move the duplicate star.* At this point, I need you to make some precise adjustments:

- Click the ⚲ icon between the W and H values to scale the star paths proportionally. Then change either the **W** or **H** value to 80 percent.

- Tab to the rotate (△) value, change it to −16 degrees, and press the Enter key. This tilts the star counterclockwise.

- Drag the shape until it appears above and to the left of the larger star, as in Figure 9-25. Assuming the △ value is no longer active, you can nudge the star with the arrow keys.

When the new star appears in the proper position, press the Enter key to confirm the transformation.

Figure 9-25.

15. *Repeat the last transformation three more times.* This means pressing Ctrl+Alt+T to duplicate the latest star and enter the transform mode. Again scale the star proportionally to 80 percent, rotate it −16 degrees, press Enter, move it to the left, and press Enter again. Repeat the process twice more. It's a bit tedious, but the result—the arcing sequence of five stars shown in Figure 9-26 on the next page—is worth the effort. I mean, really, how often are you rewarded with five stars?

16. *Name the new layer.* Double-click the Shape 1 layer name in the **Layers** palette and enter the new name "Stars."

17. *Turn on the Field layer.* Click the empty box in front of the **Field** layer in the Layers palette to display a slanted blue shape layer. I created this layer by drawing a plain old rectangle with the rectangle tool and distorting it in the free transform mode.

18. *Set the Field layer to Hard Light.* Click the **Field** layer in the Layers palette and choose the **Hard Light** mode or press Shift+Alt+H. Press the Esc key and then press 8 to lower the **Opacity** value to 80 percent. Even though Field is a vector shape layer, it's subject to the same blend modes and transparency options that are available to all layers in Photoshop Elements.

Figure 9-26.

19. *Turn on the Stripes layer.* Click in front of the **Stripes** layer to display a sequence of red stripes. I created the top stripe by distorting a rectangle. Then I duplicated and transformed the other four.

20. *Set the Stripes layer to Multiply.* Click the Stripes layer to make it active and press Shift+Alt+M to burn the stripes into the background image, as in Figure 9-27.

Figure 9-27.

21. *Select the line tool.* The next step is to draw a rule under the word *Election*. The best tool for this job is the line tool. You can select it in any of the following ways:

    - Choose the line tool from the shape tool flyout menu, just as you chose the polygon tool back in Step 3.

    - Assuming a shape tool is active (most likely the arrow tool), click the line tool icon in the options bar, as you see me doing in Figure 9-28.

    - Alt-click the shape tool icon in the toolbox or press the U key as many times as it takes to advance to the line tool.

Figure 9-28.

22. *Increase the Weight value to 12 pixels.* The **Weight** value determines the thickness of lines drawn with the line tool. You can modify the value directly in the options bar, or press Shift+⬆ to raise the value by 10 and ⬆ to raise it another 1.

23. *Select the Stars layer.* Click the **Stars** layer in the **Layers** palette. This tells Elements to create the next shape layer in front of the Stars layer and pick up the Stars layer's attributes.

24. *Draw a line under the word* Election. I want the rule to extend beyond the left edge of the canvas, so it's easiest to draw from right to left. Begin your drag below and just to the right of the last letter in *Election*, as illustrated in Figure 9-29. *After* you begin dragging, press and hold the Shift key to constrain the rule to precisely horizontal. (If you press Shift before you

Figure 9-29.

start to drag, you run the risk of adding the line to the existing Stars layer.) Drag beyond the edge of the canvas before releasing the mouse and then release Shift.

If you don't like the position of your line, change it. To move the line as you draw it, press and hold the spacebar. To nudge the line after you draw it, Ctrl-click the shape outline to select it and then press Ctrl along with the appropriate arrow key (↑, ↓, ←, or →).

25. *Name the new layer.* Again, Elements automatically names the new layer Shape 1. Double-click the layer name and enter the new name "Underscore." Then click the **2032** layer to accept the name and hide the vector outlines around the shape layers. The final artwork appears in Figure 9-30.

Figure 9-30.

The beauty of this design is that most of it is scalable. For example, to turn this into a piece of tabloid-sized poster art, choose **Image→Resize→Image Size**, turn on the **Resample Image** check box, and change the **Width** value in the **Document Size** area to 17 inches. Make sure all three check boxes at the bottom of the dialog box are selected. To heighten the effect, change the Bicubic setting to **Nearest Neighbor** and then click **OK**. The background image and the pixel-based *2032* become jagged. But as witnessed in Figure 9-31 on the facing page, everything else remains supersmooth, a testament to the power of vector-based shapes in Photoshop Elements.

Figure 9-31.

Bending and Warping Type

The distortions we performed back in Step 13 of the "Applying a Special Text Effect" exercise (see page 287) aren't possible with live, editable text layers. But that doesn't mean live text distortions are entirely out of the question. Elements offers a text-specific distortion function called Warp Text. And it's so fantastic and easy to use, I lament that it can't be applied to shapes and images.

This exercise shows you how to work with distorted type in Photoshop Elements. We'll start things off by editing text wrapped around the perimeter of a circle. Then we'll stretch and distort letters inside the contours of a predefined free-form shape. All the while, our text layers will remain live and fully editable.

1. *Open a layered image.* This time around, the file in question is *Radio-free space.psd*, which you'll find in the *Lesson 09* folder inside *Lesson Files-PE4 1on1*. If the program complains that some layers need to be updated, click the **Update** button. Pictured in Figure 9-32, the composition contains several layers of shapes and live type. We'll modify a couple of the text layers in the upcoming steps.

Figure 9-32.

2. *Select the text in the Bottom Type layer.* Among the text layers are two—Top Type and Bottom Type—that I aligned to a circle inside Photoshop CS2. As the fates would have it, Photoshop Elements lacks any means for creating text on a circle, but it does let you edit it. For example, let's say we want to reverse the order of the words *utter & complete* along the bottom of the circle. To select this type, double-click the T thumbnail to the left of **Bottom Type** in the **Layers** palette. Elements switches to the type tool and highlights the text.

3. *Edit the text.* While a versatile tool, the type tool is not adept at selecting type along a curve. Better to select the text from the keyboard as follows:

   • Press the ← key to move the insertion marker to the beginning of the text.

   • Press Ctrl+→ three times in a row to advance to the word *utter*.

   • Press Ctrl+Shift+→ three times to highlight *utter & complete*, as shown in Figure 9-33.

   Now replace the type with "complete & utter," which I believe is the more conventional word order—here on Earth, at any rate. Feel free to enter the words as lowercase characters; Elements will automatically change them to uppercase thanks to a special formatting attribute that I assigned in Photoshop CS2. When you finish, press the Enter key on the numeric keypad to accept your changes.

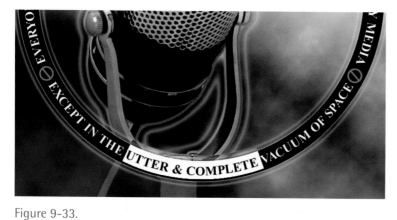

Figure 9-33.

4. **Select the Radio-Free Space! layer.** Press Alt+⬚ to drop down to the layer. Right now, the text treatment at the top of the page is almost comically bad. Cyan letters, wide leading, big thick red strokes, Verdana—how much worse could it get? We'll start by spicing up the text with a blend mode, and then we'll warp the text for a classic pulp fiction look.

5. **Change the blend mode to Overlay.** Select **Overlay** from the pop-up menu at the top of the Layers palette. Or press Shift+Alt+O. The already much improved result appears in Figure 9-34.

6. **Click the warp icon in the options bar.** Press T to reselect the type tool. Then look to the far right side of the options bar for an icon that looks like ⊥ (labeled in Figure 9-35). Click this icon to bring up the **Warp Text** dialog box.

Figure 9-34.

7. **Apply the Arc Lower style.** The Warp Text dialog box features these options:

   - The Style pop-up menu defines the shape inside which the text bends. The icons provide hints as to what the effect will look like. But if in doubt, choose an option and watch the preview in the image window.

   - Change the angle of the warp by selecting the Horizontal or Vertical radio button. With Western-world text like the stuff we're working with in this exercise, Horizontal bends lines of type and Vertical warps the individual letters.

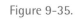

Figure 9-35.

   - Use the Bend value to change the amount of warp and the direction in which the active text layer bends. You can enter any value from –100 to 100 percent.

   - The two Distortion sliders add a hint of perspective to the warp effect.

For example, Figure 9-36 shows four variations on the Arc Lower style. The icon next to the style name represents the effect as flat on top and bent at the bottom. Assuming Horizontal is active, this means the warp is applied exclusively to the bottom of the text. A positive Bend value tugs the bottom of the text downward (first image); a negative value pushes it upward (second image).

To achieve a strict perspective-style distortion, choose any Style option and set the Bend value to 0 percent. Examples of purely horizontal and vertical distortions appear in the last two images in Figure 9-36.

Figure 9-36.

For this exercise, choose **Arc Lower** from the **Style** pop-up menu. Then set the **Bend** value to −40 percent. The resulting effect looks awful—easily the worst of those shown in Figure 9-36—but that's temporary. Have faith that we'll fix things in future steps and click **OK**.

8. ***Increase the size of the word Space!*** Triple-click the word *Space!* with the type tool to select both it and its exclamation point. Press Ctrl+Shift+⟩ to increase the type size incrementally until the width of the selected text matches that of the text above it. (To resize faster, press Ctrl+Shift+Alt+⟩.) Or just change the type size value in the options bar to 88 points, as in Figure 9-37.

Figure 9-37.

9. ***Increase the leading.*** Although the selected word better fits the horizontal dimensions of its layer, it overlaps the line above it. Click the A̲ icon in the options bar to highlight the leading value. Change it to 76 points and press Enter (see Figure 9-38).

10. ***Accept your changes.*** Press the Enter key on the keypad to exit the text edit mode and accept the formatting adjustments.

Figure 9-38.

11. ***Scale the text vertically.*** One of the byproducts of warping is that it stretches or squishes characters, thus requiring you to scale them back to more visually appealing proportions. In our case, the text is *really* squished, so some vertical scaling is in order. Choose **Image→Transform→Free Transform** or press Ctrl+T. Then change the **H** value to 167 percent and press the Enter key twice in a row to make the letters taller without making them wider, as in Figure 9-39.

Figure 9-39.

12. *Nudge the text down.* The text now rides too high on the canvas. Press Ctrl+Shift+↓ three times in a row to nudge the text down 30 pixels. The final composition appears in Figure 9-40.

It's important to note that throughout all these adjustments, every single text layer remains fully editable. For example, to change the text from *Radio-Free Space!* (indicating a space completely free of radio) to *Radio Free Space!* (which suggests a broadcast organization devoted to the advancement of freedom and liberty in outer space), simply replace the hyphen with a space character. The layer effects are likewise live. To change the style of warp, select the text layer in the Layers palette and click the text warp icon in the options bar. I ask you, what in the world could be more flexible?

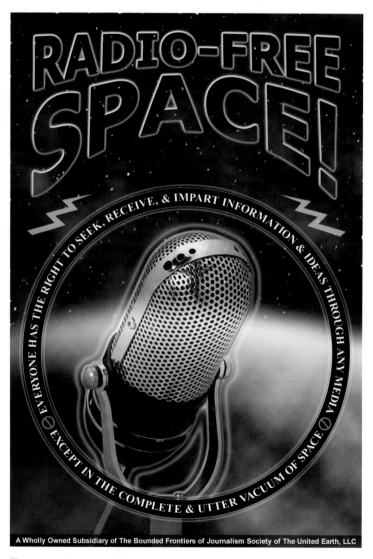

Figure 9-40.

WHAT DID YOU LEARN?

Match the key concept in the numbered list below with the letter
of the phrase that best describes it. Answers appear upside-down
at the bottom of the page.

Key Concepts

1. Raster art
2. Vector-based objects
3. Formatting attributes
4. Font family
5. Flush left
6. Leading
7. Faux styles
8. Point text
9. Area text
10. Simplify
11. Live type
12. Warp Text

Descriptions

A. Font family, type style, size, leading, alignment, and a wealth of other options for modifying the appearance of live text.

B. To convert live type into noneditable, rasterized type.

C. Lines of text that are aligned along the left side.

D. This dialog box bends and distorts live text to create wavy, bulging, and perspective effects.

E. Use these Elements-imposed formatting attributes when a font doesn't come with bold or italic variations.

F. To create the kind of type layer, first drag with the type tool in the image window to draw a rectangular bounding box and then enter your text from the keyboard.

G. A digital image composed exclusively of colored pixels.

H. Text that has no maximum column width and aligns to the place at which you clicked with the type tool.

I. Mathematically defined text and shapes that can be scaled or otherwise transformed without any degradation in quality.

J. A typeface and its multiple related styles.

K. The distance between lines of type.

L. Text that remains editable.

Answers

LESSON

10

STYLES AND ADJUSTMENT LAYERS

I LONG FOR the day when everything in Photoshop Elements is a live effect. Imagine if hours after applying the Unsharp Mask command, you elected to revisit the filter and tweak its settings. But instead of applying the new settings on top of the old ones, as happens now, you applied them *in place of* the old ones. In other words, imagine if the filter were dynamic. And not just Unsharp Mask, but every single function throughout the program. Photoshop Elements would transform overnight from a darned good photo editor to the most flexible imaging application on the planet.

Alas, that glad day continues to elude us. But that's not to say the present is bleak. Today's Photoshop Elements provides us with occasional glimpses into the world of dynamic image editing in the form of layer styles and adjustment layers. If all of Elements were this forgiving, it would be impossible to make a permanent mistake.

The Amazing World of Live Effects

Layer styles are collections of predefined color and contour attributes that let you add dimension, lighting, and texture to otherwise flat objects. *Adjustment layers* are collections of settings that correct or modify the colors of the layers behind them. As their names imply, both layer styles and adjustment layers depend on layers to work their magic. So I've assembled a simple layered document to show you how both features work:

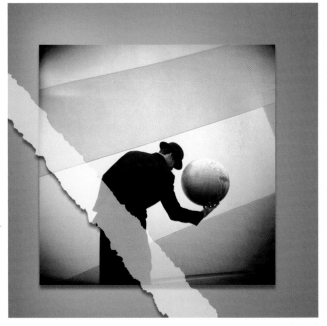

Figure 10-1.

- Figure 10-1 shows a composition with two floating layers—an image and a strip of torn paper—set against a teal background. To each layer, I applied one of the most common kinds of layer styles: a *drop shadow*, which is nothing more than a silhouette of the layer that is offset and blurred. The shadow implies a gap in

305

ABOUT THIS LESSON

Project Files

Before beginning the exercises, make sure you've installed the lesson files from the DVD, as explained in Step 5 on page xv of the Preface. This should result in a folder of images called *Lesson Files-PE4 1on1* on your desktop. We'll be working with the files inside the *Lesson 10* subfolder.

In this lesson, you'll explore the worlds of layer styles and adjustment layers, both of which enable you to modify an image composition without harming a single pixel in the original photographs. Specifically, you'll learn how to:

Video Lesson 10: Introducing Styles

If you're familiar with layer styles, you might associate them with drop shadows. But drop shadows are only the beginning. Layer styles are automated painting tools that let you not only enhance photographic layers, but also turn hand-drawn elements, text layers, and vector shapes into fully realized objects with dimension and depth.

For an introduction to layer styles, watch the tenth video lesson on the DVD. Insert the DVD, click Start, select **Set 4: Styles, Sharing, and Slide Shows** from the first pop-up menu, and then select **Lesson 10, Introducing Styles** from the second pop-up menu. In this 14-minute, 51-second movie, I tell you about the following operations and shortcuts:

Operation	Keyboard equivalent or shortcut
Show or hide the layer styles thumbnails	F7, then choose Layer Styles from pop-up menu
Append one layer style to another	Click thumbnail in Styles and Effects palette
Replace one layer style with another	Shift-click thumbnail in Styles and Effects palette
Display the Style Settings dialog box	Double-click ✿ icon to the right of layer name
Change the direction of one or more effects	Drag in image when Style Settings dialog box is open
Render out or delete a layer style	Right-click layer name and choose desired command

depth between the layers. And because the shadows drop downward, they suggest a light source that shines from above.

- Drop shadows are handy, but they are just one of several different kinds of layer styles. In Figure 10-2, I created a new layer. Using two separate layer styles, I traced a dark outline around the outside of the layer and a light outline around the inside. This results in a slight "toasting" effect, which helps separate the layer from its environment even more.

- The lower-right corner of Figure 10-3 sports an adjustment layer. Based on the Gradient Map command (see the "Colorizing an Image with Adjustment Layers" exercise, page 313), this adjustment layer inverts and colorizes the paper, photograph, and background layers beneath it.

- Figure 10-4 illustrates another Gradient Map adjustment layer. This one doesn't invert colors; it just changes them. The new adjustment layer affects everything below it, even the underlying portions of the yellow Gradient Map layer from the preceding figure. I also managed to assign a style to the layer, one that sculpts the perimeter of the layer.

Figure 10-2.

Figure 10-3.

Figure 10-4.

The upshot is that layer styles and adjustment layers possess an amazing capacity for interaction. One layer style can mix with another, one adjustment layer can modify another, and so on. You'll see examples of these interactions—and get a sense of just how useful they can be—in the upcoming exercises.

Layer Attributes Versus Layers

Layer styles and adjustment layers share many things in common. Both are *parametric*, which means that they're based on adjustable numerical settings. Additionally, both take up very little room in memory, are accessible from the Layers palette, and remain editable as long as you save them in the native Photoshop PSD format.

But layer styles and adjustment layers are ultimately unique functions, implemented in different ways:

- You assign a layer style to an existing layer. An adjustment layer exists as a layer all its own. Figure 10-5 shows examples of each as they appear in the Layers palette.

- A layer style controls the appearance of just one layer at a time. An adjustment layer affects the color and luminosity of all layers beneath it (according to your specifications, as we'll see).

Figure 10-5.

The first exercise in this lesson covers the topic of layer styles. The remaining two are devoted to adjustment layers. We'll see one highly practical use for adjustment layers and another that might be best expressed as wildly creative. Whether you intend to put them to practical or creative use, these are two amazing functions. Happily, you'll spend lots of time with both in this lesson.

Applying and Modifying Layer Styles

Layer styles serve two opposing purposes: to set layers apart and to bring them together. For example, a layer style that casts a shadow suggests that the layer is raised above the surface of its surroundings. This calls attention to the perimeter of the layer and adds depth to the image, both of which help to distinguish the layered element from a busy composition. Meanwhile, a layer style can also blend the interior or perimeter of a layer with its background. The independent layers appear not as disparate elements of a composition, but as seamless portions of a cohesive whole.

The following exercise demonstrates both capacities of layer styles. We'll take a plain composition and embellish it using a trio of predefined styles that I created in Photoshop CS2. (Photoshop Elements can only modify styles, not create them.) Before beginning this exercise, make sure that you've installed my style libraries onto your computer (see Step 5 on page xv of the Preface). In all, these libraries contain more than 80 styles that you can apply, mix, and modify as you please.

1. *Open a layered composition.* Go to the *Lesson 10* folder inside *Lesson Files-PE4 1on1* and open the file called *Paper letters.psd*. Pictured in Figure 10-6, this image features a total of four layers. The background was scanned from a brown paper bag. The other layers are filled with various shades of gray. How drab can you get? But as it just so happens, this is precisely the kind of drab art that benefits most from layer styles.

2. *Select the E layer.* Click the top layer in the **Layers** palette or press the keyboard shortcut Shift+Alt+⬚.

3. *Open the layer styles.* First make sure the **Styles and Effects** palette is available on screen. (If necessary, press the F7 key.) Then choose **Layer Styles** from the top-left pop-up menu. Most likely, you'll see a series of none-too-exciting thumbnails that represent various kinds of drop shadows. Don't let that dissuade you; plenty of exciting stuff is here—you just have to know where to look.

Figure 10-6.

Figure 10-7.

Figure 10-8.

4. *Apply the Green Glass style.* The upper-right pop-up menu lets you select a library of styles that Elements loaded automatically when you started the program. Click the pop-up menu and choose a library midway down titled **Deke Glass**. (If you don't see this option, refer to the preface for installation instructions.) You should see a total of 12 candy-colored thumbnails. Click the one called **Green Glass** to apply the shimmering, translucent effect shown in Figure 10-7.

5. *Apply the Indigo Matte style to the 3 layer.* Sometimes a style works as is, right out of the box. Such is the case with the almost liquid Green Glass effect. Other times, a style needs some help, as we'll see in this next example. Let's start by applying a base style to another layer:

   • Click the **3** layer in the Layers palette to make it active. Or press Alt+⬚ to move backward. (If the shortcut doesn't work, press the Esc key to deactivate the style name and then press Alt+⬚.)

   • Choose **Deke Surfaces** from the upper-right pop-up menu in the **Styles and Effects** palette.

   • Click the style marked **Indigo Matte**. The result appears in Figure 10-8.

6. *Edit the style settings.* I like the color and drop shadow associated with this style, but the beveled edges are just too much for this image. To modify the style, double-click the *f* icon that now appears to the right of the 3 layer in the **Layers** palette. This brings up the **Style Settings** dialog box, which lets you modify the attributes

associated with the active style. Here's a quick rundown of the options that currently confront you, along with the settings I want you to enter:

- Set the **Lighting Angle** value to 100 degrees, which shifts the light source more directly above the layer. This casts a shadow in the opposite direction, almost straight down.

- Notice that the **Use Global Light** check box is turned on. This locks in the light source at 100 degrees for all other directional layer styles for which Use Global Light is similarly turned on. At the present, no other layer is affected, so don't worry about this setting.

- Press Tab a couple of times to advance to the **Shadow Distance** option. Enter a value of 20 pixels to move the shadow 20 pixels away from the layered objects.

- Next tab to the **Bevel Size** option, which controls the thickness of the beveled edges. Reduce the value to 5 pixels to make the edges thin.

- The **Bevel Direction** should be set to **Up**, which makes the layer appear raised as opposed to recessed.

- If it isn't already on, go ahead and select the **Preview** box so you can see the results of your edits.

Click the **OK** button to accept your changes. Both the settings and the modified result appear in the resplendent Figure 10-9.

7. *Group the 3 layer with the square below it.* I want the vertical lines of the 3 layer to fit inside the gray square. And I can do that using a special function called a *clipping mask*, in which one layer fits inside the layer below it. So choose **Layer→Group with Previous** or press Ctrl+G to combine the two layers into a clipping mask, as in Figure 10-10.

8. *Apply Orange Glass to the Box layer.* Now we turn our attention to the final layer, the light gray square:

- Click the word **Box** in the **Layers** palette or press the handy shortcut Alt+☐ to make the layer active.

- Again choose **Deke Glass** from the upper-right pop-up menu in the **Styles and Effects** palette.

- Click the **Orange Glass** layer style.

Figure 10-9.

Figure 10-10.

Figure 10-11.

9. *Edit the style settings.* The result is nice, but again it needs work. Double-click ⦿ and change the settings like so:

- Set the **Lighting Angle** value to 165 degrees. The Use Global Light check box is off, so adjusting the Angle value won't affect the other layers.

- Lower the **Shadow Distance** to 10 pixels.

- Likewise lower the **Bevel Size** value to 10 pixels. Then change the **Bevel Direction** option to **Down** to create the effect of a slight depression in the background.

When your settings—and the altered effect—look like those in Figure 10-11, click the **OK** button.

10. *Change the fill opacity to 30 percent.* Photoshop Elements offers a remarkable hidden feature that lets you adjust the transparency of the pixels in a layer independently of the layer style. Termed *fill opacity,* this function is represented neither by command nor option. You can get to it only from the keyboard.

Try this: Press the V key to confirm that the move tool is active. Then press Shift+1. Notice how the layer becomes more transparent but the drop shadow and bevel remain unchanged. You just changed the fill opacity to 10 percent. Now press Shift+0. The light gray of the square returns, because you restored the fill opacity to 100 percent. Do you feel the rare satisfaction of discovering a top-secret, ultrahidden feature? You should, because that's precisely what you have just done.

Now that you've had a chance to experiment, press Shift+3 to change the fill opacity to 30 percent.

11. *Nix the Indigo Matte style on the 3 layer.* Having had time to reflect, I'm not terribly impressed by the layer style I applied to the 3 layer. So let's get rid of it. Right-click to the right of the **3** in the **Layers** palette. Then choose **Clear Layer Style** from the shortcut menu. The style and its associated fill opacity setting go away, leaving behind fully opaque black stripes.

12. *Change the standard opacity to 30 percent.* Press the 3 key without Shift to reduce the standard opacity of the 3 layer to 30 percent. Or you can adjust the **Opacity** value in the Layers palette directly. The final composition appears on the facing page in Figure 10-12.

Colorizing an Image with Adjustment Layers

We now move from layer styles to adjustment layers. These insanely practical functions permit you to apply popular color adjustments such as Hue/Saturation and Levels as well as most of the commands under the Filter→Adjustments submenu. What's more, an adjustment layer works just like its command counterpart. The Levels adjustment layer shows you the same dialog box—complete with Input Levels values and histogram—as does Enhance→Adjust Lighting→Levels. However, unlike commands, an adjustment layer affects all layers beneath it and remains editable far into the future.

Adjustment layers are so flexible that many designers use them to correct flat photographs. This way, if they later decide to tweak the colors in an image to meet the demands of a different screen or printing environment, they have their original photograph on hand with the last-applied color correction ready and waiting in the wings.

In this exercise, we'll use an adjustment layer to colorize a grayscale image. We could use the Hue/Saturation command for this purpose, but it limits you to one hue value and one saturation value per operation. My preferred approach involves a little-known function called Gradient Map, which allows you to substitute luminosity values with as many hue and saturation values as you like. Problem is, Gradient Map is fairly obscure and I haven't introduced you to it yet. Meanwhile, Hue/Saturation is familiar and commonly employed for colorizing. Hence I feel compelled to do something I don't normally do in an exercise—compare and contrast. In the following steps, we'll make use of both Hue/Saturation and Gradient Map, and you can decide for yourself which is better.

Figure 10-12.

1. *Open an image.* Open the grayscale image titled *Woman in hood.jpg*, contained in the *Lesson 10* folder inside *Lesson Files-PE4 1on1*. Pictured in Figure 10-13 on the next page, this photo was captured by Ramsey Blacklock and hails from iStockphoto. It's a swell pic, but it'll look livelier after we add some color.

2. *Convert the image to RGB color.* A grayscale image doesn't merely lack color; it lacks all capacity for color. This means an image that lists *Gray* in its title bar (as this one does) cannot be colorized without first undergoing a subtle but important transformation. Choose **Image→Mode→RGB Color**, as in Figure 10-14. Or press the Alt key and type I-M-R. The photo won't look any different, but take my word for it: It's now ready for color to blossom.

Figure 10-13.

3. *Convert to the Adobe RGB color profile.* If you followed my directions in the Preface and picked Allow Me to Choose from the Color Settings dialog box (see Step 10, page xvi), then Elements automatically assigns the newly color-capable image an sRGB profile. That's okay, but we can do better. To boost the potential range and saturation of colors in the image, choose **Image→Convert Color Profile→Apply Adobe RGB Profile**. The image is now profiled in the Adobe RGB space, just like most of the other images you have worked with throughout this book.

4. *Create a Hue/Saturation adjustment layer.* Click the half-black, half-white ◑ icon at the top of the **Layers** palette to display a menu of 11 specialty layers (3 fills followed by 8 color adjustments). Then choose **Hue/Saturation**, as in Figure 10-15. Photoshop Elements adds a layer called Hue/Saturation 1 and displays the **Hue/Saturation** dialog box.

Figure 10-14.

Figure 10-15.

5. *Turn on the Colorize check box.* Located in the lower-right corner of the dialog box, the **Colorize** check box applies the Hue and Saturation settings as absolute values. By this, I mean that all pixels are assigned one uniform Hue value and one uniform Saturation value. The moment you turn on Colorize, Photoshop Elements changes the Hue to 0 degrees (or possibly 360 degrees, same diff) and the Saturation to 25 percent, which turns the entire image a low-saturation red, as shown in Figure 10-16.

Figure 10-16.

6. *Adjust the Hue and Saturation values.* At this point, I encourage you to experiment. Enter any **Hue** value documented in the sidebar "The Visible-Color Spectrum Wheel" (Lesson 3, page 91), and you will see that very color come to life before your very eyes. Meanwhile, a **Saturation** of 0 percent invariably results in gray; 100 percent delivers the most vivid color Photoshop Elements can achieve.

For my part—and you're welcome to follow along with me if you like—I entered a **Hue** of 40 degrees and a **Saturation** of 30 percent. The result is an orange-amber *duotone,* so called because it contains two tones, black and the 40-degree amber (see Figure 10-17).

Figure 10-17.

7. *Click the OK button.* The result is a pleasant enough effect. But frankly, it's not good enough. The moment you turned on the Colorize check box, you lost all selective control. The Edit pop-up menu dimmed, and thus you lost the ability to adjust the hue and saturation of individual colors. Why sacrifice that kind of control when you don't have to?

8. *Swap Hue/Saturation for Gradient Map.* To change the Hue/Saturation layer to a Gradient Map adjustment, first make sure the **Hue/Saturation 1** layer is active and then choose **Layer→Change Layer Content→Gradient Map**. Photoshop Elements displays the **Gradient Map** dialog box, which substitutes (or *maps*) the luminosity values in the image with the colors in a gradient. If the program initially inverts the photo, as in Figure 10-18, fear not. You have my word that things will improve dramatically during the next few steps.

Figure 10-18.

Figure 10-19.

Figure 10-20.

For those who may be wondering, a *gradient* is a continuous fountain of colors. The gradient may transition from black to white, from one color to another, or between a whole slew of colors, as illustrated by the examples in **Figure 10-19**.

The great thing about Gradient Map is that it gives you so much control. You can map every single gray value, from black to white, to a specific color. And all you need to make this happen is an easy-to-create, easy-to-edit gradient.

9. *Load the custom gradients.* The predefined gradients that ship with Photoshop Elements don't work well for colorization, so I've created a handful of colorization gradients for you to play with. Here's how to get to them:

- In the Gradient Map dialog box, click the ⬛ arrow to the right of the main gradient bar. This displays a panel of small gradient swatches.

- Click the ⊙ arrow to the right of the swatches and choose **Load Gradients** from the menu, as in Figure 10-20.

- After the **Load** dialog box appears, find the *Lesson 10* folder inside the *Lesson Files-PE4 1on1* folder and open the file called *Four gradients.grd*. Four new gradient swatches appear in the Gradient Map dialog box.

10. *Select the Quadtone supreme swatch.* Hover your cursor over the first of the four new swatches. You should see the hint *Quadtone supreme*. When you do, click to select the swatch. Assuming the **Preview** check box is on (as by default), Photoshop Elements applies the colors in this gradient to the luminosity values in the image. The gradient progresses from black to very dark magenta followed by dull red, orange, and finally white, each of which finds a home over the course of the gray values in the photograph, as in Figure 10-21. That's a total of four colors plus white, hence a *quadtone*.

If your image still appears black and white, it's because you didn't convert the image from grayscale to RGB using **Image→Mode→RGB Color**, as explained in Step 2.

11. *Open the Gradient Editor.* A gradient map behaves a lot like the Levels command (see "Adjusting Brightness Levels," on page 96 of Lesson 3) in that it lets you lighten or darken luminosity values. To make brightness adjustments, click inside the gradient bar above the swatches panel to display the **Gradient Editor** dialog box.

Figure 10-21.

Although the dialog box is brimming with options, most of the action centers on the gradient bar. Labeled in Figure 10-22, the gradient bar is festooned with tiny box icons above and below. The boxes above the bar (▮) control the opacity of the gradient, and have no effect on the outcome of the Gradient Map command. The boxes below the bar (▮) let you add key colors to the gradient. Because they determine the position of the colors, they are known as *color stops*.

12. *Edit the gradient.* Click the second color stop from the left—the dark magenta one—to select it. (I know, the swatch looks purplish, but if you go by the Hue value, it's magenta. I guess I'm a stickler.) Two options, Color and Location, become available at the bottom of the dialog box. The Color swatch near the bottom of the dialog box lets you change the color; modify the Location value or drag the color stop to move the color in the gradient. Increasing the Location value darkens the colors in the image; reducing the value lightens them. (This isn't always the case—it depends on the arrangement of colors in your gradient—but that's how it works in most gradients, including this one.)

I want you to do the following:

Opacity stop
(no effect on gradient maps)

Gradient bar

Color stops

Figure 10-22.

- With the dark magenta color stop selected, reduce the **Location** value for the color stop to 15 percent. This helps to lighten the shadows and bring out details in the hair.

- Click the next color stop over—the dull red one—and change its **Location** to 50 percent. Elements darkens the midtones in the face.

- Click the final, white color stop. This time I want you to try something a little different: Press the Alt key and drag the color stop to the left until the **Location** value reads 80 percent. This duplicates the white color stop and draws out the highlights in the woman's face.

- Select the drab orange color stop, the one with a Location value of 65 percent. Alt-drag this stop to the right until **Location** reads 95 percent. Elements darkens the clouds from the overly bright background of the sky, as in Figure 10-23.

Figure 10-23.

13. *Save your revised gradient.* Enter "Quadtone Modified" into the **Name** option box and click the **New** button to add a swatch to the end of the Presets list.

14. *Click OK.* Click **OK** to accept your changes and return to the **Gradient Map** dialog box.

15. *Try out the other gradients.* To see what other gradients look like when applied to *Woman in hood.jpg*, click the ⊡ arrow to the right of the gradient bar and select a different gradient swatch. The images in Figure 10-24 illustrate three additional gradients that I provided—Cool palette, Deep sky, and Vivid contrast—as well as one of Photoshop Elements' default gradients, Copper. In the last case, I turned on the **Reverse** check box, which reverses the order of the colors in the gradient and inverts the colors in the image.

16. *Click OK.* When you arrive at a favorite gradient map, click the **OK** button or press the Enter key to accept the colorized image. (If the gradient swatch panel is visible, you may have to press Enter twice.)

You can, of course, apply more colorful gradients to an image. But the more you vary the colors, the more psychedelic and convoluted your colorized image becomes. I advise subtle changes. Even small shifts in color can make a big difference.

Using Adjustment Layers to Create Special Effects

Because adjustment layers are fully functioning layers, you can mix and match them, as well as combine them with blend modes, layer masks, shapes, and even clipping masks. Simply put, they permit you to venture into creative territories that static commands simply can't accommodate.

In this exercise, your assignment is to build a book cover for a dime-store novel using a couple of digital photos and a petroglyph silhouette that I saved for you as a selection outline. Your publisher has asked for something "dark, brooding, and suspenseful." Given that this is all the instruction you've received, it seems imprudent to make any permanent changes to the images. So you wisely decide to do everything with adjustment layers.

1. *Open a layered image.* This time the image is called *End of Road.psd*, which you'll find in the *Lesson 10* folder inside *Lesson Files-PE4 1on1*. (If the program asks to update the text layers, click the **Update** button.) Pictured in Figure 10-25 on the next page, this composition contains a text layer sandwiched between two photographic layers, both of which I captured nearly a decade ago using a 1.5-megapixel Kodak DC265. I set the layer that contains my shadow to the Multiply blend mode, thus toasting it into the orange type and drive-in movie screen.

Cool palette

Deep sky

Vivid contrast

Copper, Reverse

Figure 10-24.

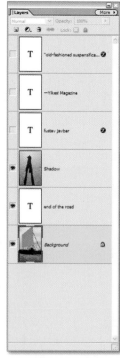

Figure 10-25.

2. *Add an Invert adjustment layer.* What's the easiest, most brain-dead way to make an image look scary? Invert it, of course. And that's exactly what we're going to do with the drive-in screen. Check that the **Background** layer is active in the **Layers** palette. Click the ❍ icon at the top of the palette and choose the **Invert** command. Elements adds a layer called Invert 1 that creates a negative version of the drive-in movie screen behind it.

3. *Change the blend mode to Luminosity.* Currently, the Invert 1 layer reverses both the luminosity values and the colors in the drive-in. This means that the blue of the sky turns to orange, and the orange of the ground turns to blue. Fine, but suppose you don't want that; suppose you want to invert only the luminosity values. Then choose **Luminosity** from the blend mode pop-up menu in the top-left corner of the Layers palette, or press the keyboard shortcut Shift+Alt+Y. Elements restores the blue sky and orange ground, as in Figure 10-26.

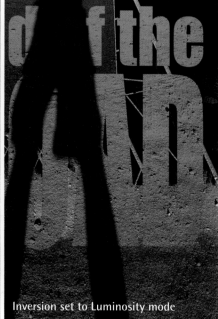

Inverted background image

Inversion set to Luminosity mode

Figure 10-26.

4. *Add a Levels adjustment layer.* Inverting the background made the image overly dark, and the best way to lighten it is with the Levels command. But you can't apply Levels to the Invert 1 layer, and if you lighten the Background layer directly, you'll darken the inverted image because the luminosity values are reversed. Solution: Click the ⬤ icon at the top of the Layers palette and choose **Levels**. Inside the **Levels** dialog box, advance to the second **Input Levels** value and change the gamma to 2.00, as demonstrated in Figure 10-27. Then click the **OK** button to apply the adjustment.

Figure 10-27.

5. *Turn on the top three text layers.* In the **Layers** palette, click the blank boxes to the left of each of the top three text layers to display the ◉ icons and the text associated with those layers. Imagine that the publisher provided these layers to you with the directive, "Keep the quote and author's name in blue, and make them leap off the page." But because blue is one of the most pervasive colors in the image, the text gets a little lost (see Figure 10-28). We need another adjustment layer to shift to color balance.

PEARL OF WISDOM

Incidentally, all the blue text is housed on editable text layers. So you might wonder how I applied those round corners to the quote and author letters. Answer: I added an Inner Glow effect to each layer and lowered the fill opacity to 0 percent.

6. *Add a Hue/Saturation adjustment layer.* Make sure the **Levels 1** layer in the Layers palette is selected because that's where you'll insert the next layer. Then press and hold the Alt key as you choose **Hue/Saturation** from the ⬤ icon at the top of the palette. This allows you to name the new layer as you create it. Call it "Color Spin," and then click the **OK** button to display the **Hue/Saturation** dialog box.

Figure 10-28.

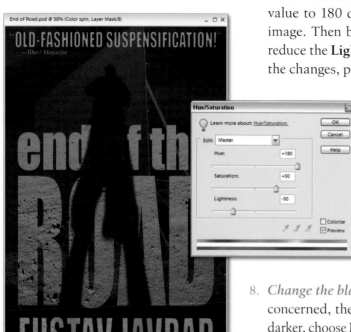
Figure 10-29.

Figure 10-30.

7. *Rotate all hues in the image 180 degrees.* Change the **Hue** value to 180 degrees to invert all colors in the background image. Then boost the **Saturation** value to +50 percent and reduce the **Lightness** value to −50 percent. Click **OK** to accept the changes, pictured in Figure 10-29.

At this point, you might quite reasonably wonder why in the world we just inverted all the colors in the drive-in movie photo when we were so careful *not* to invert the colors in Step 3. The reason is that, for the moment, all we're concerned about is making the blue text "leap off the page." After we accomplish that, we'll restore the appearance of the central portion of the image using a layer mask (see Step 9). But first . . .

8. *Change the blend mode to Multiply.* As far as the blue text is concerned, the background art remains too light. To make it darker, choose **Multiply** from the blend mode pop-up menu in the top-left corner of the **Layers** palette, or press Shift+Alt+M.

PEARL OF WISDOM

It's worth noting that so far, despite the fact that you've added three layers and applied blend modes to two of them, the size of the file has grown by just a few K, or a little more than 0.03 percent. Happily, adjustment layers are not only flexible but also models of efficiency.

9. *Select the gradient tool in the toolbox.* If you look at the Layers palette, you'll see that each one of the three adjustment layers that you've created includes a white thumbnail to the right of it. Each white thumbnail indicates a *layer mask*, which permits you to limit the portion of an image that's affected by an adjustment layer. Strange as it sounds, painting black inside the layer mask hides that portion of the color adjustment; painting white reveals the adjustment. We'll create a soft transition between adjusted and unadjusted areas of the image by painting inside the Color Spin layer mask with the gradient tool. Click the tool's icon near the bottom of the toolbox (see Figure 10-30) or press the G key to select it.

10. *Paint gradients at the top and bottom of the image.* The aim is to relegate the effects of the Color Spin layer to the areas immediately behind the blue text at the top and the bottom of the image. That means painting the central portion of the layer mask black. It's a tricky proposition, so I'll break it into pieces:

- Press the D key to make the foreground color white and the background color black, as is the default when working in a layer mask.

- Press Shift+⌐ (Shift+comma) to set the gradient tool to draw gradients from the foreground color to the background color, or white to black.

- Press the Shift key and drag from directly below the top text to the chest in the shadow, as indicated by the yellow arrow at the top of Figure 10-31. This should lighten all but the topmost portion of the image.

- Now to reinstate some darkness at the bottom of the image. Start by pressing ⌐ (period), which changes the style of gradient to Foreground-to-Transparent.

- In the image window, Shift-drag from directly above the author name (the esteemed Fustav Javbar) to the bottom of the bar of the big red *A*, as indicated by the orange arrow at the bottom of Figure 10-31. Both the top and bottom of the image should now appear dark.

11. *Invert the* **End of the Road** *text.* Now we're ready to address the book's title. The publisher has informed us that as long as we make Fustav Javbar's name prominent, we can do anything we want with the title. So let's have some fun. I want to use the letters to invert the portion of the image below them. The only problem is that Elements doesn't let you fill live text with an adjustment layer. So we first have to convert the text to a layer mask filled with an Invert adjustment layer. Here's how:

- Press the Ctrl key and click the T thumbnail for the **End of the Road** layer in the **Layers** palette. This traces the edges of the letters with selection outlines.

Figure 10-31.

- Click the ⊘ icon at the top of the Layers palette and choose the **Invert** command. Elements creates a new layer, called Invert 2, in front of the Color Spin layer. The selection outline disappears, replaced by a layer mask that traces the exact outlines of the book title.

- Click the **End of the Road** layer or press Alt+⬚ to make the text layer active.

- Press Ctrl+Shift+⬚ (or choose **Layer→Arrange→Bring to Front**) to pop the layer to the top of the stack.

- Click the ◉ icon in front of the **End of the Road** layer to hide the layer.

If the last few steps seem like a lot of busy work, take heart: They prepare you for the upcoming steps and get a few important housekeeping chores out of the way.

Figure 10-32.

Pictured in Figure 10-32, the effect is high in drama but low in legibility. One solution is to increase the contrast of the inversion effect, as in the next step.

12. *Add a Threshold adjustment layer.* Click the **Invert 2** layer to make it active. Hold down the Alt key while choosing **Threshold** from the ⊘ icon at the top of the Layers palette to display the **New Layer** dialog box. Enter the name "Black or white" because the Threshold command changes all colors to either black or white. Then turn on the check box **Group with Previous Layer** (see Figure 10-33) to clip the new adjustment layer inside the letters of the Invert 2 shape layer.

13. *Accept the default Threshold value.* Click the **OK** button to display the **Threshold** dialog box, which changes all brightness levels darker than the **Threshold Level** value to black and all levels lighter to white. As Figure 10-34 on the facing page shows, a value of 128 splits the colors right down the middle. Click **OK** to apply this setting.

Figure 10-33.

Notice that rather than making the text layer black and white, the Threshold adjustment seems to have made it black and gravelly. The text is actually black and white; the Shadow layer above it is responsible for burning the gravel into the white areas.

14. *Create a dummy layer.* The title remains difficult to read. Let's say you want to make the black portions of the text lighter by adding an inner glow. In Elements 3, you could apply an inner glow directly to an adjustment layer. Not so in Elements 4. Nowadays, you have to set up your styles on a separate dummy layer, and then copy and paste them onto the adjustment layer.

    With this in mind, press Ctrl+Shift+N to create a new layer. Name it "Dummy" and click **OK**.

15. *Apply an Inner Glow style.* When applying a style to an empty layer, you have to work blind. That's why I came up with a few specific settings to guide you on your way:

    • Make sure the **Styles and Effects** palette is visible and expanded. If it isn't, press the F7 key.

    • Choose **Layer Styles** from the upper-left pop-up menu in the Styles and Effects palette. Then choose **Inner Glows** from the upper-right pop-up menu.

    • Click the **Heavy** thumbnail in the top-right corner of the palette.

    Because the layer is empty, you won't see any change. That's okay; the style is present nonetheless.

16. *Add a Drop Shadow style.* I think the title might also benefit from a little extra definition in the form of a drop shadow. Go to the Styles and Effects palette and do like so:

    • Choose **Drop Shadows** from the upper-right pop-up menu to display a list of predefined shadow styles.

    • Click the **Low** thumbnail at the top of the palette to add a soft, subtle shadow to the existing Inner Glow style.

    Again, the empty layer makes the effect invisible. But never fear, it's there.

Figure 10-34.

17. *Change the layer style settings.* The predefined Heavy glow and Low shadow effects are rough approximations of what we want. Let's make them exactly right:

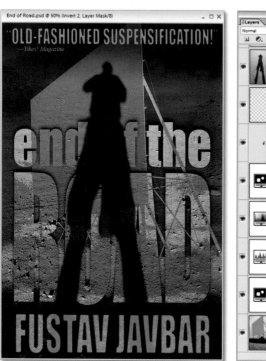

Figure 10-35.

- Double-click the ✿ icon to the right of the **Dummy** layer in the **Layers** palette to display the **Style Settings** dialog box.

- Change the **Lighting Angle** value to −90 degrees so that Photoshop Elements shines the light source from below and casts the shadow straight up. (This is the only directional effect in the composition, so the Use Global Light setting doesn't matter.)

- Change the **Shadow Distance** value to 10 pixels.

- Raise the **Inner Glow Size** value to 100 pixels.

When your settings look like those in Figure 10-35, click the **OK** button. As ever, you have to trust me that these settings will look good when applied to the title. In the very next step, you'll get to see for yourself.

18. *Copy the style and paste it on the title.* Right-click anywhere on the **Dummy** layer *except* the ✿. Then choose **Copy Layer Style**. Now right-click the **Invert 2** layer and choose **Paste Layer Style**. The dull glow and spine-tingling drop shadow appear in Figure 10-36.

Figure 10-36.

19. *Turn on the top layer and change its blend.* Scroll to the top of the Layers palette, select the **End of the Road** layer, and turn on its 👁 to make it visible. Then choose **Screen** from the blend mode pop-up menu and reduce the **Opacity** value to 70 percent. As Figure 10-37 bears witness, this combines the legibility of the orange letters with the texture and detail from the Invert 2 layer.

The final task is to add a ghost to the book cover. The publisher has supplied the ghost in the form of a saved selection. (In case you're curious, the selection hails from a several hundred-year-old Navajo petroglyph. Seriously, those guys rocked.) We'll use this selection to create one last adjustment layer.

20. *Load the Petroglyph selection outline.* Choose **Select**→**Load Selection**. In the **Load Selection** dialog box, verify that **Petroglyph** is selected from the **Selection** pop-up menu. Finally, click the **OK** button to invoke the ghostly selection outline.

21. *Add a Hue/Saturation adjustment layer.* To name the layer as you make it, press and hold the Alt as you choose **Hue/Saturation** from the ⬤ icon at the top of the **Layers** palette. Name the layer "Blue Man." Do not select the check box below the Name field in an attempt to create a Blue Man Group. (Oh, come on, that was funny.) Then click **OK**. When the **Hue/Saturation** dialog box appears, adjust the settings as follows (see Figure 10-38):

   • Turn on the **Colorize** check box.

   • Change the **Hue** to 220 degrees, a cobalt blue that matches the color of the text.

   • Increase the **Saturation** to 100 percent.

   • Raise the **Lightness** value to 80 percent. Usually, I recommend you steer clear of this clumsy option. But in this case, we're using Lightness not to correct colors but to create an effect. And in that regard, it works fine.

   • Click **OK** to apply your settings.

Notice that the Hue/Saturation adjustment stays inside the confines of the Petroglyph selection outline. Elements manages this by converting the selection to a layer mask.

Figure 10-37.

Figure 10-38.

22. *Move the layer down the stack.* The ghost needs to rest between the various title layers and any adjustment layers that might otherwise modify it. In other words, it belongs behind Invert 2 and in front of Color Spin, as in Figure 10-39. Either drag the layer to that position in the Layers palette, or press Ctrl+Shift+⬚ once and then Ctrl+⬚ three times.

23. *Save your composition.* Choose **File**→**Save As** and name the file "Bestseller in Blue.psd." Turn off **Include in Organizer**; turn on **Layers** and **ICC Profile**. Then click the **Save** button.

From here on, all adjustment layers in this composition remain editable. If you decide you want to modify the settings for an adjustment layer, double-click the layer's thumbnail in the Layers palette. The appropriate dialog box will appear, complete with the settings currently in force. (The only exceptions are the two Invert layers, which have no settings.) You can also turn adjustment layers on and off, change their stacking order, and edit their masks. The options aren't exactly endless, but they're pretty darn close.

Figure 10-39.

WHAT DID YOU LEARN?

Match the key concept in the numbered list below with the letter of the phrase that best describes it. Answers appear upside-down at the bottom of the page.

Key Concepts

1. Layer style
2. Adjustment layer
3. Drop shadow
4. Parametric
5. Bevel Direction
6. Use Global Light
7. Group with Previous
8. Fill opacity
9. Gradient map
10. Color stop
11. Layer mask
12. Threshold

Descriptions

A. Available inside the Gradient Editor, this feature determines the placement of a color within the gradient.

B. A collection of color adjustment settings that correct or modify the colors of the layers beneath them.

C. This adjustment layer allows you to specify a luminosity level beyond which darker values are changed to black and lighter values are changed to white.

D. This layer style option makes a layer appear to rise toward you or to recede.

E. Based on adjustable numerical settings and named options; layer styles and adjustment layers are examples.

F. This powerful function lets you paint inside an adjustment layer to limit the portions of an image that are affected by that adjustment.

G. This command clips a layer so that it is visible only within the confines of the layer beneath it.

H. This check box locks down the light source so that all directional layer styles in the composition cast highlights and shadows according to a consistent angle.

I. This layer style offsets and blurs a silhouette of the active layer.

J. A series of dynamic color and contour attributes that let you assign dimension, lighting, and texture to a layer.

K. This feature lets you adjust the transparency of the pixels in a layer independently of the layer style.

L. An adjustment layer that substitutes the luminosity values in the image with the colors in a gradient.

Answers

1J, 2B, 3I, 4E, 5D, 6H, 7G, 8K, 9L, 10A, 11F, 12C

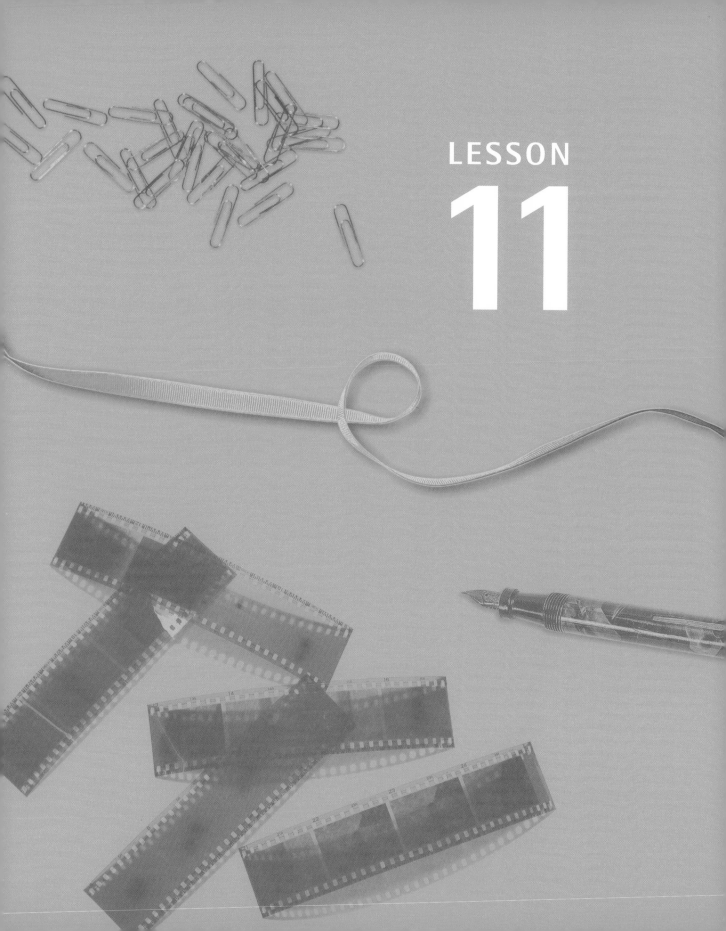

UNTIL FAIRLY RECENTLY, "sharing" photos meant bundling them into a 45-minute slide show and inflicting them on an innocent and undeserving audience of future ex-friends. The more merciful photo enthusiast might collect his or her prints into a photo album so that guests could tour them at their leisure. But the ancient conventions illustrated in Figure 11-1 are becoming increasingly uncommon and even unrealistic. Thanks to the proliferation of digital cameras, desktop scanners, and other varieties of capture devices, we create ten images for every one amassed by our parents. Many of us have too many photos to fit them into albums, and if we did, what casual visitor in his or her right mind would want to sift through them all?

Thankfully, today's notion of photo-sharing has expanded to keep up with our increasingly frenzied and eclectic habits. Certainly, we *can* print our photos; and under many circumstances, the printed snapshot remains our best and most practical image-sharing medium. (Which is why I devote the first exercise to the printing of single photographs.) But you can likewise group photos onto a page, email images to friends and colleagues, and collect the photos in an online gallery. Happily, photo-sharing is one of Photoshop Elements' strongest and best-developed features. Ecstatically, photo-sharing also happens to be the topic of this lesson.

The old ways of sharing photos were quaint

Figure 11-1.

ABOUT THIS LESSON

This lesson explains ways to share your images with other people, whether by printing or distributing the electronic files online. You'll learn how to:

- Print an image from your PC to an inkjet printer and ensure both high-quality output and accurate color. . . . . page 334

- Use photo-grade paper to produce film-quality output from an inexpensive inkjet printer . . . . . . page 340

- Combine multiple images onto a single page using the Organizer's Print command . . . . page 343

- Share pictures online for free using the Kodak EasyShare Gallery service . . . . page 351

Video Lesson 11: Emailing Your Images

Of all the ways Elements lets you share images with others, emailing is the most convenient. All you need is an email account and an Internet connection. No mysterious printer settings, no new subscription fees. Your only concern is to fire off the photos to your various friends and associates.

Elements prepares an email-friendly document with such aplomb that I devote an entire video lesson to the topic. Insert the DVD, click **Start**, select **Set 4: Styles, Sharing, and Slide Shows** from the first pop-up menu, and then select **Lesson 11, Emailing Your Images** from the second pop-up menu. During your 12-minute and 56-second journey, you'll learn about the following operations:

Operation	Keyboard equivalent or shortcut
Return to the Organizer workspace	Click the Photo Browser (⌒▦) button
Display the Properties palette (for entering captions)	Alt+Enter
Zoom an image in the Organizer workspace	Double-click the image thumbnail
Select multiple nonadjacent images	Ctrl-click image thumnails in the Organizer
Email selected images in the Organizer	Ctrl+Shift+E
Add or delete images	click the ● or ● button
Send your email to the recipients list	Alt+S

21st-Century Sharing

Don't get me wrong, nothing says you *have* to share your images. (In fact, you may prefer to keep your initial attempts at image editing to yourself.) But after you gain a sufficient degree of confidence, you'll want to let loved ones and acquaintances see what you're up to. And no program—not even the professional-grade Photoshop CS2—lets you share with the ease and proficiency of Photoshop Elements. Figure 11-2 is an illustration of a supernova, but it gives you a rough sense of the infinite ways in which Elements lets you share images. And besides, after spending two hours painting a supernova—in Elements, no less—there's no way I'm not using it in my book, however flimsy its relevance.

The new ways of sharing photos are boundless

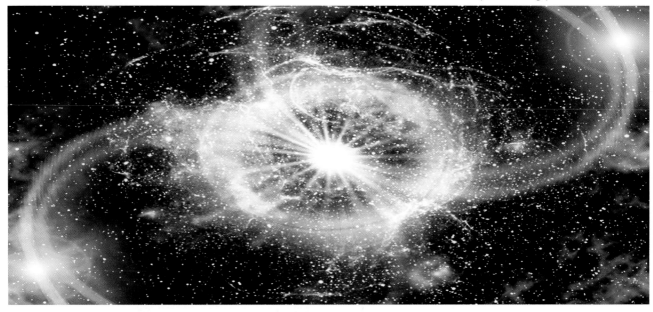

Figure 11-2.

You and I will begin this lesson by printing an image directly from the well-worn and beloved Editor workspace. But to truly exploit sharing, we must return to the workspace that launched us on this journey, the Organizer. As I show you in Video Lesson 11, "Emailing Your Images," the Organizer can assemble pages of photos and transfer them directly to your favorite email program. The Organizer is also capable of packaging photos onto pages like those you get from a professional photo studio, as well as posting images online using Kodak's EasyShare Gallery. And if that's not enough, stay tuned for Lesson 12, where I show you how to make slide shows, postcards, and a host of other creations. It's corny to say Elements gives you a universe of image-sharing options. But on a page that features a supernova, how could I resist?

Printing to an Inkjet Printer

When it comes to printing full-color photographic images, your best, most affordable solution is an inkjet printer. Available from Epson, Hewlett-Packard, and a cadre of others, a typical inkjet printer costs just a few hundred dollars. In return, you get printed images with outstanding color and definition (see the sidebar "Quality Comes at a Price" on page 340), better than you can achieve from your local commercial print house. However, you can't use a color inkjet printer to reproduce artwork for mass distribution. Inkjet printers are strictly for personal use.

In this exercise, you'll learn how to get the best results from a color inkjet printer attached to your computer. If you don't have such a devise, don't fret. You won't be able to follow along with every step of the exercise, but you'll get an idea of how the process works.

Assuming you have an inkjet device at your disposal, please load it with the best paper you have on hand. Ideally, use a few sheets of glossy or matte-finish photo paper, readily available at any office supply store (again, see "Quality Comes at a Price" for more information). If you don't have such paper, or if you simply don't feel like parting with the good stuff for this exercise, go ahead and load what you have. Just remember the kind of paper you loaded so you can make the correct selections in Steps 14 and 15 on page 338.

PEARL OF WISDOM

Obviously, I have no idea what printer you're using, so your experience may diverge from mine starting at Step 14, as I explain in the exercise. And I must leave it up to you to make sure your printer is set up properly and in working order. This means that the power is turned on, the printer is connected to your computer, print drivers and other software are installed, the printer is loaded with plenty of paper and ink, and the print head nozzles are clean. For more information on any of these issues, see the documentation that came with your printer.

1. *Open the test image.* Look in the *Lesson 11* folder inside *Lesson Files-PE4 1on1* and you'll find a file called *Y2K+10 invite.psd*. Pictured in Figure 11-3 on the facing page, this file hails from a wildly successful Y2K party some friends and I threw a few years back. In addition to making some adjustments for time—who knows what Y2010 has in store?—I expanded the range of hues and luminosity values to make it easier to judge the accuracy of our color prints. The image is sized at 4 by 5 inches with a resolution of 300 pixels per inch. But as you'll see, that can be changed to fit the medium.

2. *Choose the Flatten Image command.* This file contains a photographic background composition as well as some text layers that I converted to pixels using Layer→Simplify Layer. Although great for editability, layers require more computation and thus slow down the print process. Best solution: Get rid of them by choosing **Layer→Flatten Image**. Or press Alt and type L-F.

3. *Save the file under a different name.* You don't want to run the risk of harming the original layered image, so choose **File→Save As** or press the shortcut Ctrl+Shift+S. As long as you save the image under a different name, you're safe. But here are the settings that I recommend:

   - In the **Save As** dialog box, select the option **TIFF (*.TIF; *.TIFF)** from the **Format** pop-up menu.

   - Make sure the **ICC Profile: Adobe RGB (1998)** check box is on.

   - Click the **Save** button.

   - In the **TIFF Options** dialog box, click **LZW** to minimize the file size without harming the image.

   - For **Pixel Order**, choose **Interleaved (RGBRGB)**.

   - From **Byte Order**, select the platform you're using, presumably **IBM PC**.

   - Click **OK** to save the file.

   The original layered file is safe as houses and the flat file is ready to print.

4. *Choose the Print command.* Choose **File→Print** or press Ctrl+P. Elements displays the **Print Preview** dialog box, which shows you how the image sits on the page, as in Figure 11-4.

Figure 11-3.

Figure 11-4.

Figure 11-5.

5. *Click the Page Setup button.* Before going any further, it's important to specify the size and orientation of the paper that you'll be printing to. Click the **Page Setup** button to display the **Page Setup** dialog box.

6. *Select your printer model.* Click the **Printer** button to display a second dialog box that still goes by the name of **Page Setup**, as shown in Figure 11-5. Choose the model of printer you want to use from the **Name** pop-up menu and click the **OK** button to return to the first Page Setup dialog box.

7. *Choose the desired paper size.* If you're using special photo paper, consult the paper's packaging to find out the physical page dimensions. For example, each sheet of my paper, called Premium Glossy Photo Paper, measures 8 by 10 inches, slightly smaller than the letter-size format. Whatever the paper size, choose it from the **Size** pop-up menu in the **Paper** section of the Page Setup dialog box. Then click the **OK** button to close the dialog box and return to the **Print Preview** dialog box.

8. *Select the Fit On Page option.* The **Print Size** option at the top of the dialog box is probably set to Actual Size (4.00" × 5.00"). Click the pop-up menu and change it to **Fit On Page** to expand the image to fill the maximum printable portion of the page. Note that Elements does not resample the image; it merely lowers the resolution value so that the pixels print larger. This way, you don't waste any of your expensive paper by, say, printing a tiny image smack dab in the middle of the page.

PEARL OF WISDOM

You may notice a warning that tells you that the image will now print at less than 220 pixels per inch. This might lead you to believe that 220 ppi is a resolution threshold, above which the image looks good and below which it looks bad. Not so. It's a ballpark figure, and a rough one at that. Assuming you follow my advice in the remaining steps, your image will look fine.

The Editor workspace's Print command prints a single image file per piece of paper. If you want to print multiple images at a time, you can click the Print Multiple Photos button, which switches you to the Organizer and chooses that workspace's more versatile Print command, as discussed in the "Printing Multiple Pictures" exercise on page 343.

9. *Turn on the Show More Options check box.* The bulk of the options in the Print Preview dialog box are devoted to helping you position and scale the image on the page. But even more

important are a pair of options that can be displayed only by selecting **Show More Options** below the image preview. (If the check box is already on, all the merrier.)

10. *Confirm the source and printer spaces.* Direct your attention to the **Color Management** options, which I've circled in Figure 11-6. These options control how Photoshop Elements converts the colors in the image from your screen to your printer. To print the colors as accurately as possible, you must identify the *source space*— the color space used by the image itself—and the *destination space* employed by the printer software.

Figure 11-6.

- Below Color Management you will see the words **Source Space: Adobe RGB (1998)**. This correctly identifies the professional-level variety of RGB employed by the *Y2K+10 invite* image file.

- I have yet to encounter an inkjet printer that is calibrated to use a color space other than *sRGB*, the color-matching standard embraced by all varieties of consumer-level hardware. To accommodate this popular trend, set the **Printer Profile** option to **Working RGB — sRGB IEC61966-2.1**.

- Change the **Rendering Intent** setting to **Perceptual**, which maintains the smoothest, gradual transitions when converting colors—the best solution for photographic images.

Figure 11-6 shows the dialog box as it should appear up to this point. Only the dimmed Scaled Print Size values might read differently, to reflect the different dimensions of your paper.

11. *Click the Print button.* This closes the Print Preview window and sends you on to the main **Print** dialog box.

Figure 11-7.

12. *Verify that the right printer is selected.* It's unlikely that anything has changed since Step 6, but as long as we're here, it's worth a glance just to be sure.

13. *Display the specific properties for your printer.* Click the **Properties** button to display the options defined by your specific printer's driver software. From here on, things vary significantly from one model of printer to another, but I'll do my best to make sure everything makes sense.

14. *Indicate the kind of paper loaded into your printer.* Look for an option called **Media Type** or the like. In my case, I changed Media Type to **Premium Glossy Photo Paper** (see the arrow cursor in Figure 11-7), which happens to be a literal match of the name listed on the paper's original packaging (see the second figure on page 340). If possible, try to find a literal match for your brand of paper as well.

15. *Select the highest print quality for your printer.* This assumes you're printing to photo-grade paper. If not, choose a lower setting. The quality setting can be hard to find, so you may have to do a bit of digging. I had to forage through the following options, illustrated by the numbered items in Figure 11-8:

- I first selected **Custom** from the **Mode** options (labeled ❶ in Figure 11-8). This gave me access to a more sophisticated set of options.

Figure 11-8.

- Then I clicked the **Advanced** button (❷) to enter yet another dialog box, pictured on the right side of the figure.

- There, I found the option I was looking for, **Print Quality**. I changed it to the final setting, the printer's maximum, **SuperPhoto–2880dpi** (labeled ❸ in the figure).

PEARL OF WISDOM

If you have problems finding the print quality option (or its equivalent), consult the documentation that came with your printer. Remember: Choose the highest setting *only* if you're using photo-grade paper. Standard photocopier-grade bond cannot handle that much ink; the high-quality setting will produce a damp, smeared page, thereby resulting in a ruined print and wasted ink.

After you've selected the right paper and the correct print resolution, all that's left is to select the most accurate means of reproducing the colors.

16. *Select the best color management method.* In Step 10, you told Elements how to convert the RGB colors in the image to the color space used by the printer. Now you're presented with the trickier proposition of explaining to the printer's software how it should convert colors from the RGB space to CMYK.

Figure 11-9.

Not all printer manufacturers permit you to modify the color management method. And those that do often offer paltry controls. As it turns out, Epson's printer drivers do about the best job of it, as illustrated in Figure 11-9. Still inside the **Advanced** dialog box, I found a series of **Color Management** radio buttons. Most required me to mess with imprecise slider bars and image comparisons. But by selecting **sRGB**, I was able to identify sRGB as the source space for the color after it leaves Photoshop Elements. From there, it is up to the printing software to do the work. (As a second-best solution, I could have selected ICM, which would have used the color-matching software built into the Windows operating system.)

PEARL OF WISDOM

Thanks to the large number of printer vendors, your options may vary significantly during these last few steps. You may even encounter additional options. For example, Hewlett-Packard includes an **ICM Method** option (best set to **Host**) and an **ICM Intent** (best set to **Picture**). If none of the options I've mentioned so far is available on your screen, you'll need to experiment to find the settings that work best.

Quality Comes at a Price

Inkjet printers are cheap, often sold at or below cost. But the *consumables*—the paper and the ink—are expensive, easily outpacing the cost of the hardware after a few hundred prints. Unfortunately, this is one area where it doesn't pay to pinch pennies. Simply put, the consumables dictate the quality of your inkjet output. Throwing money at consumables doesn't necessarily ensure great output, but scrimping guarantees bad output.

Consider the following scenario:

- Of the handful of inkjet devices I own, the one I use most often is my Epson Stylus Photo 1280. It's getting to be a little long in the tooth, but it works great, the software makes more sense than most, and it can print as many as 2880 dots per inch.

- The Stylus Photo 1280 requires two ink cartridges, pictured below. The first cartridge holds black ink; the second contains five colors, including two shades of cyan, two shades of magenta, and yellow. (As the reasoning goes, the lighter cyan and magenta better accommodate deep blues, greens, and flesh tones.) Together, the cartridges cost about $60 and last for 45 to 120 letter-sized prints, depending on the quality setting you choose. The higher the setting, the more ink the printer consumes. So the ink alone costs 50¢ to $1.33 per page.

- You can print to regular photocopier-grade paper. But while such paper is inexpensive, it's also porous, sopping up ink like a paper towel. To avoid over-inking, you have to print at low resolutions, so the output tends to look substandard—about as good as a color photo printed in a newspaper.

- To achieve true photo-quality prints that rival those from a commercial photo lab, you need to use *photo-grade paper* (or simply *photo paper*), which increases your costs even further. For example, 20 sheets of the stuff in the packet shown below costs $13.50, or about 67¢ per sheet.

The upshot: low-quality-plain-paper print costs about 50 cents; a high-quality-photo-paper-print costs about 2 bucks. Although the latter is roughly four times as expensive, the difference in quality is staggering. The figure below compares details from the two kinds of output magnified to six times their printed size. The plain-paper image is coarse, riddled with thick printer dots and occasional horizontal scrapes where the paper couldn't hold the ink. Meanwhile, the photo-paper image is so smooth, you can clearly make out the image pixels. Where inkjet printing is concerned, paper quality and ink expenditure are the great determining factors.

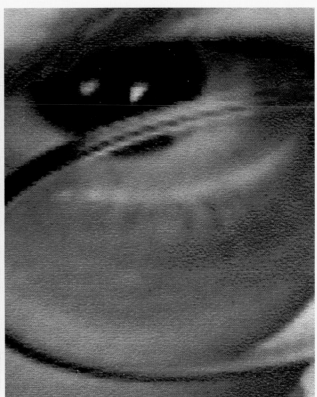

360 dots per inch, plain paper, 50¢

2880 dots per inch, glossy photo paper, $2⁰⁰

17. *Save your settings.* Whether you can save a collection of print settings depends on the software provided by your printer. In the case of my Epson device, I clicked the **Save Settings** button in the Advanced dialog box and assigned the settings a name, "Premium hi-res."

18. *Send the print job on its way.* You may have to exit a few dialog boxes to apply your changes. I had to click two **OK** buttons to navigate my way back up to the **Print** dialog box, and then click **OK** again to start the job printing.

19. *Wait and compare.* It takes a long time (usually several minutes) to print a high-quality image from an inkjet printer. But thanks to the miracle of background printing, you can continue to use Photoshop Elements and even get a head start on the next exercise. When the print job finishes, compare it to the image on screen. Assuming that your printer is functioning properly (no jams, no paper flaws, all inks intact, no missing lines in the output), the colors in the printout should bear a healthy resemblance to those in the image that you see on your computer monitor.

But there are always variations. On the facing page, Figure 11-10 shows two versions of the same image printed to photo-grade paper from my Stylus Photo 1280. The only difference between them is the Color Management setting that I assigned back in Step 16 (page 339).

- The image printed using the sRGB setting is darker and bluer than the other one. But it also happens to be a close match to what I saw on my screen. Therefore, the result is a rousing success.

- I printed the second image using Microsoft's ICM color matching. Although this version more closely matches the previous figures in this book, it strays from the image's appearance on my monitor. So I would call it the less successful print.

PEARL OF WISDOM

If the output doesn't match the screen image to your satisfaction, try experimenting with your printer-specific options (those covered in Steps 14 through 16) until you arrive at a better result. When you do, write the settings down for future reference. Feel free to scribble them down in the margins—it's your book.

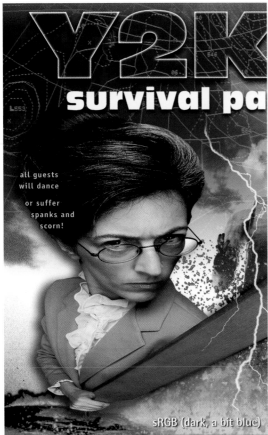
sRGB (dark, a bit blue)

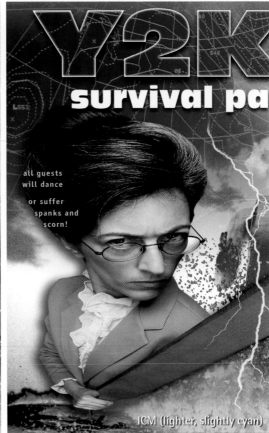
ICM (lighter, slightly cyan)

Figure 11-10.

Printing Multiple Pictures

Now that you've successfully printed a single image to your inkjet printer, it's time to learn how to print multiple photos at a time. Turns out, this is nothing short of a minor miracle. Adobe limits the senior and more expensive Photoshop CS2 to printing a single image to a single page, and yet it blesses the supposedly lesser Photoshop Elements with the ability to group multiple images at a time and even print a sequence of images, all without preparing a special file in advance (which is Photoshop's way). Does that make Photoshop Elements better than Photoshop CS2? In this particular regard, yes it does.

Multiple photo-printing is the exclusive domain of the Organizer. Even if you begin your work in the Editor, Elements transfers you to the Organizer. So whether you want to assemble quick-and-dirty proof sheets or make the most of your expensive inkjet paper, Elements does a superb job of fitting different-sized images onto a page—which is precisely what we'll do in this next exercise.

1. *Open the PE4 1on1 catalog in the Organizer.* Most likely, the *PE4 1on1* catalog that you created at the outset of Lesson 1 (see "Getting Photos into Elements," Step 2, page 6) remains the active catalog in the Organizer workspace. If not, please open it now by going to the Organizer, choosing **File→Catalog**, clicking the **Open** button, and locating the *PE4 1on1.psa* file.

2. *Open a few images in the Editor.* To ensure that this exercise appears on your screen just as it does in this book, I need you to follow these directions exactly:

   • First, make sure the Editor workspace is on the screen. (If you're still in the Organizer, press Ctrl+I to switch; there's no need to select a thumbnail in the photo browser.)

   • Close any images open in the Editor workspace.

   • Choose **File→Open** or press Ctrl+O. Go to the *Lesson 11* folder. Then click the *Burton bugs.jpg* file (it's important you click this one first) and then Ctrl+click *Puppet puppet.jpg.*

   • Click the **Open** button to make the two images appear on the screen. If one overlaps the other, don't worry about it.

3. *Choose the Print Multiple Photos command.* Choose **File→Print Multiple Photos** or press Ctrl+Alt+P. Photoshop Elements launches the Organizer (assuming it wasn't running already) and displays the **Print Photos** dialog box shown in Figure 11-11. The two images from the Editor appear in a column on the left side

Figure 11-11.

of the dialog box. You'll also see one or both of the images positioned inside the large preview window in the middle of the dialog box. To the right, you'll find the Organizer's three-step printing method. But don't rush right into step 1; the actual first step is to make sure you've successfully amassed all the photos you want to print.

4. *Add an image from the catalog.* Click the ⊕ **Add** button in the lower-left corner of the dialog box to display the dialog box in Figure 11-12. The left column of options lets you specify the images you want to add to the print queue. By default, Elements selects Photo Bin because the two photos that we've chosen thus far are open inside the Editor workspace's Photo Bin. The four other options work as follows:

Figure 11-12.

- Photos Currently in Browser lets you add a photo from those displayed in the Organizer's browser window. If you're viewing the results of a tag search, not all the photos in the catalog will be available.

- The Entire Catalog option gives you access to all the photos in the catalog, whether they appear in the photo browser or not.

- If you created any collections, the Collection radio button gives you access to them.

- If you want to add an image and you remember assigning a tag to it, select the Tag option to specify a tag and find the associated images.

For our purposes, I want you to select **Entire Catalog**. The contents of the *PE4 1on1* catalog appear on the right side of the dialog box. Click the check box next to the first thumbnail, the saber-toothed tiger skull, as in Figure 11-13. Then click **Add Selected Photos** at the bottom of the dialog box. The check mark for the skull goes away and the dialog box remains open, so naturally you think Elements is ignoring you. But not so; the photo has been added to the queue.

Figure 11-13.

Figure 11-14.

5. *Add a tagged photo.* Select the **Tag** option from the left side of the dialog box. Next choose **Max** from the associated menu to limit your view to those images that include the Max tag. Click to place a check by the thirteenth thumbnail, which shows Max wearing a crown (see Figure 11-14), and then click **Done**. Elements adds the two photos to the left column of the Print Photos dialog box (see Figure 11-15).

If you add a photo to the print queue by mistake, simply select the photo in the Print Photos dialog box and click the little minus sign icon in the bottom-left corner of the dialog box. To add more photos, click the Add button and repeat Steps 4 and 5 as the mood hits you.

6. *Choose your printer.* Choose the printer you'll be using from the **Select Printer** pop-up menu on the right side of the dialog box (identified by a gray ❶). Click the 🗒 icon to the right of the menu (circled in Figure 11-15) to display your printer's Properties dialog box, which lets you specify the print quality, paper type, and color management settings. See Steps 14 through 16 on pages 340 and 341 for more information.

Figure 11-15.

7. *Specify the printing layout.* By a remarkable twist of logic, Elements lets you print multiple images in multiple ways. To pick a way, choose an option from the **Select Type of Print** pop-up menu (labeled ❷ in the dialog box). Here are your choices:

- Choose the Individual Prints option to print your many images to many pieces of paper. You can specify the size of the photos, how many to print per page, and how many copies of each image you want to print. Use the ◐ and ◑ buttons under the large preview area in the middle of the dialog box to navigate from page to page.

- The Contact Sheet option prints small thumbnail images of the selected files, which is helpful if you want to check colors before committing to larger prints, add pages to a printed catalog, or make a hard copy of a recent photo session. You specify the number of columns you want on a page, and the Organizer adjusts the size of the thumbnails and the number of pages to make everything fit.

- Choose Picture Package to print multiple copies of one or more images onto your printed pages. Designed to accommodate portrait photographers who routinely need to print common picture sizes onto cut sheets that they can sell to their clients, I for one use it anytime I want to print multiple images at a time.

- Labels gives you access to several layouts designed to perfectly align your images to Avery-brand label sheets.

If for no other reason than that I regard it to be the most flexible of the multi-image printing functions, choose the **Picture Package** option.

8. *Dismiss the warning.* If this is your first time visiting the Picture Package option, Elements warns you that the images will print at resolutions of "less than 220 dpi at the requested print size." This extremely misleading message implies that your images don't contains enough pixels; in fact, they have plenty of pixels. Meanwhile, the Organizer tends to downsample images to 220 pixels per inch to accelerate the printing process no matter what. So what is the sense of this warning? Rhetorical, for there's nothing you can do about it. Click **OK**, as you see me doing with some small aggression in Figure 11-16.

Printing Warning

The following images will be rendered at less than 220 dpi at the requested print size.

Burton bugs.jpg
Puppet puppet.jpg
STT skull.jpg
King Max.jpg

Help   OK

Figure 11-16.

9. *Choose your desired layout grid.* Labeled ❸ in the dialog box, the **Select a Layout** pop-up menu lets you choose from 15 ways of organizing photos on the page. Choose the sixth option, **Letter (1) 5×7 (2) 2.5×3.5 (4) 2×2.5**, to see the layout pictured in Figure 11-17. The Organizer takes a stab at placing each of the selected photos inside the layout. *Burton bugs.jpg* fills the one 5×7 slot; the puppet and skull fill the two 2½×3½ slots; and *King Max.jpg* fills one of the four 2×2½ slots, leaving the other three empty. (Elements scales the image so the entire thing fits inside the slot, which is why the puppet photo has some extra white space above it.)

If you don't like the placement of the photos within the layout grid—maybe you wanted the 5×7 to be *Puppet puppet.jpg*—you can adjust this later. Choosing your layout grid simply tells the Organizer how many of what sized photos you want, whether it's two 5×7's or twenty 2×2's.

Figure 11-17.

PEARL OF ⬤ WISDOM

If your paper measures 8½ by 11 inches or smaller, Elements may warn you that the layout is too big for the paper and "some clipping will occur." Although results will vary from printer to printer, don't simply take Elements' word for it. Print a test page. With any luck, you may find that your printer is fully capable of printing the artwork without cutting off or otherwise modifying the edges of a single photo. Or not. But it's a good idea to check.

10. *Set the remaining options.* Set the **Select a Frame** option to **None**. Leave **Fill Page With First Photo** turned off. And turn on **Crop to Fit**. For those of you who want to know what the heck you're doing, I provide the following details:

- The Select a Frame option allows you to choose a frame for each photo in your picture package. These frames run from fairly stylish (Painted Edge) to downright kitschy (Strawberry Patch). Just keep in mind that the frame encircles every photo you print, so make sure you choose a frame that works well for all photos, not just one. Also note that the frame takes up some space, resulting in a cropped image.

- When turned on, the Fill Page With First Photo check box generates a separate page for each selected photo and fills each page with multiple copies of that single photo, great for creating various sizes of a single photo. Remarkably, it's still possible to swap out different photos within each page's layout, as we'll see shortly. But as I say, for this exercise, leave the check box off.

- Finally, Crop to Fit shaves away the height or width of a photo so that it conforms to the aspect ratio of the slot it occupies. The best way to understand this is to turn the Crop to Fit check box on and off and watch the effect this has on the preview. The difference is most obvious in the case of *Puppet puppet.jpg.* When Crop to Fit is on, the image appears larger on the page and the nearly square aspect of the original photo is cropped on the sides (see Figure 11-18). This option makes quick work of fitting photos to the dimensions of a real-life store-bought frame, so turn it on.

Figure 11-18.

11. *Arrange the photos within the layout grid.* Now that all the other decisions have been made, it's time to place our photos the way we want them within the layout grid:

- Let's say we want our picture package to contain one 5 by 7-inch print of *Puppet puppet.jpg* and one 2½ by 3½-inch print of *Burton bugs.jpg*. To accomplish this, drag one of these two photos in the central preview window and drop it onto the other. The images switch places.

- I want the other 2½ × 3½ slot to contain *King Max.jpg*. So drag Max and drop him onto the skull photo to switch these two images.

- Now I want to fill the four 2×2½ slots with two skull images and two of the curly-haired Burton. Drag the skull from the left column and drop it to the right of the skull thumbnail in the preview window; a green outline shows you where the photo will appear. Then drag Burton a couple of times from the left column into each of the remaining 2×2½ slots. Confused? Then just drag around thumbnails until your layout looks like the one in Figure 11-19.

1 of 1
Letter (8.5 x 11 in.)

Figure 11-19.

Figure 11-20.

12. *Set your color management preferences.* Click the **More Options** button at the bottom of the dialog box to display another dialog box, as shown in Figure 11-20. As you learned in the preceding exercise, sRGB is the standard color space for the vast majority of inkjet printers. (If there's an exception that's been manufactured in the last three years, I'd like to know about it. I know, I know, I'm repeating myself. But broken records aren't the only ones with repeating choruses.) So choose **sRGB IEC61966-2.1** from the **Print Space** pop-up menu and click **OK**.

13. *Print the images.* All that's left is to click the **Print** button in the bottom-right corner of the dialog box. A few moments later, you'll have hard copy. Or if you don't want to use your paper, click Cancel instead. Who knows, maybe you don't want to waste ink and paper printing pictures of children and puppets you don't even know. Some people are weird that way.

PEARL OF WISDOM

When you click the Print button, the Print Photos dialog box closes and you lose your layout. So be sure to select the correct number of copies in your printer options before you send the photographs on their merry way.

Sharing Pictures Online

Printing is a local sharing solution. Someone visits your home or office, you have some extra photos of the young and dear ones, and you offer them with the gladdest of tidings. So what about the remote relations? In the old days, you could toss a few snapshots in an envelope and mail them. But that was when a postage stamp cost a fifth what it costs today (see Figure 11-21) and the Postal Service accounted for the transmission of most of the country's personal missives. These days, 37 cents and slow delivery just can't compete with the alternatives.

Online is the cheaper, speedier alternative. And wouldn't you know it, Photoshop Elements helps you take advantage of this trend. Thanks to an online partnership between Adobe and Kodak, you can post photos from an Organizer catalog to an online album. At the time of this writing, there was no subscription fee to join this online album service. You just add your name to a list, and away you go. And your loved ones don't even have to do that. All they need to view your latest snapshots are a computer, an Internet connection, and a bit of curiosity.

In 1969, love was free and postage was cheap

Nowadays, love is priceless and stamps cost more

Figure 11-21.

The name of Kodak's service is the EasyShare Gallery (formerly called Ofoto). It lets you initiate an account, create an online album, notify friends about your pictures via email, and edit your album at a later date. In this exercise, we'll create an online album from three of the Victoria and Albert museum photos in the *PE4 1on1* catalog. If you decide to email an announcement to a friend, feel free to lie and say that you shot the pictures on a recent weekend getaway to London. With all that money you saved not buying stamps, you can afford it.

PEARL OF WISDOM

Although Adobe for the present endorses EasyShare Gallery, and Kodak offers reasonably priced print services, you can find a large number of similar online photo-sharing operations. This exercise is intended as an introduction to the general topic of online photo sharing, pure and simple. Also note that unlike the relatively immutable and enduring Elements software on your hard drive, an online service is fluid, so EasyShare Gallery might change by the time you try out the steps. Fortunately, it behooves Kodak to keep the process easy (as the name implies), so you should be able to navigate around any differences.

1. *Select three photos in the Organizer.* Make sure the *PE4 1on1* catalog that you used in the last exercise remains active in the Organizer. (Again, if it isn't, open it using File→Catalog.) Then click and Shift-click to select the three statue photos that I've circled in Figure 11-22.

Figure 11-22.

2. *Start the online-sharing process.* Click the **Share** button in the shortcuts bar and choose **Share Online**. Assuming that you have an active Internet connection, the screen shown in Figure 11-23 appears. In case you hadn't guessed it already, you're online.

PEARL OF WISDOM

Note the ad on the left telling you that you can order Kodak prints. This is how Kodak makes money from its EasyShare Gallery, so this won't be the last time you see an ad. And don't forget about the Order Prints palette which we dismissed in the first lesson. You can always summon it again by choosing Window→Order Prints. It provides another very easy way to obtain a hard copy of your photos.

3. *Fill out the form.* To share your photos, Kodak requires you to create a free account.

- For a **First Name**, enter whatever you want to be called, whether it's your actual name or a nickname like Scooter. But be warned that your email announcements will trumpet

"Scooter has shared photos with you," so choose your name carefully. (Case in point, here—look what my folks called me.)

- Next enter your **Email Address**. If you use America Online, note that you have to place "@aol.com" at the end of your screen name.

- Enter a **Password** at least six characters in length. The password is case-sensitive, so avoid capital letters unless you want to type them each time you enter the password.

- After confirming your password, you have a series of check boxes to contend with. If you don't want to have to reenter your password every time you go online, turn on **Remember my password**. But bear in mind, by checking this box, you permit anyone with access to your computer to go online and order a million dollars' worth of photos in your name. If that doesn't seem likely in your case, select the check box; if it does, don't.

- The next couple of check boxes reflect how much you want to be bothered—oops, make that *contacted*—by email from Kodak and Adobe. If you don't want the junk mail—er, *offers* and *promotions*—turn off those check boxes, but you might miss a sales coupon or some similar promotion.

- Finally, you have to agree to the terms of service by selecting the final check box. Click the blue **Terms of Service** link if you want to read the rules and regulations you're agreeing to. Without this option selected, things will grind to a total halt. And we don't want that.

When you've set everything up the way you want it, click the **Next** button in the lower-right corner of the screen to advance to the **Share Online** screen, shown in Figure 11-24.

Figure 11-23.

Figure 11-24.

4. *Specify the recipients of your email announcement.* Your next task is to input the contact information for the people you want to notify about your album. If you watched Video Lesson 11, "Emailing Your Images" (see page 332), you may recall that Elements maintains an email address book. Wouldn't it be great if you had access to that same address book here online? Yes, it would, but unfortunately you don't. You have to build a new address book to share photos via Kodak. A bummer to be sure, but let's get down to it.

- Click the blue **Add New Address** link and you're taken to the screen in Figure 11-25. Fill in the first name and email address of your friend. As the red asterisks indicate, these are the only two bits of info you're required to enter. (You need to fill in the other fields only if you want to send prints to your friend.) We're not going to create any groups, so skip everything else and click **Next**.

Figure 11-25.

- Your new contact now appears in the Address Book section, just below your name. Click the check boxes in front of both names to indicate that you want to email notifications of your new album to you and your friend. (You'll want an email for closure—just so you know everything worked like it's supposed to.)

Note that both names include an Edit link so that you can edit the name and address information. Your friend's info includes a trash can icon in case you guys split up and your friend issues a restraining order.

If you're feeling ambitious, enter a few more email addresses and add them to a group. An email group enables you to email photo links to an entire collection of people at once. To do this, click the Add New Group link. Then click Add New Group again, enter the name of your group, and click OK. You can then select the check boxes next to the names of the people you want to add to the group, click the Add to Group button, and the job is finished. Just remember to click Back at the bottom of the screen to return to the Share Online window.

5. *Enter a subject and a message.* The **Message** section at the bottom of the Share Online screen lets you enter a subject and message for your email. Type whatever you like here. For my part, I set the Subject to "My trip to London" and the Message to "Snapped these at the Victoria and Albert Museum. Pip pip! Cheerio!" But that's just me.

6. *Activate the security feature, if you like.* Turn on the **Require friends to sign in to view your album** check box if you want to require your friends to log into the EasyShare Gallery service to view your photos. This may sound like nothing more than a bonus for Kodak, but it's actually a security function that keeps the uninvited from crashing in on your album. Then again, how's anyone going to know the address for your album unless they get your email? So it's up to you. Personally, I favor leaving it off and clicking **Next**.

A progress bar shows that Elements is uploading the photos, one by one, from your computer to Kodak's remote servers. This screen is most noteworthy because it fails to provide you with any way to order prints.

Finally, you'll see the confirmation screen shown in Figure 11-26. (Note that you can click an Order Prints button to order prints.) I myself have problems seeing brightly colored buttons and ads, so I was worried you'd miss it.

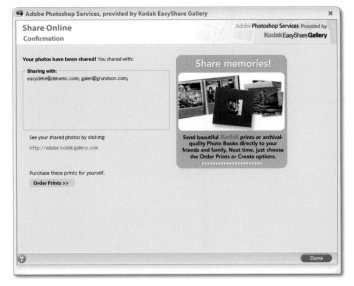

Figure 11-26.

7. *View your online album.* Click the blue **http://www** link to launch your Web browser and view your online album.

- The EasyShare Gallery might ask you to log in. If so, click the appropriate button and cheerfully enter the requested email address and password.

- EasyShare should then greet you with a screen that shows the photo album you created, like the one in Figure 11-27. You may also see a photo album created by Kodak employees that shows how attractive their children are. (I mean, what is with these folks who want to show you pictures of their kids all the time? The nerve of some people.)

- Click the album you created, and thumbnails for the three photos in the album appear as in Figure 11-28 on the facing page. Clicking one of these thumbnails takes you to a new page with a larger view of that image. Clicking the Slideshow link opens a new window that plays a simple slide show of the album's images. (Why yes, you can order prints there, thanks for asking.) But for the present, forgo those actions so we can examine the right column of links.

Figure 11-27.

8. *Experiment with the links on the right.* Because Web sites exist in an eternal state of flux, the links along the right edge of your browser window may change in name and order. But just so you have an idea of what you can do, here's a rundown of the links that I encountered:

- You probably think we've all had enough fun with the Buy Prints link for one book. You'd be wrong.

- Share This Album takes you to a screen of more or less the same options that we saw back in Step 4. The upshot is that you can send notifications to people even after your album is created and online.

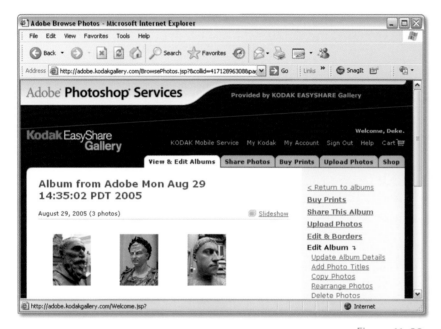

Figure 11-28.

- The Upload Photos link takes you to a page featuring a large window where it's possible to drag and drop photos straight from the Organizer (or anywhere on your hard drive) into the album. There might be a bit of software downloading, but in the end, you have an amazingly convenient way to add photos from your hard drive to an online album.

- Edit & Borders lets you apply simple image-editing commands, effects, and borders to your image. I hope you've learned enough ways to accomplish these tasks using Photoshop Elements' infinitely more powerful tools that you're not tempted to select this link.

Figure 11-29.

Album from Adobe
Mon Aug 29 14:35:02
PDT 2005
8/29/05 (3 photos)

Figure 11-30.

- Update Album Details opens a floating window in which you can rename the album, provide a description, and change the creation date—even to a date the future.

- Add Photo Titles invites you to enter a caption that will appear under a photo when you click its thumbnail to see the larger view.

- The Copy Photos link allows you to add copies of pictures to other albums you may have created. You can also create an album on the spot that contains the copied photos.

- Use the Rearrange Photos link to determine the order in which the images appear in your album. The first photo also gets the honored cover spot when you view all your albums, as we saw back in Figure 11-27. We'll rearrange our photos in just a moment.

- The Delete Photos and Delete Album links are your friends when it comes time to pare your online contributions.

Now that you have the rundown, click the **Rearrange Photos** link to display the window pictured in Figure 11-29.

9. *Edit the order of the images.* As the instructions explain, you can drag the thumbnails to rearrange the images. Let's promote the last image to the first slot. To do so, drag the last thumbnail—the one of the guy with the stitched face—and drop it on the first one. The stitched fellow assumes the first position and the other two scoot over. Now click the **Save** button. Finally, click the white **View & EditAlbums** tab to see how the stitched guy has made the cover of our album, as in Figure 11-30. Kinda makes you want to order a print of it, doesn't it?

Oh, by the way. Don't forget to check your email to see the announcement you sent yourself. And be ready to regale your friends with a few stories when they ask you all about your trip to London. Really, it was great.

WHAT DID YOU LEARN?

Match the key concept in the numbered list below with the letter
of the phrase that best describes it. Answers appear upside-down
at the bottom of the page.

Key Concepts

1. Print Preview
2. Page Setup
3. Fit on Page
4. Source space
5. Destination space
6. sRGB
7. Perceptual
8. Contact Sheet
9. Picture Package
10. Crop to Fit
11. Ordering prints
12. Online album

Descriptions

A. When printing, this signifies the color space used by the image.

B. When printing multiple images, select this option from the Select Type of Print list to combine multiple copies of one or more images onto your printed pages.

C. This dialog box allows you to specify the desired printer, as well as the paper size and orientation.

D. This Rendering Intent option in the Print Preview dialog box maintains the smoothest transitions when converting colors and is the best choice for photographic images.

E. Using the Kodak EasyShare Gallery, you can create this to share your photos with distant friends and relatives.

F. This Picture Package option crops the height or width of a photo to make it conform to the aspect ratio of the slot that it occupies.

G. The color space employed by the printer software.

H. When printing from the Editor workspace, this dialog box shows you how the image will sit on the page.

I. This Print Preview option expands the image to fill the maximum printable portion of the paper.

J. This option prints small thumbnail images of the selected files.

K. A standardized color space embraced by most consumer-level hardware, including nearly all brands of inkjet printers.

L. This exciting online service is the Kodak EasyShare Gallery's worst-kept secret.

Answers

1H, 2C, 3I, 4A, 5G, 6K, 7D, 8J, 9B, 10F, 11L, 12E

LESSON
12

SLIDE SHOWS
AND OTHER CREATIONS

AFTER 20 YEARS in the computer graphics business, I've grown accustomed to the miracles of technology. So every once in a while, I may come off as a bit jaded in my views. Just the same, I remain captivated by Photoshop Elements, especially the features of the program that are absent from the senior Photoshop CS2. Given that the latter costs so much more, it almost defies belief that Elements offers so much as a single function that's missing from Photoshop CS2, let alone an entire group of functions, particularly a group of functions as useful and just plain fun as creations. But bleach my jade and color me amazed, it's true. Across the wide range of Adobe graphics applications, creations are unique to Photoshop Elements.

Creation is Adobe's catchall term for any media project that includes one or more images. It might be an on-screen slide show, a photo album, a Web site, or even something as essential as a wall calendar (see Figure 12-1). Elements provides the templates, you provide the photos, and together you and Elements assemble the finished projects.

My guess is, Adobe is loathe to build creations or the like into Photoshop CS2 for fear that professionals will write off the application as pandering to consumers and enthusiasts. But as a professional, I need at least one wall calendar every year. And I'd rather see images that have meaning to me instead of swimwear models, Dilbert cartoons, or Thomas Kinkade paintings. Thankfully I have Photoshop Elements.

Figure 12-1.

Elements lets you assemble your images into slide shows, albums, and other creations. In this lesson, you'll use both the Organizer and Editor workspaces to assemble each of five kinds of creations. Along the way, you'll learn how to:

Project Files

Before beginning the exercises, make sure you've installed the lesson files from the DVD, as explained in Step 5 on page xv of the Preface. This should result in a folder of images called *Lesson Files-PE4 1on1* on your desktop. We'll be working with the files inside the *Lesson 12* subfolder.

Video Lesson 12: Making a Slide Show

Of Photoshop Elements's many and various creations, the most essential is the common slide show. This simple function permits you to peruse a day's photo shoot, present a group of images to friends or clients, and even export the finished piece as a Windows Media movie, complete with music and fades.

To learn all about slide shows—as well as discover the world of creations—watch the twelfth and final movie. Insert the DVD, click **Start**, select **Set 4: Styles, Sharing, and Slide Shows** from the first pop-up menu, and then select **Lesson 12, Making a Slide Show** from the Lessons list. This action-packed (and extremely fun) 18-minute, 42-second movie explains the following functions:

Operation	Keyboard equivalent or shortcut
Deselect all images in the Organizer	Ctrl+Shift+A
Play or pause the slide show	spacebar
Move from one slide to the next (or previous)	→ (or ←)
Preview a full-screen slide show	F11
Save your slide show project	Ctrl+S

How Creations Work

You make creations in a kind of mini-workspace called the Creation Setup window, accessible from both the Welcome screen and the Organizer. There, Elements walks you through the process of creating any of several kinds of creations using a hand-holding wizard. So you may wonder why I've elected to further hold your hand with a lesson full of step-by-step exercises. Three reasons:

- Things are never as easy as they seem. I have the luxury of spending hours talking to Adobe programmers and other support personnel, so I have insights to share.

- Some of the wizards deposit you into interfaces that are as complex as other parts of Elements. So long as I'm here, I reckon I might as well be of service.

- The Creation Setup wizard suffers some odd limitations, sometimes preventing you from modifying an option and sometimes only appearing to do so. Oftentimes, there are workarounds.

To enter the Creation Setup wizard, click the **Make Photo Creations** button in the Welcome screen (see Figure 12-2), or click the **Create** button at the top of the Organizer. Either way, you'll see a list of projects on the left and as many as six icons in the lower-right area of the dialog box. These are not clickable icons; they're merely informative, as follows:

- This icon means you can preview your creation on screen.

- You can save most creations to the Portable Document Format (PDF). You can open the PDF file with Adobe Reader, available for free from *www.acrobat.com*.

- If you can print a creation to your inkjet printer, you'll see this icon.

- You can order professional-quality photo books and calendars from Kodak online.

- This icon tells you that you can email the finished project.

- You can burn slide shows to a VCD (video CD), which you can play on many (but not all) set-top DVD players.

Figure 12-2.

When you complete a creation, Photoshop Elements usually adds it to the active Organizer catalog. You can then email, print, or export the project, depending on its type. I explain Elements' first and foremost creation in Video Lesson 12, "Making a Slide Show" (see page 362). I cover most of the other creations—including the Photomerge function, which is the one creation that Elements makes available from the Editor workspace—in the upcoming exercises.

PEARL OF WISDOM

The one type of creation that I skip entirely is Video CD. It's extremely finicky, the quality is poor, and readers have reported poor success with playback. If you're interested in TV playback, a far better option is to purchase Adobe Premiere Elements. If Premiere Elements is loaded onto your computer, you'll have a tenth option in your Creation Setup screen, DVD with Menu, which lets you burn a slide show onto a DVD.

Laying Out Photo Album Pages

Photo albums are generally considered low-tech affairs. But Elements gives them a modern twist. Rather than requiring you to painstakingly affix individual photos to album pages, the program lets you lay out your photos on screen and print them as fully rendered album pages. In these steps, you'll take a dozen photographs and assemble them onto picture-perfect pages.

1. *Create a catalog.* The first thing you need to do is create a catalog to hold the batch of files we're going to use for this lesson. Launch the Organizer if it isn't open already. Then choose **File→Catalog** or press Ctrl+Shift+C. In the **Catalog** dialog box, click **New**. In the resulting **New Catalog** dialog box, type "PE4 1on1 Lesson 12" in the **File name** option, and click **Save**. A new empty catalog appears on-screen.

2. *Import the files.* Click the camera icon in the shortcuts bar and choose **From Files and Folders**, or press Ctrl+Shift+G. Then do like so:

   • Navigate into the *Lesson Files-PhE4 1on1* folder, so you can see the *Lesson* subfolders.

   • Turn off the **Automatically Fix Red Eyes** check box. These photos lack human eyes, so we needn't waste time inaccurately identifying and correcting them.

   • Click on the *Lesson 12* folder to select it. Then click the **Get Photos** button.

After a moment, 19 thumbnails fill your browser window. The photographs explore details of the climbable Sea Serpents sculpture in Nashville's Fannie Mae Dees park, the product of a remarkable community project led by Chilean mosaic artist Pedro Silva. If you see a warning, click the **OK** button to dismiss it. Then press the Backspace key or click **Back to All Photos** to view the entire catalog. If you don't see all 19 images (as in Figure 12-3), resize the thumbnails so you can.

3. *Make sure your Creations are up-to-date.* From time to time, Adobe releases updates to Elements. These updates may affect the performance of the software, as well as your ability to follow along with these steps. To make sure your creations in particular are up-to-date, Choose **Edit→Preferences→Services**. Click the **Update Creations** button, as in Figure 12-4. Assuming that you have an active Internet connection, Photoshop Elements will go online and check for updates. If you see directions, follow them. When you see a message telling you that the creations are now up-to-date, click **OK** twice to accept the message and close the dialog box.

4. *Make a new creation.* Press Ctrl+Shift+A to ensure that no photo is selected in the browser window. Then click the **Create** button in the shortcuts bar to display the **Creation Setup** wizard that we saw back in Figure 12-2.

5. *Initiate the Album Pages wizard.* Click **Album Pages** on the left side of the wizard window to see a spread of folksy photo album pages. Then click **OK** or just double-click the Album Pages button.

6. *Select a page style.* Your first step is to choose a style of page. Scroll down to the **Party** section in the right-hand list and

Figure 12-3.

Figure 12-4.

click **Fun for kids**, as in Figure 12-5. It's a little garish, but given that the Sea Serpent exists for the express purpose of letting kids climb on it, I reckon it's appropriate.

When Elements lays out album pages it crops all photos to a 4-by-3 aspect ratio, whether horizontal or vertical. The exception: if you select the No Borders style from the Full Photo section at the top of the list, Elements prints the entire image on the page regardless of its proportions.

---

7. *Establish a few options.* The check boxes at the bottom of the window let you customize the appearance of your album:

   • Select the **Title Page** check box to place a page at the beginning of your album.

   • These photos include captions that I entered in the Properties palette in the Organizer workspace. Turn on the **Captions** check box to display them.

   • Select the **Page Numbers** check box to add a number to the bottom-right corner of each page.

   • The Header and Footer check boxes add text to the top and bottom, respectively, of every page except the title page. Select the **Footer** check box; leave the Header unchecked.

   • The **Photos Per Page** pop-up menu provides you with several ways to distribute your photos across pages. You can assign a specific number of images to each page. Or select a Sequence option to alternate the distribution. For this exercise, select **Sequence: 1, 3, 2, repeat**. This tells Elements to put one photo on page 1, three on page 2, two on page 3, one again on page 4, and so on.

   After you've made these choices, click the **Next Step** button at the bottom of the window.

8. *Import your photos.* Because no photo was selected when you entered the Creation Setup wizard, the Arrange Your Photos window is bare. Click the ✚ **Add Photos** button in the top-left corner of the window to change this. Elements displays the **Add Photos** dialog box. Select the **Photos Currently in Browser** option on the left to see all the images in the active catalog. We'll skip the first 7 photos (which are reserved for the panorama exercise at the end of the lesson) and select the remaining 12. Here's the easiest way: Click the **Select All** button below the thumbnails. Then click to remove the check marks from the first seven photos. When only the 12 images pictured in Figure 12-6 remain selected, click **Done**.

Figure 12-5.

9. *Acknowledge the warning.* The 12 thumbnails now appear inside the **Arrange Your Photos** window, but they are partially obscured by one of the Organizer's irritating resolution warnings. Apparently at least one of our images doesn't contain enough pixels to print smoothly. Turn on the **Don't Show Again** check box and click **OK**.

Figure 12-7 shows the culprit. The second image in the top row, the moustached Zephyr, sports a yellow ⚠ symbol, which I've circled in yellow. We'll resolve this problem in the next step.

10. *Arrange your photos.* Notice the labels that appear in the top-left corners of the thumbnails. These tell you the page numbers for the images. First comes the title page, after which the 1-3-2 sequence begins. This means our old friend Zephyr will appear big and by itself on page 1. That's a problem, because the Zephyr contains the fewest pixels of any image in the catalog. Few pixels mean low resolution, hence the ⚠.

Figure 12-6.

Turns out, I really want the last image in the group to appear on the title page. Drag the last image and drop it to the left of the thumbnail labeled **Title**, as indicated by the arrow in Figure 12-7. A vertical yellow line shows where the image will land. The image should now assume the Title spot, scooting the other thumbnails over one slot. Zephyr now shares page 2 with two other images, thus reducing its print size and increasing its resolution.

Unfortunately, the warning remains. To force an update, click the **Next Step >** button at the bottom of the window and then immediately click **< Previous Step** to return to the Arrange Your Photos screen. The ⚠ icon disappears.

---

11. *Duplicate and rearrange the images.* Between you and me, I want the title-page image to appear elsewhere inside the album. I also want to adjust the order of the images at bit:

- With the title image selected, click the **Use Photo Again** button at the top of the window.

- Drag the duplicate serpent to the right of the last image to place it at the end of the album.

Figure 12-7.

- Drag the seventh image (the second **Page 3** photo) between the first two images to promote it to the first page.

- Finally, drag the **Page 4** thumbnail to the very end of the album. When your thumbnails appear in the order shown in Figure 12-8, click the **Next Step** button.

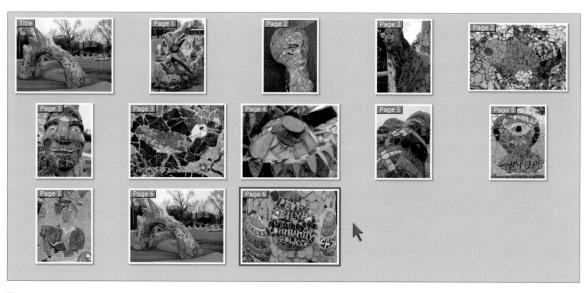

Figure 12-8.

12. *Browse the pages.* You should now see the **Customize** window. The title page appears in the middle of the window, flanked by the ❶ and ❷ buttons, which take you from one page to another. To familiarize yourself with the layout, click the ❷ button or press Page Down to page through the album. Then choose **Title** from the **View Page** pop-up menu to return to the title page.

13. *Crop the title image.* The serpent image appears small inside its frame. To enlarge the image, locate the top-right handle of the marching ants boundary, and drag it up and to the right until the handle touches the large white star in the blue balloon, as in Figure 12-9. Then click outside the image to deselect it. Elements enlarges and crops the image inside its crooked frame.

14. *Enter some title-page text.* Double-click the white **Double-Click to Insert Title** text to display the **Title** window, which lets you enter and format the text. Press Ctrl+A to select all the text and replace it with "Serpents." Set the type size to **36 pt** and click **Done**.

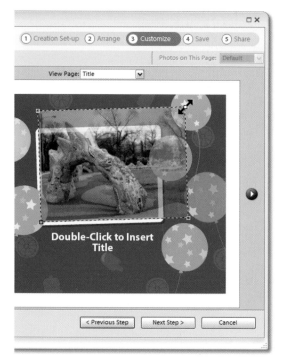

Figure 12-9.

Next click the **T Add Text** button in the upper-left corner of the **Customize** window. Again press Ctrl+A, and type "Sea." Assuming the type size remains 36 point, click **Done**. Then Shift-drag the active text block down to the position shown in Figure 12-10.

15. *Edit the footer text.* Click the ● icon to advance to the first page inside the album. The photograph appears at an angle with a caption to its right. Below the image is the faint text **Double-Click to Insert Footer**. This is the footer you requested in Step 7.

   - Double-click the footer text to display the **Footer** dialog box.

   - Press Ctrl+A to select the placeholder type and replace it with the title of this album, "Sea Serpents."

   - I want this same footer to appear at the bottom of all the pages. So turn on the **Apply to All Footers** check box.

   - Then click the **Done** button to complete the footer, as in the bottom-right corner of Figure 12-11.

It'd sure be nice if you could zoom in on a page, but the Creation Setup wizard lacks any and all forms of zoom controls. The only way to make the page bigger is to expand the wizard by dragging the bottom-right corner of the window.

---

16. *Add a caption to page 2.* Press Page Down to advance to page 2, which has just one problem: The Zephyr image lacks a caption. Double-click the small placeholder in the top-center portion of the page. Then press Ctrl+A, type "Zephyr," and click **Done**.

17. *Switch the images on page 3.* Press the Page Down key again to go to page 3. I think the page would look better if the images were switched so that the bird is on the left, looking at the face. You might reasonably assume

Figure 12-10.

Figure 12-11.

Figure 12-12.

Figure 12-13.

that you could drag and drop the images to swap their places. But try it and you'll see that dragging an image merely moves it inside its frame. Here's what you do:

- If you dragged an image, click **Reset Photos** to restore the default layout.

- Click the < **Previous Step** button at the bottom of the screen to retreat to the **Arrange Your Photos** window.

- Drag the thumbnail of the bird image and drop it to the left of the face. This swaps the two images.

- Click the **Next Step** > button to return to page 3. The ever-accommodating Photoshop Elements switches both photos and frames so that the bird is checking out the face, as in Figure 12-12.

18. *Edit page 4.* Another press of Page Down moves you to page 4, where you're met by a huge eye staring heavenward. This solitary image adheres to the 1-3-2 sequence we established in Step 7, but you can override that. Change the **Photos on This Page** option in the top-right corner of the window from **Default** to **2**. Elements adds a frame and fills it with the next image, as witnessed in Figure 12-13.

19. *View the remaining pages.* Go to page 5 and you'll see that it contains its prescribed three images. Elements has transferred one of the images from the succeeding page to fill the gap. But page 6 was slated to have two images; does that mean it will now have one photo and one blank frame? Press Page Down to find the answer. Elements has automatically adjusted the layout so that page 6 includes a single large frame. Nice.

20. *Save your photo album.* Click the **Next Step** > button to display the **Save** screen. Enter "Serpents Album Pages" into the **Creations Name** option box. Then click the **Save** > button to continue on to the final screen.

21. *Review your sharing options.* Shown in Figure 12-14, the **Share** window gives you four ways to share your album pages, which you'll see repeated in the remaining exercises in this lesson:

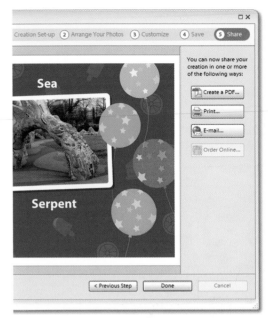

Figure 12-14.

- Click the Create a PDF button to save a PDF version of your album pages that you can later open, view, and print using the free Adobe Reader software.

- The Print button lets you print your pages to an inkjet printer or other device.

- Click the E-mail button to open a window where you can access your saved contacts and select recipients. The software then generates a PDF file and attaches the file to an outgoing email.

- Currently dimmed, the Order Online button is available when you select Album Pages' sister creation, Bound Photo Book, which offers different templates. When available, the Order Online button lets you order a small-format photo album, complete with hard-cover binding, from the Kodak EasyShare Gallery.

After you have saved a creation, you can access these options at any time by double-clicking the creation's thumbnail in the Organizer workspace. For now, there's no need to export the album to PDF or print it. Just go ahead and click the **Done** button to exit the Creation Setup wizard and save your project. If you see a message telling you that your creation has been added to the Organizer's photo browser, read the pithy prose, check **Don't Show Again**, and click **OK**. Your album is now saved to disk for your future editing pleasure.

Creating a Greeting Card

The Organizer lets you choose between two kinds of greeting cards, which you initiate by clicking the 4-Fold Greeting Card or Photo Greeting Card option. The first produces a folded card that includes a photo on the front and a place for a heartfelt, humorous, or derogatory message on the inside, much like a traditional greeting card that you buy at your local stationary store. You print the creation and fold the paper in quarters to create the finished project. Contrast that with the Photo Greeting Card option, which creates a large postcard that you can print at home or order online from Kodak, in boxed sets of 20 complete with envelopes.

Figure 12-15.

Figure 12-16.

In this exercise, we'll create a card with the 4-Fold Greeting Card option. Many of the specific settings will be familiar from the preceding exercise, so we'll breeze through this one at a brisk pace. Meanwhile, any new tips you encounter are easily adapted should you decide to try out the Photo Greeting Card option on your own.

1. *Select a photo in the Organizer.* Make sure that the *PE4-1on1 Lesson 12* catalog that you created in the first exercise is open in the Organizer workspace. Then click the thumbnail for the *Baby serpent fountain.jpg* image, which appears highlighted in the upper-right corner of Figure 12-15.

2. *Start the creation process.* Click the **Create** button in the shortcuts bar to display the Creation Setup wizard. Double-click the **4-Fold Greeting Card** option on the left side of the screen to enter the **Create a 4-Fold Greeting Card** window.

3. *Select a greeting card style.* As when making a photo album, the next step is to choose a style of greeting card from the list on the right. Our selected photo is the baby serpent in the Sea Serpents sculpture, so choose the **Baby Stork (Pink)** style from the **Baby** category, as in Figure 12-16. Even hideous monsters deserve precious birth announcements, don't you think? Click the **Next Step >** button to indicate that you do.

Some styles, such as Casual Horizontal and Spring Vertical, are designed to best accommodate photos with the specified orientation. If a style doesn't mention an orientation, it most likely automatically adapts to a horizontal or vertical photo. One exception is the Heart style in the Valentine category, which works best with a horizontal photo. Also note that if you use the Snowglobe style in the Season's Greetings category, the snowglobe image will appear on the front of the card and your photo appears *inside* the card.

---

4. *Skip the next screen.* You are now presented with the Arrange Your Photos screen, which features your preselected photo. In the preceding exercise, this screen was handy for adding photos to our album pages. But we already selected the photo we want, and one photo is all the greeting card templates can accommodate. If you were to add more photos to this window, Elements would stamp each extra thumbnail as *Not Used.* So just click **Next Step >** to move along.

5. *Edit the front of the card.* Elements presents you with the front of the greeting card. Obviously, a few changes are in order:

   • Double-click the text to open it, select it by pressing Ctrl+A, and replace the text with "It's a Girl!" Then click **Done**.

- Let's resize the photo to better display the baby serpent's winsome cuteness. Click the photo to make the selection border appear. Then drag the lower-right corner handle until the image appears more or less as shown in Figure 12-17.

- Click outside the photo to deselect it and preview how it will look inside the frame. You can click the image again and make further adjustments. When you're satisfied, click the ◐ icon to the right of the card or press the Page Down key to advance to the inside page.

6. *Customize the inside of the card.* Double-click the main **Insert Greeting** text to open the **Greeting** window. Press Ctrl+A to select the placeholder text and enter "At least, we think it's a girl." Then press the Enter key to start a new line and type "YOU check." Finally, click **Done** to return to the wizard.

Figure 12-17.

Normally, I'd have preferred to emphasize the word *You* by italicizing it. But, sadly, the Creation Setup wizard doesn't let you mix fonts and type styles within a text block. So all caps is the next best option.

Now, double-click the smaller **Insert Message** text. Select the placeholder text, type "Love, John and Marsha," and click **Done**. The inside of your card should look like Figure 12-18. Now that the card is customized to serve our new and mostly unrecognizable bundle of joy, click **Next Step >** to proceed.

7. *Save your twisted creation.* In the **Save** window, name the card "Sweet Serpent Girl" and click the **Save** button.

8. *Create a PDF of your card.* The **Share** window offers the same options we saw when creating album pages. Of these, Print is the most viable. To find out why, try this experiment:

- Click the **Create a PDF** button to display the **Save as PDF** dialog box, which presents you with three options.

- The default setting, **Optimize for Viewing Onscreen**, is fine for our purposes. So go ahead and click **OK**.

- In the **Export PDF As** dialog box, navigate to a desired folder (presumably, our very own *Lesson 12*). Accept the default filename, *Sweet Serpent Girl.pdf*, and click **Save**.

- After saving the PDF file, Elements asks whether you'd like to view the file you just finished creating. If you have the free Adobe Reader software installed on your hard drive, click **Yes**. Elements launches Adobe Reader and displays the saved file on screen.

Figure 12-18.

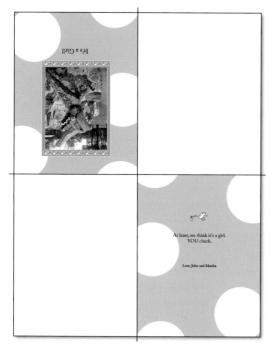

Figure 12-19.

The top-left quarter of the document is the front of the card, upside-down (see Figure 12-19). The lower-right quarter comprises the inside of the card. While the baby serpent arguably looks better on its head, this birth announcement is strange enough without half appearing upside-down. And it hardly makes for a satisfactory experience when viewed online. You really have to print the card and fold it to make it work.

9. *Print the document; call it a day.* To print the document from Adobe Reader, choose **File→Print** and work through the options. The bad news: Printing from Reader is outside the scope of this book, so I'm afraid I'll have to leave you to your own devices. The good news: Anyone with access to the free Adobe Reader can print your document for themselves.

When you finish, exit the Adobe Reader software. If need be, press Alt+Tab to return to the Creation Setup wizard. Then click **Done** to close the **Share** window.

Making a Wall Calendar

As you learned long, long ago when we explored the Date View function in Lesson 1 (see "Finding Photos by Date," page 33), the Organizer is very much concerned with knowing what day it is. So it should come as no surprise that one of the creations you can make with the Organizer is a calendar. Like photo album pages, you can either print a calendar yourself or order a professionally printed and bound calendar online. We'll look at the ins and outs of calendar creation in this exercise.

1. *Select a dozen photos.* Skipping the two saved creations, select the first 12 images in the Organizer using the sure-fire technique documented in Figure 12-20. We'll use these photographs to populate a 12-month calendar.

2. *Start the creation process.* Click the **Create** button in the shortcuts bar to display the Creation Setup wizard. Double-click the **Bound Calendar** item on the left side of the dialog box to enter the **Create a Bound Calendar** window with its list of calendar templates.

3. *Select a style.* Scroll to the bottom of the list on the right side of the screen and select **Bright Spots** from the **Playful** category. Photoshop Elements displays a sample calendar adorned with colorful clown dots.

The bound calendar styles will print split across two pages. As with a traditional wall calendar, the photo appears on the top page and the calendar appears on the bottom.

First click this thumbnail, . . .

4. *Select the desired options.* Look to the bottom of the window for a handful of options that determine the appearance and duration of your calendar:

- Turn on the **Title Page** check box to add a cover to your calendar, complete with the photo of your choosing.

- Select the **Captions** check box to display the captions that I assigned to each photo in the Properties palette. (When creating a calendar with photos that don't have captions, I recommend you turn this check box off.)

Figure 12-20.

. . . and then Shift-click this one

- The date options define the span of the calendar. If you're going to order the calendar online, you're limited to 12 months. But there are no such restrictions when you print your own—you can get a few years out of the way if you like. In our case, we'll settle for a single year. Set the two **Starting** pop-up menus to **January** and **2006** and set the **Ending** options to **December** and **2006**, which, depending on the year you read this, may be the defaults. (If you've somehow come across this book in, say, 2017, feel free to use that year instead and populate the calendar with snapshots of your space cars and servo robots.)

Your settings should look like those pictured in Figure 12-21. When they do, click the **Next Step >** button to advance to the next screen.

5. *Arrange your photos.* Once again, it's time to arrange the photographs. Elements automatically assigns a month to each thumbnail. We have 12 images, but

Figure 12-21.

somehow December is missing. This is because the first photo is slotted for the title page. Easily remedied:

- Select the first thumbnail and click the **Use Photo Again** button. Elements copies the title photo and plunks it down in January, which nudges all the other images and fills out the calendar.

- No one wants to see the title image immediately duplicated in January. So click the **January** thumbnail and drag it to the end of the list. The serpent switches to December and the other photos shift forward a month.

That crazy Zephyr still has his "I'm too tiny!" warning sign (⚠), but we shall blithely ignore it. Assuming that your thumbnails appear in the quantity and order pictured in the meticulous Figure 12-22, you are cleared to click the **Next Step >** button.

Figure 12-22.

6. *Customize the title page.* The **Customize** screen appears, showing the title page for our calendar. Follow the advice of the tiny yellow **Double-Click to Insert Title** text—that is, double-click it. Press Ctrl+A and replace the placeholder text with "Sea Serpents 2006 Calendar." Click **Done** to see the new title below the cover photo.

7. *Add a holiday.* Click ● or press Page Down to advance to the month of January. The top page shows the baby serpent with its caption below it; the bottom page shows the calendar itself. If you look closely, you'll notice that the calendar has no holidays—no New Year's Day, no Martin Luther King Day, no

National Folic Acid Awareness Week, no nothing. But just because Elements is holiday-unaware doesn't mean you can't add a few holidays if you like. Here's how:

- For the sake of example, click ◐ or press Page Down three times to advance to April.

- Click the T **Add Text** button in the top-left corner of the window.

- Press Ctrl+A and type "April Fool's Day."

- Set the type size to **10 pt**.

- Click the color swatch, select a dark blue from the **Color** dialog box, and click **OK**.

- Click **Done** to exit the Text dialog box and create your custom holiday text.

- The text block appears centered above the photo on the top page. That's no good, so drag the text down until it appears fully inside the April 1 cell, as in Figure 12-23. If you plan to add other holidays to this month, you might want to reduce the text box size so it doesn't interfere with other dates.

Admittedly, it's a pain in the neck to have to position tiny text like this for each and every holiday. (And boy, do I wish there was a zoom tool!) But this method does at least afford you the option of jotting down a few personal events, such as birthdays, anniversaries, dental appointments, and other celebratory occasions.

Figure 12-23.

If holidays are important to you and you don't feel like entering them manually, you can bypass the Creation Setup wizard and order a calendar from Kodak using images from your online photo album (see Lesson 11, "Sharing Pictures Online," page 351). If you go this route, you'll get a calendar with the standard holidays. No birthdays or anniversaries, but you can always write those in.

---

8. *Fix November.* Choose **November 2006** from the **View Page** pop-up menu above the page preview. The top portion of this month has a problem: I forgot to include a caption with *Zephyr full.jpg.* Double-click the teeny-weeny caption text and press Ctrl+A to highlight the placeholder text. If you're like me, you've had enough of this creature, so type "I curse thee, Zephyr!" Then click **Done**. The new caption is too small to read this far away from the page, but it was cathartic nonetheless.

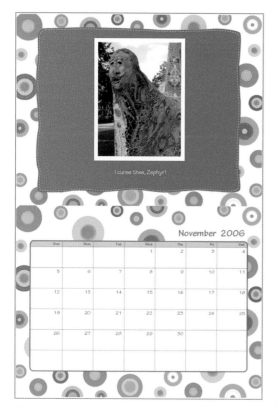

November 2006

Figure 12-24.

When you finish, you should see something that resembles Figure 12-24. If so, click **Next Step** to proceed to the **Save** screen and breathe a sigh of relief.

9. *Save the creation.* Click the **Use Title for Name** check box, and let Elements automatically name the file *Sea Serpents 2006 Calendar.* Then click the **Save** button.

10. *View your sharing options.* The final screen presents you with the same sharing options we encountered when creating photo album pages (see Step 21, page 371), only this time, the Order Online button is active. If you click the Print button to print the calendar from your inkjet printer, Elements will combine the top and bottom pages for each month onto a single upright sheet of paper. If you order a calendar online, you'll receive a standard spiral-bound booklet that measures approximately 10¼ by 15½ inches when open.

After you finish sharing your calendar to any and all extents you desire, click the **Done** button to save your latest creation to disk and post the file in the Organizer.

Designing a Photo Gallery for the Web

In the preceding lesson, you learned how to share your photos online using the Kodak EasyShare Gallery (see "Sharing Pictures Online," page 351). While Kodak generously provides you space on its servers for free, you have limited options for customizing the appearance of your gallery. Worse, you're stuck with the random Web address that Kodak assigns you.

Happily, the Organizer lets you create an online photo gallery that you can post as a fully functioning Web site. The site starts off with a page of thumbnails, which link to larger versions of the images. Elements currently offers more than 30 Web site styles, as well as an assortment of options to customize your gallery. The only catch is that you have to procure space with an Internet service provider (or set up your own server, if you're adept in that department) so that you can upload your gallery for public viewing.

In this exercise, you'll learn how to create your own online photo gallery with the Organizer. And don't worry if you don't currently have a way to post the site to the Web; the Organizer lets you preview the finished gallery directly from your hard drive.

1. *Add a caption to the Zephyr.* Start inside the Organizer. We're going to use the same 12 photos in our online gallery that we used in the preceding exercise. And you well know by now, one of the photos, *Zephyr full.jpg*, doesn't have a caption. You were able to add a temporary caption while assembling the photo album and calendar, but you won't get the chance to do this while creating an online gallery. So let's add a permanent caption now and avoid some heartache later.

   Select the Zephyr image in the Organizer workspace. Then double-click it to fill your screen with the strange Salvador Dali-headed creature, as in Figure 12-25. Make sure the **Properties** palette is visible in the lower-right portion of the screen. If it isn't, press Alt+Enter to make it so. If necessary, switch to the **General** panel of the palette and type "Cursed Zephyr!" into the **Caption** field, as the figure shows. Alternately, you can just click the **Click here to add caption** text under the image and type away.

Figure 12-25.

2. *Start the creation process.* Assuming you zoomed in on the creature like I did, press the Backspace key to zoom back out. Click the Zephyr to select him, and then Shift-click the first image in the photo browser (skip the three saved creations) to select the same 12 photos we used in the calendar exercise. (If you forget which ones I'm talking about, refer to Figure 12-20 on page 375.) Click the **Create** button in the shortcuts bar to launch the **Creation Setup** wizard. Double-click the final option along the left side of the dialog box, **HTML Photo Gallery**, to open the independent **Adobe HTML Photo Gallery** interface. In Figure 12-26, I dragged the edge of the interface outward to expand it slightly and reveal thumbnails for all 12 images. I suggest you do this, too.

HTML stands for HyperText Markup Language, the language in which most Web sites are coded. But don't worry; you don't really need to know that.

Figure 12-26.

3. *Arrange the images.* As usual, I want to adjust the order of the photos. (In case you're wondering, "Why didn't you put these in the right order in the first place?" remember that you can reorder photos only inside a collection. Besides, we're working through these steps so *you* can get the experience.) The good news: I'm going to make you swap only one image. I want what is currently the final image, the wide view of the serpent, to be the first. Make sure that you can see all 12 images, as in Figure 12-26 on the preceding page. (Seeing the thumbnails in a single column makes it difficult to arrange them freely.) Then drag the serpent and drop it in front of the first thumbnail.

4. *Select a style.* The next step is to choose a Web gallery template from the pop-up menu at the top of the window. With so many styles to choose from the decision can be difficult. To preview the styles, try this:

   • Make sure the **Simple** option in the **Gallery Style** pop-up menu is highlighted dark blue, as it is back in Figure 12-26. If it isn't, press the Tab key as many times as it takes to highlight the option.

   • Press the ↓ or ↑ key to switch from one style to another. As you do, keep an eye on the preview below the pop-up menu. It updates to show you a sample version of the first page in the active gallery.

Gallery styles fall into two categories: The first features an index page with thumbnails that link to different pages with larger images. Simple and Antique Lace are examples. The second features an ever-present row or column of thumbnails and displays a larger image within the same page. Fall and Horizontal Frame are examples of this category.

Worth singling out is the Horizontal Slide Show style, which is programmed to switch between large images automatically, creating a continuous parade of images in your Web browser.

Choose **Hello** from the **Gallery Style** menu. Or, with the Gallery Style option highlighted, just press the H key. The amber of the Hello template contrasts nicely with the mosaic serpents, plus it tosses in a bit of animation for good measure. As with most of the Gallery Style settings, this one has available several options that don't have any bearing on the final outcome of your site.

5. *Choose your banner settings.* Below the amber gallery preview are four tabs, each of which takes you to a different panel of options. We'll start with the default panel, Banner. Most gallery styles, Hello included, don't actually include a banner. However, some of the information in the **Banner** panel will appear on your Web pages anyway.

- The contents of the Title option appear in the title bar of the Web browser and within the Web page itself. Note that Adobe includes a placeholder in the Title as a kind of free publicity missive. Don't let them freeload off you. Assuming that the Gallery Style option remains highlighted, press the Tab key thrice to select the **Title** entry and change it to "Sea Serpents Shots."

- The **Subtitle** option lets you add a second line of text to your Web page. Our Hello style doesn't utilize this option, so leave Subtitle blank.

- If you enter an address into the E-mail Address field, it appears as a clickable link in the site. This is good and bad. When a person clicks the link, Outlook or another email program automatically launches and creates an outgoing piece of mail addressed to you. By the same token, professional spammers can harvest these links using industrious little "bot" programs that eternally rummage through the world's Web pages, thus leading to an increase in junk email. For now, go ahead and enter your address in the **E-mail Address** field, if only to see how it lands on the page.

- The **Font** option presents you with three fonts that reside on every computer sold in the last several years. Choosing the fourth option, Default, lets the Web browser determine the typeface. Leave this option set to **Arial**.

- The Hello template ignores the **Size** setting, so there's no sense even bothering with it. For reference, my suggested settings appear in Figure 12-27.

Figure 12-27.

6. *Adjust the settings for thumbnails.* Click the **Thumbnails** tab to advance to the next panel. The thumbnails in question appear on the first page of the gallery. When a person clicks a thumbnail, the browser goes to a page that features a larger version of that image.

- First up is the Thumbnail Size menu, which determines how large the thumbnails will be. At one extreme, Small scales the image so that the larger of its height or width is a scant 64 pixels. At the other extreme, X-Large permits a maximum of 160 pixels. Turns out, using the largest thumbnails with the Hello gallery produces an interesting side effect. To see it for yourself (in a few steps, that is), choose **X-Large** from the **Thumbnail Size** menu.

- Next are a handful of options that add captions under the thumbnails. Keep the **Font** set to **Arial**; stylistically, it's probably best not to mix fonts within a gallery, especially fonts that don't go together such as Arial, Times, and Courier. Again, the Hello template ignores the **Size** menu, so I invite you to ignore it, too.

- You can include the image's filename and caption with the thumbnail; the Hello style ignores the Date option. For our purposes, turn on the **Filename** check box; leave Caption and Date off.

Figure 12-28 shows the settings.

Figure 12-28.

7. *Set the large image options.* Click the **Large Photos** tab to display a panel of options that control the size of the full versions of your photos. The large images are the meat of a photo gallery site, the main attraction. You might wonder, then, why you would want to resize your images at all. Why not let your viewers enjoy every single pixel?

PEARL OF WISDOM

The reason we resize images is because when an image appears in a Web browser, a one-to-one correspondence exists between the pixels in the image and the pixels on the monitor. In other words, it's like viewing an image in the Editor at the 100 percent zoom factor. With the exception of the smallish Zephyr, the images we're using (like most digital photos) are far too large to display in their entirety at a one-to-one zoom factor. The standard solution is to shrink the image so that the whole thing fits on the screen. Many browsers do this automatically, but they don't do it well. (The image typically looks choppy.) Better to size the images yourself in advance.

Nevertheless, your first decision in the Large Photos panel is whether or not you want to resize the photos. If you deselect the Resize Photos check box, the Organizer won't downsample the images. They'll appear on the Web in all their hugeness, and folks will have to do a lot of scrolling to see every single pixel. Consider the cyclops image in Figure 12-29. On the printed page, I can scale it and retain all the pixels; on the Web, I cannot. At a one-to-one zoom ratio, the eye alone consumes the entire width of the page, as in the dimmed background behind this text. Not only that, consider that if you give your visitors the original photo, in all its glory, they'll have everything they need to print and otherwise repurpose high-resolution versions of your work. From a simple copyright perspective, this might not be something you want to encourage.

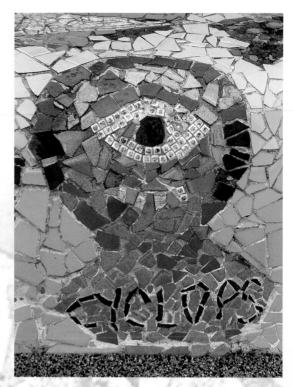

Figure 12-29.

As tempting as preserving your enormous images may sound, I recommend that you leave the **Resize Photos** check box turned on. Then set the other options like so:

- The default Resize Photos setting of Large is, in truth, a little too large for portrait-oriented images to be fully displayed on most computer screens. So set the **Resize Photos** option to **Medium**. Elements will resize the images so that the larger proportion is 400 pixels.

- The Photo Quality slider determines the amount of JPEG compression that Elements applies to large photos. A Low setting gives you very small file sizes (about 15K each) and fast loading times. But the image looks awful. A High setting gives you much larger file sizes (about 200K each) and more prodigious load times over slow Internet connections, but the images look great. I advocate that you leave the **Photo Quality** slider set to the halfway point, which is a swell compromise.

- Finally, Elements presents you with some more **Captions** settings. As always, leave the **Font** set to **Arial** and ignore the **Size** option. You have lots of room to display info beneath a large image, so make sure the **Caption** check box is selected. Turn on **Filename**, but ignore the **Date** check box; the Hello template pays it no nevermind.

Figure 12-30.

Between you and me, I've a special affinity for Figure 12-30. How come? It shows you my recommended settings.

8. *View (but don't change) the Custom Colors options.* Click the **Custom Colors** tab to display the final panel. Only a handful of HTML templates fully utilize the Custom Colors settings. A few others pick up the Text and Visited Link options. But *all* the options are ignored by the Hello template, just as they are by most other gallery styles. So leave the **Custom Colors** settings alone.

9. *Save your Web photo gallery.* When Elements creates your Web site, it stores the pages and images in a folder on your hard drive. The **Destination** options let you specify that folder's name and where it's placed.

   • Click the **Browse** button, navigate to your computer's desktop, and click **OK**.

   • Name the folder by entering "Sea Serpents Gallery" into the **Site Folder** option box.

   • Click the **Save** button.

   A progress bar appears while the Organizer creates your gallery. A moment later, you'll see the **HTML Photo Gallery Browser** window, as in Figure 12-31. This window is the Organizer's built-in browser, made especially for viewing Web galleries.

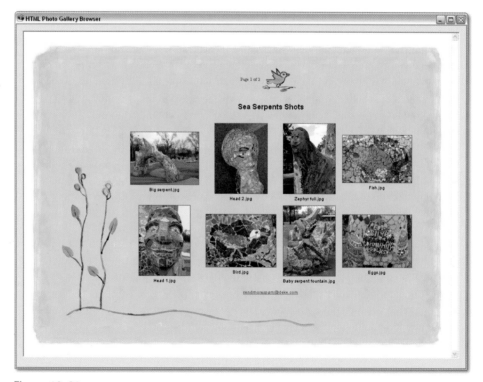

Figure 12-31.

10. *View the gallery.* Click the maximize button (▢) on the far right side of the title bar to maximize the window. Notice the *Sea Serpents Shots* text above the thumbnails; if you were viewing this gallery in a browser such as Internet Explorer, this text would appear in the browser's title bar as well. Notice also the clickable email address below the thumbnails. Finally, notice that there are only eight thumbnails on this page. With the thumbnail size set to X-Large, the Organizer fits just eight thumbnails on an index page, regardless of the size of your monitor.

- To access the other four thumbnails, move your cursor over the little orange birdie at the top of the page. Just hover for a moment and watch. I'll let you enjoy his animated performance for yourself. Now click the bird to reveal the second index page with the remaining thumbnails.

- Click the *Eye.jpg* thumbnail to display the full page pictured in Figure 12-32.

The left- and right-facing birdies above the photograph let you navigate through the gallery. Click the plant between the birds to return to the index pages.

Figure 12-32.

Continue to explore the gallery at your leisure. When you're through, click the ✖ icon to close the HTML Photo Gallery Browser window. Be aware that the Web site isn't saved as a creation document in the Organizer workspace. However, the actual HTML files and accompanying image files are saved on the desktop level of your hard drive, permitting you to copy the site to an Internet server and post it for all to enjoy. Plus, the next time you create an HTML photo gallery, the last settings you used will remain in effect, making it easy to go back and tweak things if you're not entirely happy with your initial results.

Creating a Panoramic Picture

And what about those seven photos that we imported in the first exercise and have neglected ever since? Fret not: In this, the final exercise of the book, the time for those photos has come at last. Coauthor Galen Fott shot these photos with the intention of stitching them together into a panoramic "big picture" view of the Sea Serpents sculpture. Naturally, the ready-for-anything Photoshop Elements has just the tool for the job.

The surprise is where this tool is located. Unlike the other creations we've explored in this lesson, panoramic pictures can't be created from the Organizer. For that task, you have to return to that *yin* to the Organizer's *yang*, that *Chang* to the Organizer's *Eng*, that *Sid* to the Organizer's *Marty Krofft*—the Editor. In this last exercise, you'll learn how to create a panoramic picture using the Editor's Photomerge command, plus pick up a few tips on shooting suitable source pictures.

1. *Select the seven partial serpent photos.* Since we've spent the last five exercises in the Organizer, let's start there. Click to select the first photo that bears the date 2/15/2004. Then Shift-click the last thumbnail dated 2/15/2004. The facing page's Figure 12-33 tells the whole story.

2. *Send the photos to the Editor.* Next, click the **Edit** button in the shortcuts bar and choose **Go to Standard Edit**. Or better yet, press the keyboard equivalent Ctrl+I. Elements launches the Editor workspace (if it isn't running already) and opens the seven photos.

3. *Begin the merge.* Creating a Photomerge panorama is one of the Editor's neatest tricks, but for some reason the good people at Adobe have chosen to bury the command in what seems to this humble author to be a remote location. Then again, who

cares? I know where it is, and my job is to pass along that info to you: Choose **File→New→Photomerge Panorama** to display the first **Photomerge** dialog box, shown in Figure 12-34, which gives you a place to gather photos that you want to merge. By default, any images open inside the Editor are added to the Source Files list, hence the inclusion of our seven serpent JPEGs. You can click the Browse button to add more photos. But we're full up, so click **OK**.

Click this thumbnail

Figure 12-33.

. . . and Shift-click this one

Figure 12-34.

Suddenly the Editor swings into action as if there were a ghost in the machine. A glance at the Layers palette reveals that the Editor is busy at work copying the seven images and pasting them into a single document. Soon enough, the truly massive second Photomerge window appears. An alert message tells you that Elements tried valiantly to do all the work for you, but a slight problem occurred. What can you do? Some jobs you just have to do yourself. Click **OK** to cordially dismiss the message.

4. *Add the problematic photo.* Obviously we have a small problem. But first, a quick tour around the Photomerge window, depicted in Figure 12-35. The upper-left corner of the window features a smattering of tools helpful for merging images. The long thin strip across the top underneath the light bulb-laden help section that currently houses a lone disenfranchised photo, is known as the *light box*. If Photomerge can't automatically reckon how to merge an image with its brethren, to the light box it goes. You can also use the light box to store photos that you decide to exclude from the final rendering.

Figure 12-35.

On the right side of the window, below the OK, Cancel, Undo, Redo, and Help buttons, are controls for manipulating your merge. The first of the controls is the Navigator panel, which behaves almost exactly like the Editor's Navigator palette, permitting you to move around the main work area.

Press the spacebar to temporarily access the hand tool, which lets you scroll the image inside the work area. Photomerge did a pretty good job fitting the photos together, but scroll to the left and notice an obvious problem: The big serpent is missing its head. Let's reattach it:

- If you still have the spacebar down release it for heaven's sake, to reactivate the arrow tool. Then drag the lone photo from the thin light box into the larger work area.

- Notice that as you drag the head, the overlapping portions of the head and body appear translucent, helping you to see how the photographs will merge.

- Drag the head to the far left side of the merged composition. Try to line up the bottom rightmost spike on the serpent's head with the corresponding one underneath. Because the Snap to Image check box is selected (see the right side of the window), you may feel a "snap" as the image jumps into place, but don't worry if you don't. Just try to line up those spikes as best as you can.

PEARL OF WISDOM

Photomerge wasn't able to automatically merge the first two images because there wasn't enough overlapping area between them. Image overlap is one of several issues to keep in mind when shooting images for Photomerge. Adobe recommends an overlap of 15 to 40 percent, a big range. Even so, Galen's experience was a bit different. The six images that Photomerge combined automatically overlap by an average of 50 percent each, which seems to work well. My recommendation: Shoot for around 50 percent overlap and you should be fine. You may also find it helpful to use a tripod to keep the camera level and stationary. And finally, turn off your camera's automatic exposure setting and meter the scene manually. This eliminates the chance that some images will come out lighter or darker than others. The Photomerge function can account for slight differences in brightness, but the more similar your photos, the better.

5. *Adjust the blending.* Use the zoom tool to magnify the front of the serpent, as in Figure 12-36. You may see a diagonal shift in brightness as Photomerge tries to blend one image into another. Or you may see a sudden shift in detail, most evident in the blue and orange stripes in the ground. In the figure, I've highlighted the transitional area with a yellow circle.

Figure 12-36.

To better blend between one image and the next, turn on the **Advanced Blending** check box in the **Composition Settings** along the right side of the window. Then click the **Preview** button and wait a few seconds to see the revised results. The transitions may not look perfect, but they should be better.

You can't continue to work in the Photomerge window while previewing the Advanced Blending function, so click the **Exit Preview** button to return to the normal mode. But leave Advanced Blending turned on; although it may not preview the effect, Elements will apply Advanced Blending to the final render.

---

6. *Apply some perspective to the merged scene.* Scroll a bit to the right and you'll notice a problem in the row of bricks next to the small tree in the foreground (circled in Figure 12-37 on the opposite page). Photomerge did a great job of merging the serpent and other background details, but it pretty well missed the mark with those bricks. By default, Photomerge positions and rotates images to help align them, but it doesn't distort them. Clearly some distortion is needed to fix the bricks.

Go to the **Settings** section of the controls and click the **Perspective** radio button. Photomerge takes a minute or so to calculate the perspective distortion and then displays the results in the work area. Alt-click with the zoom tool to take in the entire merge. As witnessed in Figure 12-38, the Photomerge function has distorted the images so that the bricks meet seamlessly. However, the perspective results in the dreaded "bow-tie effect," where the ends flair outward as if the photo were projected on the inside of a cylindrical wall. That's great if you want to create the effect of an image projected onto a museum wall. But we're supposed to be outside, for heaven's sake. There must be a better way.

Figure 12-37.

7. *Fix the bow-tie distortion.* Turn on the **Cylindrical Mapping** check box in the Composition Settings area. Again, this effect is too complex to preview automatically, so you'll have to click the **Preview** button to see it work. As shown in Figure 12-39 (see the next page), Photomerge avoids the inverted cylinder effect by wrapping each image around its own gradual cylinder. It may not be exactly right, but it's better—and better is as good as things get in Photomerge.

Figure 12-38.

8. *Merge the images.* All that's left to do is to click **OK**. After a couple minutes of calculation and tomfoolery, Elements generates the nearly seamless panorama you first saw in the preview (see Figure 12-39). Okay, it's not perfect, but it is amazing.

If the Keep as Layers check box is activated when you exit the Photomerge dialog box, Elements will render each photo to a different layer. This can be helpful if you want to adjust a particular photo independently, but it comes at an expense. Keep as Layers cancels the Advanced Blending option, and therefore produces less satisfactory results. Unless you have a very particular reason for doing otherwise, leave the Keep as Layers check box turned off.

Figure 12-39.

EXTRA ★ CREDIT

Having arrived at a reasonably successful stitched panorama, you might be ready to call it a day, close this book for the last time, and get on with your life. (Life beyond this book—is there such a thing?) Or, possibly, you're wondering what you could ever do with the oddly curving image on your screen. If you want to see how to turn this image into something printable, read on.

Figure 12-40.

9. *Rotate the image.* The Editor workspace offers a great function for reversing the curvature of an image. Unfortunately, it works vertically, not horizontally. So, to fix what ails this serpent, we first need to rotate it. Choose **Image→Rotate→90° Right** to turn the image onto its side.

10. *Apply the Shear filter.* Now it's time to apply one of the simplest, oldest, crudest, and most practical distortion functions available to Elements. Choose **Filter→Distort→Shear** to display the tiny dialog box with the squalid, entirely inadequate preview pictured in Figure 12-40.

Okay, enough bellyaching—here's the best way to approach our tricky but fetching serpent:

- Turn on **Repeat Edge Pixels**. This prevents the filter from wrapping pixels from one side of the image to the other.

- See that vertical line at the top of the dialog box? Adding and moving points along that line bends the image. The problem is that its middle bends up—or to the right when on its side. So click in the middle of the line to add a point. Then drag that point three or four pixels to the left. That's right, *just three or four screen pixels*. Lean in close to your monitor and squint. The Shear filter is absurdly sensitive, so *very* slight changes produce big effects.

- Drag the top point one pixel to the right. Sounds crazy, but that's enough to add some lift to what will be the left side of the panorama.

- Drag the bottom point two pixels to the right.

If you're feeling ambitious (or merely fussy), you could try adding a few more points to the line. But given that single pixel movements equate to about 10 percent of bend in the image, you're not likely to achieve much more control. When your dialog box looks more or less like the one in Figure 12-40, go ahead and click the **OK** button.

11. *Un-rotate the image.* Choose **Image→Rotate→90° Left** to return the image to its original landscape orientation. Figure 12-41 shows the much more acceptable results.

Figure 12-41.

12. *Crop the image.* Press the C key to select the crop tool. Drag around the opaque portion of the image. The idea is to preserve as much of the image as possible, especially above the serpent, where the space is tight. So feel free to press Ctrl+⊞ or Ctrl+Alt+⊟ to zoom in nice and tight. When you're confident that you've cropped the image with all the care of a mother burping her newborn, press the Enter key to accept the results.

Figure 12-42.

13. *Flatten the image.* The Photomerge command delivers a single layer against a transparent background. Frankly, that doesn't do us any good; it just prevents us from saving the panorama to some common file formats. So choose **Layer→Flatten Image** to fuse the layer into a flat image file.

14. *Save the panorama.* After all this work, you'll want to save the results. Choose **File→Save** or press Ctrl+S. Name the file "Serpentmerge" or something equally clever and trademarkable. Then set the **Format** option to **JPEG (*.JPG; *.JPEG; *.JPE)**. Click the **Save** button, and then click **OK** in the **JPEG Options** dialog box.

The figures on this page show the merged, sheared, and cropped result. You might be able to make out some slight alignment problems in the close-up view (indicated by the arrows in Figure 12-42), but it looks great from a distance (Figure 12-43).

Congratulations! You've sewn up a sea serpent and polished off a book to boot. Time to give yourself a well-deserved break. But before you do, don't forget to take the last quiz. Otherwise, how will you know what you know?

Figure 12-43.

WHAT DID YOU LEARN?

Match the key concept in the numbered list below with the letter of the phrase that best describes it. Answers appear upside-down at the bottom of the page.

Key Concepts

1. Creation
2. Premiere Elements
3. Update Creations
4. Header and footer
5. 4-Fold Greeting Card
6. Create a PDF
7. Add Text
8. Banner
9. Photomerge
10. Light box
11. Advanced Blending
12. Cylindrical Mapping

Descriptions

A. Printing is by far the best way to share this creation type.

B. This Web page feature doesn't appear in most HTML photo gallery styles, but any information that you enter into it can be used elsewhere on the page.

C. Unused images are placed in this portion of the Photomerge interface.

D. Adobe's catch-all term for any media project that includes one or more images.

E. This companion program from Adobe lets you burn your Photoshop Elements slide shows to DVD.

F. Click this button to add holidays to a wall calendar.

G. These album page options add customizable text to the top or bottom of every page except the title page.

H. This Photomerge feature helps smooth rough transitions in your final panorama.

I. The only Elements creation type that you access through the Editor, this function lets you stitch photos together into a continuous panorama.

J. If your Photomerge suffers from the "bow-tie effect," this option can help unknot it.

K. This command in the Services panel of the Preferences dialog box ensures that all components of the Creation Setup wizard are up-to-date.

L. One of the sharing choices for several creations, this option generates a file that you can distribute online or output to a printer.

Answers

1D, 2E, 3K, 4G, 5A, 6L, 7B, 8F, 9I, 10C, 11H, 12J

INDEX